A Land Made from Water

A Land Made from Water

APPROPRIATION AND THE EVOLUTION OF COLORADO'S
LANDSCAPE, DITCHES, AND WATER INSTITUTIONS

Robert R. Crifasi

UNIVERSITY PRESS OF COLORADO
Boulder

© 2015 by University Press of Colorado

Published by University Press of Colorado
5589 Arapahoe Avenue, Suite 206C
Boulder, Colorado 80303

 The University Press of Colorado is a proud member of
Association of American University Presses.

The University Press of Colorado is a cooperative publishing enterprise supported, in part, by Adams State University, Colorado State University, Fort Lewis College, Metropolitan State University of Denver, Regis University, University of Colorado, University of Northern Colorado, Utah State University, and Western State Colorado University.

∞ This paper meets the requirements of the ANSI/NISO Z39.48-1992 (Permanence of Paper).

ISBN: 978-1-60732-367-9 (cloth)
ISBN: 978-1-60732-587-1 (pbk)
ISBN: 978-1-60732-382-2 (ebook)

Library of Congress Cataloging-in-Publication Data
Crifasi, Robert. R.
 A land made from water : appropriation and the evolution of Colorado's landscape, ditches, and water institutions / Robert. R. Crifasi.
  pages cm
 Includes bibliographical references.
  ISBN 978-1-60732-367-9 (cloth) — ISBN 978-1-60732-587-1 (pbk) — ISBN 978-1-60732-382-2 (ebook)
 1. Water resources development—Colorado—History. 2. Hydraulic engineering—Colorado—History. 3. Water-supply—Colorado—History. I. Title.
 TC424.C6C75 2015
 333.91009788—dc23
                    2015011293

Cover illustration: Boulder, Colorado, situated at the foot of the Front Range in a detail from an 1890s Union Pacific Railroad advertisement.

To my parents

Contents

Preface

There is something uniquely western about wielding a pitchfork while standing shin deep in water shoveling wet leaves from an irrigation ditch that was turned on a only few hours earlier. It is hard labor. But it is also rewarding in a uniquely western way. Wet leaves weigh a lot more than they look. You need to get them out of the ditch. If you do not, they collect at any number of places and cause the water to back up until the ditch overtops and breaches. This is dirty work. But everyone involved is excited that the water is being turned on for the season. Hopefully, you will not encounter a putrefying skunk carcass that you have to fish out of the water and place on the bank. With luck, someone else will deal with the skunk before you do.

For the most part, pitching leaves is monotonous, repetitive work. At least it is for me. Inevitably I start talking about the ditch and its history with the people working around me. If you are lucky, and you have an old-timer who has lived along the ditch for a long time, you can learn a lot about your community. When you are knee deep in water, it is enlightening to hear about the people who came before you, their exploits and arguments, and how they built the ditch. As I move along, I often wind up talking about the trees, the ditch easement, and perhaps water law with some unhappy person on whose lawn I just pitched those wet leaves.

I can get quite philosophical when pitching leaves. I think about the role ditches and their builders played in colonizing the West. Invariably, I come around to thinking about appropriation and the labor theory of property, as my sense of ownership in the ditch increases with every toss of wet leaves. The thought of writing a book grew out of all those pitchfork throws. So the idea for this book was really born in a ditch.

This book is about how Boulder Valley's landscape ended up looking as it does after several centuries of rapid change. Water and rivers connect people and places. Water touches on all aspects of life and the environment.

To make sense of Boulder's water history, I find it helpful to situate it within the context of local and regional ecological and environmental change. I believe that we cannot disaggregate human from environmental history. Both are inextricably entwined and intermingled. The interconnectedness of society and ecology are inseparable, especially when considering water development. Standing knee deep in ditch water, these are the kinds of things I decided I would discuss should I ever write a book. You may find that a tad strange; my wife surely does, but it makes a long day of pitching wet leaves go a bit faster.

Introduction

Let me begin by telling you a little bit about my initiation into water management in Boulder. I started by making a mistake. With just a couple of weeks on the job as the new water resources specialist for Boulder's Open Space Department, I sent a "letter of introduction" to the many ditch companies that the city has an ownership interest in announcing that I was their liaison to the city. I was eager to jump into my new responsibilities and develop positive working relationships with these companies. I thought that the letter was a professional way to begin that relationship. To my surprise, I learned that people at several ditch companies reacted with great suspicion when they received this letter. Some were troubled by the letter and thought that the city was going to try to take control of their ditches. Why is the City of Boulder writing us a letter to tell us that someone is going to work with us? they groused. Others thought the city was being arrogant and was preparing to steamroll them with some new but as yet unknown agenda.

Little did I know, I had inadvertently stepped into a local crucible for a whole range of contentious water issues. I had never experienced firsthand

DOI: 10.5876/9781607323822.c000

the deep distrust that many ditch company shareholders have toward city employees. Until I walked into annual meetings for these ditches and found myself the lightning rod for the frustration many rural people feel toward the municipal governments that surround them, I had no on-the-ground knowledge of the many fault lines that trouble rural and urban water users in the West.

My hope is that this book conveys a number of interconnected messages. One is the sense of what it is like to work on a small irrigation ditch. Another is to weave together various histories. In Colorado, mining history seems far more romantic and colorful than our agricultural legacy. But how many active mines remain in Colorado? There are literally thousands of small ditch companies that still move water to a wide host of uses. In 2000, the Colorado Division of Water Resources listed a remarkable 22,800 ditches and canals that are active in the state. Anyone who thinks about sustainable economic development in Colorado cannot ignore our ditches as these companies are the gold standard for what is possible for intergenerational development. Mines were never nor ever will be sustainable economic institutions. Ditches have proven that they are.[1]

I also hope to convey that the ecological history of ditches and their lasting effect on the character of the region is nothing short of remarkable. Often water development is painted as having overall negative effects on landscapes. Environmental literature and magazines are rife with laments about all the bad things that water development brings. But when we look at ecological and landscape history from the perspective of small irrigation ditches, the picture becomes very fuzzy. Many ecological problems are evident. However, small irrigation ditches have produced wetlands, expanded riparian forests, and supported native biodiversity in numerous ways. It is impossible to paint black and white pictures that depict ditches as either good or bad. Rather, we find judgments of what is "good" or "bad" has far more to do with one's perspective than with anything inherent in empirical data. It is this complex interaction of people and the environment over time that is perhaps the overarching theme of this book.

It is difficult to predict the future of ditches. However, their rich history will forever remain a central part of Colorado's legacy. They enabled agriculture in this semiarid state. Water management institutions and legal doctrines that developed here have propagated across the American West. And, at least for now, unique environments coproduced by the agency of man and nature have spread out along our streams and ditches.

NOTE

1. Holleran, *Historic Context for Irrigation*, 106.

A Land Made from Water

ONE

Making the Great American Desert

"I do not hesitate in giving the opinion, that it is almost
wholly unfit for cultivation, and of course uninhabitable by
a people depending upon agriculture for their subsistence."
—*Stephen Harriman Long, 1822*[1]

The City of Boulder's Forestry Division estimates that there are about
650,000 trees in Boulder's urban forest, including about 38,000 trees in city
parks and public street rights-of-way. Just twelve miles south of Boulder, on
Rocky Flats, there are virtually no trees, save those that grow along Coal
Creek. This is no coincidence. Urban development skipped Rocky Flats.
The shortgrass prairie on Rocky Flats looks much as it did when Major
Stephen Harriman Long passed near here in 1820. Boulder Valley, on the
other hand, is a landscape transformed. It is an urban oasis by virtue of
water development.[2]

Over the last few centuries, people have extracted, others say plundered,
the resources from Colorado's riparian corridors. Regardless of one's

DOI: 10.5876/9781607323822.c001

perspective, these actions have transformed Colorado's Front Range rivers and shaped the character of the landscape we see in places like Boulder Valley.

TIMELINES AND BASELINES

Boulder's landscape history is written on its streams and riparian areas. For at least the last 200 years, and perhaps for a long time before that, change and transformation was the overriding feature of Front Range streams. Streams present in the Front Range bear little resemblance to what once existed. People have appropriated the water and dug lakes within the floodplains. They have introduced dozens of new species of vegetation, fish, insects, and algae while at the same time they have eliminated many others. And stream channels have been bridged, channelized, modified by flood control structures, inundated by reservoirs, and encroached by urbanization. There is no hint that this process of development and environmental change will slow. Development has shifted the riparian ecosystem to the point that new, hybrid ecosystems have emerged.

It is hard to pick a date to begin a story about change when change itself is arguably the normal state of affairs. Although somewhat arbitrary, I think we can select two interconnected points of departure. The first starting point involves the Native Americans who were here until they were brutally expelled by American invaders from the east. They lived and hunted here and adapted the environment to suit their needs. One really cannot do justice to 10,000 years of history in a few pages, so I hope you forgive me for making omissions and broad generalizations. However, to ignore the Indians would be a far graver sin, so abbreviate I will. What is critical here is that the Indian influence on the landscape that the Europeans first saw when they arrived was so fundamental that it blurs, almost beyond resolution, any distinction between what was "naturally" here versus that which was created through the action of Native Americans. Indeed, I maintain that it is impossible, and often counterproductive, to even attempt segregating the "manmade" from the "natural" when describing the evolution of contemporary landscapes.

The second is some people who, as far as we know, never actually visited Boulder Valley: the Spanish conquistadores. Although never directly present, their impact rippled across the region and through the centuries by their introduction of horses and cattle, the establishment of irrigation institutions, and the realignment of trade. And so it was that the Indians and Spaniards set the stage that the Americans would later walk upon and rearrange.

The First Americans and the Legacy of Coronado

In the fall of 1860 a band of about 400 Arapahoe Indian pony riders made the last great antelope roundup in Boulder Valley. They started their hunt by forming themselves into a large circle to enclose a tract of land near South Boulder Creek on which "thousands of antelope" were grazing. During the day the Indians rode a relay of ponies in an ever tightening circle. As the day wore on, the frightened antelope became so tired that they began lying down with exhaustion. By nightfall, the Indians came in and slaughtered all the antelope they wanted. Some 500 antelope were killed that day for use as winter meat by the tribe. This hunt took place near a hollow where Charlie Pancost would soon build Boulder Valley's first reservoir. Today, Xcel Energy's Valmont Power Plant stands at that site.[3]

It is tempting to overlook Indian impacts, such as the antelope hunt, on the Front Range. After all, history belongs to those who write it. If the hunt were not recorded in an early Boulder history, all memory of this hunt would now be lost. Without a written record from the Native Americans, it is tempting mark the beginning of changes to the land with the arrival of those who wrote down their observations. Once the Indians were removed, it became easy to overlook the legacy of Native Americans.

The Indians of the High Plains and Mountain West were nomads. For the most part, their lifestyle was one of cyclic seasonal movement centered on the availability of grass, game, water, and shelter. Their lifestyle demanded movement, not year-round sedentary occupation. This is in stark contrast to the Spanish settlement of New Mexico, where the Spanish conquistadores had to contend with Indians living in well-established and sedentary villages. In Colorado the settlers stayed and expelled the Indians to less desirable areas.

In 2009, workers digging a garden pool unearthed a Clovis point cache in the yard of a west Boulder residence. The tools place aboriginal occupation of the Boulder Valley to the late Pleistocene, or at least 13,000 years ago. Biochemical analysis of proteins on the points indicates that the implements were used to butcher now-extinct ice-age camels and horses. Protein evidence from the tools also suggests the presence of bear and sheep. Other excavations show that Colorado contained both Columbian and American mastodons, dire wolf, horses, saber-toothed cat, Harlan's ground sloth, and other large mammals in the centuries before human occupation. Although the reasons for extinctions of these animals remain hotly debated, there is no reason to doubt that these animals were hunted and consumed by aboriginal populations up until their extinction.[4]

Native American occupation continued uninterrupted from the late Pleistocene to the present. Archeologists describe Native American occupation in northeastern Colorado in terms of several cultural periods. Throughout that time, a gradual cultural and economic evolution took place. The earliest phase was a Paleo-Indian period that extended from about 9500 to 5500 BC and was characterized by gathering and big-game hunting. After that, a Plains Archaic period spanned from about 5500 BC to AD 1. A Late Prehistoric period followed until about 1550. During this time the Native American hunters and gathers likely moved seasonally between the mountains and plains.[5]

In 1540 everything changed for the Indians of the American West. That year Captain-General Francisco Vasquez de Coronado, the Spanish conquistador, began his journey in search of Cibola, the fabled Seven Cities of Gold. Traveling with his army of conquerors from the city of Mexico, Coronado and his men became the first Europeans to ascend the Rio Grande into what is now New Mexico and then push beyond to the Central and High Plains in what are now parts of Texas, Kansas, Nebraska, and possibly Colorado. Coronado's party was enormous for its time. With him were over one hundred Spaniards, including at least three women, six Franciscan friars, and more than 1,000 Indian allies supported by about 500 horses and pack animals.[6]

This was the first time American Indians saw horses and the first that Spaniards saw the American bison. When Coronado traveled to the plains, they encountered small settlements of Indians who "live in tents made of tanned skins of the cows." The Indians communicated with them via sign language and said that there was a very large river in the land of the rising sun, and that one could go along this river for ninety days without a break from settlement to settlement.[7]

Coronado's expedition through the High Plains is one of the most remarkable events in the European conquest of the Americas. After traveling all the way from Mexico City, they set out anew from somewhere near modern-day Pecos, New Mexico, and then headed east for twenty-two days with the full army. Realizing the vast distances involved, Coronado turned the foot soldiers around and continued onward with a select group of horsemen for another forty-two days. Along the way Coronado encountered so many buffalo that it was "impossible to number them." Traveling the plains "there was not a day that I lost sight of them," Coronado reported. Based on his travel distances, Coronado's expedition easily went past the Arkansas River and perhaps beyond to the Platte River in central Nebraska or even the Missouri.[8]

Coronado's epic journey marked the beginning of Hispanic occupation in the Southwest. The Spanish and later Mexican settlers that followed (notwithstanding their brief expulsion during the Pueblo Revolt) transformed the western landscape. They introduced horses, cattle, sheep, and other domestic animals and plants. Eventually Spanish and Indian peoples learned to coexist. The Spaniards and later New Mexicans developed a unique agrarian culture centered on irrigation via the *acequia* or ditch systems. Their irrigation technology was eventually dispersed around the West as Anglo-American settlers later flooded in. Their cultural and ecological impacts resonate to this day. When Anglo-Americans began trickling in during the early 1800s to what is now eastern Colorado, the Spaniards had already acquired some 270 years' experience in the area, and left in their wake an environment that was permanently altered.

In the seventeenth and early eighteenth centuries, the Comanche Indians, who by then were acquiring Spanish horses, spent much of the year between the Colorado Front Range and the Sawatch Mountains. The Comanches and their Ute allies gathered wild seeds, nuts, and berries and snared jack rabbits and other small mammals. During the summer and fall they spent time on the plains hunting bison. Sometimes they headed farther south to raid the Spanish Pueblos or trade for corn.[9]

By the time Colonel Henry Dodge commanded a troop of Dragoons on a march up the South Platte to the foothills in 1835, the distribution of Indians along the Front Range and High Plains had markedly changed. Significantly Dodge described what we now know as the High Plains in the vicinity of Boulder as "Snakes and Crow's War Ground." Dodge also reported that Blackfeet Indians occupied the area between the North and South Platte Rivers, and the "Gros Ventres Indians of the Prairie" lived in what is now Weld and Adams Counties, Colorado. Farther south, the "Chiennes Indians" occupied the north bank of the Arkansas River near Bents Fort. The Indians he encountered were nomadic, and each group would sweep across vast tracts of the High Plains during any single season.[10]

For the Arapahoe and Cheyenne, coming to the Colorado High Plains was a dramatic event. Prior to 1700, the Arapahoe and Cheyenne were farmers living on the Upper Mississippi. They lived in earth lodges and were more or less sedentary. Beginning in the early 1700s, the Arapahoe and Cheyenne were in what is now North Dakota. In the early nineteenth century, the Cheyenne were living in the lake district of western Minnesota. It is around this time that they may have acquired horses from the Kiowa. Concurrently, the Europeans were pushing westward in a relentless quest for furs. It seems that a series of wars over the control of the fur trade motivated the Arapahoe and Cheyenne to begin a slow migration southwest onto the High Plains. Eventually, the Arapahoe and Cheyenne exchanged their sedentary lifestyle for a nomadic existence based on the horse and bison. It was only after the Long Expedition that the Arapahoe and Cheyenne began spending considerable time along the Front Range. The Cheyenne and other plains Indians intentionally set fires, held communal hunts, grazed horses, transplanted beneficial species, and took whatever was useful for their survival. It is through their efforts that plants like the American groundnut (*Apios americana*) were likely introduced to Boulder Valley.[11]

Introduction of guns in the early 1600s by the Dutch, French, and English on the East Coast of North America and even earlier by the Spaniards in Mexico began a long transformation of Native American hunting practices across the continent. To acquire guns and other European trading goods, the Indians accelerated their hunting and trapping of animals. The introduction of the horse and European trade goods led to radical adjustments in the Indian social structures and resource strategies. Once horses became widely available, tribes had new flexibility for dealing with the changes that were affecting them. Horses facilitated a transition of the tribes from mostly sedentary lifestyles to a wholly nomadic existence based on bison hunting. Trade with the whites provided them with the items they could not produce while on the move. By the early 1700s the Indians depended on hunting and trading to support their lifestyle. Thus, Indians became an extension of the European's extractive commodity trade in furs and hides. The Indians were not idle bystanders as the populations of fur- and hide-bearing animals were decimated throughout the nineteenth century.[12]

These Indians had no permanent homes, but were not homeless. They circulated widely through the seasons between favorite summer and winter camps. Their travels were guided by seasonally available water, game, and pasture. Their environment was very unpredictable. Reliance on mammal hunting did not provide the security of a sedentary farm life. The short- and medium-grass prairies over which the nomadic hunters wandered evolved in concert with marginal and highly variable annual rainfall. Wildlife populations that the Indians relied on fluctuated with the weather and the grass. Include extractive practices such as hide and fur hunting by both Indians and Americans, and there is no surprise that the animal populations in the Foothills and High Plains experienced a long precipitous decline. At almost the very moment that the hunting pressures completely undermined the Indians' nomadic lifestyle, white prospectors discovered gold on the Front Range, leading to a flood of settlers onto the Indians' critical winter camping ranges. Even if the brutal campaign of ethnic cleansing by whites to remove the Indians from the High Plains in the 1860s had never taken place, it is doubtful that the Indians' nomadic ways could have survived for much longer.[13]

Once the ethnic cleansing of Indians was complete, the space for Americans to build their farms, towns, mines, and ditches was opened. The landscape that the Americans entered may have been wild but it was not pristine.

MAJOR STEPHEN HARRIMAN LONG AND THE UNITED STATES TOPOGRAPHICAL ENGINEERS

In the aftermath of the Louisiana Purchase, Americans began tracing the footsteps of Lewis and Clark to fill in the blank places on the maps of the American West. Prominent among the explorers was Major Stephen Harriman Long of the United States Topographical Engineers. In 1819 and 1820 Long mounted a scientific exploring expedition to the watersheds of the Mississippi and Missouri Rivers. Long's unusually broad mandate included reporting on peoples his party encountered and collecting information on the region's topography, geology, and biology. In February 1820, Secretary of War John C. Calhoun ordered Long to make an overland exploration of the country from the Missouri to the Rocky Mountains and then proceed along the base of the mountains and return via the Arkansas and Red Rivers.[14]

The mission, which came to be known as the Long Expedition, was the first government-sponsored scientific and topographical survey to reach the base of Colorado's Front Range. Long's expedition had about twenty-two men. A key member was Edwin James, who later published the expedition's journal. In early June 1820, the expedition departed Council Bluffs and headed upstream along the Platte River. The party remained vigilant for hostile Indians and often posted sentinels through the night. While traveling, they hunted buffalo and encountered numerous "deer, badgers, hares, prairie wolves, eagles, buzzards, ravens, and owls." On typical days they traveled twenty to twenty-five miles, and did so for months at a time. As they progressed westward, the number of trees along the river diminished and eventually disappeared altogether. By June 21, they noted that wood was so scarce that they could find no poles to pitch their tents. On June 22 they reached the confluence of the North and South Platte, where they saw elk wading in the river. The next day they started up the South Platte and encountered signs of Indians. That day they noted a "narrow fringe of timber" along the South Platte, much of it killed by old age or beaver. On June 24, the party saw "immense herds of bisons, blackening the whole surface of the country."[15]

On June 26, the expedition camped near a recently occupied Indian fortification that could have protected up to thirty men. The breastwork was a circular form about five feet tall composed of logs and bison skeletons. Nearby was a semicircular row of sixteen bison skulls arranged to point downriver. One of the skulls was painted with red lines. A rod stuck in the ground held evidence of four human scalps. One of the interpreters thought that the camp was built by a war party of Pawnee Loup Indians.

Long later wrote that the "Great Desert is frequented by roving bands of Indians who have no fixed place of residence but roam from place to place in quest of game." By June 30, the expedition had ascended the South Platte far enough to make out their first distant view of the mountains. Rapid progress and the first sight of the mountains cheered them. By July 3, they began finding more and more wood, eventually encountering an "uninterrupted stripe [sic] of timber, extending along the immediate banks of the river, never occupying a space of half a mile in width." Of the ground they just covered, Long noted that the Platte and South Platte was "almost entirely destitute of woodland, scarcely a tree, bush, or even a shrub, making its appearance."[16]

The South Platte "is seldom navigable, except for skin canoes, requiring but a moderate depth of water, and for these only when a freshet prevails in the river," Long noted. It was so shallow that few attempts were ever made to ascend the wide river in canoes.[17]

By moving fast, they left little time for detailed survey or exploration. One day they passed three large creeks coming in from the northwest. These creeks were likely the Cache la Poudre, Thompson, and St. Vrain. Long named one of these streams the Elk, probably for what we now know as the St. Vrain. Sometime on July 4, 1820, they crossed the fortieth parallel, which would have placed them directly east of what is now Boulder near modern-day Brighton, Colorado. On July 4 they did not even pause to celebrate, but Major Long ordered an extra ration of maize and distributed of a small portion of whiskey to the men. By now, the expedition was commonly seeing both longleaf and narrowleaf cottonwood. On July 5, they passed another stream that they named "Canon-ball Creek" for its stone cobbles. Continuing upstream, they passed more creeks. "Vermillion Creek" came in from the south, and nearly opposite to it was a much larger creek that they called "Medicine Lodge Creek," named after an Indian medicine lodge that once stood near its mouth. Based on their position, distances traveled, and the expedition map, the most likely modern candidates for Vermillion and Medicine Lodge Creeks are Sand Creek and Clear Creek respectively, which join the South Platte nearly opposite from each other.

About noon on July 5, 1820, the party had traveled over 1,000 miles and camped at the base of a "range of naked and almost perpendicular" rock. They halted in front of the "chasm through which the Platte issues from the mountains." The diversity of wildlife at the foot of the mountains was striking. Beaver, otter, mink, and muskrat were abundant along the rivers, and "badgers, raccoons, hares, polecats, porcupines, many varieties of squirrels, panthers, wild cats, lynxes and foxes of several species" were in residence. At other times they reported elk, deer, prairie dogs, eagles, wolves, rattlesnakes, and grizzly bears.[18]

After exploring in the vicinity of what we now call Waterton Canyon, the expedition continued on toward the Arkansas, traveling south along a tributary of the South Platte, most likely Plum Creek. Long's expedition provides the earliest reliable descriptions of the Colorado High Plains and was the first to map the South Platte and its tributaries near the foothills. Perhaps most significantly, on the expedition's map, Long prominently displayed the words "GREAT DESERT" across Colorado's High Plains between the South Platte and Arkansas Rivers. "I do not hesitate in giving the opinion, that it is almost wholly unfit for cultivation, and of course uninhabitable by a people depending upon agriculture for their subsistence," Long wrote. "Although tracts of fertile land considerably extensive are occasionally to be met with," he added, "the scarcity of wood and water, almost uniformly prevalent, will prove an insuperable obstacle in the way of settling the country."[19]

Thus the Great American Desert was born. Later writers only reinforced the notion of a vast inhospitable, waterless plain. When Thomas Farnham, a British traveler, journeyed to the High Plains in 1839, the landscape had become even more fearsome: "It is a scene of desolation scarcely equaled on the continent, when viewed in the dearth of midsummer from the base of the hills. Above, rise in sublime confusion, mass upon mass, shattered cliffs through which is struggling the dark foliage of stinted shrub-cedars; while below you spreads far and wide the burnt and arid desert, whose solemn silence is seldom broken by the tread of any other animal than the wolf or the starved and thirsty horse which bears the traveller across its wastes."[20]

For the generation that followed Major Stephen Harriman Long, the waterless and treeless plain across a barren prairie occupied by hostile Indians was seen as holding little prospect for settlement. But the harsh aridity implied by the word "desert" was an exaggeration fostered by a series of dry years that occurred at the time of Long's expedition. It would take other travelers with different motivations to begin challenging Long's view of the region.[21]

JOHN C. FREMONT AND THE CORPS OF TOPOGRAPHICAL ENGINEERS

Trappers and traders traveling among the Indians were the vanguard of America in the trans-Missouri West in the first decades after the Louisiana Purchase. Outside of the Mississippi River Basin, Spain (and later Mexico) claimed all of the land south of the Arkansas River, the Colorado River Basin, and land in present-day Nevada, Utah, Arizona, and California. North of the forty-second parallel, in what was known as Oregon, was a contested territory between the United States and Great Britain. The area that became Colorado was a destination for trappers and traders and was a thoroughfare for travelers to the Oregon and Spanish territories. Trappers, traders, and later settlers led the way in the long process of Americanizing the region. When the United States government wished to extend its reach, an obscure branch of the War Department, the Corps of Topographical Engineers, often found itself in the forefront in of those efforts. Through the Corps, exploration and mapmaking by the young Unites States government gave substance to its geopolitical claims.

Today the Corps is all but forgotten to most Americans. In the 1840s, however, the Corps was famous. It created the maps that led migrants west. It gathered intelligence ahead of the Mexican-American War. It helped lift the veil of western topography and affixed names to landmarks that remain in use today. Exploits of the Corps sparked intense public interest. Presidents and Congress employed the Corps in the cause of American expansion.

Among the heroes of the Corps, John C. Fremont remains the most famous. Rivers and mountains across the American West remain associated with Fremont's travels. He named the Golden Gate and the Great Basin as well as many mountains, lakes, and rivers. Fremont's work helped inspire the Mormon migration to Utah. His maps guided the overland emigrations to Oregon and California.

Through several expeditions mounted in the 1840s, Fremont was charged with mapping routes for overland migration to the American West. His detailed maps of routes along the South Platte and Arkansas would aid settlers as they rushed to Colorado during the Gold Rush a few years later. Figure 1.1 is the map produced as part of the Fremont Expedition to New Mexico and the Southern Rocky Mountains. This map later helped settlers reach the Pikes Peak area during the Gold Rush. The closest Fremont came to Boulder Valley was to Fort St. Vrain on the South Platte. His report of the area was influential in convincing easterners that the valleys along the Front Range held great agricultural potential.

Fremont employed Lucien Maxwell of Taos, New Mexico, to serve as the chief hunter to the expeditions of 1842 and 1843–44. Also joining the party was a young William Gilpin, later to serve as a bodyguard to Abraham Lincoln and the first territorial governor of Colorado. Rounding out the party was Maxwell's brother-in-law, Christopher "Kit" Carson. Broad-shouldered and with clear blue eyes, Carson would go on to become a lifelong friend of Fremont. In time Carson's fame would eclipse that of all other western trappers and mountain men and perhaps Fremont himself.[22]

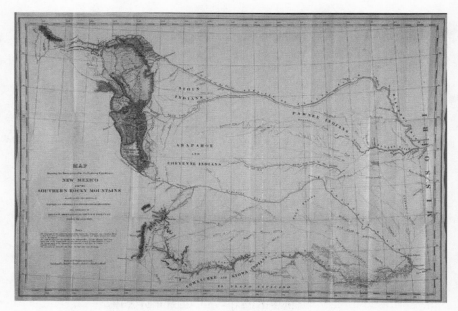

FIGURE 1.1. A map produced in 1845 from information collected during the Fremont expedition to New Mexico and the Southern Rocky Mountains.

Fremont helped dispel Long's declaration that much of the American West, and in particular what would become Colorado, was a barren desert, devoid of potential. In vivid contrast to Long's "Great American Desert," Fremont spoke glowingly of Colorado's great agricultural potential. Fremont's observations of the rich grasslands along the base of the "Black Hills," mountains we now call the Front Range, helped inspire the westward migration to Colorado as soon as gold was found.

On his first expedition, Fremont arrived at Fort St. Vrain on July 10, 1842, where he was warmly welcomed by Ceran St. Vrain, a French Canadian from St. Louis. The trading fort was built using Mexican laborers that Ceran St. Vrain employed to make adobe bricks in the style of New Mexico. The stream directly across the South Platte from the fort now bears the St. Vrain name. When Fremont's expedition arrived, trade along the Front Range was dominated by the Bent, St. Vrain & Company, which worked the eastern plains of Colorado and traded between St. Louis and Taos. Ceran St. Vrain was one of the three partners in the company, the others being brothers

Charles and William Bent. St. Vrain and his partners were energetic, having established their trading network, two forts, a couple of ranches in northern New Mexico, and homes for themselves at Taos.[23]

Fremont regretted that he did not have the time to visit the mountains to the west. On leaving the fort on July 12, the party headed down the South Platte for some distance, "which resembled a garden in the splendor of fields of varied flowers, which filled the air with fragrance." After crossing Thompson Creek, the Cache la Poudre, the expedition headed north toward Fort Laramie.[24]

A year later, Fremont returned during a second expedition and arrived at St. Vrain's fort on July 2, 1843. While there, they extend the reconnaissance upstream from the previous year. Several days later they approached what is now lower downtown Denver, surprising "a grizzly bear sauntering along the [South Platte] river." Later they halted for the night a little above Cherry Creek, likely near present-day Confluence Park in Denver.[25]

Fremont's enthusiasm about the region grew. Where the South Platte emerges from the mountains, Fremont found "excellent grass and rushes for the animals" and many "beautiful flowers, which we had not hitherto met." A day later Fremont had more good things to say, noting that they passed "little valleys, with pure crystal water, here leaping swiftly along." These valleys contained "green spots of luxuriant grass."[26]

Farther south the exploring party had another encounter with the local fauna. Riding quickly, they came upon a large grizzly bear that was busy digging roots. On seeing them, the grizzly "charged upon us with such sudden energy that several of us came near losing our saddles." In short order, the explorers put six rifle balls in the bear, killing him. Not wishing to waste any meat, Fremont found that he "was miserably poor, and added nothing to our stock of provisions."[27]

Notwithstanding the excitement of a grizzly bear encounter, Fremont liked what he saw. On July 11, 1843, he summed the impressions that were gathering in his mind over the last few days. "The soil of all this country is excellent, admirably adapted to agricultural purposes, and would support a large agricultural and pastoral population," Fremont wrote. "A glance at the map, along our several lines of travel, will show you that this plain is watered by many streams. Throughout the western half of the plain, these are shallow, with sandy beds, becoming deeper as they reach the richer lands approaching the Missouri river."[28]

Here Fremont forcefully contradicts Long's view that the region was "almost wholly unfit for cultivation." Boosters of western migration welcomed Fremont's revisionist reports. Nevertheless, it would be another fifteen years before the Gold Rush and the flood of migrants to Colorado began. But when they did come, it was Fremont's words and maps that led the way.

NOTES

1. James, *Account of an Expedition*, 3:236.

2. City of Boulder Forestry Division, https://bouldercolorado.gov/parks-rec/the-benefits-of-trees.

3. Bixby, *History of Clear Creek*.

4. "Clovis-era Tool Cache"; Dell'Amore, "Ancient Camels Butchered in Colorado"; Yohe and Bamforth, "Late Pleistocene Protein Residues."

5. Gleichman and Gleichman, *Prehistoric Paleo-Indian Cultures*; G. C. Frison and M. L. Larson, *Prehistoric Hunter-Gathers of the High Plains and Rockies*, 3rd ed. (Walnut Creek, CA: Left Coast Press, 2009); Gleichman, Gleichman, and Karhu, "Excavations at the Rock Creek Site."

6. This section utilizes the translation of Coronado's journals from Winship's *Journey of Coronado*. Winship does not assert that Coronado entered what is modern-day Colorado, but I think that it is highly likely. Coronado's was the second group of Spaniards to see the American Southwest. The first known were Cabeza de Vaca and three others, lone survivors of the 300-man Navarez expedition that marooned near Tampa Bay, Florida, on April 15, 1528. Also see Weber, *Spanish Frontier*.

7. Winship, *Journey of Coronado*, 65.

8. Ibid., 201, 214. The expedition used dead-reckoning methods to estimate latitude. Dead reckoning is a navigation method that was known to the Spaniards of the time so the statement that they reached fortieth parallel is probably quite accurate. Coronado reported the distances they traveled using the obsolete Spanish unit of distance, the league. A Spanish league is equivalent to about 4.2 kilometers, or about 2.6 miles.

9. Isenberg, *Destruction of the Buffalo*, 34.

10. This information comes from one of two maps that were attached to Dodge, *Journal of the March*.

11. Hyde, *Life of George Bent*; see also West, *Contested Plains*, 74.

12. Dolin, *Fur, Fortune, and Empire*; Isenberg, *Destruction of the Buffalo*.

13. Isenberg, *Destruction of the Buffalo*, 45.

14. James, *Account of an Expedition*, 1:2.

15. Ibid., 2:160, 180; 3:227.

16. Ibid., 2:180.

17. Ibid., 3:228; The term "freshet" refers to increased streamflows seen after a storm.

18. Ibid., 3:236.

19. Ibid.

20. Farnham, *Travels in the Great Western Prairies*, 137.

21. Lawson and Stockton, "Desert Myth and Climatic Reality." These authors used tree ring data to establish a statistical relationship with known climate conditions to infer climate conditions on the High Plains back to 1700. They concluded that when Stephen Long passed through in 1819–20 and John Fremont in 1842–44, severe drought conditions were prevalent.

22. Fremont, *Report of the Exploring Expedition*, 9.

23. In 1842, Taos and New Mexico were still part of Mexico.

24. Fremont, *Report of the Exploring Expedition*, 32.

25. Ibid., 112.

26. Ibid., 113.

27. Ibid., 114. The encounter was on July 11, 1843.

28. Ibid.

Juggernaut of Change

"In the hills, where the bear, the lion, and the wolf
once roamed, there are cities, towns, and innumerable mining camps, where thousands dig, and delve,
and toil for gold that glitters, and silver that shines. In
the valleys, where streams with limpid currents once
ran unfettered to the plains on their journey to the
sea, there are towns, where industries flourish."
—*William E. Pabor, 1883*[1]

In the years immediately surrounding Charles Fremont's visits to the Front
Range, pelt trapping reached its peak and quickly declined. Buffalo hide
hunting replaced the beaver as the most exploited commodity in the West,
and it too went into steep decline. Then the momentous discovery of gold
by three brothers from Georgia, William, Oliver, and Levi Russell, in 1858 set
in motion a juggernaut of human migration that one can argue has never
ended. All these events were motivated by one common underlying theme,

DOI: 10.5876/9781607323822.c002

the appropriation of natural resources for private gain. Colorado's watersheds were changed forever.

EARLY IMPACTS OF TRAPPING AND HUNTING ON WESTERN RIVERS

The scarcity of beaver, river otters, and numerous other fur-bearing animals is a lingering outcome of a concerted and systematic extractive trapping effort culminating in the 1820s and 1830s. With overtrapping, the populations of these animals quickly collapsed in Colorado. To this day, the legacy of trapping has suppressed the populations of many of these animals. In many river basins, some of these animals were entirely trapped out and have not returned. Due to the scarcity of records we will never know the full extent of trapping. As late as 1911, a lone female mink was trapped on Boulder Creek, five miles west of Boulder. Mink would not be seen on Boulder Creek for nearly one hundred years until they began making a slow comeback in the early 2000s.[2]

It is difficult to piece together the magnitude of trapping on Front Range streams. As early as 1810, trappers worked the Front Range. In 1828, French fur trappers reportedly made a rendezvous on the Cache la Poudre at a site known as LaPorte. In 1836 a trapper's caravan worked its way up the Cache la Poudre toward the Green River. A man by the name of Antoine Janis was with his father at the time and later staked a squatter's claim at LaPorte in 1844 at the site of their old camp. How much trapping these groups performed, however, remains obscure.[3]

Other whites soon trickled into the area. From about 1838 to 1840, four competing adobe trading forts were established on the banks of the South Platte. These forts were little more than private trading stockades that were hardened to withstand Indian attacks. On the South Platte, this chain of forts was concentrated in a twelve-mile cluster around the mouth of the St. Vrain River.[4]

The largest and best-known trading fort on the South Platte was owned by Ceran St. Vrain and his partners, the brothers William and Charles Bent. The Bents and St. Vrain are most famous for their American Fur Company outpost (Bents Fort) on the Arkansas River. The Bents and St. Vrain built their South Platte post around 1837 or 1838 to better stay ahead of threats to their business. By this time, their business had largely shifted toward buffalo hide extraction.

That four forts could operate along the banks of the upper South Platte a few miles apart demonstrates the growing economic significance of the region. There were apparently enough fur- and hide-bearing animals to sustain several years of intense trapping and hunting in the headwater region of the South Platte to justify the construction of forts.

As mountain men kept few records, we can only speculate on the actual number of furs and hides taken along the South Platte and its tributaries. Statistics from other areas in the West give us a sense for the magnitude of the trapping industry. For example, over a four-year period from 1823 to 1827, about sixty British trappers employed by the Hudson Bay Company working streams in Montana took "no fewer than eighty thousand beaver, weighing in all about one hundred sixty thousand pounds." Likewise in 1825, William Henry Ashley and a group of 120 men trapped the headwaters of the Green River in what is now Wyoming. Ashley's party took about 6,000 pelts that fetched $50,000 when they reached St. Louis.[5]

In North Park during the fall of 1827, the young Ceran St. Vrain assumed charge of a trapping expedition to Colorado when its leader fell ill and died. The party set out from Taos and trapped the headwaters of the North Platte along the present Colorado-Wyoming border. Eventually St. Vrain's party crossed to the Front Range and ended back in Taos in May of 1828. On reaching Taos, Ceran St. Vrain and his party sold their take of furs for $5,708.50.[6]

While the beaver population plummeted, traders began turning their sights toward the great hide-bearing animal of the plains: the American bison. Ascending the Arkansas River in November 1806, Pike saw so many buffalo that the "the face of the prairie was covered with them, on each side of the river, their numbers exceeded imagination."[7]

In 1800 there were perhaps some 28 to 30 million buffalo grazing across the Great Plains. Of that, it is estimated that there were about 8.2 million buffalo grazing in the southern grasslands, "blackening the whole surface of the country." Bison sought water and grass along their annual migratory path. Their consumption of grass and water dictated the vegetation assemblage present along streams throughout the region.[8]

"Between 1824 and 1836 a traveler might start from any given point, south or north, in the Rocky Mountain Range, journeying by the most direct route to the Missouri River, and during the whole distance this road would be always among large bands of buffalo," Fremont said. However, by the middle of the nineteenth century, the buffalo were already in steep decline. Few remained east of the Mississippi River. In 1843 Fremont, who himself enjoyed the buffalo hunt, observed that the "extraordinary rapidity with which the buffalo is disappearing from our territories will not appear surprising when we remember the great scale on which their destruction is yearly carried on."[9]

Throughout the mid- to late eighteenth century, the Great Plains was essentially a vast bison killing factory. Each year from the 1830s through the 1860s about 90,000 to 100,000 buffalo robes were sent to St. Louis alone. Across the entire Great Plains during the peak years of the early 1870s, some 5.5 million bison were killed every year. Buffalo were killed for local consumption, export of hides, and more odiously to bring about the eventual starvation and submission of Plains Indians. Historians generally agree that Generals William T. Sherman and Philip Sheridan "viewed the eradication of the buffalo as 'the critical line of attack' in the struggle with the plains tribes," and that these men actively encouraged their subordinates to carry out a policy of exterminating the buffalo.[10]

With the decimation of the bison, the species reached its lowest ebb in 1889. The last wild bison in northeastern Colorado was also killed that year. So few bison remained in Colorado that William T. Hornaday, superintendent of the national zoo, resorted to counting phantoms. "There is a rumor that there are ten or twelve mountain buffaloes still on foot in Colorado," Hornaday wrote, "in a region called Lost Park." Sounding desperate, he noted that while the rumor "lacks confirmation, we gladly accept it as a fact." By 1897 not a single wild bison remained in all of Colorado.[11]

Hornaday's grim survivor tally of January 1, 1889, included 25 in the Panhandle of Texas, 20 in Colorado, 26 in southern Wyoming, 10 in Montana, and 4 in western Dakota. Add in another 550 animals remaining in the Northwest Territory of Canada, and the total number of wild bison for all of North America was only 635. Another 256 were in captivity, and 200 were under US Government protection in Yellowstone Park. This meant that, including members of phantom herds, only 1,091 bison remained. In under a century, a mammal that reigned as the keystone species over large swaths of North America since the close of the Pleistocene was eliminated as an ecological force.[12]

By 1909, the only way a biologist working with the US Biological Survey could piece together the former range of buffalo in Colorado was by looking for their bleached skulls. Without any nostalgia in his language, Merit Cary wrote, "the bleached skulls, now rapidly disintegrating after more than 20 years' exposure may still be seen in considerable numbers." In the same survey Cary estimated that "considerably fewer" than 3,000 elk remained in the entire state of Colorado. Moreover, the "huge piles of antlers at many of the ranches in the northern mountains are mute testimony to the former abundance of this noble animal."[13]

It was not just buffalo that were shot into near oblivion. All large native grazing animals had gun sights trained on them. In 1870, William Henry Jackson could have shot the photo of bleached animal skulls from Albany County, Wyoming (Figure 2.1), anywhere in the American West. In the most vivid way, Jackson's photograph demonstrates that all large animals, not just the buffalo, were gunned down by hunters across the plains and mountains. Although the overall number of animals killed is unknown, Jackson's photograph hints at the carnage. The grainy image of buffalo, elk, deer, mountain sheep, and wolf skulls and bones heaped up in a trophy pile celebrates the kill.

Historians have asserted that the "social, economic, and environmental transformations that contributed to the demise of the bison were not separate categories of change, but embedded in each other." The eradication of the buffalo and their systematic replacement by cows transformed the rivers and valleys of the High Plains. Vegetation that coevolved with the bison began adapting to the needs of cows and other species introduced by the settlers.[14]

Predators fared even worse than either the beaver or buffalo. The fate of these animals would be sealed with the discovery of gold. Among those to encounter predators was the early settler Morse Coffin, who was among the first to Boulder Valley. In the winter of 1859, Coffin and a friend lived in a shack on mesa about three miles south of Boulder, on land that is now part of Boulder Mountain Parks. They were sawing lumber nearby and often encountered the local wildlife. One morning a helper by the name of Abe Cronk went to work in the woods alone. Coffin later heard Cronk shouting excitedly. Apparently, Cronk "had encountered a small pack of large grey wolves." The wolves soon became aggressive and "hung around and snapped their jaws and snarled as though they might try to make a breakfast of him." Cronk was able to escape but came close to becoming a meal for the gray wolves. But that risk was not to last.[15]

FIGURE 2.1. William Henry Jackson's 1870 photograph of bleached animal skulls in Albany County, Wyoming. Photograph courtesy of US Geological Survey.

Settlers quickly shot as many of these animals as they could. By 1906, only a few gray wolves remained in scattered corners of the state. Those that did remain had bounties on their heads of up to $25 per animal. Today, the gray wolf's presence in the Front Range is only a memory buried in yellowing biological surveys.[16]

Similarly, when Charles Fremont encountered a grizzly bear during his 1843 expedition in what is now Denver, he could scarcely guess their fate over the next few decades. By the early 1870s grizzly bears were only present in the upper reaches of Front Range watersheds and were in decline across the rest of the state. At the turn of the twentieth century grizzly bears were all but absent from the Front Range.[17]

The demise of the large grazers and predators likely led to secondary changes in the flora. From work in Yellowstone Park, researchers know that major vegetation alterations occur as changes in predator population impact grazing animals. Once native grazing animals were eliminated, the pressure they exerted on native grasses, shrubs, and trees ended and likely caused a shift in vegetation patterns. However, the story is not so simple. Complicating the pattern of change is the nearly simultaneous introduction of cattle and horses where few existed before. Change in vegetation patterns clearly occurred, although the details remain murky.[18]

While hunters were killing off native wildlife, early settlers were importing cattle and sheep. As emigrants crossed the plains, they often used oxen to pull their wagons. Emigrants also brought milk cows to supplement their diets. When the Gold Rush began, settlers had only a vague idea how their livestock would fare once in Colorado. Among the early settlers was Colonel Jack Henderson, who crossed the plains with oxen in late 1858. When he arrived at Auraria, Colorado, he had no place to keep the oxen, so he put them out to pasture and hoped for the best. The next spring, while hunting buffalo near Bijou Creek, Henderson came across the oxen grazing on native grasses. Over the winter they had grown fat and were in fine condition. With favorable reports from people like Henderson, Colorado's livestock industry was born.[19]

By 1862 Denver butchers were boasting that "no fatter cattle can ordinarily be found on the markets of the eastern states." It was soon clear that a lucrative homegrown cattle industry would emerge in Colorado. As hunters exterminated the last of the buffalo, ranchers moved in to fill the vacated ecosystem with cattle, sheep, oxen, horses, and mules brought from the East.[20]

Joining the deliberately imported animals were numerous unwanted creatures. Animals such as the brown or Norway rat (*Mus norvegicus*) and house mouse (*Mus musculus*) hitchhiked in with settlers to make homes in Colorado towns and along nearby waterways. By 1910, rats and mice were found in all large towns such as Denver, Boulder, Longmont, and Greeley.[21]

More recently, other species such as white-tailed deer, mourning doves, and bobolinks migrated up newly expanding riparian forests along the South Platte. These animals were formerly unknown or rare on streams like Boulder Creek, but are now fairly common. And perhaps most interesting, the Canada goose, which was introduced up and down the Front Range by the Colorado Division of Wildlife in the 1960s, is now so common that many people think they have been here forever.

From the earliest days of active settlement, newcomers have systematically, both deliberately and incidentally, changed the composition and distribution of animals living along Colorado streams and surrounding watersheds. The changes wrought were dramatic and irreversible. Virtually every stream experienced impacts. As buffalo hunting accelerated, an event of even greater import initiated landscape transformations that linger to this day.

THE GOLD RUSH AND ITS LEGACY

For a number of years, unconfirmed rumors of gold along the Front Range circulated among trappers and traders. However, through most of the 1850s tension between the whites and Indians made travel along the Front Range seem suicidal for anyone thinking about prospecting. Then in the late spring and summer of 1857, Colonel Edwin V. Sumner, under orders from Secretary of War Jefferson Davis, led the First Cavalry against Cheyenne camps on the Platte and Arkansas Rivers. A series of inconclusive engagements ensued, but reports in the East made it seem that the Cheyenne were vanquished. A window opened for people wishing to investigate the gold rumors.[22]

In the spring of 1858, a party of Cherokees and whites from Georgia headed west under the lead of William Green Russell and John Beck. Their goal was Ralston Creek, near present-day Denver. When they arrived, they almost immediately found some gold, but it was not in the quantities they had hoped. Moving farther upstream past Cherry Creek and on to Dry Creek, they finally found what they were seeking. Each man began gathering up to ten dollars per day. Word quickly spread.

Discoveries by William Green Russell and John Beck were teasers, but did not really amount to much. The Gold Rush itself got under way in 1859 when John H. Gregory discovered a major placer (gravel bar) gold deposit on Clear Creek near where the town of Black Hawk now stands. Once the magnitude of Gregory's discovery was understood, prospectors fanned out across the Front Range trying to replicate his success. In Boulder County the first commercially viable discovery was at Gold Run, near the town of Gold Hill. Once gold was found, the mining effort that unfolded was monumental.[23]

FIGURE 2.2. A placer mining operation near Alma, Colorado. This photograph was likely taken sometime between 1880 and 1900. Photograph courtesy of the Denver Public Library, Western History Collection, X–60090. Reprinted with permission.

The western experience in mining began about ten years earlier with the 1849 California Gold Rush. For the first few years of the California Gold Rush, and to some extent the Colorado Gold Rush, mining was largely a primitive affair. All that changed in 1853 when Edward Matteson developed the hydraulic mining process in California. Matteson directed water under high pressure through a hose and nozzle to wash alluvial sediment down into pits or streams for processing. With this invention, hydraulic mining became a major transformative activity throughout streams in the western United States. The technology evolved quickly, and eventually miners used water cannon with nicknames like the "Little Giant" to wash away entire hillsides in a day. Waste gravel ended up in the creek or along the stream banks. Never before were western streams so rapidly altered as with hydraulic mining. As Stuart Udall described it, "hydraulic mining companies set a record for industrial land abuse unparalleled in the nineteenth century."[24]

Technologies and practices perfected in California were soon employed in the Colorado gold fields. Hydraulic mining on streams like Clear Creek, Four Mile, and Left Hand Creeks in the Front Range left lasting impacts. To this day, anyone driving up Clear Creek along US Highway 6 will see spoil piles from the placer mining. A photograph of a placer mining operation near Alma, Colorado, is shown in Figure 2.2.

To enhance gold recovery efficiency, gold miners added mercury directly into the sluice boxes. A description of placer mining from the 1860s summarizes the process:

> [Hydraulic mining] requires a considerable stream of water, in such a position that it will permit a fall of from twenty to one hundred feet. This stream is conducted through an artificial aqueduct composed of sluice boxes . . . The sluice boxes have riffle-bars or clusters of slates with spaces between . . . to catch the gold and fine dirt, and to give the quicksilver an opportunity to come in contact with the fine particles and form an amalgam with them. The quicksilver is usually put in near the head of the sluice . . . [and] the washing of the gold goes on without cessation, usually from three to ten days, when the miners "clean up" by taking out a portion of the riffle-bars at a time, and collecting the coarse gold and the amalgam, pressing the gold from the mercury by straining it through cloth or buckskin . . . As water is not over-abundant . . . the miners . . . resort to blasting to bring down and loosen large quantities of the earth so that it can be more rapidly thrown into the sluice while the water is running.[25]

Hydraulic mining had obvious impacts on the streambed, and as the quote suggests, enormous impacts on water quality, too. Considerable amounts of mercury passed out of the sluices and into the stream. Also, the miners often cooked the amalgam to evaporate mercury to further concentrate the gold. In the absence of environmental regulations, both the miners and the stream likely suffered.

With the advent of the twentieth century, millers began switching to a more cost-effective but equally dangerous substance to extract gold. Cyanide came into use because it could extract upward of 95 percent of the available gold. The first cyanide mill in Boulder County was opened in 1905 at the Cache Mine near Magnolia. Environmental controls on the use of cyanide were nonexistent. The solubility of cyanide meant that mill tailings contaminated with the substance would leach into the ground and eventually reach nearby streams. Its danger notwithstanding, by 1910 cyanide mills were operating at Ward, Caribou, Sunshine, and other sites across the county.[26]

Although hydraulic mining ravaged many creeks, hard-rock mining and milling had even greater impacts on streams, especially in Boulder County.

In these sites miners and millers dumped huge volumes of mine waste and mill tailings on the slopes and canyon floors below their operations. Miners dammed creeks to operate the water mills, further altering the stream. Sediment from the various operations soon choked streambeds as storms washed material downhill away from the mining operations.

At the height of California's placer mining boom, geologists reported that the amount of "material annually overturned was reckoned in the scores of millions of cubic yards" of boulders, cobbles, sand, and silt. Sediment choked creek valleys and river canyons and reduced effective channel capacity. This resulted in increased flood intensities all the way from the Sacramento River to San Francisco Bay. With so much sediment, the magnitude of flood events increased because water had nowhere to go but over the banks. These increased flood events lasted for many years. However, as time passed, the sediment slowly worked its way down the river. Although overbank flooding would occur due to constricted channels, the large flows also flushed sediment from the system. Once this material passed downstream, some equilibrium returned and fewer out-of-bank events occurred.[27]

The experience in California provides an analogy for the Front Range. I suspect that the large Boulder Creek floods of 1894 and 1897 were so damaging in part because they were the first really large flow events since debris from milling and hydraulic mining choked the channel in the years following the 1858 discovery of gold.

Mining impacted the whole Boulder Creek Watershed. From the timber cutting that supported the industry to the tailings, mill waste, and other pollutant discharges, the stream experienced drastic changes. Between denuded hillsides and sediment-choked stream channels, it is little wonder that Boulder experienced several devastating floods in the late nineteenth century. With fewer trees to hold back the water and nowhere for the water to go once it arrived, the magnitude of late nineteenth-century floods were likely out of the ordinary in their potential to cause destruction. Figure 2.3 shows a railroad bridge in Boulder during the 1894 flood. This is not to say that large storm events (such as the Big Thompson flood of 1976 or the flooding of 2013) will not strike other area streams and cause major flooding. Rather, given the state of the watershed at the time, it is no surprise that those particular floods were so destructive.[28]

FIGURE 2.3. A railroad bridge in Boulder that was damaged during the 1894 flood on Boulder Creek. Photograph courtesy of Carnegie Branch Library for Local History, Boulder Historical Society Collection. Reprinted with permission.

PROPERTY RIGHTS, BARBED WIRE, AND THE FENCING OF THE AMERICAN WEST

Thomas Jefferson was a man of the Enlightenment who actively used the tools of science for the betterment of society. One of his signature achievements was the imposition of Cartesian geometry on America's vast western domain. By introducing the Public Land Survey System, Jefferson employed Cartesian principles to survey "township," "ranges," and "sections," revolutionizing land ownership patterns in the United States. Jefferson's initial motivation for improved surveying was to facilitate the sale or disposal of the public domain in the West. He implemented these ideas with the Land Ordinance of 1785 and the Northwest Ordinance of 1787. Jefferson probably never imagined how successful his idea would be in facilitating organized western settlement.[29]

Jefferson's Public Land Survey System resulted in the familiar rectangular property boundary patterns seen across the American West. Once Congress enacted the Homestead Act of 1861, settlers could claim title to 160-acre tracts of land provided they file an application, improve the land by living on it, and then file for deed of title. With the enactment of these laws, a quilt-like network of rectangular land parcels entered private hands in the West.

As western migration accelerated, the destruction of the bison opened the way for a flood of cattle to replace them. The migrating bison were owned by no one and taken by all. Cattle were private property that required confinement and identification by their owners. This meant one needed to control their wanderings. Control in turn required fencing. On the Great Plains where there were few trees, fence building was a herculean task. In most instances the costs and labor needed to import wood for fences or to build stone walls was beyond economic sense. Only small enclosures were practical. Where there were sufficient trees, one might build a post and rail fence. Sometimes settlers built sod fences or planted hedgerows. However, all fence options available to early settlers had serious limitations. In the late 1860s wood such as cottonwood, oak, and walnut were selling for premiums of $20 to $40 per thousand feet. Insufficient lumber for fencing quickly became a drawback to rapid settlement. For settlers to exploit the great western plains, a better fence was needed.[30]

In 1873 Henry Rose of Waterman Station, Illinois, conceived a plan to keep cattle from slipping through loose fences. The idea was to employ control through pain. Rose attached sharp wires to a board along his fence at about the height of his cows' heads. If the cows pressed up against the board, the pointed wire would cause sharp pain and the cow would recoil. Joseph F. Glidden refined Rose's invention by taking two wires and coiling them with metal barbs in between. Wire could be spun like rope, and the wire could be fixed to fence posts. Far less wood was needed, and coils of wire were relatively easy to transport. It was a good idea and a number of patents were quickly filed.[31]

Barbed wire was an immediate success. As early as 1882, barbed wire became one of the major types of fence being employed across the Great Plains, and by 1885 it was dominant. Ranchers soon adopted it across the Mountain West. It was now possible to control the motion of cattle without having cowboys keeping watch day in and day out.[32]

Barbed wire imprinted the Jeffersonian land grid on the West's ecology. Prior to its introduction, cattle could roam much as they pleased. With barbed wire, cattle were confined to the lands bounded by their owners. And those boundaries are defined by the land survey system. The Jeffersonian grid remains a legal and cultural construct that worked in concert with technology to reorganize the migration patterns of animals across the continent.

Barbed wire facilitated migration and settlement of the High Plains as never before. Barbed wire allowed people to dictate where animals migrated. Vegetation patterns soon adapted to the new land grid. Controlling the grazing location, timing, and intensity was now feasible. Once a rancher installed a barbed wire fence, he could compartmentalize his range, manage access to water, and rotate his cattle from plot to plot. Cartesian geometry now dictates cattle migration patterns.

The use of barbed wire spread as larger numbers of farmers settled former open ranges and stream corridors. Homesteaders selected the best government land, often along streams or near water sources. Cattlemen, who could previously graze the open range, soon found their herds restricted from the best grass and water sources. Accelerating settlement in turn encouraged cattlemen to acquire, settle, and fence their own land.

According to the commissioner of the General Land Office, in the 1880s whole "counties have been fenced in by cattle companies, native and Foreign." Large operators did not care if their fences forced small farmers to travel long distances for water or market. Where farmers once fenced their vegetable crops to protect them from their neighbor's cattle, now capitalists used fences to enclose large tracts to exclude all others. Some ranchers even fenced public lands to reserve the best grazing and water sources for themselves. Eventually a fence-cutting war erupted in Texas and spread to Montana before the situation stabilized. Along the way, people were killed, properties were destroyed, and neighbors became enemies.[33]

Historian Reviel Netz has called barbed wire one of the signature ecological innovations in modern times. The ecological impact of barbed wire extended to river ecology as it controlled access to water. Concentrated grazing localized waste and runoff into rivers. Erosion and vegetation patterns along water courses changed. Concentrations of cattle resulted in overgrazing in some areas and none in others. Overall, the introduction of barbed wire represents one of the most profound alterations ever to have affected the western ecological landscape.[34]

THE VANISHING FOREST

With the discovery of gold in California in 1849, a great rush of people moved up the Platte to Wyoming and across the Continental Divide. With that, almost all remaining grass, wood, and game was gone from the river corridor, so the Argonauts, as the California gold seekers were known, began heading west on a southern route along the Arkansas River where some resources remained. Cottonwood groves along the Arkansas where the Indians camped for generations were cut down in a single season by settlers heading west. Even the Big Timbers of the Arkansas began to thin, and the Indians reported that the grass for miles on either side of the river was eaten down to the ground by the Argonauts' livestock. Then with the 1858 gold strike the rush to Pikes Peak began. As settlers stampeded in, they cut down almost all remaining cottonwood groves while their cattle, horses, and oxen grazed the grass along streams to the earth. Once they reached the mountains, Colorado's primary forests came under siege.[35]

Among those exploiting the forest was twenty-two-year-old Morse Coffin, who arrived in Boulder in 1859. He quickly gave up on mining and began seeking other sources of income. Coffin learned to whipsaw and hired himself out cutting lumber for $30 per month. His first whipsaw job was cutting lumber on Four Mile Creek to build mining sluices. Later he cut lumber on the road to Gold Hill and in the foothills south of Boulder. In 1860, Coffin hiked to Left Hand Canyon and helped build a sawmill there. Coffin's experience was fairly typical for the time: new settlers needed work and mines needed lumber. As the forests began to thin, the impacts on local streams increased.[36]

As the mining camps grew and small farms started to dot the plains, timber was needed for just about everything. Miners and settlers needed it for their cabins, for burning as fuel, producing charcoal, for fences, smelting, mine construction, bridges, and flumes, and any number of other uses. Accidental fires were common and extensive. Charcoal makers even deliberately set forest fires in order to gain the right to cut burned-out areas. The High Plains fared no better. There everything was cut, and even the tender bark of cottonwood trees was used for horse feed. In short, any tree in sight with a possible use was fair game for cutting. But that was just the beginning; once railroad construction began, an insatiable demand emerged for ties to lay rails. Initially the region around Laramie, Wyoming, became a center of tie cutting when the transcontinental Union Pacific Railroad was built. Later mountain forests of Boulder County supplied many of the ties for the railroads extending into Colorado. The number of ties used in railroad construction was staggering, ranging from about 2,300 to 3,000 ties for each mile laid. If that was not enough, once constructed, the railroad itself enabled the export of wood products from across the region.[37]

Many tie cutters were migrant laborers ready to work wherever they might find a payday. A laborer might cut fifty ties in a single day. One such itinerant laborer was John Lord, who late in life wrote about his experiences in the West. Lord fought in the Civil War, worked as a rancher and miner, and even met Teddy Roosevelt. And during the late 1860s Lord spent a season as a "tie hack" cutting railroad ties along the North St. Vrain.[38]

John Lord and another knockabout, a twenty-seven-year-old partner that he knew only as Pool, agreed to cut 10,000 railroad ties at eighty cents each for a railroad construction contractor. They would cut the ties and then float them out of the mountains where they were to be loaded onto wagons for the contractor. With the onset of August, Lord and Pool headed up the North St. Vrain. As Lord described it:

> The country was virgin. There had never been an axe struck into a piece of timber and game was in abundance—elk, two kinds of deer, black and white-tail mountain sheep, cinnamon and black bear, and plenty of small game. Every stream, no matter how small, was simply alive with mountain trout. It was a paradise for two such chaps such as we. We found an abundance of the finest timber on the narrow, low, rich bottoms along the creek. The trees stood as thick on the ground as there was room for them to grow, very tall and straight. We didn't make any split ties and we never cut a tree that didn't make five ties eight feet long. Some trees made eight, hewed on both sides to a seven inch face and not under eight or over ten inches thick. We didn't make a tie over seventy-five yards from the creek bank.[39]

Lord and Pool got busy and made all their ties by Christmas of that year. Since they couldn't float their ties until the following May, they hunkered down for winter to "hunt, fish, and prospect." In the spring they got ready to move the ties:

> When the first of May came around we had all our ties piled on the bank and ready to throw into the creek. We hired men and went to throwing in ties. From the first of May until the tenth there were icicles hanging from the grass, weeds, and small bushes near the water's edge. We were in the water

every morning before sunrise up to our chins and in and out all day. And let me tell you, it wasn't every man who had the nerve to drive timber in a Rocky Mountain stream full of rapids and rocks. Many times every day the ties would lodge and pile up and if we didn't get in there and break the jam thousands of ties would pile up and wedge until we never could get them out. We had to cut or saw the ties that were the keys to the whole jam and when the ties began to pop and the rocks groan then a fellow had to fly for his life. Sometimes the ties would snap like matches. You had to run back and keep on top of the ties and get ashore where it was safe before the jam went to pieces.[40]

Danger to life and limb was never far away. "I saw one man working in under the front end of a jam. I yelled at him to get out, but the water was making so much noise he couldn't hear me or the timbers breaking," Lord explained. Then when "the timbers begin to move he saw he didn't have time to get back on top, so he jumped into the rapids and went down ahead of the jam and outswam it until he struck water smooth enough so could get back on the bank."[41]

Once they got the ties out of the mountains, it took thirty horse teams to haul them away. After making the delivery, the contractor tried to stiff Pool and Lord for the money he owed him. Pool and Lord were unperturbed, and after a calm discussion involving a well-placed gun, the contractor paid them in full. Figure 2.4 shows tie hacks throwing newly hewn ties into a Front Range creek at the kickoff of the spring tie drive.

Many others had their hand at cutting ties along local streams. Captain George Brown, who was sent to Burlington, Colorado, by the army in 1865, was one of them. Brown liked the area and decided to stay. Searching for a place to settle, Brown started a ranch on the North Fork of the South St. Vrain River. Brown would cut, stockpile, and later float wood to market at Burlington, the hamlet that was later absorbed into the town of Longmont. High-quality wood was worked into useable timbers, and the waste wood went to a charcoal kiln located on an island in the St. Vrain River.[42]

Tie drives took place up and down the Front Range. Figure 2.5 shows a tie drive on a river somewhere along the Front Range. The number of logs hints at the magnitude of deforestation. This logging affected both the stream corridor and surrounding watershed. Placing the logs in the river caused additional channel impacts.[43]

FIGURE 2.4. Tie hacks throwing newly hewn ties into a Front Range creek. Undated photo from Wroten, "Railroad Tie Industry." 332.

During the winter of 1868 to 1869 over 200,000 ties were cut and floated out on the Cache la Poudre. In 1874 tie hacks had to wait for the water to come up to float out about 25,000 ties that were stranded. South Boulder Creek had plenty of timber in its narrow boulder-strewn canyon. To get at the timber there, a company called the South Boulder Flume company built a mile-and-half-long flume. One of the company's first contracts was to run 20,000 ties to a Golden-based railroad contractor. In other areas of Boulder County where timber was thick, such as near Jamestown, Sunshine, Ward, and Nederland and along Boulder and South Boulder Creeks, tie operations were carried out from about 1870 until after 1900.[44]

Log runs also damaged ditch diversions of farmers and ranchers. Sometimes this led to violence. In 1886 tie drivers bringing 20,000 ties down South Boulder Creek made arrangements to cross most properties along the creek. When the tie drivers arrived at a ranch owned by a Mr. Connelly, he objected, saying they had made no arrangements, and forbade them to cross his property. The tie drivers persisted, and on entering Connelly's land he took up a shotgun and stationed himself behind an old stone house and fired a warning shot. The angry tie drivers charged Connelly with their spiked tie poles and drove him off. Connelly and seven tie drivers wound up getting arrested over the incident.[45]

FIGURE 2.5. A tie drive on a Front Range river. Undated photo from Wroten, "Railroad Tie Industry." 334.

Timber fed bustling lumber mills around Boulder County. Figure 2.6 shows a dam on Boulder Creek at the junction with Four Mile Creek in Boulder Canyon. On the right is the Hunt-Barber Mill. A train of the Greeley, Salt Lake & Pacific Railroad is heading up Four Mile Canyon for Sunset. Clinton Tyler and James P. Maxwell built the dam in 1865 to catch logs that they floated down Boulder Creek to the mill. Notice the wood flume that carried water to operate a power wheel at the mill. This image gives one a sense of the logging industry's scale on Boulder Creek. By 1870 Tyler and Maxwell had moved on to other endeavors and the Hunt-Barber Smelter had replaced the former sawmill.[46]

"Thirteen active saw-mills are kept in active operation" within Boulder County, boasted the *Rocky Mountain Gazetteer* in 1871. Sawmills operated at the mouth of Boulder Canyon, in Gregory Canyon, along South Boulder Creek, and elsewhere along the base of the foothills. One mill at Caribou alone employed "thirty men constantly."[47]

FIGURE 2.6. The Hunt-Barber Mill and its diversion dam on Boulder Creek. Photograph courtesy of Carnegie Branch Library for Local History, Boulder Historical Society Collection. Reprinted with permission.

Tree cutting in the first decade of active settlement was so extensive that we are really not sure what the "pre-development" conditions of forests along the streams and in the mountains were. It was soon clear that the deforestation was not sustainable. Cyrus Thomas of the Hayden Expedition became alarmed over the extent of tree cutting in the Colorado Territory. He believed that if it continued unabated, cutting could inhibit the development of the entire region. Of the wood supply he had this to say:

> I do not think the supply inexhaustible. The rapid increase of the mining operations and population in the mining sections, which are in the heart of the pine regions, is rapidly consuming, for building purposes, fuel, &c., the pines around these points. And the numerous fires which occur here, and sweep up the mountain side with a wild fury, like that of a burning prairie, are destroying vast quantities of this timber. Even now we can scarcely travel a single mile along the mountain canons where we do not see the slopes on either side marked by broad strips of burnt timber, which appear as somber spots on the otherwise beautiful scenery.[48]

Accounts such as this help explain why we see so few trees on the hill-sides above Boulder and other communities along the Front Range in photographs from the 1870s and 1880s. The situation was so severe that the US Department of Agriculture reported that by 1883 the "eastern slope of the mountains, including the counties of Laramie, Boulder, Gilpin, Clear Creek, Jefferson, Douglas, El Paso, Fremont, Lake, Park, and Chaffee have been stripped of from two-thirds to three-fourths of their lumber." Even then, active logging continued for many more years.[49]

By the mid-1870s the cutting was so extensive that some people started taking note and began clamoring for a change. An old 1831 federal law made it a crime to "cut, destroy, or remove live oak or other trees" on government land. However, the government simply lacked the manpower—and will—to enforce the law on the vast public domain.[50]

Responsibility for monitoring cutting was in the hands of the underfunded and undermanned General Land Office. Even with the authority to regulate timber cutting, the General Land Office rarely took action. Individuals simply enriched themselves at the expense of the public domain without giving anything back from their windfall. As the magnitude of cutting became apparent, the situation began to change. Starting in 1871, timber cutters in Wyoming were required to pay a fee on the wood they cut. For the first few years the fee was largely overlooked or ignored. Throughout the 1870s a "stump tax war" simmered in Wyoming as the issue of forest conservation garnered more public attention. During those years most people in Colorado supported the loggers. Lumber in the public domain was still seen as available for appropriation, not conservation. Finally, on the eve of Colorado statehood, the first prosecutions took place for illegal cutting. Then on being admitted to statehood, the Colorado Constitution authorized the legislature to issue laws to protect the new state's forests.[51]

In 1877 editorials in Denver papers began complaining that small operators were pursued by government agents while railroads and their contractors "are never molested." This emboldened a federal government that had previously looked the other way. Special Agent Marshall Wilcox of the US Department of the Interior announced that he would arrest parties in the habit of devastating large tracts of land or cutting lumber. In September 1877, Wilcox seized 120,000 ties in Boulder County owned by railroad magnate David H. Moffat and his associates, claiming that they were taken from government land without payment. The tie affair quickly became a legal entanglement involving both the federal and state governments. Complicating matters was the uncertain ownership of the ties. To make the situation even worse, while the guards were absent, the Colorado Central Railroad coupled an engine to fourteen carloads of ties and ran them off, asserting that it had bought them from Moffat. All this time the impounded ties delayed railroad construction. Eventually, the various parties stipulated to a settlement and the ties were released to the Denver Pacific.[52]

The tie affair further heightened awareness about the state of Colorado and Wyoming forests. Interior Secretary Carl Schurz warned that "the rapidity with which this country is being stripped of its forests must alarm every thinking man." By November 1877, the tie affair had amassed such attention that President Rutherford Hayes promised that the subject would be fully investigated. This and similar abuses elsewhere eventually led Congress to create the US Forest Service.[53]

Once the newly assertive federal government began enforcing timber laws, one of the first to feel the heat was John C. Teller, nephew of Colorado senator Henry Teller. At least six criminal and civil cases were brought against Teller in the United States District Court in Cheyenne over his attempts to dodge paying stumpage fees. Nevertheless Teller managed to escape punishment even though there "was little doubt of his guilt in either civil or criminal cases."[54]

Then in 1891 a law was enacted that authorized the president to "withdraw" federal land for forest reserves. These withdrawals allowed the government to withhold land from sale, settlement, leasing, or other kinds of access. President Benjamin Harrison soon withdrew lands for a forest reserve near Yellowstone and a month later withdrew land for the White River Plateau Reserve in Colorado. The issue festered for much of the 1890s. During that time the impacts of logging on the West's streams and watersheds came into better focus. As trees were removed, the ability of the mountainous hillsides to retain water diminished. Settlers noticed that snowmelt in logged-out areas occurred earlier than in the forests. Farmers, now well established, began to see their former allies as damaging their water rights. The progressive era was in full swing by then too, and there was a growing backlash to the laissez-faire attitude of westerners who saw it as a birthright to plunder the public domain. The laissez-faire era featuring unfettered appropriation of forest resources came to a close on June 4, 1897, when President McKinley signed the Organic Act creating the US Forest Service. The new service's mission was "to improve and protect the forest within the reservation, or for the purpose of securing favorable conditions of water flows, and to furnish a continuous supply of timber for the use and necessities" of the American people.[55]

As soon as fossil fuels came into wide use, deforestation for domestic fuels decreased. To be sure, wood was still needed for construction, but loggers became more discriminate with the trees they selected. By the turn of the twentieth century, and more so by about 1920, cutting slowed while fire suppression efforts expanded. This provided some relief to Colorado's forests. The logging industry had also moved on to untapped forests on the western slope and to other states altogether. Within a few decades dense stands of secondary forests began filling in barren hillsides. Eventually, the secondary forest had grown to such an extent that catastrophic forest fires and pine beetle outbreaks became common. Forest changes in the watershed undoubtedly affected area streams. Forest removal likely increased sediment and runoff rates, and once the forest grew back, sediment and runoff rates would have decreased. Precise impacts on the streams will never be known. It is certain, however, that the decades of forest cutting and recovery are part of the legacy of appropriation on the region's rivers.

NOTES

1. Pabor, *Colorado as an Agricultural State*, 10.

2. Cary, *Biological Survey of Colorado*, 183. Ellen Wohl carefully traced the history of trapping and described the ecological consequences of trapping in Front Range Streams. See Wohl, *Virtual Rivers*.

3. French-speaking fur trappers originating from towns such as St. Louis were commonly referred to as French into the 1830s and 1840s, even though the Mississippi Basin transferred to US control in 1804. Also see Steinel, *History of Agriculture*, 176.

4. For information on the early fur-trading posts, see Hafen, "Early Fur Trade Posts."

5. Harrison Clifford Dale, *The Ashley Smith Explorations and Discovery of a Central Route to the Pacific 1822–1829* (Cleveland: Arthur H. Clark Company, 1918), 98; Dolin, *Fur, Fortune, and Empire*, 226.

6. See Lavendar, *Bent's Fort*, chap. 4.

7. Hart, Hulbert, and Gardner, *Southwestern Journals*.

8. James, *Account of an Expedition*, 160; Flores, "Bison Ecology"; Isenberg, *Destruction of the Buffalo*, 25.

9. Flores, "Bison Ecology"; Fremont, *Report of the Exploring Expedition*. The quote is from the August 28, 1843, entry.

10. Dolin, *Fur, Fortune, and Empire*; Netz, *Barbed Wire*; quote from Smits, "Frontier Army," 312.

11. Armstrong, *Distribution of Mammals*; Hornaday, *Extermination of the American Bison*, 523.

12. Hornaday, *Extermination of the American Bison*, 525; see also Hornaday, *Our Vanishing Wild Life*, 180.

13. Cary, *Biological Survey of Colorado*, 51, 53.

14. Isenberg, *Destruction of the Buffalo*, 111.

15. Coffin, "Reminiscences," *Longmont (CO) Ledger*, July 26, 1907.

16. Cary, *Biological Survey of Colorado*, 169.

17. Ibid., 198.

18. Beschta, "Reduced Cottonwood Recruitment."

19. Steinel, *History of Agriculture*, 108–9.

20. Ibid., 110.

21. Warren, *Mammals of Colorado*, 137–40.

22. West, *Contested Plains*, 97–100.

23. Ibid., 103–4.

24. Udall, *Forgotten Founders*, 134–35.

25. *American Annual Cyclopaedia and Register of Important Events of the Year 1863*, vol. 3 (New York: Appleton, 1864), 170.

26. "Successful Cyanide," *Boulder (CO) County Miner* 1, no. 4 (June 22, 1905).

27. Grove K. Gilbert, *Hydraulic-Mining Debris in the Sierra Nevada*, US Geological Survey Professional Paper, no. 105 (Washington, DC: Government Printing Office, 1917).

28. On South Boulder Creek, I have measured vertical down-cutting of up to about five feet that is visible by comparing photographs taken in 1907 and present-day conditions.

29. US Geological Survey, "The Public Land Survey System," accessed June 30, 2011, http://nationalmap.gov/small_scale/a_plss.html#two.

30. Netz, *Barbed Wire*, 24; see also Hewes and Jung, "Early Fencing."

31. Netz, *Barbed Wire*, 26–27.

32. Hewes and Jung, "Early Fencing."

33. Earl W. Hayter, "Livestock-Fencing Conflicts."

34. Netz, *Barbed Wire.*

35. See Hyde, *Life of George Bent,* 96, 108.

36. Coffin, Letter to *Longmont* (CO) *Ledger,* July 12, 1907, and August 2, 1907.

37. Wroten, "Railroad Tie Industry," 158; Veblen and Lorenz, *Colorado Front Range.*

38. Lord, *Frontier Dust*; Wroten, "Railroad Tie Industry," 248.

39. Lord, *Frontier Dust,* 93.

40. Ibid., 97.

41. Ibid., 98.

42. Benedict, *Left Hand Canyon,* 43–44.

43. Undated photo from Wroten, "Railroad Tie Industry." 334.

44. Wroten, "Railroad Tie Industry"; also Wohl, *Virtual Rivers,* 94.

45. *Rocky Mountain News,* June 19, 1885.

46. Wohl, *Virtual Rivers,* 98.

47. *The Rocky Mountain Directory and Colorado Gazetteer for 1871* (Denver: S. S. Wallihan and Company, 1871), 41.

48. Report of Cyrus Thomas, in Hayden, *Preliminary Field Report,* 150–51.

49. Baker, "Report by States."

50. Wilkinson, *Crossing the Next Meridian,* 121.

51. Wroten, "Railroad Tie Industry." 172.

52. Ibid., 182–87.

53. Schurtz quote from Wilkinson, *Crossing the Next Meridian,* 122; Wroten, "Railroad Tie Industry."

54. Wroten, "Railroad Tie Industry," 202.

55. Forest Service Organic Administration Act (Act of June 4, 1897) (16 U.S.C. §§ 473–78, 479–82, and 551).

THREE

From Desert to Oasis

"The Changes wrought by irrigation in the last half century have been little less than marvelous. The highest-priced farming lands on this continent are found in areas once regarded as desert and worthless, and great cities have been reared in regions once believed would always be dreary solitudes."

—*Elwood Mead, 1903*[1]

COLORADO'S FIRST DITCHES

When settlers began digging ditches along the Front Range in 1859, they became part of a long chain connecting Indians and Spaniards to enable agriculture in Colorado's semiarid climate. To make a go of life on this new frontier, they quickly adopted irrigation methods and technologies developed in southern Colorado and northern New Mexico.

DOI: 10.5876/9781607323822.c003

Sizeable canal systems began appearing in southern Arizona around 1200 to 1000 BC and influenced the entire region. The earliest known water works within Colorado were built by the Ancient Puebloans or "Anasazi" of Mesa Verde. Their ditches and reservoirs made sedentary farming viable in the arid Southwest and date from about AD 900. Near modern-day Kayenta, Arizona, the ancient Puebloans used a wide variety of water-control devices from about AD 1150 to 1300. Around the same time ditches, diversion dams, and other structures were actively used at New Mexico's Chaco Canyon. Irrigated agriculture was critical for the ancient Puebloans, and their technologies spread across the ancient Southwest to places like the Rio Grande Valley.[2]

Once the Spanish arrived, they quickly appropriated the indigenous knowledge of the Pueblo Indians and blended it with the traditions and technologies they had brought from Spain. The Spanish added organizational knowledge and brought tools and technology that took Indian irrigation practices to new levels, resulting in the emergence of the *acequia* systems that remain in use to the present.

Acequia is a Spanish word derived from the Arabic *al saqiya*, and means "water conduit" or "water carrier." The Arabs and Moors brought irrigation technology to Spain during their occupation of the Iberian Peninsula. The Spanish in turn exported the technology to the Americas. By necessity, *acequias* were often the first form of government implemented in the Hispanic Southwest. *Acequia* governance often remains synonymous with local government in rural Hispanic communities. Then, as now, communities organized themselves to build and maintain ditches and to create rules to allocate water.

The Spanish farmers used locally available materials to build their diversion works. They manufactured wood and metal tools to excavate ditches. They organized their labor to first dig and then enlarge and maintain the *acequias*. The common sense and basic hydraulic engineering that went into these structures are often one and the same.[3]

In the Hispanic communities, *acequias* represent both the physical infrastructure of the ditch and the social organization that keeps it operating. Both are inseparable. The *acequia* is the glue that keeps communities together. The main ditch that runs through a community is often called the *Acequia Madre*, or mother ditch. Water carried in the *Acequia Madre* is quite literally the lifeblood of the community.

By the time Americans began regularly traversing the Santa Fe Trail, New Mexicans had been irrigating from *acequias* for generations. American visitors were impressed by the Mexicans' use of ditches. Josiah Gregg, one of the earliest chroniclers of the Santa Fe trade, documented the need for irrigation in the arid West for his American readers. The *Acequia Madre* could "convey water for the irrigation of an entire valley, or at least for all the fields of one town or settlement," wrote Gregg in 1857. He compared the system of labor used to maintain these ditches as analogous to the Americans' shared labor for maintaining county roads. Gregg explained that the "principal ditch is of course proportioned to the quantity of land to be watered," and noted that it is positioned in the higher part of the valley and that minor ditches branching from it serve individual farms. In times of scarcity or on small streams, "each farmer has his day, or portion of a day allotted to him for irrigation; and at no other time is he permitted to extract water from the *acequia madre.*" Farmers, Gregg explained, "after letting the water into his minor ditch, dams this, first at one point and then at another, so as to overflow a section at a time, and with his hoe, depressing eminences and filling sinks, he causes the water to spread regularly over the surface." This way, a typical farmer could irrigate a five- or six-acre field during a single day. It was through the stories and writings of travelers like Josiah Gregg that future American migrants to Colorado became aware of the potential to support themselves through irrigated agriculture.[4]

Another American traveler, William W.H. Davis, explained that in New Mexico's *acequias* "the supply of water necessary for cultivation [was considered] a matter of public interest." Annually, justices of the peace would call together "the owners of ditches, and the proprietors of the land watered by them, to elect one or more overseers" to supervise the "erection and repairs of ditches; to regulate the number of laborers to be furnished by each proprietor," and perhaps most importantly "distribute and apportion the water among the several proprietors, and see that no one gets more than his share." Although Colorado's settlers took a different direction for managing ditches, the New Mexico experience clearly informed what would evolve in Colorado in just a few years' time.[5]

Eventually, American traders became entrenched in Taos and Santa Fe. Kit Carson, the Bent Brothers, and their partners Ceran and Marcellin St. Vrain all had interests in New Mexico. At both Bents Fort on the Arkansas River and St. Vrain's Fort on the South Platte, the traders helped support their operations using agricultural and irrigation practices learned in New Mexico.

Irrigation in Colorado was also practiced at short-lived Spanish and Mexican settlements. The earliest of these was at San Carlo de Jupes, an aborted settlement next to the Arkansas River about eight miles east of present-day Pueblo. This ditch was started in 1787 but abandoned within months.[6]

Perhaps the earliest ditch in what was to become Colorado is one constructed at the confluence of the Arkansas and Purgatoire Rivers by Bent, St. Vrain and Company. There the Bents decided to establish a ranch between their trading fort and Taos. To do this they enlisted John Hatcher, a mountain man, trapper, trader, and sometime partner. In September 1846, Hatcher left Taos for the Purgatoire with fifteen or sixteen Mexican laborers. They took three wagons, sixteen yoke of oxen, and all they supplies they needed to dig a ditch and farm the land. Under Hatcher's supervision, they began digging later that month.

Work was interrupted when word arrived of Charles Bent's murder in the Taos Revolt. Some 300 US dragoons under the command of Colonel Sterling Price together with 65 volunteers organized by Bent's partner Ceran St. Vrain soon put down the revolt. In the battle that ensued at Taos the outgunned rebels retreated to a church, but the dragoons soon breached its wall and directed cannon fire from mountain howitzers into the interior, killing about 150 and wounding many more. Surviving rebels inside the church eventually surrendered and were arrested. Hatcher missed the climactic battle at the church, but arrived at Taos in time to participate in the trials of the captives. Five rebels were found guilty of murder and one for treason. Hatcher served as a guard and watched them hang from a tree in the Taos town square.

When things settled down, Hatcher returned to the ranch at the Purgatoire with William Bent and resumed building the ditch. Joining him was an eighteen-year-old traveler by the name of Louis H. Garrard, who would later write a book about his adventures in the West. Garrard described how William Bent and the others set about completing the ditch: "They had plows, and the *acequia*, by which the land would be irrigated, was nearly finished; the dam to elevate the water in this was yet to be constructed, so the following morning we went hard to work. For two days we labored as though the embryo crop depended upon our finishing within a specified time. When the water flowed in the *acequia*, we watched the bits of wood and scum floating with the first tide with intense interest and satisfaction."[7]

With this modest beginning, Colorado's irrigation age began. However, tensions with the Indians made farming risky. The Indians killed all of the cattle at the fledgling ranch. Hatcher and the others were warned that they would be next. With that, the first effort at operating a ditch in Colorado stalled. Hatcher and the others retreated to Taos. About five and a half years later, Hispanic settlers moving north from New Mexico established the San Luis People's Ditch. Theirs became and remains the longest continuously used ditch in the state, and was eventually rewarded the number one priority for all ditches in Colorado. Only in the 1860s did a new rancher by the name of J. W. Lewelling restart the Hatcher Ditch.[8]

Even before the Pikes Peak Gold Rush began, enough Americans had traveled back and forth on the Santa Fe Trail that the irrigation practices of New Mexico were well known. American settlers quickly adopted Hispanic ditch digging and irrigation practices. During the early years of the Gold Rush, Mexican irrigation practices were employed by the new settlers and many even referred to the works as *acequias*. But as the number of settlers increased, English terms replaced the Spanish, and the memory of the Spanish and Indian origins of ditches faded.

WORKING WITH THE LAND

The discovery of gold set in motion a rush to settle stream valleys up and down the Front Range. Many came for mining but soon switched to farming. Fremont's observations that the region was "admirably adapted to agricultural purposes" were quickly tested by thousands of migrants looking for prime land to build farms. In 1859 newcomers began settling land along Boulder Creek and got busy cutting hay and growing crops to cash in on the demand coming from the gold camps.

When the first settlers arrived in Boulder Valley, they found a nearly blank slate as they contemplated how to build the ditches that would bring water to their farms. With the prospect of hand-digging ditches through gravely soil ahead of them, it was only natural that a prospective ditch digger would carefully survey the landscape so that he might use any natural advantage it presented. It was completely logical that settlers dug the first ditches on easy-to-irrigate bottomlands. The combination of minimizing labor and maximizing the advantages presented by the local geomorphology neatly explains where most early and many subsequent ditches were built.

In Boulder Valley, Hank, Lute, and Vane Wellman were the very first settlers to irrigate their land. When they arrived on August 1, 1859, the three Wellman brothers ended up about two and one-half miles east of town where they settled on 640 acres. They chose à level site next to Boulder Creek. When Boulder Creek rose, which happened frequently before many of the other ditches were built, it would overflow the bank and water would flow into the side channels and onto their farm. The Wellmans did not need to even build a ditch from the creek. All they needed to do was dig smaller laterals to distribute water when it came to them. Only after ditches were built upstream from them did the Wellmans need to construct a ditch from the stream to their farm.

Other settlers also selected good bottomlands. Norman Ross Howard, Marinus Smith, and John Rothrock settled on prime land next to Boulder and South Boulder Creeks to take advantage of ready access to water. The ditches they built did not stray far from the creeks to reach their land and were shorter and easier to construct. Many of them incorporated natural depressions or abandoned stream channels to reduce the amount of digging needed.

Coal Creek's modern geomorphology may give a clue to how creeks like Boulder and South Boulder looked in the years before settlers began digging their ditches. Although Coal Creek has a significantly smaller watershed and lesser annual flows, it does possess the cobble-strewn features of other Front Range and High Plains streams. Because the annual flow in Coal Creek is less than in nearby streams, it is tapped by fewer ditches. Coal Creek has what geomorphologists call a straight channel, meaning that it has few meanders. However, next to the main channel are a series of secondary channels that contain water only when the flow in Coal Creek reaches flood stages. As flows increase, Coal Creek's appearance changes from a straight channel to one that looks like a braided stream. Before settlement, water likely flowed primarily within the main channel of Boulder and South Boulder Creeks as depicted in an early survey plat shown in Figure 3.1, and like Coal Creek only at flood stage did the other channels convey water. Because these "dry" channels crisscrossed the floodplain, they were easy to modify to serve as ditch channels.

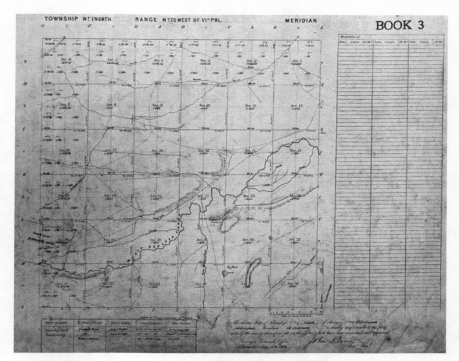

FIGURE 3.1. This is a survey plat from August 1863 in the area of what is now Boulder, Colorado. A branch of Boulder Creek, formerly known as Dry Creek, is depicted here as a "slough." This channel was eventually converted into the Boulder and White Rock Ditch. Photograph by author.

David Nichols built the Dry Creek Ditch (later part of the North Boulder Farmers Ditch) to serve his property near Boulder Creek. The headgate for the North Boulder Farmers Ditch is located on a former channel or branch of Boulder Creek known during pioneer days as "Dry Creek." Government surveyors referred to this channel as a "slough" when they produced the first township plat map for the area in 1863. Use of the word "slough" by the surveyors suggests that this channel actively carried water during high flow periods until it was converted into a ditch. Before the photograph in Figure 3.2 was taken, the channel extending away from the viewer behind the headgate was straightened and deepened and people referred to it as a ditch. It was Nichols and others who enlarged and converted this channel

FIGURE 3.2. An early view of the Boulder and White Rock Ditch at its headgate on Boulder Creek. This is the site of a former slough that was converted into the upper part of the ditch. Photograph courtesy of the Carnegie Branch Library for Local History, Boulder Historical Society Collection. Reprinted with permission.

into a ditch. In time Dry Creek was naturalized in people's minds as an irrigation facility.

The North Boulder Farmers headgate was eventually expanded and became one of the main water diversion facilities in Boulder Valley. This headgate is located in downtown Boulder at Central Park. Figure 3.3 is a photograph of the headgate looking across the diversion dam. Today the structure is shared by North Boulder Farmers, Boulder & White Rock, Smith and Goss, McCarthy, and Boulder & Left Hand ditches. This headgate and associated diversion structure was designed by the well-known landscape architect Frederick Law Olmsted Jr., the son of the famed landscape architect who designed New York City's Central Park. Frederick Law Olmsted Jr. also designed the reflecting pool at the Jefferson Memorial in Washington, DC. His firm drafted the street layout for Mapleton Hill in Boulder and wrote the city's first master development plan. Olmsted's elegant arch dam has subsequently been marred by the installation of a grouted rock kayak shoot.

Like Nichols on Boulder Creek, Norman Ross Howard adapted the local geomorphology to his advantage when he built the Dry Creek No. 2 Ditch

FIGURE 3.3. Photograph of the Boulder and White Rock diversion and headgate that was designed by Frederick Law Olmsted Jr. Photograph courtesy of the Carnegie Branch Library for Local History, Boulder Historical Society Collection. Reprinted with permission.

on South Boulder Creek. George Chase, an early shareholder in the ditch, remarked that "Dry Creek #2, runs through my place. This ditch isn't a 'made' ditch all the way through. The water is let into an old channel, and goes down through all these farms. Probably that's the reason it's named Dry Creek."[9]

A little farther downstream from the Dry Creek No. 2, settlers incorporated other parts of the local geomorphology for ditch service. As early as 1863 the settlers building the Original Cottonwood Ditch realized that by digging through the upper reach of Dry Creek by nearly two miles they could efficiently and easily capture South Boulder Creek water and irrigate lands within the Dry Creek basin. Dry Creek itself was described as "a fork or branch of South Boulder Creek, like as a bayou of former channel of . . . South Boulder Creek."[10]

Timothy Shanahan, who homesteaded in the valley, recalled that the "old Dry Creek Channel was a natural channel." Shanahan added, "Water ran [in] the old channel in times of high water." By excavating Dry Creek the settlers established what may be one of the earliest (if not the earliest) transbasin diversion in Colorado. This was an ingenious and efficient use of geomorphology to facilitate irrigation. When settlers arrived in Boulder Valley, Dry Creek was an ephemeral stream that could not support irrigation. By converting the upper reach into what is now known as the New Dry Creek Carrier, the settlers were able to establish the Original Cottonwood, Andrews Farwell, Dry Creek Davidson, Leyner Cottonwood, Coal Ridge, and Lewis H. Davidson ditches. All this early ditch work began to bend the environment toward the intensively managed ecosystem that exists today.[11]

After the best bottomlands were taken, ditch diggers realized that by routing their canals to reach nearby stream terraces they could irrigate lands and grow bountiful crops. But for early settlers like Morse Coffin, it was not immediately obvious that lands outside the rich valley bottoms held potential:

> We, in 1860, '61, and '62, considered these little valleys—Boulder, St. Vrain, Thompson, and Cache la Poudre—of more real value for farming purposes than all the high dry land between these streams; an illustration of the ignorance and short-sightedness of puny man.
>
> We expected—or many people did—that these between lands would be useful as a stock and game range, but we did not anticipate a time when there would be people enough in this country and with capital enough to construct irrigating ditches ten or twenty miles long—not to say hundreds of miles—to irrigate high land, tho' we soon learned the soil was all right if it had water.[12]

Settlers such as William H. Davidson and Jonathan A. Tourtellot were among those who saw the potential that Morse Coffin overlooked, and they dug ditches to lands beyond the floodplain. Tourtellot and others began working on Farmers Ditch in October of 1862. They started their ditch near the north bank of Boulder Creek just east of the canyon mouth, and by using a slight gradient were able wind their ditch along contours to irrigate 3,000 acres of land north of Boulder. To the south William H. Davidson began irrigating stream terraces, greatly improving the value of his property.

Eventually settlers built hundreds of ditches around Boulder Valley and beyond. Boulder County is now crisscrossed by dozens of ditches, as depicted in Figure 3.4. But Boulder was not the only place where this occurred. Throughout the 1860s, first on the bottomlands and then on the terraces, settlers dug ditches on the Cache la Poudre, Big Thompson, Little Thompson, Left Hand, Coal, Clear, Ralston, and so on south. Settlers

FIGURE 3.4. Map showing the extent of ditches and agricultural lands around Boulder, Colorado, in 2009. Prepared for the Ditch Project, courtesy City of Boulder Open Space and Mountain Parks, 2009.

claimed bottomlands so rapidly that by 1860 people like Morse Coffin had to travel out beyond the confluence of Boulder and St. Vrain Creeks to acquire property along the creek. By 1870, anyone contemplating making a go of agriculture was forced even farther east.

Over the past 150 years all of this water development replumbed first the tributaries and then the South Platte itself. Multitudes of water right changes and transfers have subsequently taken place. Within the Boulder Creek Watershed alone, thousands of water rights now exist and serve a myriad of uses. Expansion in water rights tracks the expansion of irrigated land. In 1860 there were only about 35,000 irrigated acres in all of Colorado. By 1900 there were about 1 million acres; by 1950 the number had grown to 3.2 million acres. Finally, by 2000, the number of acres had leveled off at about 3.4 million.[13]

Digging Ditches

In the fall of 1859 settlers like Marinus Smith and John Rothrock grabbed some picks and shovels, gathered some friends, perhaps a spouse or some hired hands, and walked down to the creek. They brought teams of horses or oxen and a plow. At the stream's edge, they began digging. First they would dig a hole four or five feet wide and about one or two feet deep, or just deep enough so that water might flow in. They would lengthen the hole into a trench, first ten feet long, then twenty, eventually a hundred feet long. Every day, day after day, they dug. By this point, their back muscles must have screamed why people call this place "Boulder." The soil was hard, and they had to continually lift out cobbles that were often one or two feet across.

They attached plows or scrapers to the oxen or a horse team to break up the soil and haul it out of the trench. If they had some extra money, they commonly paid itinerant laborers to help out. When digging they were careful to slope the ditch so that water runs down it, but not so fast that it erodes the bottom. The new ditch would follow the contour of the land and gradually migrated toward the side of the valley floor or possibly onto a bench-like terrace that lay fifteen, twenty, or more feet above the creek. In just a month or two, they had a ditch a mile or more long that snaked along to the edge of their property that could irrigate all the land between it and the stream.

Edwin Baker, an early Greeley Colony settler, recalled how the horses used to dig ditches "were gotten from nearby herds, and looked large and

FIGURE 3.5. Horse teams using Fresno scrapers dig Community Ditch along a hillside south of Boulder. Photograph courtesy of Carnegie Branch Library for Local History, Boulder Historical Society Collection. Reprinted with permission.

beautiful on the range, but when put on the scales they did not demonstrate the avoirdupois they appeared to have . . . Frequently the scraper caught and the holder vaulted over it into the heels of the animals. . . . In the course of a week or so the force would get settled down to something like decorum."[14]

This intense activity is hinted at in Figure 3.5, which shows horse teams pulling Fresno scrapers to dig Community Ditch across a hillside south of Boulder. Here they employed at least four teams of four horses led by one or two men per team. Horses and men were spread out along the ditch and made broad sweeps with each full scoop.

It is no wonder that farmers remain so possessive toward their water. Once the backbreaking process of digging the ditches and establishing their homestead was completed, the experience was seared into their psyche, and the labor they expended served as proof enough of their right to use their water and control their ditch. Building the ditch and the labor expended during many subsequent years of maintaining and upgrading it reinforced the farmers' and ranchers' tie to the land and water and renewed the ownership they feel toward that water and the lifestyle it enables.

Before you could divert water into a ditch, you also needed to build a diversion dam across the stream to capture water. Settlers usually waited until the ditch was complete so that water would not flow in and make a mess. In the 1860s ditch diversions were primitive affairs. Concrete diversion dams would not be built for decades to come. Horace Greeley described how farmers at his colony diverted water from the Cache la Poudre. "Taking the water out of the river is here a very simple matter," Greeley said. "At the head of an island, a rude dam of brush and stones and earth is thrown across the bed of the stream, so as to raise the surface two or three feet when the water is lowest, and very much less when it is highest. Thus deflected, a portion of the water flows easily into the canal."[15]

Although relatively easy to build, these primitive diversions often washed out during the spring snowmelt. On the Left Hand Ditch, for instance, the diversion dam washed out in 1864, 1867, and 1868. The Left Hand Ditch Company eventually built a diversion dam of boulders that was three or four feet high and spanned the entire South St. Vrain River.

For water to flow down a ditch, a steady slope is needed. This slope has to be slightly less than the gradient of the nearby stream. By maintaining this gradient, the ditch slowly migrates farther away from the stream and may eventually reach terraces that parallel the stream, or even cross a divide to the next watershed. If it is too steep, the channel erodes; if it is too flat, water moves slowly and seeps into the bed. To achieve the proper grades, settlers resorted to some simple but ingenious technology. One innovative device is a ditch level. In Figure 3.6, two longtime Boulder ranchers, brothers Babe and Leo Hogan, stand alongside one of these devices. On it, one leg is set longer than the other and a carpenter's glass bubble level is attached. The ditch diggers periodically check the level to make sure they are maintaining the proper grade as they dig. Eliza Rothrock, wife of John Ramsey Rothrock, who built the Lower Boulder Ditch, recalled that the ditch diggers "had a two-by-six board, a rod long, with a level in the center of the length. At each end they nailed an up-right, one end of which was one inch shorter than the other. This was to give a one inch fall every 16½ feet." But surveying required supervision: "One day while John was absent, the workmen got the pole turned about, and when John returned part of the ditch was running up hill. Of course it had to be surveyed over. Can you imagine surveying a ditch six or eight miles long in this manner!"[16]

I have often been very impressed at the accuracy of grades established using ditch levels. On several occasions I have had to redig old laterals because

FIGURE 3.6. Two Boulder ranchers, brothers Babe and Leo Hogan, stand alongside an original ditch level. Photograph by author.

they were filling in with sediment. On resurveying them, I have found that the alignment made with the old surveying methods needed no correction.

Before the advent of mechanized machinery, ditch digging was basically backbreaking labor. The tools used were essentially shovels and hoes modified for use with draft animals. Buck scrapers and slip scoops were the preferred tools to move earth. A simple buck or dirt scraper (Figure 3.7) allowed a man with a team to move larger quantities of earth a greater distance than he could under his labor alone. Nevertheless, buck scrapers and slip scoops were very hard to control, extremely heavy to dump, and of limited use in rocky soil.

An invention that dramatically improved ditch digging came from the Central Valley of California. An immigrant, James Porteous, was working as an agricultural laborer and immediately saw the need for a better earth-moving device to dig canals around Fresno, California. Porteous was inspired to design four generations of scrapers, and his final design came to be known as the Fresno Scraper, which he patented in 1883 (Figure 3.8).

Fresno scrapers became very popular and were used across the United States to build canals, ditches, roads, railroads, dams, and reservoirs. Its

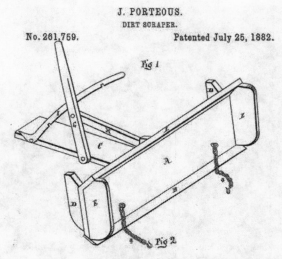

FIGURE 3.7. A simple buck or dirt scraper. US Patent No. 261,759.

biggest advantage was that a single man could operate the scraper while managing a four-horse team. Within a few years ditch digging equipment became mechanized. Initially, steam engines were fitted with Fresno scrapers. Descendants of the Fresno scraper became standard equipment on tractors and bulldozers.

Early Colorado visitors noticed all the ditch digging. In 1869 Cyrus Thomas, of the Hayden Survey, traveled along the Front Range when many people were still calling ditches by their Spanish name, *acequias*. He noted that the largest *acequia* then in Colorado was near Denver, on the south side of Platte River. It was several miles long, and cost $14,000 to construct.[17]

In 1867, one of Colorado's first tourists arrived. At the time of Bayard Taylor's trip, Colorado tourism was so novel that a person could write a book about his experience. Taylor remarked that the "the farmers have adapted themselves to the new conditions of their occupation. They seem already to prefer the secure yield which irrigation offers to the uncertain prospects of a more variable climate."[18] Taylor contrasted the promise of irrigation against the expense and difficulty of digging ditches. The rapid pace of ditch and reservoir construction clearly made an impression:

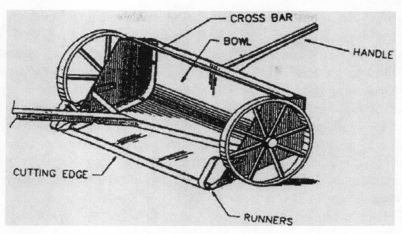

FIGURE 3.8. The Fresno scraper. US Patent No. 275,075.

Ditches are being carried from Clear Creek over all parts of the undulating slope stretching down from the mountains and it was a cheering sight to find a large field of the greenest wheat upon one of the highest points in the midst of a plain studded with cactus. A short distance from Denver one of the ditches has been turned into a natural basin a mile in diameter forming a lake of that extent around which large herds of cattle were grazing. We found a number of men at work constructing new ditches by a very simple process. Several furrows are first ploughed and then the dirt is shoveled out rapidly by a broad frame of timber drawn by horses in a lateral direction. Our course was sometimes impeded by the number of these ditches which are not yet bridged."[19]

Workers on the Left Hand and McGinn ditches received about $2.00 to $2.50 per day to build these ditches. Along the way Taylor managed a side trip to Boulder Valley before returning east to write his book. His first stop was Marshall's mine and furnace, and then he headed on north to the town of Valmont, where he remarked that the "extent and beauty of the cultivated land watered by the two streams [Boulder and South Boulder] was a new surprise. For miles farm followed farm in uninterrupted succession the breadths of wheat black green in its richness or overrun with a yellowing gleam dotted with houses and clumps of trees like some fenceless harvest plain of Europe . . . Here I saw again how much Civilization improves Nature."[20]

Virtually all available level land was cultivated. On approaching Valmont, Taylor "turned a corner where the fields had almost forced the road off the level and there stood perhaps a dozen new cabins and a few scattering cotton woods. But of these cabins one was a store one a printing office and one a Presbyterian church." Residents informed Taylor that "the farming on the St. Vrains is fully equal" to what he had seen on the Boulder and that "the valleys of the Big and Little Thompson and even of the Cache la Poudre are settled and cultivated and will this year produce splendid crops." He added that the "line of settlement is thus not only creeping northward and southward from Denver but also following the tributaries of the Platte it advances eastward to meet the great tide approaching it."[21]

THE COURSE OF DEVELOPMENT

It is tempting to organize different phases of development into neat categories. Doing so helps clarify our understanding of events. The problem, however, is that history is messy and not easily categorized. Time periods overlap or blend, and categories that make sense from one perspective break down when viewed from another. People seldom see themselves as belonging to a specific time period or lump themselves within one or another category. It is with this in mind that I trace the progress of water development along the Front Range.

One convenient way to look at early western development is by dividing it into an "Old West" and a "Post-Railroad West." In the Old West an agrarian economy prevailed where settlers lived in small villages. Although these settlers relied heavily on trade with the East, they were remote from markets in ways that forced them to utilize craftwork performed by local artisans and blacksmiths. Farm products were consumed locally. Urbanization was slow, with exceptions such as Denver and Salt Lake. In the Old West, animals provided the energy to move goods, plow fields, and move carriages. Draft animals were the major source of energy within the economy. The guns the settlers carried were single-shot muzzle-loading rifles, and animals were herded by family groups. Corporate organization of the labor force had not yet become pervasive. This characterization of the Old West provides a pretty good description for Colorado prior to the arrival of the railroads.[22]

In contrast, once the railroads arrived at settlements, the character of local economies changed dramatically. In the Post-Railroad West, a cash and commodity economy quickly became dominant. The railroads precipitated rapid growth of communities. Resource extraction and development began in earnest as spur lines reached remote sites. Industrialized mining and agriculture rapidly became dominant forces in these economic sectors. With this, labor relations changed as more farmers and miners found themselves beholden to distant markets. Many became paid laborers working for others. Labor relations emerged as major concerns. Formerly isolated communities soon became closely linked to eastern markets via railroad and telegraph. Railroads expanded the demand for timber and fossil fuels and allowed the importation of kerosene and turbines. Railroads brought machinery to towns and reduced the need for craft industry. With the advent of cattle cars, the once isolated cattle industry became highly profitable as it exported to eastern markets.

Many pioneers lived to see the railroads built, and they enthusiastically participated in the economic transformation that followed. William Davidson, the Boulder-based miner and ditch builder, was typical. He came as a pioneer and later rode the wave of industrialization to great personal profit. Davidson helped invent the corporate model for ditch building and was quick to partner with other likeminded entrepreneurs to bring the railroad to Boulder.

It is common to see Colorado's ditch history described as if it happened in discrete eras. Starting with Colorado state engineer Edwin S. Nettleton in 1882 and expanded by historian Alvin T. Steinel in 1926, ditch development was traced along "pioneer," "corporate," and "colony" lines. These descriptions have had remarkable traction and good descriptive value, but they have limited use when one contemplates why development proceeded as it did.[23]

I prefer to think of pioneer ditches, agricultural colonies, corporate ditches, and governmental efforts as part of an evolution in governance that developed as people grappled with environmental conditions that forced them to build increasingly more complicated water projects. As the best diversion and dam sites were appropriated, it became necessary to craft more sophisticated governance, organization, and financing systems to build successive projects.

Water rights administration and governance evolved in response to environmental conditions along each river. Legal institutions allocating water between water users evolved simultaneously with the ditches. At first it was sufficient to administer water rights between ditches on streams such as

Boulder or St. Vrain. Water users began by asking the state to intervene and hire the first water commissioners. Later they asked that the state coordinate the administration of water between the tributaries of rivers such as the South Platte. It was no longer sufficient to know if your neighbor on Boulder Creek was in or out of priority as calls from beyond the stream affected your operations. Again at the urging of water users, the state hired a state engineer to coordinate administration. Eventually administration and management necessitated coordination between river basins, then between states, and eventually between countries. As demands on the resource increased, other factors such as water quality, fish and wildlife, and urban planning concerns added layers of complexity to water development governance and legal institutions. The result is almost as if we built an onion by adding layer upon layer until we achieved the interconnected institutions and infrastructure that exist today.

Water institutions and administration can be visualized as nested within successively larger basins and watersheds. Activities at each level inform and influence other levels to a greater or lesser degree. In time it became necessary to link other aspects of water use and development such as water quality, instream flows, and endangered species to water administration and management. Although rivers continue to be overused or polluted, the governance structures we developed have helped mitigate some of the worst inefficiencies and destructive tendencies along the way. These successive institutional innovations took place as water infrastructure was built on the rivers.

In using the term "nested," I refer to organizations that are essentially linked and dependent on one another from individual creeks to entire watersheds. Thus ditches along one stream must coordinate their use through a water commissioner, and in turn water use in whole watersheds is coordinated with other watersheds through district engineers. And so management steps up and down levels and between watersheds. It is through this nested water administration system that events in one watershed have ripple effects elsewhere. My views are informed by economist Elinor Ostrom, who maintains that establishing resilient and meaningful rules between various levels is an essential ingredient for establishing successful irrigation systems. Here the rules range from individual operating guidelines within ditch systems, to the Prior Appropriation system that allocates water between ditches, to interstate compacts that guide use between states.[24]

Nineteenth-century ditches were first among nested irrigation institutions that developed in Colorado. In tracing the evolution of these ditches, it is useful to begin by considering the ditches built by the first pioneers and then move on to more complicated organizations like the corporations, agricultural colonies, and municipalities. As ditch organizations developed, they evolved a progressively more sophisticated governance structure.

Water project development followed a similar trajectory. Although settlers did not discuss their activities in these terms, over time they found the need for more complicated and multilevel governance. At first, it was sufficient for individual settlers to divert water from streams under their own effort. However, as water was diverted from larger streams or to irrigate land farther from the streams, better organization and access to greater capital was needed. As time went on, developing ditches became more technically sophisticated and water users began building dams that required even more capital and expertise. Similarly, financial arrangements became more complex as individual farmers gave way to corporate financing and later governmental subsidy. Seen from this perspective, development evolved in response to environmental conditions (streamflow and geography), which led from pioneers to corporations and colonies to governmental organizations building and managing ditches.

As construction continued, each successive water project both constrained and influenced what came next. Once an earlier settler selected a prime site, the next person had to work around or build on earlier projects or contend with successively more difficult physical conditions to get the project built. This "path dependency" in building the ditches along the Front Range means that earlier water developments influence how and where later projects were designed and operated. Writers such as Bruce Colten and Martin Melosi point out that built infrastructure is often quite influential beyond its functional obsolescence. Likewise, pioneer ditches with secure water rights often impose design constraints on subsequent high-dollar projects. Because the first projects often occupy prime locations, new developments had to contend with more difficult site conditions elsewhere. Existing infrastructure affects environmental conditions and constrains future events. Not only do the earlier ditches occupy prime real estate and hold superior water rights, but those who follow must also live with lower water yields and less favorable cost benefits for their projects.[25]

DOCUMENTING A DESERT'S DEMISE

With the end of the Civil War, the attention of the US government followed the thousands of war veterans who began drifting westward in search of a better life. The desire for more and better information about the vast trans-Missouri West became insatiable. Previous efforts, such as the maps prepared by Fremont and others, were largely summaries of reconnaissance missions along key rivers and trails. The general outlines of the region were by then well known, but many details needed to facilitate development were missing. Critical information like the basic land surveys needed to define property boundaries were entirely absent. It was into this information vacuum that the government sponsored various geographical and geologic surveys. One Department of Interior survey directed geologist Ferdinand Vandeveer Hayden (the Hayden Survey) generated some of the most detailed information about Colorado then available.[26]

During the spring and summer of 1867 Hayden made some initial investigations along the Front Range. In 1869 the expedition returned to travel south from Cheyenne, Wyoming, along the foot of the Front Range of Colorado and over Raton Pass to Santa Fe, New Mexico. Two years later, Hayden gained wide notoriety for his geological survey into the Yellowstone region.[27]

Hayden, the scientist, was, in the words of historian Donald Worster, "no great figure; his mind was a jumble of facts, his powers of reasoning limited. As a human being he was even less impressive: vindictive, insecure, manipulative, self-promoting, a plagiarist." Personal failings aside, the output and information generated from Hayden's expeditions remain one of the signature accomplishments of nineteenth-century US government scientific exploration. The Hayden Survey produced the most accurate maps then available for Colorado, such as Figure 3.9, which depicts the river drainages of the Territory. Reports coming out of the survey described a Colorado that was in a state of flux as settlers sought to mine gold and cash in on resources like water, timber, and coal. He described widespread deforestation and stream diversions. During his travels, he encountered an eager public intent on learning about soils and water resources in Colorado. Hayden's 1869 report holds some the first detailed scientific descriptions of geology, flora, and fauna along the Front Range, including Boulder Valley.[28]

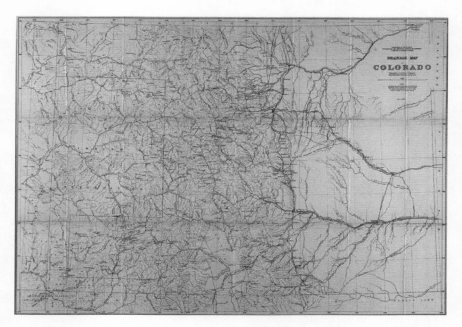

FIGURE 3.9. River drainage map of the Colorado Territory published in 1877 by the Hayden Survey.

Changes due to ditch digging were dramatic. Hayden remarked that as "we come from the north to the south side of the plateau [known today as Table Mountain], we can look across the valley of Left-hand Creek to near Boulder Valley, at least ten miles, dotted over with farm-houses, fenced fields, and irrigating ditches, upon one of the most pleasant views in the agricultural districts of Colorado."[29]

Expedition member Cyrus Thomas held the dual roles of entomologist and botanist to the expedition. In addition to reporting on the nascent agricultural development, Thomas spent a considerable amount of time thinking about how to control plagues of locusts then afflicting Colorado's farmers, a task that seems particularly befitting as he was also a preacher.

Thomas was greatly impressed by the rapid expansion of irrigation in the territory. He recognized the irrigation potential on the alluvial terraces east of the mountains. He observed that the heavier and larger sediment (boulders and gravel) preferentially remained near the mouth of the canyons and that finer-grained sediment was transported and deposited farther downstream.

On South Boulder Creek, Thomas foretold the future of Colorado:

> [Here] I may justly say, is found the link that unites the agriculture of
> the plains with the mining of the mountains, the two great interests of
> Colorado . . . Sinking into the bluff on which we have been standing, we pass
> alternating strata of coal and iron ore. Here they quietly rest, rich, thick, and
> abundant—the fuel and the metal. The one to convert the other into instru-
> ments to till the soil, to harvest the grain, to thresh and garner it, to convert it
> into food, to make the highway of transportation, and carry it to the miners
> of the mountains and the snow-bound dwellers in the far north. Such a com-
> bination is seldom seen.[30]

For Thomas mining, agriculture, and transportation were linked. The mines would produce the metals and tools to build farms and railroads. The railroads would transport the farm's bounty, and the farms would become some of the most important agricultural districts in the country. Thomas accurately predicted that development would commence on the eastern slope of the Rocky Mountains and gradually move eastward. Thomas saw the interconnectedness of land and water, mountains and prairie. He under-stood the critical role that water would play in Colorado's future. As long as there was water, the possibilities seemed endless:

> "the great problem of the development of the agricultural capacity of the vast
> western plains is the supply of water. Furnish this, and the fertile prairies and
> valleys east of the Mississippi will soon find a strong rival contending with
> them in the grain marts of the world for precedence. Furnish this, and the
> "Great American Desert" of old geographers will soon become one mighty
> field of flowing grain. Furnish this, and the few other minor impeding factors
> will soon be eliminated. The streams rushing down from the mountains
> slacken their course on the level plains where the great battle between mois-
> ture and aridity begins. Is there any power in the human grasp to assist nature
> in this struggle, and turn the scale in her favor?"[31]

Thomas was perhaps the first scientist to notice that as farms and ditches were dug, water somehow lingered in the streams later into the season. Some people would take this as proof that rain follows the plow. However, severe droughts in the 1880s brought many people back to reality and shook their notion of a link between rainfall and cultivation. For anyone suffering from selective memory, the droughts and dustbowls of the 1930s forever dismissed any remaining notion that there was a link between rainfall and the expansion of agriculture.

Thomas's observations are noteworthy for other reasons. More water was likely present in the streams when he visited than there was just a few years earlier. Decades later, CSU engineering professor Ralph Parshall documented how water running through ditches and off irrigated fields would affect streamflow days, months, or even years after its application to fields. Irrigation return flow, as it is now known, occurs after a field is irrigated, and the water percolates into the ground and works its way back to the stream as groundwater, and then later daylights in a creek to prop up late-season streamflows. With the number of ditches and farms steadily increasing, the amount of water appearing as irrigation return flows also increased. Other factors likely contribute to Thomas's observation. Foremost is the widespread deforestation taking place at the time of Thomas's visit. With deforestation, there were fewer trees available to consume soil moisture or slow runoff, and the result is that streamflow and streamflow peaks increased. With fewer trees, streamflow increased due to less evapotranspiration, but the people on the plains did not necessarily recognize deforestation as contributing to the increased streamflow.[32]

Climate change and cyclical weather patterns likely contributed to the conditions for the increased flows. By 1869, the year Thomas visited, white settlers had only ten years of experience with Colorado's climate. This limited frame of reference meant that any change they observed would naturally be interpreted as a shift away from the "normal" conditions that they experienced early on. As it turns out, it appears that the Hayden Survey arrived in the Colorado Territory during a short spurt of wet years. It is very possible that Thomas and the settlers he encountered experienced conditions that were the wettest since active settlement began in 1859. For the next thirteen years conditions remained significantly drier.[33]

Writing for an eastern audience, Thomas emphasized that irrigation was critical. Although ditch building was expensive, the farmer would have the satisfaction of knowing that, when complete, "he may feel himself forever secure from loss through drought."[34]

Thomas described how Colorado farmers used the local geomorphology to their advantage. Farmers would dig a ditch at a grade less than the creek and so, over the course of a mile or two, bring water to otherwise dry terraces. By irrigating terraces Thomas became "satisfied that there is but a small quantity of land between Cache a la Poudre and South Platte which cannot be irrigated." And he added, "when these terraces have been irrigated and cultivated for a few years I feel confident that the soil on them will prove as productive as that of the bottoms." Without ditches these terraces were perched too far above the streams to receive water from the yearly spring floods. When Thomas visited Boulder Valley, he found some "of the finest farming and grazing lands north of Denver," much of it located on formerly dry terraces.[35]

Cyrus Thomas's predictions proved prophetic. Over the course of about fifty years, the United States sponsored expeditions and surveys that documented the transition of Colorado from an Indian space that was almost unknown to Americans to one that was firmly part of the United States. By the end of the 1860s, Colorado was integrated into the American nation. It is doubtful that Stephen Harriman Long could have foreseen the rapid demise of his "Great American Desert."

In the years between Long's declarations that Colorado would never serve as a site of civilization to Fremont's enthusiastic report of well-watered valleys, a western desert of magnificent scale grew in the minds of Americans. Not deterred, trappers and hunters exploited the wealth of the rivers and plains. Then with the discovery of gold as its spark, an unparalleled human migration to Colorado began that led to the settling of farms and digging of ditches along with the concurrent subdivision of land and consumption of forests. By the time Ferdinand V. Hayden visited Boulder Valley, the Great American Desert was in rapid retreat in both minds and on the ground. By then people were digging ditches, and the landscape would never be the same.

NOTES

1. Mead, *Irrigation Institutions*, vi.

2. Frazier, *People of Chaco*, 95–104; Lekson, *History of the Ancient Southwest*.

3. The information about the history, culture, and management of *acequias* in this section relies on Jose A. Rivera, *Acequia Culture: Water, Land, and Community in the Southwest* (Albuquerque: University of New Mexico Press, 1998).

4. Gregg, *Scenes and Incidents*, 151–52.

5. Davis, *El Gringo*, 198–99.

6. Holleran, *Historic Context for Irrigation*, 9.

7. Garrard, *Wah-to-yah*, 242.

8. McHendrie, "Hatcher Ditch."

9. Testimony of George Chase, Boulder District Court Case CA1280, 1881.

10. The Dry Creek discussed here is different from the one that David Nichols ditched on Boulder Creek or N. R. Howard ditched on South Boulder Creek. Numerous other streams and gulches throughout Colorado possessing the name "Dry Creek" create a constant stream of confusion for people discussing various waterways; see also Boulder County District Course Case CA6524, 5.

11. Testimony of Timothy Shanahan, Boulder County District Course Case CA1345, 1881; the original excavation of Dry Creek was rerouted around Base Line Reservoir when it was constructed and that is when it received the name New Dry Creek Carrier.

12. Coffin, "Reminiscences No. Four."

13. Holleran, *Historic Context for Irrigation*.

14. Edwin Baker's quote appears in Laflin, *Irrigation, Settlement, and Change*, 17.

15. Greeley, *What I Know of Farming*, 263.

16. Quote from Romer, "The Heritage and the Legacy of John Ramsey Rothrock," 64.

17. Thomas in Hayden, *Preliminary Field Report*, 150.

18. Taylor, *Colorado*, 44.

19. Ibid., 46. The natural basin that turned into a lake is possibly Church Lake, the first reservoir in the South Platte Watershed.

20. Ibid., 157–58.

21. Ibid., 158.

22. Udall, *Forgotten Founders*.

23. Nettleton, *Biennial Report*; Steinel, *History of Agriculture*.

24. Ostrom, *Crafting Institutions*.

25. Colten, *Unnatural Metropolis*; Melosi, *Sanitary City*.

26. Bartlett, *Great Surveys*.

27. Hayden, *Preliminary Field Report*.

28. Worster, *River Running West*, 204; F. V. Hayden, *Drainage Map of Colorado* (Washington, DC: US Geological Survey, Department of Interior, 1877).

29. Thomas in Hayden, *Preliminary Field Report*, 28.

30. Ibid., 136.

31. Ibid., 140.

32. Parshall, *Return of Seepage Water*.

33. Lawson and Stockton, "Desert Myth and Climatic Reality."

34. Thomas in Hayden, *Preliminary Field Report*, 149.

35. Ibid., 135.

FOUR

The Ditch

"I am standing in a bank overseeing a row of
men bent double as they dig. Mutterings and
grunts pass up and down the line, the clang of
shovel blades, the clack of handles, the hiss of
dry brush being pushed or kicked away."
—*Stanley Crawford*[1]

Perhaps more than any other place in the American West, the headgate of a
ditch is the site where nature and society intertwine. At the headgate people
control the flow of water. But nature supplies the water and has more control here than any of us. Although humans and all our handiworks are part
of nature, the headgate represents a conceptual divide between nature controlled and uncontrolled. The combined action of climate, weather, geomorphology, and hydrology directly influence the activities and business of man
at and beyond the headgate. All our actions, from writing the legal doctrines
we use to manage water to the concrete and steel we pour into the river to

DOI: 10.5876/9781607323822.c004

manipulate flow, impact the hydrology, watershed, ecology, chemistry, and character of the stream and surrounding landscape.

Conversations about water can easily start or end at the headgate. If your interest is limited to fish and aquatic organisms, the headgate may be the terminus and the site that threatens those things you most value. For others it is the place to divert and use water. It enables a way of life and distinctly western economies. Issues that arise on either side of the headgate may threaten someone's property and way of life. Either way, the headgate is a location of active engagement with a river. What happens here influences the stream ecology on one side and the urban and agricultural ecologies on the other.

Although the headgate, like the Enterprise Ditch headgate shown in Figure 4.1, may represent a conceptual boundary, in reality it is not much of a barrier at all. It is certainly not an ecological barrier. Water passing the headgate delivers many organisms and seeds down the ditch, and although modified by active management, the ecology along ditches often resembles that of the stream from which the water comes. It is not a management barrier either, as the hydrology on both sides of the headgate is affected by all the other dams and headgates stretching along the river. But it does make sense to begin considering ditches with their headgates, as they symbolize the purpose and operation of the entire system.

The headgate is of course the structure that we open and close to divert water from a stream into the channel of a ditch. Diversion dams (also known as weirs), sand sluices, trash gates, and other structures surround and support the operation of the headgate.

During the early years of settlement, building a diversion dam was often a simple matter of piling rocks in the stream. This worked, but the ditch company often had to rebuild the diversion every year after the spring flood. Later efforts involved constructing log dams that were somewhat more permanent. By the mid-twentieth century, most of these old structures were replaced by far more permanent and robust concrete structures.

Once water flows beyond the headgate, it enters the ditch itself. Other common synonyms for "ditch" include "canal," "aqueduct," and "acequia." I am not sure why people settled on using the word "ditch" for the vast majority of these structures in Colorado, as words like "canal" and "acequia" sound far more interesting and important than "ditch." Certainly anyone naming

FIGURE 4.1. Headgate of the Enterprise Ditch. Photograph by author.

their facility a ditch was not thinking about marketing. They were not promoters like Leaf Erickson, who named Greenland. After all, in the newspapers ditches are where people crash their cars and dump bodies. Canals have

romantic associations with Venice or Panama. Would you rather live next to a ditch or a canal? It sounds important to say you manage a canal, but I doubt many people have landed a date by saying they clean ditches for a living. And the word *acequia*, besides simply being exotic for English speakers, gives those who are familiar with it mental connotations of villages having deep community roots that one sees across New Mexico.

It seems to me that many ditches take on the some of the characteristics of the people who manage them. Considering a ditch this way, a ditch is much more than a trench across the landscape. As I walk down a ditch in my hip waders pitching leaves and debris, I am deeply engaged with the landscape. I feel solidarity with Stanley Crawford's *mayordomo*, and I certainly appreciate Richard Wright's perspective of how labor creates landscape and a sense of ownership.[2]

There is no ideal ditch. It is not surprising to see a ditch that is well graded, perhaps with a well-maintained maintenance road next to it, and no trees or willows along its bank. We also see ditches lined with trees and choked with willows that make it look more like a creek than a canal. Usually, a willow-choked ditch is managed by a small company run by a few fiscally tight farmers who have few resources to spare and even less time to deliver water without doing more than they absolutely have to. It should also not surprise anyone to learn that the well-manicured canal is operated by a large, well-funded company, city, or district that can afford to hire contract labor and full-time managers. Just compare any canal managed by the Northern Colorado Water Conservancy District to a small Boulder Creek ditch, and you will immediately see the distinction between a ditch run by a well-financed professional institution and one run as a shoestring operation.

Figure 4.2, from a *Harper's Weekly* magazine, depicts the basic outline of a ditch system that remains essentially the same as it was when this illustration was published in 1874. Physical infrastructure in a ditch system includes its headgate, diversion dam or weir, measuring device, the canal itself, laterals and a number of other structures used to divert and move water. An institution runs a ditch, and by that I mean the water right owners that are responsible for building and maintaining a ditch. The institution can be a giant organization, like the City of Denver, or a large quasi-public water conservancy district that operates a diverse system of canals and reservoirs, or small ditch companies run by a few shareholders, or even an individual or

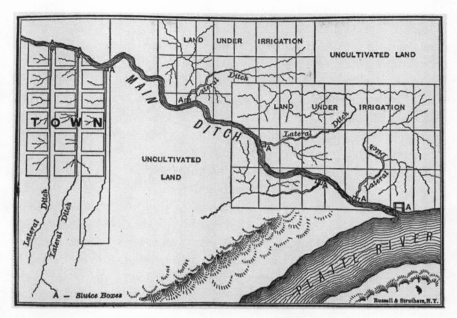

FIGURE 4.2. An illustration of a typical Colorado ditch system from the June 20, 1874, edition of *Harper's Weekly*.

family who owns a single ditch. It is not uncommon for individuals, companies, schools, government agencies and municipal water providers, churches, and even cemeteries to have ownership in a single ditch.[3]

Along with roads and property lines, ditches create linear patterns across the landscape. This visual character is something beyond the essential hydrologic services that ditches provide. Ditches help organize western cultural landscapes much as fenced fields. In conversations I have had with historian Michael Holleran, he eloquently describes how ditches visually enrich the urban and rural fabric. Ditches add visual complexity and enliven otherwise dull views. So often in the West, our cities and county roads are laid out in a Cartesian grid. For organization this is great, but it's uninteresting. Because ditches follow winding topographic contours, they bisect otherwise sterile road patterns and introduce visual interest into neighborhoods. Once vegetation grows along the banks, the winding ditch provides communities subtle enhancements to their visual makeup.

DITCH COMPANIES

Many people outside of ditch companies only see ditches as the trench that crosses a field or hillside. But ditches are as much about the people who run them as the physical infrastructure. People manage ditches and use the water that they deliver. Without the aspirations, cooperation, labor, and ideas of people, water would not flow to fields. Most Colorado ditch companies are small affairs whose sole purpose is to get water delivered to its shareholders.

Every ditch company varies in size and organization. The least complex ditch organizations are those that are unincorporated. This means that that the owners are either tenants-in-common or partners. No formal structure exists to manage the ditch. It's common to hear shareholders on one or another of these unincorporated ditches complain how they seem to do all the work and the other owners seldom get involved. Another aspect of unincorporated ditches is that the ownership transfers by deed. I am never surprised when I hear that one owner does not even know who else has an interest in their ditch or lateral.

A more complicated ownership structure is found within mutual irrigation ditch companies. These are almost always incorporated under state law. Most are nonprofit companies and charge assessments to their shareholders to meet company overhead. A few are for profit in which the company leases water to its users.

Shares of stock in a mutual ditch company represent the stockholder's interest in water rights. An example of a stock certificate from the Dry Creek No. 2 Ditch Company is shown in Figure 4.3. Ownership of ditch company stock includes the exclusive right to use the water it represents. The water managed by the mutual ditch company is divided on a pro-rata basis according to the number of shares held by each shareholder and the total number of shares in the company. The ownership of shares in a mutual ditch company is incidental to the ownership of the water rights by the shareholders. Each share represents a definite and specific water right. A shareholder's interest in the water rights cannot be altered by any action of the ditch company or other shareholders. Mutual irrigation ditch companies were first incorporated under territorial and then state laws. Incorporation allowed owners to raise money and issue shares of stock.[4]

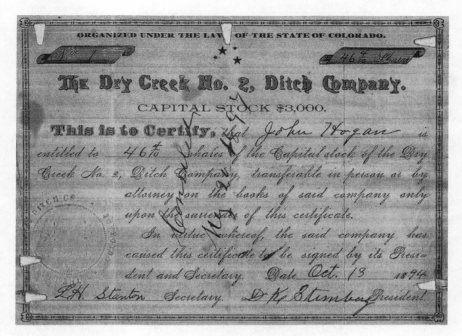

ORGANIZED UNDER THE LAW OF THE STATE OF COLORADO.

46 ⁷⁄₁₀

The Dry Creek No. 2, Ditch Company.

CAPITAL STOCK $3,000.

This is to Certify, *That John Hogan is entitled to 46 ⁷⁄₁₀ shares of the Capital stock of the Dry Creek No. 2, Ditch Company, transferable in person or by attorney on the books of said company only upon the surrender of this certificate.*

In virtue whereof, the said company has caused this certificate to be signed by its President and Secretary. Date Oct. 13 *18*94

L. H. Stanton *Secretary.* D. K. Stimber *President*

FIGURE 4.3. A stock certificate from the Dry Creek No. 2 Ditch Company. Photograph by author.

Among the first orders of business for settlers was to get water. Details like organizing and incorporating the ditch often waited until after the digging got under way. The Star Ditch, a lateral that carries Left Hand Ditch water, was more or less typical. Thomas Richart, A. R. Brown, and George C. Batchelder began digging the Star Ditch on April 1, 1871, and completed their work about four weeks later. It was only after they began digging that they organized the company on April 11, 1871.

Richart, Brown, and Batchelder knew they would get around to incorporating, so they kept track of expenses related to the ditch. Their intention was that people using the ditch before the company incorporated would pay $40 in cash or labor to get a share. Their secretary tallied how much various people spent in time, labor, or materials to offset the initial $40 per share to buy into the company. For instance, sometime in 1871 or 1872, George Batchelder performed labor worth $13.55 and paid $26.45 to receive one share. At that time, Star Ditch was paying about $2.00 per day for labor, so

Batchelder probably worked nearly seven days on the ditch. During the mid-1870s another shareholder by the name of J. G. Rutter performed labor worth $24.25, bought nails worth $2.88, and then paid a balance of $12.87 to get his share in the Star Ditch.[5]

Although organized in 1871, it was 1878 when Richart and E. C. Ereckson incorporated the Star Ditch. Their stock subscription book is reproduced in Figure 4.4. They authorized issuing twenty-five shares, capitalized at $100 per share, but they were able to sell only fourteen. After incorporating, the plan was that you would have to have to pay $100 to acquire a share. Just like an initial public offering for a modern technology company that might take place today, entrepreneurs getting in before the launch saw the value of their interest increase from $40 to $100 per share. Although Thomas Richart paid $80 for his two shares, stock certificate numbers 2 and 3, once the company was incorporated they were theoretically valued at $200.

Once incorporated, Thomas Richart became the president, and A. R. Brown became the company secretary. One of Brown's first expenditures was to purchase a corporate seal for $8.50 from the Novelty Manufacturing Company of Denver. With the seal, they began issuing stock certificates. The Star Ditch secretary still uses the $8.50 seal when he issues new stock certificates after a share is sold.

Besides mutual irrigation companies, there are other types of ditches. One is the "carrier ditch." This ditch transports water through it for a fee. Carrier ditches typically have no water rights of their own, but move water owned by others through them. Several incorporated carrier ditches transport water around Boulder County. The Agitator Ditch is one of them. This company, incorporated in 1908, transports water from the McGinn and Davidson ditches to farms in the eastern part of the county.

Other organizations manage and operate ditches. These include irrigation districts, water conservation districts, and water conservancy districts. These organizations are quasi-governmental and have taxing power to raise money for construction and operating expenses. No irrigation districts operate in Boulder County; however, the St. Vrain and Left Hand Water Conservancy District and the Northern Colorado Water Conservancy District both provide water and services in the county. Water districts and conservancy districts are generally large organizations and serve both farmers and cities. Many operate reservoirs and ditches.

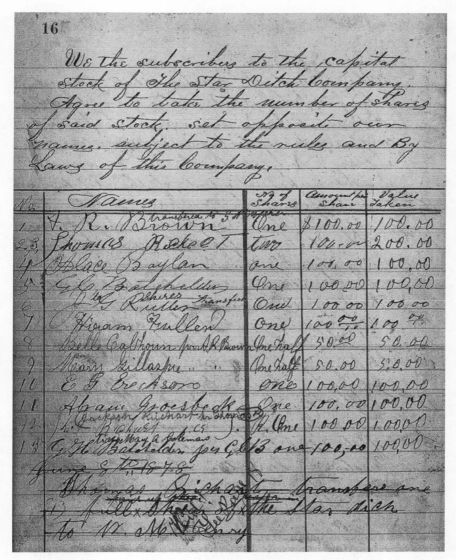

FIGURE 4.4. The stock subscription book for the Star Ditch. Photograph by author.

ANNUAL MEETINGS

Perhaps nowhere is each ditch company's personality and culture on display more than at its annual shareholder meeting. The annual meeting is where much of the business is conducted and decisions made for operating the ditch over the coming months. At the meeting the shareholders review the events of the past year, decide what maintenance is needed in the coming year, examine finances, set assessments, discuss whatever needs to be discussed, and elects its directors or officers. If ditch companies have a personality, this is where you see it.

Take the South Boulder and Bear Creek Ditch Company, whose majority shareholder is the City of Lafayette. Lafayette controls about 85 percent of its shares. Because of this, four of the five directors are Lafayette employees. For the most part, the minority shareholders get to sit back as Lafayette employees make all the decisions for the company. This company's annual meeting is brief. Peter Johnson, an engineer with Lafayette and the South Boulder and Bear Creek president, calls the meeting to order. Brad Dallam, a Lafayette engineer and company secretary, rips through the business agenda. Staff makes a game of keeping it short and sweet. Brad will ask, "Has everyone read last year's minutes and can I have a motion to approve?" Mark, another Lafayette employee, barks, "Motion to approve." Just as quickly, Peter adds, "Second." And then back to Brad, "Approved." Brad then moves on to the next agenda item. In 2007 the South Boulder and Bear Creek meeting was convened one Tuesday in February at 11:03 a.m. and adjourned at 11:12 a.m. And if I recall correctly, the 2008 and 2009 meetings were even shorter. It always took me more time to get to the meeting than it did to attend it.

The annual meeting for the Green Ditch was always a mix between a social event and family affair. For many years until he passed away, Drake Sullivan was the president and ditch rider. Drake was a former World War II flying fortress pilot. Like true war heroes, he never spoke about his exploits. Drake's wife Berene was the longtime company secretary. Until she retired from her duties, I could anticipate having a delicious slice of homemade apple pie as an inducement to attend. For years, she passed out meticulously handwritten minutes and an accounting of expenses down to the penny. Often joining the meeting were Berene and Drake's daughter and son, Rosamond and Floyd. Meetings of the Green Ditch were always relaxed but efficient. After Drake passed away, Rosamond stepped up and became the ditch rider, and Floyd pitched in with his backhoe when bigger equipment was needed.

Not all annual meetings and companies are a model of efficiency or friendship. In my mind, the Original Cottonwood Ditch of the 1990s and 2000s was the poster child for troubled management. For many years, the shareholders would meet in the unfinished basement of Bob Pherson, then company president. Bob would set up some metal folding chairs and a poker table to conduct the business. About the only other thing in Bob's basement was a corrugated metal stock watering tank set up as a giant goldfish bowl. We ate doughnuts, sipped coffee, and settled in for the meeting.

One year when the Original Cottonwood Ditch business meeting began, Margaret, the company secretary, read the minutes and financial report. The 2008 annual meeting appeared to start well enough, and we muddled through the prior year's minutes even though it was never clear from the minutes what actually transpired at the previous meeting. When it was time to read the financial report, Margaret said something approximating, "The company has about $7,300 dollars and that is about right." One of the shareholders present asked Margaret what she meant by that, and requested a more specific figure. Margaret then picked up the sheet of paper on which the finances were written and looked at it. Next, she brought the paper a bit closer to her face and then rotated the sheet 90 degrees. Then she rotated the sheet another 90 degrees and then rotated it back 180 degrees. Margaret finally admitted that she wasn't quite sure how much money the company had. Needless to say, the shareholders did not approve the financial report. Margaret resigned from the board shortly after that. Eventually the whole board was replaced. The company has been struggling to sort out the records and finances ever since.

Many years ago, a former colleague of mine, Delani Wheeler, attended the annual meeting of the Howard Ditch. At the time, the company was undergoing many changes. The cities of Lafayette and Louisville had bought multiple shares and transferred them out of the ditch. Some of the land along the ditch was being developed. The future of the ditch company itself seemed in doubt. Tension among the board and shareholders ran high. At one annual meeting, Delani witnessed an argument between the ditch president and a developer that ended up with the president throwing a chair at the guy. Years later, I ended up serving on the Howard Ditch board, and fortunately, by then, all the meetings I attended were civil.

Most ditch annual meetings are rather uneventful, even boring. The Left Hand Ditch annual meeting is typical. On the first weekend of February Richard Behrmann, the company president and lifelong farmer, calls the meeting to order. Richard has an honest, folksy sense of humor that puts everyone at ease. He seems never to get angry, and if he does, it does not show. He sticks to the agenda and keeps the meeting moving. Terry Plummer, the company superintendent, describes operations for the past year. Terry is a no-nonsense, gun-carrying preacher and former builder who spends his time allocating water to shareholders, smoothing ruffled feathers, and keeping the water moving. Usually about thirty or forty shareholders attend the annual meeting in Boulder County's old Altona Grange. Terry and Richard discuss operations at the various ditches and reservoirs that the company owns. The attorney gives his report and works in a bad PG-13 joke, and then one or another invited speaker makes some comments. Then each board member gives his report. Next the company holds its board of director elections. Only one or two board seats are up for election each year, so there is a lot of continuity on the board. Because elections are based on the number of shares each shareholder owns, the election results are fairly predictable. The annual assessment is discussed and voted on, and soon after that the meeting adjourns to a lunch of barbecued beef or chicken.

A big part of each annual meeting is setting the company assessments. Since most of these companies are not-for-profit corporations, it is the shareholder assessments that generate most of the operating funds. Occasionally, additional money comes in from fees to nonshareholders, such as payments from developers or someone else who wishes to modify the ditch easement. But companies cannot rely on outside fees, so the conversation about the budget is important, as it determines what each stockholder pays to keep the ditch running for another year. In this regard, the Dry Creek Davidson Ditch is pretty representative. Its annual meeting is usually in late February. Shareholders discuss cleaning needs and set aside funds to do necessary work. In 2010 the company raised about $21,500 in assessments. It spent about $2,200 on overhead like worker compensation, insurance, bank fees, state corporation fees, and postage. It also paid the president, secretary-treasurer, and ditch rider about $5,400 for their time. The other board members do not receive any compensation. Hand labor, backhoe work, equipment rental, structural repairs, and other related costs ran about $9,000. The money that was not spent went into a capital replacement fund to save for infrequently needed major repairs. Capital items for the Dry Creek Davidson include repairs to the main headgate or other large structures on the ditch. After the annual meeting is held, ditch companies start working to get the ditch going in the season ahead.

DITCH OPERATIONS

Once shareholders hold their annual meeting, it comes time to start the ditch. This involves cleaning it, performing any necessary maintenance, and then getting the water going. By setting assessments the company president and superintendent know what resources they have for operations in the coming year. The budget allows them to determine what maintenance they can perform before the ditch is turned on for the season. I've served as the president of several ditches, and that is one of the main tasks I handled each year. On the McGinn Ditch, for example, maintenance generally fell into to two categories, annual and long term. Annually, I walked the entire ditch to determine the biggest maintenance needs. Then the ditch rider and I would get together to compare notes and set maintenance priorities. We paid special attention to areas where the ditch was eroding or where vegetation was encroaching. These were addressed annually. We also worked on one or more larger projects, such as infrastructure replacement or more comprehensive mechanical cleaning at specific sites. Because the company had limited funds, it performed comprehensive cleaning only on high-priority reaches and left the rest for another year.

Some amount of annual cleaning occurs along almost the entire length of each ditch. This usually entails pitching out leaves and debris from the bottom of the ditch or from trash grates. When I helped clean the Silver Lake Ditch, I spent hour after hour pitching wet leaves from the ditch. On a couple of occasions I have scooped a putrefying skunk out of the ditch. Those were usually existential moments when I questioned my chosen line of work.

The hardest work, but frankly the most rewarding, is when the company turns the ditch on for the season. If the ditch is in priority, the state water commissioner will allow the users to turn the ditch on. Seeing the water flow down the ditch from its source at the headgate as the season launches is magical. Each company goes about getting its ditch turned on slightly differently. Some let the superintendent hire labor and get the ditch going. Other companies are more frugal and solicit help from shareholders.

The Dry Creek Davidson Ditch asks its shareholders to help get the water running. Depending on river calls, it is usually turned on around the third week of May and runs until the end of August. Figure 4.5 shows Jess Alexander, the now retired Dry Creek Davidson ditch rider, pitching weeds

FIGURE 4.5. Jess Alexander, ditch rider for the Dry Creek Davidson, pitching weeds during the spring water run in May 2004. Photograph by author.

during the spring water run in May 2004. Jess is a rancher who has lived on the ditch for decades. He rode the ditch to keep it clear of debris and to make sure the other shareholders got their water. When it was time to run water, a number of shareholders put on hip waders and grabbed pitch forks. When Jess turned the water into the ditch, leaves or branches started floating down it. Shareholders spread out and pitched debris out as the water advanced. It was a struggle to keep up with the flowing water. It did not flow very fast, as much of it seeped into the dry bed. However, wading through the water and pitching soaked leaves for hour after hour was very tiring. It was hard work, but seeing the flowing water generally put everyone in a very good mood.

After the first few days, things settle in for the season. The ditch rider usually checks the main headgate every day during the season. This is to make sure that no debris blocks the headgate and that the permitted amount of water is in the ditch. The water commissioner also comes around to make sure the headgate is set correctly. Each ditch rider also checks various watch-spots. These are places that he or she knows will accumulate trash when the wind blows or where a fence or trash grate collects debris. Checking these sites is especially important after storms. Running a ditch is all based on judgment and experience. Getting a ditch rider on board that is responsible, has common sense, and is willing to work for next to nothing is one of the biggest challenges ditch companies face. Long-term ditch riders get to know a ditch much like you get to know an old car. Each one (ditch and ditch rider) is different and temperamental. If the ditch is maintained poorly, it won't run. Then the ditch president starts fielding angry phone calls about the ditch. If the ditch rider is competent, things run smoothly and the president's phone remains quiet.

Another job that the ditch rider does is to check and set the lateral headgates. This varies from company to company. On the organized side of things is the Left Hand Ditch, where Terry Plummer takes water orders via the Internet and keeps track of shareholder accounts. Terry then fills orders and releases water into the various lateral ditches for shareholders. Each lateral headgate has a measuring device so he can make sure each shareholder gets what he or she ordered. Terry keeps records of water deliveries, and the company directors monitor operations when they get together for their monthly board meeting.

Many ditches on South Boulder and Boulder creeks are far less rigorously managed. Every ditch has a measuring device at its main headgate because this is mandated by state law. Some companies have measuring devices on their laterals and others do not. It is often left to the shareholders to monitor what they get down any particular lateral. On these ditches, the ditch rider knows how many shares each user has and visually estimates flows into laterals. If shareholders feel that they are not getting what they own, they let the ditch rider know. When problems arise on ditches or if drought strikes, the measurement of water becomes critical. Measurement, after all, is the only way to determine if you are receiving the water you own. As water administration tightens, it is easy to imagine a day when each lateral will have a measuring device.

The need to measure water flows developed along with ditches and the legal doctrine governing water rights. Throughout the latter half of the nineteenth century and well into the twentieth, engineers struggled to invent reliable structures that could accurately measure quantities of water. It wasn't until the 1920s that Ralph Parshall, an engineering professor at Colorado State University, perfected a simple and accurate water measurement device that now bears his name: the Parshall flume. These flumes use simple instrumentation to record flows, and the instruments are housed in weatherproof sheds attached to the structure.

A vernacular architecture to house the measuring devices has emerged from the need to protect the gauge instruments. "Chart" or "gauge" houses are small buildings about the size of old-fashioned outhouses that contain these measuring devices and are found almost everywhere that the flow of water is recorded. Gauge houses are simple and utilitarian. The gauge house located on the Original Cottonwood Ditch, and shown in Figure 4.6, is constructed out of an old boiler. It is sturdy and was very inexpensive to construct. It sits right on the concrete wall of the Parshall flume. I know that the water commissioner for Boulder Creek dislikes this gauge house because he sees lots of spiders living in there, and he also finds plenty of mouse droppings that make him worry about catching Hantavirus.

LATERALS: GETTING WATER TO DITCH USERS

Once the water passes the headgate and moves down the ditch, it is distributed to water users. This is accomplished by sending water down laterals, which are just smaller distribution ditches that branch off the primary ditch. As water runs down the main ditch, the ditch rider opens and closes smaller

Figure 4.6. The gauge house on the Original Cottonwood Ditch. Photograph by author.

headgates or division boxes to send water into laterals. I have heard analogies of the main ditch to an artery, and laterals to capillaries. One difference between the main ditch and a lateral is that the laterals are seldom operated or maintained by the ditch company. Laterals are owned by the individual shareholders that use them. While there are always exceptions to the rule, most laterals are unincorporated and are managed by its users. Confusion often creeps into discussions among ditch shareholders when someone wants to run water down a lateral and finds out that he or she needs permission from a single shareholder or group of shareholders and not the ditch company that the water originates from.

In 1999 the lines between the main ditch run by the South Boulder Canon [*sic*] Ditch and one of its private laterals became blurred. It turns out that several members of the board of directors lived along a single lateral. Bob Pherson, the ditch rider and company president (he was also the president of the Original Cottonwood Ditch), began maintaining the lateral at the behest of the directors who lived along it. After some years, a landowner along the lateral—who was not a shareholder—placed an undersized culvert in it to improve his driveway access. Bob and the landowner got into a heated exchange over the culvert. Before long, the South Boulder Canon Ditch and the landowner were in court over the lateral. The company nearly bankrupted itself spending upward of $90,000 in legal fees over the culvert. Eventually a settlement was reached in 2002, and a new culvert of the correct dimensions was installed for several hundred dollars. At the next annual meeting I watched as angry shareholders shouted pointed questions about how the company got into a lawsuit over a lateral that the company did not even own. The upshot of this was that the ditch president was replaced, a new board was elected, and a new ditch rider was hired. The new ditch rider has strict orders not to maintain any of the private laterals along the South Boulder Canon Ditch.[6]

On Left Hand Creek there is a lateral named the North Tollgate Ditch. For years, the North Tollgate Ditch operated as an unincorporated lateral ditch that distributes water from Left Hand Ditch. What this generally meant is that a couple of the owners, usually longtime ranchers Larry Strear and Harold Steel, would walk the ditch from top to bottom and throw out knapweed and debris before turning it on in the spring. Once they finished cleaning and the ditch was turned on, other folks would call for water too. Most people just piggybacked on their work. Now and then, sediment would build up, and they would hire a contractor to clean parts of the ditch.

Things became strained on the North Tollgate in 2004 when Larry and Harold were walking the ditch and an adjacent landowner told them they would be trespassing on his land if they cleaned the ditch. No amount of reasoning could persuade the landowner that they had the right to access the easement to clean the ditch. The landowner even called the sheriff. I became involved because the City of Boulder had an ownership interest in that ditch. The lateral owners were seething. All the North Tollgate owners knew they had a right to do the work, but the threat of legal action made them act with caution. No matter what the lateral owners proposed, the landowner refused to consider. Eventually we incorporated the North Tollgate so that the company, and not each individual owner, could press its legal rights. After incorporating, the new company hired an attorney. It then wrote a letter to the landowner and stated its intention to clean its easement. This motivated the landowner to seek an injunction to prevent the company from proceeding. A hearing was held in Boulder County District Court, and the judge ruled from the bench that the suit had no merit and reaffirmed the company's right to clean the ditch and access its easement. It cost the company over $30,000 to protect its interest in court and another $900 to actually clean the ditch. Figure 4.7 shows the ditch-cleaning operation after the ruling.[7]

Beyond the laterals lie the users' fields, crops, ponds, and aspirations. Be it a lawn, truck garden, or ranch meadow, the water moves on to its actual point of use. Here water evaporates, transpires, soaks in, and runs off. Anything left to reach the stream flows down to the next headgate, where it is diverted anew.

FAILED DREAMS

Occasionally, ditches fall into disuse. The Hatcher Ditch, Colorado's first ditch, fell into disuse because hostilities with the Indians made it too dangerous to irrigate. For the most part, the reasons for abandoning a ditch are far less gripping. Perhaps all the water rights were sold off and transferred elsewhere. Maybe irrigation ceased when the land was developed. Sometimes the water user simply gets too old to maintain the system or finds that the water right is so junior that the effort is not justified. When this happens, a water user may just walk away with the intent of never using the ditch again. This is outright abandonment. Sometimes ditch users simply stop irrigating and think that someday they will try again.

Over time, disuse can mature into abandonment and the loss of water rights. In order to avoid having dozens of dormant or abandoned water rights clogging water rights tabulations, Colorado enforces a "use it or lose it" criterion for maintaining water rights. Every ten years, the Colorado state engineer reviews water use from ditches and prepares a list of water rights that it believes are no longer used. It then drafts an abandonment list. The state publishes the list, and if the owner does not protest, the court signs the decree and the right is abandoned.

Some fairly major ditches have been abandoned this way. The South Boulder and Foot Hills Irrigating Ditch Company was a latecomer to the ditch-building business in the Boulder Valley. Construction of the South Boulder and Foot Hills Irrigating Ditch began in 1883. Because of its junior decree, users received water very inconsistently.[8]

The South Boulder and Foot Hills Irrigating Ditch, as shown on Figure 4.8, once extended along a winding path from its headgate on South Boulder

FIGURE 4.7. Mechanical cleaning on the North Tollgate Ditch. Photograph by author.

Creek east of Eldorado Springs all the way north to what is now the Green Mountain Cemetery in Boulder. It served water to farms that were later annexed and developed as subdivisions. Because it had no reservoirs to add extra water, the ditch could not provide a reliable supply of water to shareholders during the critical late-irrigation season.

As recently as 1956 there were still nearly 600 acres under irrigation from the South Boulder and Foot Hills Irrigating Ditch. Farmers grew alfalfa, pasture grass, corn, beans, some grain, and even sugar beets. However, as Boulder developed, land was converted to subdivisions, and shares in the company fell into disuse, leaving fewer and fewer shareholders to maintain

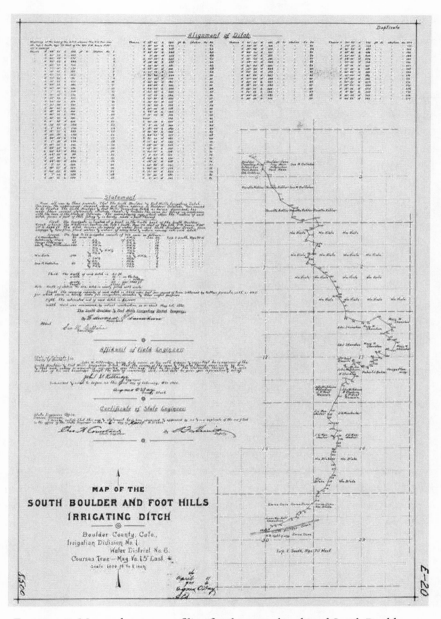

FIGURE 4.8. Map and statement filing for the now abandoned South Boulder Foothills Irrigating Ditch. Colorado state engineer, Map and Statement Filing, South Boulder Foothills Irrigating Ditch, 1911. Permission pending.

the company. By the late 1970s the ditch ceased operations, and in 1984 the State Engineer placed the ditch on the abandonment list. The ditch was formally abandoned by the water court in 1988.[9]

Traces of the ditch remain visible near the City of Boulder Open Space and Mountain Parks' Mesa Trail off of Eldorado Springs Drive. Several years ago Lynn Shanahan, whose grandfather homestead the land he farms in south Boulder, showed me a South Boulder Foothills Ditch stock certificate he found in a safe deposit box. He was wondering what it might be worth. "Sorry, Lynn," I said, "That is just paper now."

NOTES

1. Crawford, *Mayordomo*, 1.

2. Crawford, *Mayordomo*; White, *Organic Machine*.

3. *Harper's Weekly* 18, no. 912 (June 29, 1874).

4. Jacobucci v. District Court, 189 Colo. 380, 541 P.2d 667 (1975).

5. *Secretary Report of the Star Ditch Company, December 1, 1877, Boulder County, CO*, prepared by A. R. Brown, Secretary. Star Ditch Company, Care of City of Boulder Open Space and Mountain Parks.

6. See Boulder County District Court Case 99CV413-3. In literature of the American West up until the 1880s, it was common to see the word "canyon" spelled in its original Spanish, *canõn*, or Anglicized as "canon," as in the ditch name. By the 1890s the current spelling was in widespread use. Some ditch companies retain the Anglicized form: South Boulder Canon Ditch.

7. Boulder County District Court Case 2004 CV 1235.

8. Boulder County District Court Case CA6672.

9. Colorado state engineer's Structure Summary Report for the South Boulder Foothills Ditch, accessed November 17, 2010, http://cdss.state.co.us/onlineTools /Pages/StructuresDiversions.aspx. Then search for South Boulder Foothills Ditch; Colorado Water Court Case 84CW293.

Boulder's Pioneer Ditches

> "Irrigation is a miracle!"
> —*William E. Smythe*[1]

Dreams of gold and grain converged in Boulder Valley in 1859 and 1860. Swarms of young men scoured the mountains for elusive gold dust west of the new mining supply camp of Boulder. Seeking riches in minerals, most found only disappointment. Others, mostly country boys from the Midwest and Europe, turned to what they knew, and looked to the fertile valley bottoms east of the mountains for choice farmland. Soon many were cashing in supplying food and hay to the bustling mining camps. But to do so, most first built ditches, for without water there was no hope of raising a crop, supplying food for themselves, or creating a surplus to sell.

At the time, the prospects for successful irrigation were far from certain. The results turned out to be better than anticipated, leading later generations to call irrigation the "miracle" that enabled farming in Colorado's semiarid climate. Almost all ditch digging during the first years of the Gold Rush

DOI: 10.5876/9781607323822.c005

took place within the active floodplains of streams. "We, in 1860, '61, and '62, considered these little valleys—Boulder, St. Vrain, Thompson, and Cache la Poudre—of more real value for farming purposes than all the high dry land between these streams," settler Morse Coffin explained. For early settlers such as Coffin, simply getting the valley bottoms irrigated was a sufficient challenge. The dry terraces beyond the valley bottoms were seen as useful for grazing and little else.

For the earliest settlers, irrigation's full potential was not obvious. As Coffin put it, "When Horace Greeley was through this country in June 1859, he gave it as his opinion that farming in this country would be limited to gardening along the streams. So it is no special wonder that we common people fell into the same error."[2]

Boulder's earliest irrigation ditches were short and hand-dug. On Boulder Creek, the Wellmans were the first to irrigate through field laterals, and the Smith-Goss and Lower Boulder ditches were dug soon after. Howard Ditch was the first on South Boulder Creek in 1860. Within a few months other settlers moved to the South Boulder Creek valley to dig the McGinn, Schearer, and others. Similarly, the William C. Hake and Autrey Eggelston Ditches on nearby Coal Creek were dug 1860 to serve small farms. Generally, these ditches are named after the settlers who dug them. Together, these ditches map the early history of Boulder Valley and the expansion of farming during the first years of the Gold Rush.

ANDERSON DITCH AND THE GROWTH OF A CITY

One can find many themes that run across the history of the American West on the Anderson Ditch. Settlement, war, the growth and decline of farms, and the rise of a city are all traced along banks of this one ditch.

Among those who were in the vanguard of settlement during the early days of Colorado settlement was the family of Jonas Anderson Sr. In 1859, forty-seven-year--old Jonas Anderson Sr. arrived in Boulder with his wife Sarah and two sons, Fred and Jonas Jr., from Sweden. An accomplished stonemason, Jonas Sr. settled on 160 acres just south of the fledgling town of Boulder. Anderson and his neighbors squatted on land that belonged to the Arapahoe and Cheyenne Indians. In 1860 he, his sons, and his neighbor, Marinus Smith, began digging the Anderson Ditch, diverting water from

Boulder Creek at the canyon mouth at a site that allowed water to flow by gravity around the foot of Flagstaff Mountain to their lands on what would become University Hill. Over the next several years, the Anderson family set about building their farm and improving the ditch. Among his various enterprises, Jonas Anderson Sr. bought land close to the foothills and developed a stone quarry. He is credited with building many buildings in Boulder, including the railroad depot and the homes of his sons, Fred and Jonas Jr. The elder Anderson ended his days suffering from cancer that ate away his jaw. He died in 1894 at eighty-two, just months after being declared insane from senility.[3]

FIGURE 5.1. Jonas Anderson Jr. Photograph courtesy of the Carnegie Branch Library for Local History. Reprinted with permission.

Eventually, the ditch became closely associated with Jonas Anderson Jr., whose photo is shown in Figure 5.1. Perhaps this is because he is buried right on the ditch bank in Boulder's Columbia Cemetery. Jonas Jr., a naturalized American, served in the Civil War at Glorieta, New Mexico, and later under Chivington at the massacre of Cheyenne and Arapahoe Indians at Sand Creek. Several years ago, the Anderson Ditch Company lined the ditch through the cemetery, in part because erosion was threatening to wash Jonas's grave into the ditch. It seems as if Anderson and his ditch will not be separated. Jonas Jr., like his father, ended up senile, dying in 1919.

The Anderson Ditch Company was first incorporated in 1871 by Jonas Anderson Sr., Marinus G. Smith, and George A. Andrews. Like Anderson, Smith and Andrews were prominent Boulder citizens. Smith previously built Boulder's very first ditch, the Smith and Goss. Although Smith dug his ditch first, John Rothrock of the Lower Boulder Ditch was first to file a claim, which left Smith with the number two priority water right on Boulder Creek. Smith, a veteran of the 1849 California Gold Rush, spent some time in Illinois before heading to Colorado in 1859 at the start of the Pikes Peak Gold Rush. Smith realized that there was more money in supplying miners than in being one. He started a stage and mail line between Denver, Boulder, and various mining towns. Smith then focused his attention on Boulder and acquired a large tract of land on the southern outskirts of town. In 1863, Smith helped build what would become the North Boulder Farmers Ditch. He also sold the land for Boulder's Columbia (or Pioneer) Cemetery. Smith's early irrigation efforts helped prove the viability of irrigated agriculture along the Colorado Front Range and inspired subsequent efforts elsewhere. An early Boulder historian extolled Smith's effort, declaring that irrigation could "make the desert rejoice, and blossom as the rose."[4]

Water from Anderson Ditch played a critical role in fostering Boulder's development. In the early 1870s, Marinus Smith donated ten shares of Anderson Ditch to irrigate the future University of Colorado campus. Smith also joined Jonas Anderson Jr., George Andrews, David Nichols, and others in donating land and money to bring the university to Boulder.

It is hard to understate Smith's impact on Boulder's early development. Beyond his irrigation efforts and donations for the university, Smith provided land for the depot (which Jonas Anderson Sr. built) to lure the first railroad, the Colorado and Southern Railway, to town. As Smith aged, his mental health declined. By 1894, Smith began experiencing hallucinations and fearing imaginary enemies. In June 1894, Smith was declared insane and taken to Pueblo Asylum, where he spent time convalescing before returning home to Boulder. Smith died in 1901 at the age of eighty-two.[5]

Anderson Ditch became an important fixture in Boulder's early agricultural life. Eventually, the Anderson family sold off most of their shares and land. D. K. Sternberg bought shares in 1872. Thirty years later, Sternberg was still irrigating a fruit orchard that he planted under the ditch. During those years small farms produced vegetables for local consumption using ditch water.

Originally, Anderson Ditch irrigated about 425 acres. In time the irrigated area increased to nearly 1,500 acres of small productive farms on the outskirts of Boulder. Among them was the Vineland Fruit Farm. It had twenty-four acres planted to small fruit, including raspberries and strawberries. The Vineland Fruit Farm also had an orchard featuring apples, pears, and peaches. One year during the late 1890s, this farm reportedly produced about 14,000 quarts of raspberries.[6]

Like all early ditches in Boulder Valley, Anderson Ditch was initially used for more than irrigation. It provided water for drinking, household uses, and livestock. Laterals from Anderson Ditch paralleled city streets and brought water to homes. Domestic use of Anderson Ditch water continued until the city of Boulder began developing its municipal water system. As late as 1907 there were still about 200 households located beyond Boulder's municipal system using Anderson Ditch water for domestic purposes.[7]

Because of the seniority of Anderson Ditch, it proved a very reliable water supply. That, coupled with the ditch's convenient location at the mouth of Boulder Canyon, made it a logical water source for Boulder. Starting in 1886, Boulder began buying shares. Boulder obtained shares through direct purchases and acquisitions when land was annexed or developed. Simultaneously, the number of irrigated farms decreased. By 1925, the city owned 14¾ shares in the Anderson Ditch. Like most ditch water rights, the original decree only specified irrigation as the authorized use. Once Boulder purchased shares, it began changing their use from agricultural to municipal, which allowed the city to transfer the water to the municipal water intake. Boulder completed its first transfer in 1925. Other transfers followed in 1942, 1963, and 1989. By the early 2000s, only a small percentage of Anderson Ditch shares remained in private hands. About two-thirds of the water in Anderson Ditch is now owned by the City of Boulder, one-quarter by the University of Colorado, and the remaining by other public entities and a few private shareholders.[8]

In the 1940s and 1950s development on Boulder's University Hill began to encroach Anderson Ditch. Though various agreements, the company granted permission to developers to pipe sections of the ditch. As a result, various buildings, including Boulder's landmark Fox Theater, were built over the ditch.

In the 1980s, other Boulder Valley communities were experiencing unprecedented growth. One of these, the city of Lafayette, was looking to expand its domestic water supply. Farmers realized that they could sell their shares in ditches and reservoirs and make a significant profit. One company, the Base Line Land and Irrigation Company is situated between Boulder and Lafayette and owns the moderately sized Base Line Reservoir. In 1986, Base Line shareholders approached the City of Boulder with an offer to sell the company. No deal was concluded because Boulder believed the asking price was too high. About a year later, a major subdivision developer, M.D.C. Holdings, Inc., a corporation that later built a major subdivision at Superior known as Rock

Creek, offered to buy Base Line. M.D.C.'s $20,560 per share offer was rejected by the Base Line Company. But the scramble to buy Base Line was on. By 1996, the cities of Boulder and Lafayette determined that purchasing Base Line Reservoir was in their interest. To the Base Line shareholders' delight, a bidding war between the two cities ensued. Lafayette prevailed and ended up paying around $34,000 per share to get about 300 shares of stock and the controlling interest in the company. After acquiring its interest, Lafayette filed numerous water court applications to allow it to store water in the reservoir for its municipal system.

Once Lafayette gained a controlling interest in Base Line, the city began exploring ways to expand water supplies available to Base Line. An obvious source was the Anderson Ditch. Base Line had a contract with Anderson Ditch dating to 1911 that allowed it to run Boulder Creek water down the ditch to the reservoir. Once Lafayette took control of Base Line, it sought to increase the amount of water flowing through Anderson Ditch. The ditch company became alarmed about the prospect for dramatically increased maintenance costs, and Boulder residents fretted about the possibility that Boulder Creek would dry up as Lafayette diverted more water. Lafayette's leveraging of Base Line to carry more water through the Anderson Ditch quickly brought it into conflict with Boulder.[9]

In 1996 and 1997 a dizzying series of lawsuits were initiated in Boulder County District Court between Lafayette, Base Line, the Anderson Ditch, and Boulder. In the first lawsuit, Lafayette asserted that it could use excess capacity in Anderson Ditch to carry Lafayette's water to Base Line. Then the Anderson Ditch terminated the 1911 carriage agreement, claiming that Base Line violated the contract. Base Line responded by countersuing to reinstate the 1911 carriage agreement. The legal proceedings became so acrimonious that at one point presiding Judge Morris Standstead charged the Anderson Ditch board with contempt of court for refusing to run Base Line water through the ditch. Although those charges were later dropped, the legal tabs reached nearly $1 million per city.

Further confusing matters is that Lafayette and Base Line are separate entities, just as Anderson Ditch and Boulder are separate entities. However, the staff of each city represents majorities of each respective board. In the public's eye, the legal battles between the two companies were seen as proxy wars between Boulder and Lafayette.[10]

The issues between the cities and companies finally played out in the Greeley Water Court when Lafayette's water rights application went to trial. The trial court's decision was eventually appealed all the way to the Colorado Supreme Court, which held that Lafayette "had no legal right to use water from the point of diversion [Anderson Ditch]." This was a major blow to Lafayette, but the matter was not finished.[11]

Eventually Judge Standstead reinstated the 1911 Base Line agreement, but found that the Anderson Ditch Company had no obligation to enlarge Anderson Ditch. During this time legal costs rose, and both Lafayette and Boulder staff received increasingly negative press over what seemed like an arcane issue to the general public. Political pressure mounted on both city councils to settle. Lafayette and Boulder entered into an Intergovernmental Agreement in 2001 that settled the case. This settlement authorized infrastructure changes that allowed Lafayette to better operate its water supply system. Boulder, in turn, moved its wastewater discharge several hundred feet downstream of its historic location to keep effluent out of a new pipeline that Lafayette constructed to divert water from Boulder Creek. In exchange, Lafayette dropped all of its claims to an ownership interest in the Anderson Ditch and any right to use the ditch to carry Lafayette's water. However, Base Line was allowed to continue transporting water through Anderson Ditch under the 1911 carriage agreement. The drawn-out legal battle between the two cities, Anderson Ditch, and Base Line finally concluded when Boulder and Lafayette completed building their new facilities in 2003.

The contest over the use of Anderson Ditch underscores the great value and ongoing relevance that pioneer ditches retain today. Although the settlers are long gone, their legacy reverberates as cities grow around their ditches.

THE FIRST WATER RIGHT: THE LOWER BOULDER DITCH

At the commencement of the Gold Rush, the first known diversion of water in the South Platte Basin took place out of Clear Creek in mid-1859 to irrigate two acres of land. But it appears that no water rights claim was ever filed for this diversion. Several weeks later on Boulder Creek Marinus Smith, William Pell, David Nichols, and others dug the first ditch, but they took their time filing the paperwork for their claim, waiting until mid-November 1859. Farther down the creek, John Ramsey Rothrock and William R. Howell started dig-

ging a week after Smith and Pell. But Rothrock and Howell were more atten-
tive to legal matters, so they filed their claim first, paying the $25 filing fee,
on October 1, 1859. With that, Rothrock and Howell received the very first—
most senior—water right appropriation in the South Platte Basin.[12]

In the spring of 1859, William R. Howell became an early member of the
westward surge. Howell crossed the plains from Illinois and spent a season
prospecting west of Boulder. He then acquired land on the broad and fertile
bottomlands along lower Boulder Creek. Howell recognized that irrigated
agriculture offered a better future than mining. Among his first tasks, Howell
helped build and organize Lower Boulder Ditch, and when it was incorporated he became the company's first president. He also developed two other
ditches that bear his name, the Howell and Beasley Ditch and the Howell
Ditch. In December 1859 he dug the Howell Ditch and started the other with
James Beasley in March of 1865. Beasley, in turn, is best known for building
the Boulder and White Rock and other ditches. Howell lived on his 160-acre
homestead twelve miles below Boulder until 1877. He then bought a larger
spread two miles farther down the creek and eventually acquired over 1,000
acres. Howell married Cornelia A. Sheldon and had two daughters with her.
Howell entered politics and was elected Boulder County sheriff in 1869.[13]

The other founder of the Lower Boulder Ditch, John Ramsey Rothrock
(Figure 5.2), was also in the throng of gold seekers heading west. Of German
and Scotch ancestry, Rothrock was born in Center County, Pennsylvania, but
by 1855 was living on the frontier in Nebraska City, Nebraska. For the next
couple of years Rothrock worked for a government surveying party that was
laying out the sixth principal meridian. This survey would later become the
basis for all future land claims in Boulder Valley. Rothrock's surveying work
put him in a good position to cross the prairie when word came of the gold
discoveries, and he likely learned how to file a claim during this time. Rothrock
joined thirty-one settlers led by Captain Thomas Aikens to travel with ox and
horse teams to Colorado. Aiken's party started out from Nebraska City, and
Rothrock joined later near Kearney, Nebraska. By the fall of 1858 Rothrock
was in Colorado, where he erected some cabins on Platte River below Denver.
Nineteen of his party returned to Nebraska, but thirteen of them, including
Rothrock and Aikens, relocated to Boulder Creek at the base of the foothills,
where they overwintered. When the settlers formed the Boulder City Town
Company in February 1859, Rothrock was one of its founding shareholders.[14]

Later, Rothrock and an associate, John Hall, surveyed the public square where Boulder's courthouse was later built. Rothrock surveyed the first one hundred lots in Boulder and set the grade for the Leggett and Leyner ditches. In early 1859, Rothrock helped discover the Gold Run placer and spent the season working the claim. That same spring Rothrock acquired 160 acres of land on Boulder Creek where he built a log cabin, planted potatoes, and built a toll bridge over the creek. Rothrock continued prospecting, but seeing the demand for hay in the mining

FIGURE 5.2. John Ramsey Rothrock.

camps, he cut natural hay and brought it to Central City and Black Hawk, netting $100 per ton profit. The work on his ranch put him at the leading edge of agriculture in Colorado. Rothrock was soon building up his farm. During this time, Rothrock and Howell built the Lower Boulder Ditch. It was here that Rothrock came the own the first stock issued in the region's most senior ditch. An image of Rothrock's stock certificate is reproduced in Figure 5.3. In 1867 Rothrock married Eliza C. Buford, of Lancaster, Missouri, and they began their family on the farm.[15]

Although Rothrock and Howell made the first claim for water in the South Platte Basin, they waited nearly twelve years to incorporate the ditch. The mission of their company was "to run water from Boulder Creek . . . for irrigating lands, household purposes and other uses and purposes generally." They capitalized their company at $600 divided into twelve shares of $50 each.[16]

Eventually the Lower Boulder Ditch Company was reorganized as the Consolidated Lower Boulder Reservoir and Ditch Company. The company has 200 shares of preferred capital stock and 200 shares of common capital stock outstanding. The company's original decree calls for the irrigation of about 1,500 acres. Shareholders eventually lengthened the Lower Boulder Ditch to over thirty-two miles. The ditch also obtains supplemental water

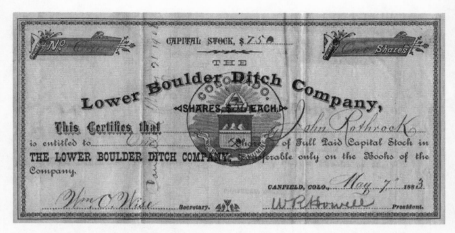

FIGURE 5.3. A stock certificate of the Lower Boulder Ditch Company, the company with the most senior water right within the South Platte Basin.

from Base Line Reservoir and the Bureau of Reclamation's Colorado–Big Thompson system.[17]

With its great seniority, Lower Boulder Ditch shares are extremely valuable. This was demonstrated during the 2002 drought when it was the only ditch on Boulder Creek that was not curtailed due to low flows. Not surprisingly, various cities have purchased shares and transferred them to municipal use. At least twenty separate court cases have altered the Lower Boulder Ditch water right through various transfers, exchanges, and augmentation plans. Consequently, flows into the Lower Boulder Ditch are significantly reduced. Only about 22 percent of the land originally irrigated by Lower Boulder Ditch still receives ditch water. Cities owning shares include Boulder, Lafayette, and Louisville.

In 1882, there were about 14,980 acres under irrigation from the ditch, and with transfers this figure had shrunk to about 3,365 acres by 2005. The remaining farmers grow a variety of crops, including alfalfa, corn, beans, pasture grass, small grains, sugar beets, and vegetables.[18]

As with other pioneer ditches, its great seniority has proven both a benefit and a burden. Farmers irrigating with this right know their water supplies are secure. They also know that their shares are extremely valuable and can cash in on their investment. Municipalities will happily buy shares to expand their water supply. But any shares that are sold will invariably reduce the amount of land irrigated by this legacy ditch.

FARMS TO INDUSTRY

Some of the best bottomlands in Boulder Valley were once located near the confluence of Boulder and South Boulder Creeks. Fertile alluvial soils and access to ample water made this area prime farmland. Of course, that was long before aggregate companies bought up most of the area, stripped the topsoil, and extracted the sand and gravel. It was also before power plants and light industry took root. What remains of the floodplain are abandoned mining pits holding steeply sided, oddly rectangular lakes. Nearby sits the Valmont Power Plant and several reservoirs that deliver cooling water to it. But this was not the case in 1860. The confluence was something of a cross-roads for people traveling up one or the other stream. Location, excellent grades, good soil, and ample water meant this land was quickly settled. A village soon sprang up under the landmark Valmont Butte just to the east of the confluence. The town of Valmont would, for a time, rival neighboring Boulder as the main community in the county. Thriving farms lined the two creeks on either side of the town.

Among the first to capitalize on Valmont's potential were two men, Ed Donnelly and Thomas (Tommy) Jones, who partnered to build the ditch that now bears their names. At less than two miles long, the Jones and Donnelly is a short ditch. An image of the headgate taken about 1908 at its diversion on South Boulder Creek is shown in Figure 5.4. Work on the ditch began on May 1, 1860. I always found it interesting that the court records are so precise in record-ing the start dates for ditches such as the Jones and Donnelly. In truth, I think that these dates are somewhat uncertain, but they fulfill the all-important role of establishing the relative priorities of the ditches that came before and after.[19]

Tommy Jones was the first settler in Valmont and helped plat the town. Prior to his move to Colorado, Jones operated a wagon factory in Rock Island, Illinois. Jones came to Boulder in May 1859 carrying a wagonload of goods, which he sold off immediately, and went to mining at Gold Run. But before he headed to the mountains, Jones acquired a ranch at Valmont as a fallback if the gold mining did not work out. It didn't, and he returned to Valmont in 1862 to start a stage stop and hotel.

FIGURE 5.4. The Jones and Donnelly headgate around 1908. Photograph courtesy
Carnegie Branch Library for Local History. Reprinted with permission.

Ed Donnelly worked odd jobs trying to make ends meet before settling
down to farming. When Donnelly first arrived in Boulder, he and a partner
built the town's first general store. Donnelly also operated a sawmill at the
mouth of Boulder Canyon and later donated money toward the first school-
house built in the county.

Just to the south of Valmont, a settler by the name of Charles Pancost
began digging a ditch to serve the farm that he shared with his wife Catherine.
They needed water and began work on the East Boulder Ditch on April 1,
1862, and later incorporated it in 1865. Pancost dug his ditch seven feet wide,
three feet deep, and extended it for about four miles. Back then, East Boulder
Ditch was also known as the Pancost Ditch. The Pancosts' thriving farm
grew prize-winning wheat and boasted nearly 700 grapevines. George Chase
and other neighbors helped Pancost build the ditch. They later enlarged it in
1872. The ditch extended from South Boulder Creek to the Pancost farm on
what is now the site of Xcel Energy's Valmont Power Plant.[20]

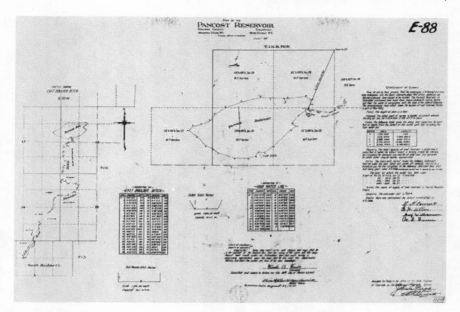

FIGURE 5.5. Pancost Reservoir is the first reservoir built in Boulder Valley. This map and statement filing from 1915 was completed fifty-two years after the reservoir was built. Map and Statement Filing, Pancost Reservoir, 1915. Courtesy of the Colorado state engineer.

To get more water, Charles Pancost built the first reservoir in Boulder County in 1863. Figure 5.5 shows the map and statement filing for Pancost Reservoir. This was only the second since American settlement began. Henry Church, who settled on Clear Creek, was first, and he "conceived the idea of making artificial lakes and holding water to be used for irrigation." The problem of irrigation and water was on every settler's mind, so Church's innovation was likely widely discussed. Perhaps Pancost knew from Henry Church's brother, Boulder resident J. L. Church, about the artificial lake. Originally, Pancost's lake was little more than a dam in a swampy slough that he filled with water from the East Boulder Ditch. Pancost eventually received a storage decree for 93 acre feet, which is small compared with reservoirs that followed. Besides irrigation, Pancost profited from his reservoir by stocking "sun-fish" that he raised and sold to miners.[21]

FIGURE 5.6. The wood crib diversion structure for the East Boulder Ditch in 1909. Photograph courtesy of the Carnegie Branch Library for Local History, Boulder Historical Society Collection. Reprinted with permission.

Figure 5.6 shows the East Boulder Ditch diversion in 1909. Bulky wood crib diversion dams were typical at the time. In the mid-twentieth century, shareholders replaced it with a more robust concrete dam. Since this photo was taken, South Boulder Creek has eroded several feet downward and a riparian forest has grown around the site.

In the 1920s the Public Service Company of Colorado (PSCo, now a subsidiary of Xcel Energy) began building its Valmont Power Plant. A key component of the project was developing water supplies for plant cooling.

The Pancost farm was swept up in this industrialization. The power plant occupies the farm site, and Pancost Reservoir is now submerged under the Leggett-Owens Reservoir, which itself is part of the Valmont Lake complex. Weisenhorn Lake was the second lake built at the complex after Pancost Reservoir and takes its name from Frank Weisenhorn, the owner of a nineteenth-century Boulder institution, the Crystal Springs Brewing and Ice Company. Figure 5.7 is a detail of Drumm's Wall Map of Boulder County

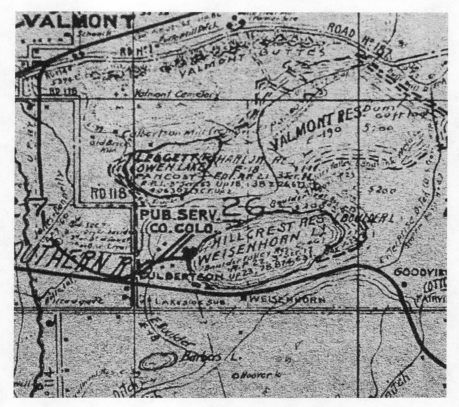

FIGURE 5.7. A detail of Drumm's Wall Map of Boulder County from 1926 showing the ditches and reservoirs in the Valmont area, courtesy of the Carnegie Branch Library for Local History.

from 1926 showing the ditches and reservoirs in the Valmont area. Various names are associated with the site, including Pancost Lake, Owens Lake, Leggett Reservoir, Weisenhorn (now known as Hillcrest) Reservoir, Harlow Reservoir, Leggett-Owens Reservoir, and Valmont Reservoir.[22]

To supply the lakes, PSCo constructed a new inlet (now called the Leggett Inlet) on South Boulder Creek and relocated the Jones and Donnelly Ditch headgate to the inlet canal. Figure 5.8 shows the inlet diversion under construction in 1925. This diversion was completely refurbished by Xcel Energy in 2009.

Because of its proximity to the Valmont Lake complex, PSCo began seeking additional water to cool its coal-fired turbines at its Valmont power

MAIN FEEDER PAVING
EAST OF HIGHWAY BRIDGE
NORTH OF PILING
APR-21-1925
L-701

FIGURE 5.8. Construction of the Leggett inlet diversion in 1925. Photograph courtesy of the Carnegie Branch Library for Local History, Boulder Historical Society Collection. Reprinted with permission.

station. PSCo began buying East Boulder Ditch stock and now owns about 90 percent of the company. In the 1970s PSCo purchased about half of the Jones and Donnelly Ditch and also bought shares of other area ditches.

Most of the Jones and Donnelly Ditch water still used in irrigation is delivered down the Butte Mill Ditch to various properties. Originally, the Butte Mill was a project of John DeBacker and Peter M. Housel that they began in 1865. The ditch derives its name from the flour mill that DeBacker and Housel constructed near Valmont. Housel traveled east to acquire milling equipment, and by 1866, their mill and ditch were operational. Eventually the mill was abandoned, but the water still serves farms along the ditch.[23]

Among the Jones and Donnelly's shareholders is longtime ditch rider Gene Sawhill. Gene is also the ditch rider for the Butte Mill Ditch. "My father used to be the ditch rider," said Sawhill in a 2009 interview, and in "1972 I started taking care of the ditch, cleaning it and making sure that we could get the water down it. I could see that things needed to be done, and there were not too many folks wanting to do it, so I just kind of got into it."[24]

Sawhill's account is typical for many ditches: a company shareholder sees a need and steps up to keep things operating. For shareholders, the senior water rights provide reliable water to their lawns, ranches, and farms. In a unique arrangement, the shareholders of the Jones and Donnelly and the Butte Mill operate both ditches jointly. The boards overlap, and many shareholders own stock in both companies. This pattern of use has likely occurred since both ditches were built. The Jones and Donnelly water allows operations such as CURE Farms to raise late-season vegetables for the local farmers' market and area restaurants. Although it is a small ditch, it is fairly typical: first built by enterprising pioneers, much of its water was eventually sold for industrial uses, and only a few irrigators remain.

Walk along the Jones and Donnelly Ditch today, and you would scarcely know a ditch was present. Its headgate is tucked behind a recycling facility in industrialized east Boulder. To reach it, you must cross the creosote-soaked railroad tracks that bring coal trains to the Valmont Power Plant. Beyond the headgate on the Leggett Inlet Canal, the ditch winds through a composting facility and passes in and out of pipes under a series of ball fields and industrial pads. It emerges only long enough to collect leaves from overgrown cottonwood trees before dipping under roads and railroads to dump its water into the Butte Mill Ditch. But more change is coming. Recently, Xcel Energy announced that it would shutter its two coal turbines around 2016. Although electricity production at a natural gas turbine will continue, this generator does not require the nearly as much cooling water as the coal turbines. Xcel will undoubtedly begin seeking new uses for the water that once grew prize-winning wheat.

McGinn Ditch and the End of Domestic Water Use on Ditches

South Boulder Creek emerges from its narrow canyon at Eldorado Springs almost as large as Boulder Creek just to the north. Like Boulder Creek, South Boulder flows across a wide boulder-strewn floodplain. On old aerial photographs, wide arcs of former meanders and old oxbows are visible paralleling the modern channel. For settlers arriving at the commencement of the Gold Rush, it was the valley bottom several miles east of the canyon that attracted their initial attention. Here the stream valley was wide and the gradient low. The effort needed to build a ditch along this reach would be far less than farther upstream. It was an ideal place to start a farm.

The first person to dig a ditch on South Boulder Creek was Norman Ross Howard, and his ditch now bears his surname. A few weeks after Howard arrived, three brothers, John, Edward, and James McGinn, came to the valley and liked what they saw. Each brother started a farm, and in May of 1860 they began digging their ditch. In 1870 they incorporated, issuing forty shares of stock.

Little did they know how valuable their water right would eventually become. Their initial ditch carried at a little over three cubic feet per second (cfs) of water, but they had the number two priority on South Boulder Creek. Several years later, in June of 1865, the McGinns enlarged their ditch and obtained a second appropriation for nearly 11 cfs. When the McGinns incorporated the company, they capitalized it at $4,000.[25]

Figure 5.9 shows the home of James McGinn (the company secretary) during the 1880s. The rocky soil in front of his cabin suggests a hardscrabble existence on the Colorado frontier. They used the ditch for all their household needs, for stock watering, and of course for irrigation. By the late 1880s, other well-known Boulder settlers had bought into the ditch, including Louis Stengel, John DeBacker, Timothy Shanahan, L. F. Spicer, James B. Viele, the Burke Brothers, and Florence Clyncke.

Many of these settlers were European immigrants. John DeBacker, who was born in Belgium in 1827, was typical. He apprenticed as a carpenter and millwright and in 1855 immigrated to the United States. He worked for a time in Virginia, New York City, and then Iowa City, where he remained until 1859. During the Gold Rush, DeBacker migrated to Colorado and worked sawing lumber in the mountains. Once here, DeBacker acquired 100 acres on South Boulder Creek and became involved in the dairy and flour milling businesses.

James B. Viele, his wife, and three small children came to Boulder in 1865. Sadly, James's wife soon died, so his youngest son, Albert, had to go live with his nearby older sister. Despite these hardships, Viele thrived by bringing the first threshing machine to Boulder County. Previously all threshing in Boulder Valley was done by intensive hand labor.

Work on Boulder Valley ditches was often a communal affair. Shareholders could either work themselves, supply labor or a team, or pay an assessment

FIGURE 5.9. The home of James McGinn during the 1880s. Photograph courtesy of the Carnegie Branch Library for Local History, Boulder Historical Society Collection. Reprinted with permission.

and have the company do the work. Minutes from the McGinn Ditch annual meeting in 1889, reproduced in Figure 5.10, show how shareholders worked twenty-five days maintaining the ditch. That year the company did not assess stockholders because everyone pitched in and completed the work without hiring outside labor. Today it is necessary to levy annual assessments because few shareholders work on the ditch.

By the early 1900s towns and cities served their citizens through an expanding network of reservoirs and pipelines often far removed from urban centers. In rural areas, however, domestic water supply still came from ditches. As late as 1907 there were about fourteen families using the McGinn Ditch for their domestic needs. After the irrigation season ended, the McGinn shareholders continued diverting about 6.5 cfs for domestic purposes throughout the winter. Families on other ditches also diverted water in the winter. Constant flows of water down ditches depleted the winter flows in South Boulder Creek. As reservoirs were constructed, irrigation companies wanting to fill their lakes in the winter could obtain little water since they were junior to ditches like McGinn, and their water calls seldom came into priority. The wisdom of diverting water down ditches all winter long to meet domestic needs came under increased scrutiny. Consequently, when a stream adjudication proceeding for the Boulder Watershed got under way in 1907 to

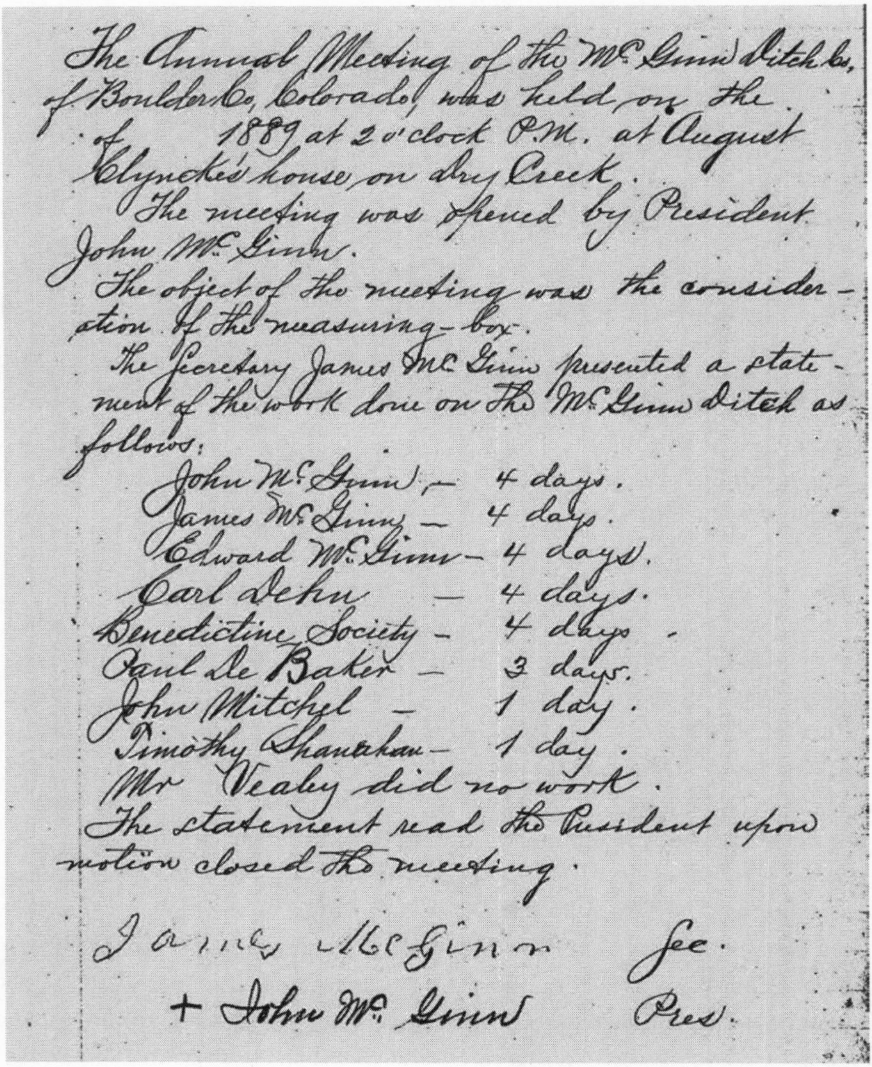

The Annual Meeting of the McGinn Ditch Co,
of Boulder Co, Colorado, was held on the
of 1889 at 2 o'clock P.M. at August
Clyncke's house on Dry Creek.
The meeting was opened by President
John McGinn.
The object of the meeting was the consider-
ation of the measuring-box.
The Secretary James McGinn presented a state-
ment of the work done on the McGinn Ditch as
follows:
John McGinn, – 4 days.
James McGinn – 4 days.
Edward McGinn – 4 days.
Carl Dehn – 4 days.
Benedictine Society – 4 days.
Paul De Baker – 3 days.
John Mitchel – 1 day.
Timothy Shanahan – 1 day.
Mr Vealey did no work.
The statement read the President upon
motion closed the meeting.

James McGinn Sec.
+ John McGinn Pres.

FIGURE 5.10. Notes from the 1889 annual meeting of the McGinn Ditch showing a tally of work done during the previous year. Photograph by author

sort out all the new rights claimed since the prior 1882 adjudication, reservoir companies vigorously contested the winter use of ditches for domestic purposes. Community Ditch, a unit the Farmers Reservoir and Irrigation

Company (FRICO), had a singular stake in the outcome since diversions by the McGinn and others meant that its newly built Marshall Lake was not receiving as much water as hoped. Community Ditch called diversions by McGinn wasteful and pushed for their curtailment.[26]

Judge James E. Garrigues, the presiding judge in the adjudication, struggled with how to reconcile ostensibly legal winter diversions with their inherently inefficient use of water. In what became a groundbreaking decision, Garrigues agreed with FRICO. He reasoned that the benefits coming from the public use of the water must be commensurate with the draft on the stream. He concluded that if a user needed to divert a very large amount of water compared with "the good resulting from the diversion, it cannot be said that the diversion was for a beneficial purpose."[27]

Judge Garruges noted that the McGinn Ditch shareholders used only one-half of 1 percent of the water they diverted, wasting the other 99.5 percent. Judge Garrigues wrote that he did not believe the law authorized so much wastefulness. He then not only ruled that the McGinn Ditch Company had no right to divert water for domestic purposes in the winter but also ordered several other ditches on South Boulder Creek to cease diverting during the winter. The needs of fourteen families who had historically used the ditch were dismissed in favor of filling a large reservoir that could serve many. FRICO's shareholders likely applauded the decision.[28]

During the first half of the twentieth century, the McGinn Ditch continued to provide agricultural water in Boulder County. Then in the early 1950s the McGinn Ditch found itself in the path of the single most important transportation project to affect Boulder Valley since its settlement. The Colorado Department of Transportation (CDOT) proposed building the Boulder Denver Turnpike, and the McGinn Ditch's headgate was right in the middle of the proposed road alignment. In 1951 shareholders approved relinquishing part of the ditch easement in exchange for allowing CDOT to build a new diversion dam some yards to the north on South Boulder Creek.

Figure 5.11 shows the diversion built by CDOT as it looked in March of 2000. This diversion dam was typical of structures built around Boulder County during the mid-twentieth century. In the foreground, a nearly five-foot-high concrete diversion dam or weir spans the creek. A concrete apron is visible at the bottom of the dam. At the far side of the creek is a sand sluice that passes sediment around the dam. The ditch itself is hidden by willows

FIGURE 5.11. The McGinn Ditch diversion dam in March 2000. Photograph by author.

in the distance. This structure effectively blocked fish migration on South Boulder Creek. As the City of Boulder began acquiring open space along the creek, public awareness of the modified South Boulder Creek ecosystem expanded. Boulder began retrofitting diversion dams to improve connectivity for fish migrating along the stream. The McGinn Ditch was retrofitted with a fish passage in the fall of 2008. Looking downstream, Figure 5.12 shows the completed structure in the fall of 2009.

In a recurring theme, the McGinn Ditch's seniority has made it an appealing acquisition target. As the city of Louisville began growing in the 1980s, it began purchasing McGinn Ditch shares and transferring them to municipal use. Similarly, Boulder's open space program eventually acquired fourteen shares, making it the single largest shareholder in the company. With a demand for shares, stock prices skyrocketed. In the early 2000s, shares reportedly sold for more than $250,000 each.

With acquisitions by Louisville and Boulder, the number of private shareholders in the McGinn Ditch Company has steadily declined. In 1975, 100 percent of ditch shares were private, but that number has decreased to less than 40 percent today.

FIGURE 5.12. The McGinn Ditch diversion dam in fall 2009 after it was retrofitted with a fish passage structure. Photograph by author.

THE FIRST BECOMES LAST

Many ditches in Boulder Valley bear the name of the settler who first dug it. The Wellman Ditch, known today as the Wellman Canal, is no exception. Built by three brothers, Hank, Lute, and Vane Wellman, they were likely the very first settlers in Boulder Valley to plow land, plant seed, and sow wheat. Natives of Susquehanna County, Pennsylvania, Hank Wellman was born in December 1821, Lute Wellman in March 1826, and Vane Wellman in 1834.[29]

While growing up in Pennsylvania, the Wellmans learned how to farm and process lumber. For about six years starting in 1845, the oldest brother, Hank, became a tanner and currier's apprentice in Hamilton, New York. Around the same time, Lute left and found employment building bridges on the New York & Erie Railroad. Vane, the youngest, left home in 1848 to join Lute and Hank. After the discovery of gold in California, the three brothers began thinking about prospects out west. So in 1850 Lute took a ship to California via the Isthmus of Panama. Hank joined him a year later. They stayed in California mining, ranching, and stock raising until 1856, when they returned to Pennsylvania and joined Vane in the cattle business.

When the Wellmans heard of the discoveries of gold in the Pikes Peak region, their attention once again turned west. So in March 1859 all three left for Colorado. The three brothers outfitted themselves with three yoke of oxen and a wagon loaded with mining tools and a year's worth of pro-visions. Beginning their journey in Dixon, Iowa, they crossed the Missouri River and headed across the plains. Along the way they met hundreds of disappointed parties returning east with discouraging news from Pikes Peak. Disheartened, they thought they would skip Pikes Peak and push through to California to make a go at farming. They were so dejected that they even dumped their mining tools along the road. However, arriving at Fort Laramie, they encountered Horace Greeley of the *New York Tribune*, who was just then returning from a tour of Colorado's mines. Contrary to the downcast parties returning east, Greeley waxed ebullient about Colorado's prospects. Greeley advised the Wellman brothers, and anyone else willing to listen, that Colorado was the place to settle.

Perhaps the Wellmans were inspired by Horace Greeley's reports that "corn is four dollars per bushel in Denver, and scarce at that; oats are not to be had; there is not a ton of hay within two hundred miles, and none can ever be brought hither over the present road at a cost below forty dollars per ton." There was money to be made in Colorado, and for the Wellmans that money was to be made through farming.[30]

So, instead of heading to California, the Wellmans stuck with their initial plan and headed south, prospecting along the Colorado foothills. Around August 1, 1859, the three Wellmans reached Boulder. After a quick reconnais-sance they ended up about two and one-half miles east of town where they settled on a 640-acre tract. They wasted no time. On August 4, 1859, Vane Wellman recorded in his diary that they "Finished ploughing the first acre of land plowed in this country." The day was "pleasant and warm, evening played euchre, cattle gone; sowed three quarters of an acre of turnips, some lettuce, onions, and cucumbers." By the middle of August, the Wellmans were securing poles for fences and lumber for a home.[31]

In the August and September heat, the turnips grew rapidly. But that was not to last. One evening, neighbor George Nichols visited as they ate dinner and asked, "Boys, did you ever see it rain grasshoppers?" They ran out of the cabin to find so many grasshoppers falling from the sky that they made a pile nearly a foot deep. The Wellmans' first turnip crop was devoured in a matter of minutes.[32]

At the time the Wellmans arrived, Boulder Valley still had vast herds of wildlife. They commonly saw around 500 elk grazing near their place. Their cabin, built in 1859, was the first in Boulder Valley with doors, windows, and floors.[33]

Any farmer who could bring a crop to market stood to profit. In 1859 the nearest flour was packed in from New Mexico (likely from Ceran St. Vrain's Mora mill). It was said to be of an inferior quality, even gritty, as it was threshed on the ground. The flour arrived in dressed elk skin sacks, each bag weighing 200 pounds, and was shipped to Colorado by burros.[34]

In 1862, the Wellman Brothers harvested forty acres of wheat, averaging sixty bushels per acre. There were sixty-three pounds per bushel, and their grain was worth about $20,000. Albert Viele, whose father James settled along the McGinn Ditch, described how the Wellman brothers farmed:

> They got out a ditch about where the 24th Street bridge crosses Boulder Creek. This was on the south side of the creek and it irrigated part of their land. They didn't have to put much of a dam, if any, across the creek there at first. The creek ran high then.
>
> After they broke the sod and got the ground ready for planting, they sowed that first wheat broadcast. That is, a man walked across the field in a straight line with a bag of wheat across his shoulder secured by a strap. He would take a handful and scatter it out, then another. When he got to the end of the field, he'd go over a ways and walk back. A good man could sow the wheat even.
>
> When the wheat was ready, they cut it with a cradle. That's a scythe with a light wooden frame that we called a cradle to catch the stalks. Those early farmers had to use the cradle until the first binders came out. . . .
>
> The Wellman boys probably threshed it with a flail (a staff with a club hinged to one end that swings freely). They beat the grain with this until the kernels were out of the heads. Then they tossed it up in the air with forks, letting the wind carry away the chaff. Then they gathered the grain up . . .
>
> They raised a wonderful crop of wheat that first year (1860) though they didn't have much planted. It convinced them and others that they could farm this land if they got water on it.[35]

The Wellmans' other cash crop was hay. Beginning in August 1859, Van Wellman and others realized that the lush native grasses along Boulder Creek were a potential quick buck. Hay netted as much as $125 per ton when delivered to the miners in Blackhawk and Central City. They got busy and cut five stacks of hay weighing twenty-five to thirty tons each. Miners paid a premium because they relied on their mules to do much of the heavy work, such as moving ore and timber, and hay was the indispensable fuel their mules needed to keep the mines operating.

The Wellmans quickly figured out that irrigation was essential. They selected a nearly perfect spot to farm. It was on the nearly level valley bottom close to Boulder Creek. Water was plentiful. A system of small alluvial channels, likely braids of Boulder Creek that became active only with high water, branched through their property. When the water level on Boulder Creek rose, which happened frequently before many of the other ditches were built, it overflowed its bank and water moved into the side channels. As Al Viele recalled decades later, the Wellmans did not need to build a dam across Boulder Creek to get water because high water naturally overtopped the stream bank. In 1859 all they needed to do was extend a number of "small ditches" (today we call these "field laterals") to collect water and irrigate. At the time, their actions made complete sense. But delaying the construction of a diversion eventually caused the Wellmans major damage to their water rights. But those problems were unforeseen, and for the time being they had ample water to irrigate. Within a year, the Wellmans had about 400 acres under irrigation and were well on their way to becoming a successful farming family.[36]

While the Wellman brothers went about farming, other settlers built ditches that tapped into Boulder Creek upstream from them. Farmers, Boulder and White Rock, North Boulder Farmers, and Boulder and Left Hand are just a few of the ditches that were built after the Wellmans began irrigating. Diversions for these ditches progressively captured more and more flow of Boulder Creek, making it harder for the Wellmans to get water. Finally, in June of 1870 they set about digging a three-foot-wide, eighteen-inch-deep ditch to Boulder Creek so they could continue farming. Even then it seems that the Wellmans were slow to claim rights for the water. When the general stream adjudication for Boulder Creek took place in 1882, Judge Chester C. Carpenter awarded the Wellman Ditch a priority date of May 1, 1878, a full nineteen years after they first started irrigating. During the adjudication proceeding, the Wellmans argued that their "small ditches" mattered, but Judge Carpenter concluded that the Wellmans failed to build a diversion on the creek. He set the date of their appropriation as the date he thought the Wellmans finally built their diversion. In Judge Carpenter's ruling, the

Wellmans lost their position at the front of the line as the earliest irrigators from Boulder Creek. The Wellmans ended up with an appropriation date later than most of the water rights granted in the adjudication. This bitter blow must have landed hard on the Wellmans.

Long after the Wellman brothers were gone, the modern Wellman Canal came into existence with the construction of Hillcrest Reservoir by the Leggett Ditch and Reservoir Company. In 1917, planning for the construction of Hillcrest Reservoir began. It is seems that the Leggett Ditch and Reservoir Company acquired the Wellman Ditch around this time. As part of the reservoir project, the company enlarged and extended the old Wellman Ditch to carry water from Boulder Creek to South Boulder Creek and on to Hillcrest Reservoir. It is this enlarged ditch that acquired the term "canal." Actual construction likely began sometime in the early 1920s. At that time the headgate for the Wellman Canal was rebuilt. The project allowed the company to divert water from Boulder Creek into the Wellman Canal, where it flows east and discharges into South Boulder Creek. Water then flows down South Boulder Creek, where it is rediverted into the Hillcrest Reservoir.[37]

As the Leggett Ditch and Reservoir Company worked on the Hillcrest Reservoir, the Eastern Colorado Power Company began developing reservoirs for its expanding electricity business. Electric companies soon went through a series of consolidations, and the Eastern Colorado Power Company became part of PSCo. Then when PSCo built its Valmont Power Station, it contracted with the Leggett Ditch and Reservoir Company so that it could enlarge the reservoir to provide cooling water for its coal-fired power plant. During that time, PSCo bought the Wellman Canal. This allowed PSCo to release water from Barker Reservoir, where it would travel on down Boulder Creek to the Wellman Canal and on to the Valmont Power Station.

Because of the junior decree for the Wellman ditch, the water right itself had little value and fell into disuse. Ironically, the value ended up being the ditch itself, a facility that the Wellmans built only as an afterthought. In 1985 PSCo let the court abandon the water rights for the Wellman Ditch.[38]

The era of pioneer irrigation began with Hank, Lute, and Vane Wellman's digging of small ditches to irrigate their fields. That same era essentially ended with them when they built a diversion so that they might continue getting water as supplies diminished along Boulder Creek. Near Boulder the time that pioneers could build ditches lasted scarcely four years before the good bottomlands were claimed. Among the last settlers who built a ditch without raising significant capital was Lemuel McIntosh with his South Boulder and Bear Creek Ditch. After that, new irrigators had to adopt fresh strategies and raise large sums of money and labor to get water. These early efforts planted the seeds for the corporate ditches and agricultural colonies that followed. In the meantime, settlers had to first consolidate control over land and water in Colorado.

Notes

1. Smythe, *Conquest of Arid America*, 42.

2. Coffin, letter to *Boulder* (CO) *County Miner*, January 8, 1914.

3. *Boulder City Herald*, July 2, 1890.

4. Bixby, *History of Clear Creek*, 389.

5. The breadth of Marinus Smith's holdings is hinted within the *Map of Lands Belonging to the Heirs of Marinus G. Smith, Dec.*, prepared on his death by James P. Maxwell and Henry Drumm, filed with the Boulder County Clerk and Recorder, May 17, 1902, accessed January 28, 2011, http://www.bouldercolorado.gov/index.php?option=com_content&task=view&id=2413&Itemid=75.

6. With the Farmers and Fruit Growers of Boulder County, *The Irrigation Era*, August 1898, 33; Boulder County District Court Case CA1269.

7. Boulder District Court Case 4842 (1907), 23. Corporate filings have variously referred to both the New Anderson Ditch and Anderson Ditch. To avoid confusion here, the company is simply called the Anderson Ditch.

8. City of Boulder, *Source Water Master Plan* (2009), 3–10; testimony of D. K. Sternburg, Boulder County District Court Case CA4842.

9. City of Lafayette v. New Anderson Ditch Company, Colorado Supreme Court No. 97SA2, June 29, 1998.

10. See City of Boulder, *Source Water Master Plan*, for a summary of the Base Line Anderson Ditch issues.

11. City of Lafayette v. New Anderson Ditch Company, Colorado Supreme Court Case No. 97SA2, 4.

12. Colorado Water Resources Research Institute, South Platte Team, *South Platte River System in Colorado: Hydrology, Development and Management Issues Working Paper* (Fort Collins: Colorado Water Resources Research Institute, Colorado State University, 1990); Dyni, *Pioneer Voices*.

13. Bixby, *History of Clear Creek*, 643, 713; Boulder County District Court Cases CA1301 and CA1302.

14. Rothrock photograph, Stone, *History of Colorado* 4:414.

15. Romer, "Heritage and Legacy"; Bixby, *History of Clear Creek*, 678.

16. Lower Boulder Ditch, Articles of Incorporation (May 15, 1871). Colorado State Archives, Incorporation Records, Book D, 268.

17. The names Lower Boulder Ditch and Consolidated Lower Boulder Reservoir and Ditch Company are often used interchangeably; Colorado Water Court Case Numbers 79CW0387 and 90CW0108. In Boulder County District Court Case CA1300, the Lower Boulder Ditch was awarded an appropriation date of October 1, 1859 (priority number 1) for 25 cfs and a later enlargement on June 1, 1870, for 97 cfs.; Today the ditch shares its headgate with the Northern Colorado Water Conservancy District's South Platte Diversion Canal.

18. Colorado state engineer Structure Summary Report for Lower Boulder Ditch, accessed April 23, 2015, http://cdss.state.co.us/onlineTools/Pages/Structures Diversions.aspx. Then search Lower Boulder Ditch.

19. The Jones and Donnelly Ditch was likely originally known as the Donnelly Ditch. The Donnelly Ditch was incorporated for twenty years with a $3,000 capitalization and fifty shares of stock valued at $100 each. However, that Donnelly Ditch corporation status lapsed, and the Jones and Donnelly appears to have taken its place.

20. Testimony of George Chase, Boulder County District Court Case 4842, 1881; *Boulder News*, July 18, 1870.

21. Boulder County District Court Case 4842, 1881; see also Henry Church, interview by Hubert H. Bancroft, February 5, 1887, University of Colorado Archive, Boulder.

22. Colorado Water Court Case W 9308.

23. The water right for the Jones and Donnelly Ditch was adjudicated on June 2, 1882, for 14.36 cfs. At the time, Ed Donnelly testified that there were about 360 acres under the ditch when it was first constructed; Boulder County District Court Case CA1298; Jones and Donnelly Ditch Structure Summary Report, accessed November 18, 2010, http://cdss.state.co.us/onlineTools/Pages/StructuresDiversions.aspx, then search for Jones and Donnelly Ditch.

24. Gene Sawhill, interview by Elisabeth Black for the Ditch Project, 2009.

25. Boulder County District Court Case CA1357; http://cdss.state.co.us/online Tools/Pages/StructuresDiversions.aspx, then search McGinn Ditch accessed December 20, 2010; State of Colorado, Division 1 Water Court Cases 85 CW 137 and 87 CW 327.

26. Testimony and ruling for Boulder County District Court Case CA4842.

27. Ibid., 72. Judge James E. Garrigues eventually sat on the Colorado Supreme Court.

28. Ibid., 74.

29. Excerpt taken from Forest Crossen, "Pioneer Farmers and Farming Methods Recalled by 'Al' Viele," *Daily Camera*, November 15, 1954. Sources for the Wellmans include Bixby, *History of Clear Creek*; "Wellman Brothers, First Farmers in Valley, Arrived Here in July, 1859," *Daily Camera*, August 2, 1954.

30. Greeley, *Overland Journey*, 122.

31. "Wellman Brothers, First Farmers in Valley," *Daily Camera*, August 2, 1954.

32. Bixby, *History of Clear Creek*; 389.

33. Ibid., 380.

34. Coffin, letter to *Boulder* (CO) *County Miner*, January 8, 1914.

35. Excerpt from Crossen, "Pioneer Farmers."

36. Testimony of Sylvanus Wellman, 1881, Boulder County District Court Case CA1279.

37. Boulder County District Court Case CA6672; Amended Map and Statement Filing for the Hillcrest Reservoir, February 15, 1918, Boulder County Clerk.

38. Colorado Water Court Case 84 CW 357.

SIX

Taking Colorado

"Of course, the first settlers in this whole
region were squatters on Indian lands."
—*Morse Coffin*[1]

A number of years ago I was elected to the board of directors of the Anderson Ditch Company. At the time, I was working for the City of Boulder, which is the majority shareholder in the company. My experience in operating ditches made me a logical fit for the board. Soon afterward, the ditch board held its spring ritual of walking the ditch to prioritize its annual maintenance work. So out five of us went along the ditch. As we hiked, we crossed into Columbia Cemetery, which Boulder locals also call Pioneer Cemetery. Some of Boulder's earliest settlers are interred here. The ditch runs through the cemetery, and about three-quarters of the way through we came to the tombstone of Jonas Anderson Jr., the fellow after which the ditch is named.

Jonas Anderson Jr.'s tombstone is just a couple of short paces from the ditch bank. Here we have a man and his ditch (Figure 6.1). The placement of

FIGURE 6.1. The military tombstone for Jonas Anderson Jr. memorializing his service in Company D of the Third Colorado Cavalry. Anderson Ditch flows in the background. Photograph by author.

Anderson's grave had to be intentional. That's interesting enough, but what drew me in was his tombstone. It is a standard marble military tombstone of the type issued to those who have served our nation. There on the tombstone was Anderson's name and the unit in which he served, Company D of the Third Colorado Cavalry.

Only a few months before, I had finished reading Elliott West's excellent history of the Gold Rush, *The Contested Plains: Indians, Goldseekers, and the Rush to Colorado.* So standing there looking at Anderson's grave, I immediately knew that he was one of the so called "100 Days Men," members of Colonel John Chivington's cavalry who had massacred Cheyenne and Arapahoe Indians in November 1864. This event from the Indian Wars became variously known as the Sand Creek Massacre, the Chivington Massacre, or the Battle of Sand Creek. This connection to the massacre created in me both a sense of fascination and horror that has only grown over time. After all, I was now a member of a board of directors to a company whose founder participated in one of the most brutal and infamous massacres of American Indians in our nation's long history.[2]

It turns out that Jonas Anderson Jr. enlisted as a private and that quite a few other founders of Boulder ditches had roles in the events of 1864. Boulder volunteer George C. Green founded the ditch bearing his name. Also volunteering were James Arbuthnot and neighbor Lorenzo D. Dwight, who helped found the Left Hand Ditch Company. Another was Morse Coffin, who developed ditches near Longmont (years later, Morse's brother Rubin became famous for destroying the headgate for the Left Hand Ditch). Porter M. Hinman, who along with his father Porter T. built the Hinman Ditch and worked on the Left Hand, had joined too. Another was Onsville C. Coffin, who settled along the Marshallville Ditch and was involved with its early years. Granville Berkley, who helped work on the North Boulder Farmers Ditch, volunteered. And perhaps most notably, leading the Boulder volunteers was Captain David H. Nichols, himself well known for helping found the University of Colorado. Nichols's lesser-known accomplishment is his founding role in the North Boulder Farmers Ditch. All these men served as United States Volunteers with Company D, one of six companies under the command of a former Methodist minister, Colonel John M. Chivington.

The connection to Chivington, the Sand Creek Massacre, and Boulder's ditches is wider still, as Lemuel McIntosh, (South Boulder and Bear Creek

Ditch) and Judge Peter Housel (Butte Mill Ditch) helped build Fort Chambers, the site where Company D trained before joining Chivington. And Joseph McIntosh, Lemuel's brother, served with Company D. Also, Clinton Monroe Tyler (whose brother-in-law, James P. Maxwell, founded the Silver Lake Ditch and much of Boulder's water supply) served as a captain of a volunteer troop from Black Hawk nicknamed the "Tyler Rangers." Tyler headed a military unit on the South Platte that provided protection for the wagon trains coming to Denver. These are just some of the direct connections; I have little doubt that there are others.

Of course, many other Boulder Valley volunteers joined besides those involved with the ditches. Chivington's volunteers represented a wide cross section of the Boulder community. One of the best known was Captain Thomas A. Aikins, who led the first party of settlers to Boulder. Although he was by then fifty-six years old, Aikins was likely a welcome addition as he had reportedly fought Indians when he was a volunteer with a brigade in Illinois during the Black Hawk War of 1832.[3]

In addition to the Anderson Ditch, I have served on the boards or as an officer on the Green, Butte Mill, Left Hand, and South Boulder and Bear Creek ditches as well. So I hope you can appreciate that I feel a very real and unsettling, if somewhat indirect, connection to this dark chapter of Colorado's history.

It seems that there are just too many links between the Sand Creek Massacre and Boulder's ditch founders to wave off their connection as simple coincidence. In the early 1860s these men were building their farms, ranches, and community. Historian Jeff Campbell, who has compiled extensive biographical information on members of the Third Colorado Cavalry, identified 383 farmers among the regiment. To them the Indians represented an existential threat, and nothing less than the Indians' elimination or removal would guarantee that the land they came to occupy would remain theirs. Farmers were the most common occupation of volunteers, with miners coming in second at 309 men. After that, the next most common occupation was laborers with 85 members. There were fewer still for other occupations, such as carpenters, mechanics, brewers, lawyers, stone masons, and so forth. Their numbers and occupations defies the common presumption that the volunteers were predominantly frontier toughs and lowlifes. Rather, these people were well regarded and represented a broad spectrum of the community. This alone opens up space to question intent and complicity. The events surrounding the Sand Creek Massacre point to a generally overlooked aspect of appro-priation: that is, in the early 1860s, the appropriation of land and water as resources by Americans was also synonymous with the appropriation of Indian land and water by the Americans.[4]

Events surrounding the Sand Creek Massacre have been recounted in numerous books. Standing out in this field of works includes Elliott West's *The Contested Plains,* which I have already cited. Margaret Coel's *Chief Left Hand* presents a biography of the Southern Arapahoe chief who died from wounds received at the massacre. Storyteller Patrick M. Mendoza's *Song of Sorrow* gives us a much-needed Indian perspective on the matter, and Stan Hoig, in his *The Sand Creek Massacre,* makes a compelling argument why this event is appropriately called a "massacre" and not a "battle," as Chivington loyalists would assert. And most recently is Ari Kelman's, *A Misplaced Massacre,* which recounts the massacre and the struggles over memorializing this event.[5] My goal here is not to simply rehash this well-documented tragedy. Although providing certain background for the events is necessary, I wish to focus on two aspects that appear missing or apparently neglected in these other works. First, I provide some detail regarding the activities of the Boulder volunteers with Company D that is not widely reported. Second, I believe there is more than the simple hatred of Indians (as repugnant as that is) that motivated both the leaders and foot soldiers during this time. Specifically, I assert that these people knew that by killing off the Indians and driving away survivors (genocide and ethnic cleansing in today's language), the government and settlers would secure firm title to the land, water, and other resources this region had to offer.

PROMISES AND BROKEN PROMISES

It is said that if you look behind all great fortunes, you will find a crime. For the great and small fortunes that came out of Colorado in the 1860s, that crime took place in what the Cheyenne call the Month of the Freezing Moon, or November 1864. That a crime would take place became all but inevitable at Fort Laramie when the Indians and Americans gathered to talk peace and make a treaty that they concluded on September 17, 1851. At the very height of the Plains Indian horse culture a remarkable gathering took place between the US government and the Sioux, Cheyenne, Arapahoe, Crow, Assiniboine,

Mandans and Gros Ventres, and Arickaree tribes. The purpose was to establish routes across the Plains for the whites and to delineate tribal lands extending from the Yellowstone and Missouri Rivers on the north to the Arkansas River on the south. For the Cheyenne and Arapahoe, the Fort Laramie Treaty demarcated their territory as the lands between the North Platte and the Arkansas. With the ratification of the treaty, the United States recognized that the Cheyenne and Arapahoe had legal title to most of the land that would someday comprise much of eastern Colorado and southeastern Wyoming.

Even though the Fort Laramie Treaty recognized the Indians' territorial rights, the United States seemed intent on ignoring that part of the agreement almost from the moment it was signed. In 1854, Congress created the territories of Kansas and Nebraska to facilitate westward migration. This set the stage for the conflict that followed. Even so, the US government was bound to recognize the Indians' legal title to these lands. It was only a matter of time before some event would bring white migrants rushing headlong into the heart of the Cheyenne and Arapahoe territory. Just four years later that event occurred when William Green Russell and his party of Cherokees and whites from Georgia discovered gold near what is now Denver. Soon afterward, John Gregory's party struck placer gold on Clear Creek on May 6, 1859, and there was no turning back. White migration went into high gear, and the Indians soon looked on with dismay as Americans began building settlements in heart of the Indians' traditional winter camping grounds on lands that the United States had said would be theirs forever.

In short order, American migrants and the Indians began to cross paths. The traveler Bayard Taylor described one of these early encounters near the mouth of Boulder Canyon:

> I was introduced to one of the original eight squatters in Boulder Valley. He tells a singular story of their experience with the Indians when they first settled here in 1859. Where the town of Boulder now is was one of the favorite camping grounds of the former. They not only warned the intruders away but threatened to exterminate them if they remained. The eight men however constructed a rude fort and made preparations to stand a siege. Hostilities commenced and were carried on for some time when one day the besieged noticed signs of commotion in the Indian camp. Toward evening a warrior arrived demanding a parley. They hesitated for a while but finally admitted

him whereupon he stated that the medicine man of the tribe had dreamed the night before of stars falling from heaven and a flood from the mountains sweeping away their camp. This he interpreted as a warning that they should leave and the tribe therefore were preparing to depart. The next morning they packed their tents and after uttering in concert a mighty howl of lamentation went out on the Plains and never afterward returned.[6]

The Indians we know were Arapahoe, perhaps even Left Hand's band. Their lamentations seemed to anticipate the tragedy that would befall them at the hands of some of these same settlers at Sand Creek in just a few years. Nearly concurrently to this, settlers in what is now Denver established the Provisional Territory of Jefferson. Although this territory was an extralegal entity, it served notice to the US government of the settlers' intent to stay. The federal government supported the squatters by its actions too. In 1859 it surveyed a baseline along the fortieth parallel into Boulder Valley that provided a necessary precursor for the land grid settlers would need to file land claims in the region.

The first Americans establishing farms and towns knew full well they had no legal basis for taking up residence. But they were not deterred. Morse Coffin, who settled nearby, recalled the situation existing in 1859 and 1860: "Of course, the first settlers in this whole region were squatters on Indian lands, as the Indian title was not extinguished for two or three years later, and in the meantime we used to hear that the Indians desired very much to retain this portion of the country as a permanent reservation and so we were uneasy about it and many declared they would never vacate, if so ordered, without being forced to do so. But when surveyors came in the fall of '63 we felt at rest."[7]

Coffin was of course relieved when surveyors, using the 1859 baseline, began recording squatters' claims in 1863. In short order, two events occurred that helped make landowners out of squatters. The first was the Treaty of Fort Wise, which was negotiated in 1860 and finalized with revisions on February 18, 1861. The second was when Colorado became an official territory on February 28, 1861. At Fort Wise, William Bent and later Albert G. Boone (grandson of Daniel), on behalf of the United States, and Arapahoe and Cheyenne chiefs including Little Raven, Storm, Shave-Head, Big-Mouth, Black Kettle, White Antelope, Lean Bear, Little Wolf, and Left Hand (a

Cheyenne, not the Left Hand associated with Sand Creek) agreed to cede many of the territorial rights in the Fort Laramie Treaty of 1851 that pertained to them. Notably the Northern Cheyenne and Northern Arapahoe plus other bands among the Southern Cheyenne and Arapahoe who opposed changing the treaty were absent. In a lopsided exchange in which the Indians were to receive annuities, southern bands who were seeking peace agreed to a smaller reservation in eastern Colorado. By entering into the treaty, peaceful factions among the Southern Cheyenne and Arapahoe acknowledged the reality on the ground that they had already lost control of the High Plains along the Front Range. The treaty played to the interests of the United States well, because it could claim that Indian title to the lands of the Pikes Peak Gold Region were extinguished. Since many Indians boycotted the Fort Wise treaty negotiations and rejected the agreement, the likelihood for conflict was enhanced. Nevertheless, between the treaty and the establishment of the new territories, the US government apparently felt it had sufficient legal basis to allow the surveyors that Coffin saw in 1863 to begin their work along the Front Range. Farther east the situation remained unsettled, and the title to lands in what is now northeastern Colorado remained clouded to the extent that the government held off privatizing large tracts for several more years.[8]

Outside the High Plains, the early 1860s were turbulent times as the United States headed into the Civil War. Once that conflict began, Colorado settlers were drawn in, and became increasingly concerned about Confederate designs on the Pikes Peak gold mines. Among the Colorado settlers many held strong abolitionist sentiments. In Boulder, Swedish immigrant Jonas Anderson Jr. was among them and looked to support the Union cause. When the call came, Jonas Anderson Jr. stepped forward to serve his adopted country, joining the Colorado Volunteers in the New Mexico Campaign. In 1862 Anderson held the rank of private in Company K under Silas S. Soule. He participated in the decisive battle of Glorieta Pass where they crushed the Confederate bid to invade Colorado and take the gold fields. It was at Glorieta Pass that one of the officers, Colonel John Chivington, had the lucky stroke of intercepting and destroying the Confederate supply train, which contained nearly all of the Southerners' supplies and ammunition. The Confederate advance collapsed, and Southern forces never again threatened Colorado. Chivington became a hero to many in Colorado. Not long afterward, Anderson was back in Boulder where he resumed farming.

Over the next couple of years white migration into Colorado continued unabated. This migration consumed what little forage was left along the South Platte and Arkansas Rivers. As hunters decimated buffalo herds along the migration routes, the Indians were stricken by diseases and drought that put them under severe stress. Conditions on the new reservation went from poor to worse, as game thinned and promised annuities often fell short or came late. Indians from bands who had signed the treaty felt that they had no choice but to hunt outside the reservation, while others joined militant bands as conditions deteriorated. Many young Cheyenne men gravitated toward the Dog Soldiers and other militant groups like them who wished to expel whites from Colorado and would not answer to head chiefs like Black Kettle. To add insult to injury, Indians looked on as white settlers such as John Wesley Iliff began moving cattle into former prime hunting grounds at Bijou and Kiowa Creeks, Fremont's Orchard along the South Platte, and other sites, further limiting hunting opportunities. Soon frustrated Indians began stealing livestock from the settlers and migrants along the South Platte. It was only a matter of time before open warfare would erupt.[9]

As historian Elliott West asserts, conditions on the High Plains in the spring of 1864 provided the ideal context for an ugly conflict. Whites and Indians with a history of discord were now living in close proximity, and both relied on many of the same resources. The well-meaning but not universally accepted Fort Wise Treaty brought only embitterment and confusion to both sides. Hungry Indians began taking settlers' livestock. Whites began fighting back against Indian raids.

1864

With many young men having volunteered for the Union Army and away at the war, settlers were feeling anxious and exposed to perceived Indian threats. In places like the Boulder and St. Vrain Valleys, settlers began organizing militias. In early 1864, a short lived sixty-two-man "Lower Boulder and St. Vrain Valley Home Guards" formed near Burlington (Longmont). They built "Fort Junction," a 100-foot by 130-foot sod-walled fort near the confluence of Boulder and St. Vrain Creeks. The guard wished to deter any Indians that might come up either valley. In support of their efforts, the federal government supplied cap and ball six-shooters, rifles, and ammunition to each guard member. When in August of 1864 Territorial Governor John Evans made a call for United States Volunteers to raise a "100 Day Cavalry" to fight Indians, many militia men from Lower Boulder and St. Vrain Valley Home Guards joined.[10]

By late June 1864, tensions were reaching a breaking point for many settlers in Colorado. Some bands of Indians had made raids to steal property and livestock. A number of whites were killed, and some women and children taken hostage. However, in retrospect, the actual numbers of depredations that can be tied with certainty to the Indians are actually very few. In the most notorious incident, the killing of the Hungate family southeast of Denver, the Indians were blamed by hawkish citizens in Denver, but the actual culprits—white or Indian—were never established. It seems that the fear of raids loomed larger than actual attacks. By early summer jumpy soldiers had killed a number of Indians. Then on June 27, 1864, Evans made an appeal to the "friendly Indians of the Plains." In it he said that the "Great Father is angry" for the attack by Indians on soldiers and whites. He urged friendly Indians to stay away from those who were at war. He called on friendly Arapahoe and Cheyenne to muster at Fort Lyon where the US Indian agent would "give them provisions, and show them a place of safety." He asked friendly Indians from other tribes to gather at additional safe havens. The object of his pronouncement, Evans said, was "to prevent friendly Indians from being killed through mistake."[11]

Over the summer, Governor Evans made several requests to Washington to raise a cavalry for use against the Indians on the High Plains east of Denver. Two other Colorado cavalries were already deployed in the Civil War and were unavailable for local duty. In arguing for the new cavalry, Evans exaggerated depredations by the Indians and fanned anti-Indian frenzy among settlers. Although initially rebuffed, President Lincoln relented and granted Evans the authority to raise additional volunteers. The recruitment poster calling for volunteers is reproduced in Figure 6.2. Immediately after receiving permission, Evans issued a proclamation on August 11, 1864, to raise a 100-day United States Volunteer force among citizens of the Colorado Territory "to go in pursuit of all hostile Indians on the plains, scrupulously avoiding those who have responded to my said call to rendezvous at the points indicated; also to kill and destroy, as enemies of the country, wherever they may be found, such hostile Indians." His proclamation authorized citizens to keep any property they captured from the hostile Indians.[12]

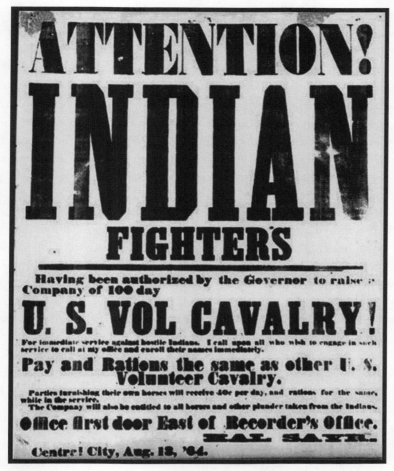

FIGURE 6.2. A recruitment poster for the Third Colorado Cavalry. Notice that the governor authorized volunteers to "be entitled to all horses and other plunder taken from the Indians." Image courtesy Colorado State Archive.

As the hysteria over Indians increased, panicked settlers in Boulder started digging trenches on Twelfth (now Broadway) and Thirteenth Streets. In mid-August, volunteers were recruited from Boulder, the mining camps west of town, and the surrounding valleys. The government circulated posters calling for "Indian fighters" to volunteer for the 100 Day Cavalry. For Jonas

Anderson Jr., recently returned from New Mexico, life did not settle down, as he, Morse Coffin, the Arbuthnot brothers, David Nichols, and many others from the Boulder, Left Hand, and St. Vrain Valleys answered Evans's call.

Evans's Third Colorado Cavalry was raised with a 100-day authorization at the same pay as other US Volunteer cavalries. Governor Evans's personal secretary, Samuel Hitt Elbert, who would go on to become Evans's son-in-law, governor, Supreme Court justice, and a major figure in water law, issued the proclamation to raise troops. Colonel John M. Chivington was placed in overall charge of the Colorado troops. Lieutenant George L. Shoup, who led the Third Colorado Cavalry under Chivington, was appointed by Evans and confirmed and commissioned by US military authorities.

John Evans was fabulously wealthy by the time he became Colorado's second territorial governor in 1862. Born in Waynesville, Ohio, on March 9, 1814, Evans became a doctor after studying in Pennsylvania and Ohio. While practicing medicine, Evans helped found Indiana's first insane asylum and school for the deaf. He relocated to Chicago and eventually became a professor at Rush Medical College. Other achievements include helping found Mercy Hospital and the Illinois Medical Society. Evans, according to son-in-law Elbert, was "about 5 ft. 11 in. rather a large frame, but little flesh; mild in his demeanor, patient, determined and utterly without fear." Perhaps his fearlessness led Evans to make the prudent investments in the Chicago & Fort Wayne Railroad and the Chicago & Evanston Railroad that made him rich. Evans soon became politically active where he served on the Chicago City Council, helped found the Illinois Republican Party, and became friends with Abraham Lincoln. The town of Evansville, Illinois, is named after him.[13]

Once in Denver, Evans took an interest in the work of Captain Edward L. Berthoud to develop a railroad and wagon route from Denver to Salt Lake City. Evans worked with the Territorial Legislature to incorporate the Colorado and Pacific Wagon, Telegraph and Railroad Company to lure investors. With Evans's encouragement, President Lincoln signed the Pacific Railway Act of July 1, 1862, which created the Union Pacific Railroad Company. Evans's lobbying was not philanthropic: the act named Evans as a charter director of the Union Pacific Railroad Company. Two years later, President Lincoln signed an amendment to the act that initiated the first transcontinental railroad. To encourage construction, these two railroad acts granted prospective railroad builders a total of 6,400 acres of federal land for each mile of railroad they built. Further sweetening the incentives was the issuance of thirty-year government bonds to build the railroad. In addition, the act directed the United States to "extinguish as rapidly as may be the Indian title to lands required." All the railroad men knew, Evans included, that extinguishing Indian titles was a prerequisite for opening the door to lucrative federal land grants. As such, Evans and others would need to address Arapahoe and Cheyenne Indian rights in the 1851 Fort Laramie Treaty. Moreover, Evans was a political insider well aware of the financial windfall awaiting anyone who could build a railroad into Denver. Indeed, this provided Evans with a financial motive to use his powers as territorial governor and ex-officio superintendent of Indian affairs for Colorado to pressure the Indians into new treaties that would extinguish Indian land claims along railroad routes and other resource-rich areas.

During the summer and fall of 1864, Cheyenne Indians, under the leadership of Black Kettle, tried to negotiate peace with the Americans. On September 4, a Cheyenne, Ochinee (One-Eye) went to Fort Lyon with his wife and another man to deliver a letter from Black Kettle and other chiefs to its commanding officer, Major Ned Wynkoop. Jumpy soldiers shot at Ochinee when he first tried to deliver the letter. In it, Black Kettle reported that his people were hungry and fearful of raids. As a sign of his peaceful intentions, Black Kettle offered to turn over white captives that he had acquired. He invited Wynkoop to meet to discuss peace. An apprehensive Wynkoop accepted, placed Ochinee, his wife, and comrade under guard, and with their guidance led a force of 127 men in a four-day ride to the Cheyenne and Arapahoe camp near the Smoky Hill River. When he arrived he was "confronted by from six to eight hundred Indian warriors, drawn up in line of battle, and prepared to fight." After some nervous moments in which hostilities nearly erupted, the Indians went to parley with Wynkoop in his camp. He later said that had a fight started, he would have been overwhelmed. Wynkoop met with various Indian chiefs, including Black Kettle of the Cheyenne and Left Hand of the Southern Arapahoe. At the meeting the Indians turned over four white women and children that they had purchased from hostile bands. The chiefs professed a desire for peace, but Wynkoop stated that he did not have the authority to conclude a treaty. Wynkoop convinced the chiefs to travel with him to Denver to meet with Governor Evans and Colonel Chivington for peace negotiations.[14]

Wynkoop and the Indian delegation soon set out for Denver. On September 28, 1864, Black Kettle, White Antelope, Bull Bear of the Cheyenne and Neva, Bosse, Heap of Buffalo, and Na-ta-nee, all Arapahoe chiefs, met with Governor Evans, Colonel Chivington, Wynkoop, and other whites at Denver's Camp Weld. Left Hand stayed behind but sent close relatives in his stead. At their peace council, Black Kettle implored that all "we ask is that we may have peace with the whites." Black Kettle carried weight within the tribe as an influential chief within Cheyenne's council of forty-four chiefs. During the meeting Evans remained scornful of the Indians' peace overtures. He claimed that since war had already begun, making peace was out of his hands and the responsibility of the military authorities. As territorial governor, ex-officio superintendent of Indian affairs, and commander in charge of the Territorial Militia, Evans seemed to unnecessarily and self-servingly downplay his command responsibilities. Ominously, Evans stated that the "time when you can make war best, is in the summer time; when I can make war best is in the winter . . . my time is just coming." Near the conclusion of the council, Colonel Chivington added that he was not the "big war chief," but that his rule of fighting whites or Indians was to fight "until they lay down their arms and submit to military authority." Chivington then directed the chiefs to camp near Major Wynkoop (at Fort Lyon) if they were ready to lay down their arms. A photo of Black Kettle and other Arapahoe and Cheyenne chiefs taken at the time of Camp Weld Council in September 1864 is shown in Figure 6.3. Black Kettle is seated on the lower left, and a man mistakenly identified as Left Hand is standing in the top row center.[15]

Several days after the meeting, Evans left for Washington, leaving the territory's affairs in the hands of Acting Governor Elbert and Colonel Chivington. Evans did not return to Colorado until the following April. By mid-October Black Kettle, Left Hand, and various other chiefs and their bands relocated to Fort Lyon as directed by Chivington. Then in early November Wynkoop was suddenly and unexpectedly relieved of command and replaced by Major Scott Anthony. For a time the Indians remained at Fort Lyon, but Anthony had trouble feeding them. So with Anthony's permission, the Indians moved to a camp on Sand Creek where they could hunt more game.[16]

It is not known if Governor Evans spurned the peace overtures to further his railroad dreams (after all, he was far too smart to put something like that in writing), but it is known that he was angry with Wynkoop for bringing

Bosse. Left Hand. White Wolf,
Black Kettle, White Antelope, Bull Bear, Neva
Chiefs of Arapahoe, Sioux, Cheyenne & Kiowa tribes

FIGURE 6.3. Black Kettle and other Arapahoe and Cheyenne chiefs taken at the time of Camp Weld Council in September 1864. Contrary to the note on the photograph, Left Hand was not present. Photo courtesy of the Denver Public Library, Western History Collection, X–32364. Reprinted with permission.

the Indians in to discuss peace. Regardless, Evans, Chivington, and others in Denver held strong, often overtly racist anti-Indian sentiments and desired outright elimination or removal. That the militantly abolitionist Methodist minister John Chivington could so hate the Indians has never been adequately explained. Compounding the Chivington paradox is that he was apparently one-eighth Seneca and had even served as a missionary to the Delaware and Pottawatomie. Perhaps he was just the worst manifestation among whites at all levels of government and society during the mid-1860s, which saw the Indians as an "infestation" to be exterminated like insects.[17]

Lieutenant-General William Tecumseh Sherman, writing in 1866 after a battle between the army and the Sioux, was explicit in his feelings: "We must act with vindictive earnestness against the Sioux, even to their extermination, men, women, and children. Nothing less will reach the root of the case." Sherman's chilling words reflected the sentiment held by many whites in authority toward the Plains Indian tribes.[18]

To the military leaders of the time, anything to force the relocation of the Indians—including starvation and the destruction of their nomadic economy—was encouraged. Sherman, infamous for the scorched-earth March to the Sea during the Civil War, was in the position to influence commanders across the West to implement this brutal Indian policy. In May 1868, Sherman wrote to his friend and subordinate, General Philip Sheridan, "as long as Buffalo are up on the Republican the Indians will go there. I think it would be wise to invite all the sportsmen of England and America there this fall for a Grand Buffalo hunt, and make one grand sweep of them all. Until the Buffalo and consequent[ly] Indians are out [from between] the Roads we will have collisions and trouble." Although Sherman's comments obviously postdate Sand Creek, his views were typical during the 1860s.[19]

Like the leaders, many settlers supported exterminating the Indians. "At the time the 3d Colorado regiment was raised," Morse Coffin recalled, "the idea was very general that a war of extermination should be waged; that neither sex nor age should be spared; and women held to these views in common with men." Coffin felt that "as great a per cent of the latter as the former held this view; and one often heard the expression that 'nits make lice, make a clean thing of it.' Of course there were some exception[s]." But, Coffin concluded, "such exceptions were a weak minority [that] must be well known by most residents of Colorado at that time."[20]

It was in this overtly hostile climate that Black Kettle negotiated peace. To be sure, the Indians were deeply embittered and would have preferred to see the whites go or even exterminated. Nevertheless, Black Kettle believed that they were camping under the protection of troops commanded by Major Scott Anthony. Many unarmed men, women, and children from Cheyenne and Arapahoe bands camped with Black Kettle, believing that they were under the protection of the American flag.

Morse Coffin met Left Hand sometime around 1860. Niwot (Left Hand's English transliteration of his Arapahoe name), Left Hand Creek, and the Left Hand Ditch, to name a few sites, are all named after this Arapahoe Indian chief. Left Hand was "a tall, powerful and rather good looking man in the prime of manhood and had a roman nose. I think he was counted a rather good Indian," Coffin said. But reflecting the common views of whites, Coffin added, "I guess he found himself in bad company at the battle of Sand Creek November 29, 1864, where he was wounded and died three days later."[21]

David Nichols assumed responsibility for recruiting and training the Boulder volunteers. Their training lasted barely one month, from mid-August until September 16. Company D, the Boulder volunteers, initially assembled at Fort Chambers, the small adobe fort on Boulder Creek near Valmont. By October, Company D was on the trail looking to engage any Indians they encountered. Chivington's 100 Days men were already being derided as the "bloodless third" because they had not engaged any Indians. However, those taunts would not last long.[22]

On September 18, Company D was at Camp Evans and began heading toward Fort Lupton during the night. They continued down the South Platte and joined up with Company F on September 21. A temporary camp was made at a telegraph and stage stop about 150 miles below Denver on the South Platte. Their job was to keep the highway open and to protect the nearby ranches.[23]

Then on October 9, after several weeks of monotony, an Indian came close to camp and pointed toward the south or southeast saying that "heap Cheyenne" were in that direction. Acting on that tip, Nichols quickly ordered thirty to thirty-five men to ride to a nearby ranch and stand by. As preparation, Nichols had the commissary sergeant issue three pieces of hardtack to each man.[24]

They started for the Indian camp at three o'clock in the morning, with Captain Nichols and second-in-command Lieutenant Dickson leading. All men were ordered to keep silent. Joining them at the ranch were an additional eleven men from Company D, some citizens, and a scout from the First Colorado Cavalry nicknamed "Dunk." At the earliest dawn on October

10 about forty-five troops, officers, and civilians headed out toward some springs where they thought the Indians were camping.[25]

When they arrived at the springs, the "heap Cheyennes," had "dwindled to two lodges and their occupants." The lodges belonged to the band of Big Wolf, a Cheyenne chief. After taking up positions, the excited soldiers began shooting into the lodges. Coffin says that he was at a loss to describe what came next. Some initial shots were fired through the lodges, and frightened Indians began to run toward a nearby stream bank. Several Indians were likely wounded at this time. One prominent warrior, likely Big Wolf himself, began to go through a number of strange motions that afterward some cavalry members, including Coffin, came to believe were entreaties for mercy. In short order the Indians were surrounded. Quite a few of the soldiers started firing at Big Wolf, Coffin and Nichols included, and soon he was down.[26]

Before long, two more Indians were shot. One wounded Indian was scalped while still alive. The soldiers next "found and killed four squaws, two papooses and one young warrior, say fifteen years old, or two thirds grown," recalled Morse Coffin, adding, "Two of these squaws were rather young, and two middle aged ones had the babies in their arms. One of these was killed with her feet in a pool of water, and bent over her child as if to shield it, and as we came up it opened wide its eyes and looked up at us." Mortified, Coffin continued, "I said 'boys don't kill it, it is too bad,' etc., but one of the guides (glad it was not a soldier) came up and coolly shot it, at the same time making a remark not indicative of pity." Cursing, Coffin denounced the murder. "When the shooting of the squaws began," Coffin added, "they jumped up and tried to crawl away, at the same time screaming in an agony of terror. This was too much for me, and I talked against it . . . though the general sentiment was strongly in opposition to my view of it." When their grim work was done, three men, one boy, four women, and two babies lay dead. Their bodies were then scalped, valuables taken, and the rest was set on fire. Five days later, Company D arrived in Denver. On arriving, cavalrymen Henry Blake boasted that he "had some fun showing my Indian scalps. I had the scalp of Big Woolf, chief of the Schians." These murders came to be known as the Battle of Buffalo Springs.[27]

After showing their grim trophies around Denver, various people urged the members of Company D onto other acts of barbarity. One Denver merchant asked some of the troops to save a scalp for him in case they took any more. Although Morse Coffin claimed horror at the murders of the Big Wolf band, he seemed unconflicted by taking human trophies and even agreed to procure a scalp for the merchant.

On the afternoon of November 15 Company D left Denver, with Fort Lyon as their destination. Two days later they joined Company F, where Captain Nichols assumed charge of the two units. The trail over Monument Divide to Fort Lyon was in the bitter cold of mid-November, and they often slept in the snow. As they moved toward Fort Lyon other companies began to link up. They quickly passed through Colorado City and moved on to Booneville on the Arkansas River. At Booneville they joined most of the command under Chivington and Shoup. At this point the full command was assembled, including some troops from the First Colorado Cavalry.

George Bent, a member of the Cheyenne tribe, was one of the few people who described the events surrounding Sand Creek from the Indian perspective. George, son of the famous Santa Fe trader Colonel William Bent, spent his early years at the trading fort on the Arkansas River that his father, his uncle Charles Bent, and their partner Ceran St. Vrain built. George's mother, Owl Woman, was the daughter of a renowned Cheyenne Indian chief, White Thunder, who had the honor of keeping the tribe's sacred medicine arrows. George Bent spent a number of years in St. Louis at school before returning to Colorado to live with his mother's tribe. Bent asserted that the Third Colorado Cavalry had been "hastily recruited from among the worst class of frontier whites—toughs, gamblers, and 'bad-men' from Denver and the mining camps, rough miners, 'bull-wackers,' and so on." He added that the "men were not disciplined at all, their officers had been selected by the vote of the men and had no real control over the men. The men were not even in uniform, and they were alike only in one thing: they were all eager to kill Indians."[28]

We know, of course, that George Bent's opinion was biased and his statements only partly true. These men were poorly trained, equipped, and poorly fed. Even though these men were United States Volunteers, their discipline was lax. But many members of Chivington's Third were well-known farmers, merchants, and land owners. It seems that every social stratum of frontier Colorado, from community leader to lowlife, was represented.

Under Colonel Chivington's command they left Booneville on the November 24 in good weather, but there were several inches of snow on the ground.

With over 100 wagons in tow, their procession extended over several miles. Once on the road toward Fort Lyon, Chivington enforced strict secrecy to prevent the Indians or anyone else downstream from knowing his approach. All traffic to the east was detained, and not even the mail was allowed to pass. On the morning of November 28, Chivington arrived at Fort Lyon with over 700 mounted men and two pieces of artillery. Chivington's arrival was a surprise to most at the fort. A guard was immediately placed around the fort so that no one could leave. Major Anthony's command added 125 men and two more artillery pieces to Chivington's force. Once at Fort Lyon, ammunition was handed out, and the troops were ordered to prepare three days' rations. That same evening, using intelligence from Major Anthony indicating the Indians' location, the entire force departed on an overnight ride for Black Kettle and Left Hand's camp.

Company D of the Third Colorado Cavalry was in the Second Battalion, commanded by Captain T. G. Cree. While en route, Lieutenant Pennock and some of the men of Company D were ordered to return and take charge of the camp and return the next day with the transportation.

Just about sunrise, Chivington's troops came across great herds of Indian ponies, and a company of New Mexicans were immediately sent to round up the herd. By this time the Indians had heard the clamor of the horses and artillery, and some were seen driving a different herd of horses away from the troops. On arriving about a half mile from, and in full view of, the Indian camp, the troops were halted and ordered to throw off all excess baggage. "Men I shall not dictate to you who to kill or what to kill, but remember our poor murdered woman and Children," Chivington shouted to the assembled troops.[29]

With that Chivington's troops attacked. When the firing started, Indians flocked to the lodge of Black Kettle, who quickly raised both a US flag and a white flag, in the misguided belief that these symbols would stop the shooting and protect the tribe. Troops soon "charged through the camp, driving the Indians completely out of the camp and into the creek." White Antelope, one of the chiefs at the Camp Weld peace conference, ran forward toward Chivington, perhaps to identify who they were, and was one of the first Indians shot down.[30]

Captain Nichols and Company D pursued a band of Indians that were attempting to escape toward the northeast. These Indians were overtaken, and about twenty five or thirty were killed and some ponies captured.

Escaping Indians gathered along the banks of Sand Creek to seek shelter. Some quickly dug shallow pits for protection. Those who could among the Arapahoe and Cheyenne fought back, and terrible hand-to-hand combat erupted along the banks. It was here that most of the Indians and troops were killed.[31]

Morse Coffin found himself in the center of fighting along the creek. As he advanced, he saw Company D member James Cox scalping an Indian. Then Coffin encountered "two squaws the others had left for dead, but one of these was lying face down, and writhing and groaning in great agony. She also made exclamations which sounded like O! O! and in her efforts to breathe the blood was expelled from a wound which must have been through the lungs. After thinking it over for a minute or so, and believing it an act of mercy, "I drew my revolver and shot her through the head."[32]

A short time later, Coffin came up to Henry (Hank) Farrar, who asked him for a pocket knife to scalp another Indian. Coffin explained, this Indian "was brave, but we showed him no mercy." Chaotic fighting extended into the afternoon. Coffin killed one more Indian before it was over. He was firing so often that his Smith & Wesson carbine became fouled and jammed. After that, he used his revolver. By the end of the day, Henry C. Foster and Robert McFarland of Company D were dead and another was wounded. When they found McFarland, his body was stripped and mutilated.[33]

That evening, between 150 to 500 Arapahoe and Cheyenne lay dead. Even though they had the advantage of surprise, Chivington's units sustained 70 casualties. It is variously reported that Left Hand was mortally wounded, either by shot or broken femur, and died several days later. George Bent, who was camped with relatives at Sand Creek, was wounded but escaped with other survivors. The victims of Chivington's massacre included dozens of unarmed women and children. When word of the "battle" first emerged, Chivington was hailed for his "victory" against hostile Indians.[34]

Both during the actual fighting and in the hours after the shooting ceased, many Indians were barbarically mutilated. Fleeing women and children were shot down, and many were scalped. Eyewitness John S. Smith, a white trader and founding member of the Denver Town Company, was in the Cheyenne camp trading when the attack began. He later stated that "All manner of depredations were inflicted on their persons; they were scalped, their brains knocked out; the men used their knives, ripped open women, clubbed little children, knocked them in the head with their guns, beat their brains out, mutilated their bodies in every sense of the word." Sometime during that day it is likely that Jonas Anderson Jr. acquired a scalp that was later passed down to his descendants. In addition to the scalps, some troops took body parts, including male and female genitals as macabre souvenirs. A day after the massacre, Smith's own mixed-blood son was shot and killed while being held under guard as prisoner. Some, including Morse Coffin, acquired Indian scalps that were traded for new boots on returning to Denver.[35]

Chivington and Shoup soon sent back glowing reports to Denver of their success on Sand Creek. On February 26, 1865, Acting Governor Elbert and the Territorial Assembly issued a resolution praising Chivington's actions. In it they thanked Chivington for "the able and patriotic manner in which he has discharged his duties as commandant of this District" and praised "the Colorado troops for their zeal in supporting the civil officers of this Territory, and maintaining the honor of the National Flag."[36]

But as details of the "zeal" in which the attack was prosecuted became widely known, a public outcry against the barbarity—particularly on the East Coast—was raised. Soon two investigations were opened into the matter. One was by the Congressional Committee on the Conduct of the War, a body initially set up to report on Civil War issues. This one held hearings and collected documentary evidence about the Sand Creek attack. The other was an investigation by the secretary of war ordered by a Senate resolution.

After heading west to investigate the matter, the Congressional Committee on the Conduct of the War reported its take on Chivington's actions:

Wearing the uniform of the United States, which should be the emblem of justice and humanity; holding the important position of commander of a military district, and therefore having the honor of the government to that extent in his keeping, he [Chivington] deliberately planned and executed a foul and dastardly massacre which would have disgraced the veriest savage among those who were the victims of his cruelty. Having full knowledge of their friendly character, having himself been instrumental to some extent in placing them in their position of fancied security, he took advantage of their inapprehension and defenseless condition to gratify the worst passions that ever cursed the heart of man . . . The truth is that he surprised and murdered, in cold blood, the unsuspecting men, women and children on Sand Creek, who had every reason to believe they were under the protection of the United States authorities, and then returned to Denver and boasted of the brave deeds he and the men under his command had performed.[37]

The investigation by the War Department was even more extensive, and hearings in Denver and Fort Lyon extended over seventy-six days during the spring of 1865. This hearing was wrought with drama. An early witness, Captain Silas S. Soule of the First Colorado Cavalry testified against Chivington. At Sand Creek, Soule had opposed Chivington's mission and ordered his men not to shoot. At the hearing, Soule decried the action and reported that before the attack, Major Scott Anthony had said their intent was to go out and "kill all the Indians." Chivington supporters were quick to exact vengeance on the witness. Soon after testifying, a lone gunman approached Captain Soule and assassinated him with a shot to his head in front of his new wife as they strolled along Lawrence Street in Denver. With Soule dead and unable to defend his character, Chivington introduced an affidavit at the hearing from a teamster alleging that Soule was a drunk and coward. After strenuous objections by Soule's friends, the committee refused to receive the affidavit as evidence.[38]

Soon after the hearings concluded, a soldier by the name of Charles W. Squier was accused of Soule's murder. The army ordered a close friend of Soule's, Lieutenant James D. Cannon, to arrest Squier. Cannon too had testified against Chivington. Cannon pursued Squier to New Mexico, found and arrested him, and returned to Denver. Not long after, on July, 14, 1865, Cannon was found dead in his hotel room, with his suspect cause of death being poisoning. At the same time Squier disappeared from his jail cell at Denver and was never seen in Colorado again. Thus, two witnesses against Chivington lay dead within weeks of their testimony.[39]

By the time the War Department investigation concluded, damming evidence against Chivington's actions and Evans's complacency seemed overwhelming. Chivington, however, had resigned his commission, and since he was no longer subject to military authority, he never faced charges. Evans completed his term as governor, but Sand Creek ruined his political career. Evans returned to private life and focused his energy developing Colorado's railroads.

In retrospect, it is clear that Sand Creek can only be called a massacre. It was a carefully organized surprise attack against a peaceful village. The

Cheyenne and Arapahoe believed that they were camping in an area designated by the military authorities for peaceful Indians. The Indians were given no opportunity to surrender. In fact, they attempted to fly both a US flag and a white flag to indicate their peaceful intent and submission, but those symbols were deliberately ignored by the attacking troops. When the army's intent became clear, the Indians attempted to defend themselves. Noncombatants—women, children, babies, and old men—were then deliberately and indiscriminately shot and many later horrifically mutilated. And there is no indication that their commanding officers, Colonels Chivington and Shoup, did anything to stop, restrain, or discipline their troops.

Chivington's actions infuriated the Indians. A wider war on the eastern plains broke out, with the Cheyenne, Arapahoe, and Sioux raiding forts, stage stops, and ranches up and down the South Platte. Many settlers were killed for revenge. Black Kettle was temporally stripped of leadership in the Southern Cheyenne, but was restored as his people came to understand that he was duped. Once the details emerged about the true nature of the vicious massacre, Chivington was thoroughly discredited. Nevertheless, Chivington remained a highly popular figure in Denver.

The war Chivington sparked lasted from 1865 to 1867 as militant Cheyenne bands, particularly the Dog Soldiers, attacked settlements across the eastern plains. Even with warfare ongoing, the US government apologized to the Cheyenne and Arapahoe for Sand Creek. It then went on to conclude the Treaty of the Little Arkansas on October 14, 1865. This document only served to further legally constrain the Cheyenne and Arapahoe Indians. In exchange for the usual annuities and pledges of peace, the Indians agreed that in the case of disagreement they would "submit their complaints through their agent to the President of the United States," who was to act as an arbitrator and whose decisions were to be binding on all. The Indians also expressly agreed to reduce their land claim to the unsettled portions of the country between the Arkansas and Platte Rivers. Whether the Indians realized it or not, this treaty began to make them subject to US law. Once again, Black Kettle for the Southern Cheyenne and now Little Raven for the Southern Arapahoe were the principal Indians signing.

Even with this latest treaty, peace remained elusive. The Dog Soldiers stayed away, and the war continued. The army responded by bringing in additional troops and building new forts. General William Tecumseh Sherman, by then commander of the Military Division of the Missouri, ordered Major General Winfield Scott Hancock to the Arkansas Valley with 1,400 men to suppress the Indians. Although this did not result in outright Indian defeat, it did lead to another round of negotiations and the conclusion to yet another treaty, this time on Medicine Lodge Creek on October 28, 1867.[40]

For both the Indians and whites, several critical things occurred at Medicine Lodge Creek. For it was here that the Cheyenne and Arapahoe explicitly agreed for the first time that if an Indian were to commit a "wrong or depredation upon the person or property of any one, white, black, or Indian" they would be subject to and tried *according to US law*. In other words, the Indians essentially gave up their independence at this moment and agreed that hereafter they would be subject to US justice.

Second, it was here at Medicine Lodge Creek that former Governor John Evans and his railroad partners got their big break. For the Indians agreed to live on a new reservation in southern Kansas and Indian Territory (modern-day Oklahoma) and abandon all prior land claims in Colorado and Wyoming. With this, all tribal titles from the Fort Laramie Treaty of 1851 were permanently extinguished, and the US government could now distribute former Indian lands in Colorado to railroad companies as imagined in the 1862 Pacific Railway Act. The door was wide open for a land grab in Colorado on a scale never before or since repeated.[41]

Evans, now investing in railroads, secured federal land grants and county bonds to build the railroad between the Union Pacific line at Cheyenne to Denver. Evans's railroad, the Denver Pacific Railway, opened on June 24, 1870. Evans along with partners David Moffat, William Byers, Walter Cheesman, and others, soon sold some of their land bonanza to the organizers of both the Greeley and Chicago (now Longmont) colonies in northeastern Colorado. By all accounts, Evans and his partners were wildly successful in marketing their land. As the chart from the Colorado state engineer's first biennial report in 1884 makes clear (Figure 6.4), land privatization jumped as soon as the railroads received their vast grants of former Indian lands. Evans went on to finance other railroad enterprises, including the Denver & South Park, the Denver & New Orleans, the Denver Texas & Gulf, the Kansas Pacific, and the Boulder Valley railroads. Evans worked on railroad projects up until his death on July 2, 1897.[42]

By all accounts, Jonas Anderson Jr., George C. Green, brothers James and Samuel Arbuthnot, Morse Coffin, Porter M. Hinman, Onsville C. Coffin,

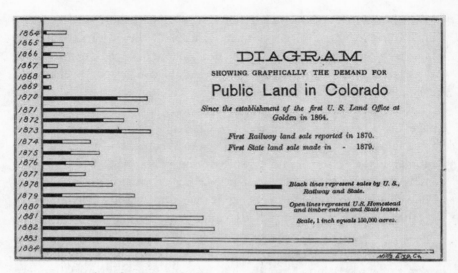

FIGURE 6.4. A chart from the Colorado state engineer's first biennial report in 1884 shows how land privatization and sales jumped soon after the railroads received their vast grants of former Indian land.

Granville Berkley, and even Captain David H. Nichols of Company D were more or less bit players in this sad chapter of Colorado's history. Nichols understood what the railroads would bring and invested accordingly. The others could rest at night knowing that the title to their land was secure.

It is clear that some Boulder settlers were enthusiastic participants in the carnage, others were horrified but nevertheless went along with their company to perform their duty, and a number served in supporting roles to the troops. The actions of these men and others like them consolidated American control over Colorado. Because the Americans won, the settlers could impose their legal systems governing water, land, minerals, and other resources in what we now call Colorado.

The United States may have had an abstract deed from France granting it the lands of the Louisiana Purchase, but until the United States wrestled control away from the Indians through war, treaties, and colonization, this land was Indian land. Actions of common men like Jonas Anderson Jr. were central in transforming the Front Range as a space dominated by the American Indian to one dominated and controlled by white settlers from the United

States. To use the language of the twentieth and twenty-first centuries, participants from Jonas Anderson Jr. to John Chivington and John Evans were accomplices to or perpetrators of genocide and ethnic cleansing.

Historian Patricia Nelson Limerick once explained that the seeming contradiction between building farms and murdering Indians was not all that contradictory from the perspective of those living through the 1860s. For people like David Nichols, Limerick wrote, "the founding of universities and the killing of Indians represented service in the same cause. The project was to 'bring civilization' to Colorado and to most nineteenth-century Anglo-Americans, that meant displacing the natives, establishing and allocating property claims, installing territorial, county, and town government, and setting up schools, colleges, and churches." For us, Limerick explains, Indian-killing and university-founding have a seemingly opposite moral meaning, "one malevolent, one benevolent." But, as she continues, "in the 1860s and 1870s, in the mind of David Nichols and many of his contemporaries, they were harmonic, two ways of pushing the region ahead to its proper destiny." Perhaps that is so, but from the perspective of any culture or any time, clubbing children to death with the intent of exterminating their kind, or failing to restrain egregious abuses by men under one's command is amoral and abhorrent, a practice that cannot be forgotten or forgiven.[43]

NOTES

1. Coffin, letter to *Boulder* (CO) *County Miner*, January 15, 1914.

2. West, *Contested Plains*.

3. Cemetery record for Aikins, accessed January 21, 2012, http://www.finda grave.com/cgi-bin/fg.cgi?page=gr&GSsr=1&GScid=57606&GRid=37762993&.

4. Campbell, *Sand Creek Massacre*.

5. Ari Kelman, *A Misplaced Massacre: Struggling Over the Memory of Sand Creek* (Cambridge: Harvard University Press, 2013).

6. Taylor, *Colorado*, 157–58.

7. Coffin, letter to *Boulder* (CO) *County Miner*, January 15, 1914.

8. West, *Contested Plains*, 281.

9. West, *Contested Plains*, 283.

10. Block, "Lower Boulder and St. Vrain Valley"; Coffin, "Reminiscences," *Longmont* (CO) *Ledger*, August 9, 1907.

11. Carroll, *Sand Creek Massacre*, 67. Note that the book contains two sets of page numbers, one for the book and another for the reports it contains. Page numbers cited here are from the book.

12. Proclamation by Governor Evans, of Colorado Territory, Denver, August 11, 1864.

13. John Evans's biographical information is derived from the Colorado State Archives, accessed January 30, 2013, https://www.colorado.gov/pacific/archives/john-evans#Biography; Elbert quote from Samuel Hitt Elbert, interview by Hubert H. Bancroft, October 21, 1884, University of Colorado Archive, Boulder.

14. Carroll, *Sand Creek Massacre*, xii; Major Wynkoop later regretted the mistake of bringing the chiefs to Denver rather than to his superior officer in Kansas.

15. It is doubtful that the Indian identified as Left Hand in the photo is him, as he was not reported at the Camp Weld Council. Transcript of Fort Weld Council in Carroll, *Sand Creek Massacre*, iv–vii.

16. Smiley, *Semi-Centennial History*, 1:418.

17. For example, see George A. Custer, *My Life on the Plains, or Personal Experiences with Indians* (New York: Heldon and Company, 1874), 5, 120; for Chivington's heritage, see "John Milton Chivington Record," accessed August 6, 2013, http://www.sandcreeksite.com/john_milton_chivington_record.htm. I believe that Evans's primary motivation to expel the Indians was to nullify their title to lands in northeastern Colorado. Railroad construction was clearly the motivation in 1865 as the Americans tried to induce the Dog Soldiers to sign treaties that would allow the construction of the Kansas Pacific Railroad in western Kansas and eastern Colorado. See Grinnell, *Fighting Cheyennes*, 245–46.

18. Letter from Lieutenant-General W. T. Sherman to General Grant, St. Louis, December 28, 1866, in Custer, *My Life on the Plains*, 85.

19. Smits, "Frontier Army," 314.

20. Coffin, "The Battle at Sand Creek," 5. Morse H. Coffin wrote a series of letters to the *Colorado Sun* in 1879 describing his experiences at Sand Creek. The letters were later republished as Coffin, *Battle of Sand Creek*.

21. Coffin, "Reminiscences," *Boulder* (CO) *County Miner*, January 15, 1914.

22. Bixby, *History of Clear Creek*, 398.

23. Unless otherwise noted, two primary sources were used to trace the movements and activities of Company D during the fall of 1864 through Sand Creek: Coffin, *Battle of Sand Creek*, and the Diary of Henry Blake, which was published in the *Daily Camera*, August 2, 1941.

24. Coffin, *Battle of Sand Creek*, 5.

25. Probably Duncan "Dunk" Kerr, a private in Company H, First Regiment.

26. Coffin, *Battle of Sand Creek*, 6.

27. Quote in Coffin, *Battle of Sand Creek*, 7–8; see also diary of Henry Blake. Others may have shared Morse Coffin's horror. Arbuthnot family history states that William Arbuthnot refused to participate and David Nichols locked him up for a night to get him to rethink his decision. But as a German Baptist, he still refused to participate. Donlyn Arbuthnot, personal communication, 2013.

28. Hyde, *Life of George Bent*.

29. Theodore Chubbuck, interview by Hubert H. Bancroft, August 30, 1866, University of Colorado Library.

30. Quote from Scott Anthony, in Carroll, *Sand Creek Massacre: A Documentary History*, 60.

31. George L. Shoup, in ibid., 57.

32. Coffin, *Battle of Sand Creek*, 21.

33. Ibid., 22.

34. Left Hand shot, in Smiley, *Semi-Centennial History*, 1:421.

35. John A. Smith, in Carroll, *Sand Creek Massacre: A Documentary History*, 131. Descendants of Jonas Anderson Jr. repatriated a scalp for burial at the Sand Creek Massacre National Historic Site.

36. Smiley, *Semi-Centennial History*, 1:425.

37. Carroll, *Sand Creek Massacre: A Documentary History*, 7.

38. Mendoza, *Song of Sorrow*, 123–25.

39. Ibid., 128. It is not clear whether Cannon's poisoning was accidental or not. See also Halaas and Masich, *Halfbreed*, 207.

40. West, *Contested Plains*.

41. Medicine Lodge Treaty, October 28, 1867. For the text of the treaty, see http://digital.library.okstate.edu/kappler/Vol2/treaties/che0984.htm.

42. Nettleton, *Report of the State Engineer*, 24.

43. Quote from Limerick, Hickey, and DiNucci, *What's in a Name?*, 6. In 1961, the Regents of the University of Colorado honored David Nichols by naming a residence hall after him for donating land on which much of the university was built. By the late 1970s the role Nichols and his cavalry played in the Sand Creek Massacre had emerged, and a controversy raged on campus whether to strip Nichols's name from the residence hall. In 1987 Nichols Hall was formally renamed Cheyenne Arapahoe Hall.

SEVEN

Left Hand Ditch and the Emergence of Colorado's Prior Appropriation Doctrine

"As has been so widely reported, Prior Appropriation passed away last month at the age of 152.
Prior was a grand man and led a grand life—by
any standard he was one of the most influential
people in the history of the American West."
—*Charles F. Wilkinson*[1]

I don't think that most western farmers realize how their livelihood depends
on nineteenth-century populist ideology. At least, if you consider recent voting patterns and listen to rhetoric coming from rural legislators, you would
never guess how beholden their economy is on socialist and populist ideology. For that matter, most city dwellers in western cities have secure water
supplies because their utilities depend on water right doctrines developed
largely during the progressive era. Environmentalists, who routinely criticize
western "water buffalo," the developers and technocrats who build water
projects, also critique Prior Appropriation in terms that overlook its populist

DOI: 10.5876/9781607323822.c007

origins. But if you use or own water rights in Colorado, you rely on institutions developed with the broadest social interest in mind. And these social principles are hidden in plain sight. The Colorado Constitution declares that the waters of the state are the "property of the people." Nowhere does it call water private property. The Colorado Constitution also has a remarkable provision (from today's perspective) that lets one person condemn another's property to access water. And the state constitution allows market intervention by county commissioners to "establish reasonable maximum rates to be charged for the use of water." That is not capitalism or libertarianism, but a nineteenth-century version of socialism that would find no easy place in today's corporatist world. Colorado's appropriation doctrine was conceived and made law during an age that rejected corporate power in the name of serving the widest public interest. So how is that we got from there to here? The irony is that today many of the biggest beneficiaries of the system are the entrenched interests: cities, farms, and industries that inherited or bought land and water rights from their populist predecessors.[2]

In 1859 the first settlers of the Gold Rush era streamed in looking for land to establish farms and ranches along Colorado's Front Range. The region that would become Colorado was first organized as the Provisional Government of the Territory of Jefferson. This new territory was not recognized by Congress and existed from October 24, 1859, until Congress created the Colorado Territory on February 28, 1861. The Jefferson Territory included parts of the Kansas, Nebraska, New Mexico, Utah, and Washington territories. Settlers elected a provisional governor and general assembly that met for three months between November 1859 and January 1860. Access to water was one of the issues on everybody's mind. Recognizing this need, the assembly gave the explicit right to divert water to fields for those who did not own land along a stream. Once Congress created the Colorado Territory in 1861, the new Territorial Legislature granted a similar right to irrigators.[3]

For most settlers everything about irrigation was new. They knew that they could not depend on rain to grow crops in Colorado. The smart farmers knew that Colorado's climate necessitated irrigation. Some believed the adage that rain followed the plow, but they invariably failed, while those who tried their hand at irrigation succeeded. Both writers and government chroniclers passing through New Mexico before and after the Mexican War saw and wrote about irrigation in those regions. Similarly, Mexican War veterans returning to eastern cities described the ditches they saw in New Mexico's Hispanic communities.[4]

Settlers, some of them traveling east from California, were veterans of the 1849 Gold Rush. These former miners had direct experience managing and diverting water in the gold fields of the Sierras. They knew that because water was limited, placer miners created and enforced various rules to allocate the limited supplies among miners to assure that everyone received a share of the resource, or allocate the water should the supplies fall short.

California forty-niners developed the first rough water law in the American West. They applied the same "first-in-time" rule to water that they used at their gold diggings. In this doctrine of prior appropriation, water or gold belonged to the first man to stake a claim. By 1855 this concept gained the force of law when the California Supreme Court ruled that once water was diverted, someone arriving later "has no right to complain, no right to interfere with the prior occupation of his neighbor, and must abide the disadvantages of his own selection." The 1849 California Gold Rush also provided on-the-job engineering training to thousands of gold seekers. Every gold-extraction process required water to wash gravel from the heavier gold ore. In California, forty-niners dug many miles of ditches and built massive flumes to move water to and from mining claims. Over a ten-year period, they learned practical engineering skills and brought this expertise to bear when gold was discovered in Colorado.[5]

To stake mining claims, miners "posted notice" by tacking up claim signs at their diggings. They initiated a similar practice of posting water claims along the creek. Others could divert available water from the same stream, but their rights were junior to the first man to "post."

Although aspects of mining camp practice later appeared in water law, there was a remarkable variability between mining camps in how they allocated water. Some mining camp regulations referenced priority, others distributed water proportionately, and a few even placed strict limits on total diversions. Occasionally, miners employed riparian principles for water distribution. What this tells us is that miners were largely inventing rules as they went along. Each district was experimenting with ideas they thought would work best.[6]

The mining camps also brought us the notion of "use it or lose it." Stated simply, you had to actively work your mining claim to maintain your right to it. If you walked away from the claim, others could preempt it. Miners needed to keep up the use of water for milling to maintain their rights to it. This concept extended to the responsibility of using only what was needed so others could get water too. In later years, notions of water right abandonment and nonwaste were embraced by the courts and are now considered in every water right transfer.[7]

Settlers realized that to access water, they often needed to cross other people's land. Without this critical right-of-way, a person or corporation owning land along a stream could exclude everyone else and monopolize water resources for themselves. Historian Hubert Howe Bancroft called these monopolists "water-grabbers" who "fenced off the rivers from the common use of the people." Many settlers coming to Colorado resented the corporate elite and the privileged few who could buy up the best land for themselves. What most settlers wanted was to make sure that water was distributed to as many people as possible. Monopolizing water jeopardized Colorado's continuing development. Tensions over access to water came to a head on Bear Creek, west of Denver, in 1871 when Jason Yunker, a farmer who owned land away from the creek, sued Andrew Nichols, who owned land along Bear Creek, for preventing his access to water. Yunker, Nichols, and another farmer had built a ditch and verbally agreed to equally share in the water it carried. However, after they completed the ditch, Nichols decided not to pass the water along to Yunker. The case eventually ended up in front of Chief Justice Moses Hallett of Colorado's Territorial Supreme Court. Hallett, a gold prospector turned lawyer, understood the critical need for access to water in a place like Colorado. Hallett made a radical departure from the riparian laws in the eastern United States by crafting a uniquely western solution. In his decision, Justice Hallett wrote: "In a dry and thirsty land it is necessary to divert the waters of the streams from the natural channels, in order to obtain the fruits of the soil, and this necessity is so universal and imperious that it claims recognition of the law." Hallett ruled in favor of Yunker to grant him permission to take water across Nichols's land. Several years later, in 1876, Hallett's decision was embodied into Colorado's new constitution: "All persons and corporations shall have the right of way across public, private and corporate lands for the construction of ditches, canals, and flumes."[8]

Colorado's new constitution enshrined other principles of water distribution that evolved during the territorial days. It declared all unappropriated water "to be the property of the public" and also declared that water was "subject to appropriation." Water provisions in the constitution encapsulate the idea that the widest distribution of wealth is a necessary foundation for democracy.

As legal scholar David B. Schorr notes, water law "did not materialize out of thin air as a spontaneous response to geographic conditions in the arid west." Water law came about as "expressions of an agrarian, populist world view widespread in the western United States in the nineteenth century, an ideology locked in a secular struggle with corporate capitalism and speculative investment, particularly in western lands."[9]

For Colorado's miners and farmers "monopoly" was a vulgar word. As Schorr put it, monopoly was "an epithet for all the institutions agrarian reformers disliked or feared." Monopoly, Schorr continued, represented "the accumulation of property on a scale beyond what was practical for personal use, particularly for purposes of speculation or deriving income from tenants." Monopolies, from the perspective of farmers, violated the ideals of the founding fathers, including Thomas Jefferson, and philosophers like John Locke, whose natural-law, labor theory of property was instrumental in the founding of the United States. Rejection of monopolistic practices was another expression of the ideals that inspired the Homestead Act in the hopes of distributing the public domain to the greatest possible number of people.[10]

In 1861, when the Colorado Territory was created, eastern states followed a riparian legal doctrine to distribute water. This "riparian doctrine" was in turn based on English common law. In the riparian system, property owners owning land bordering a stream or lake had a right of access to the water and its use—for instance, to drive mills, hunt, fish, or consume reasonable quantities of water. Settlers in the West knew that under the riparian doctrine, wealthy individuals or corporations could buy riverfront property and exclude all others from access to water. If one person were to buy all the land bordering a river, he could effectively control far more land than he owned by denying all others access to water. In the arid West, where water is life, application of a riparian doctrine represented an existential threat to development, democracy, and the future of the region.

Colorado's arid landscape demanded a different approach to water management from the wetter East. Pioneers were digging ditches up and down the Front Range. By 1864, there were already thirty-two ditches on Boulder Creek. Gold miners were building flumes for sluicing operations from Left Hand

Creek south to Clear Creek and beyond. Miners faced the problem of allocating limited water supplies on these creeks. Actions pioneers took in the new agricultural communities and mining camps often preceded legislative action. In short, the Territorial Legislature was playing catch-up with the miners and farmers. And the courts made judicial law in the absence of legal precedents for their actions. Ever innovative, the settlers adapted mining rules to use with water. This created a sense of security and provided a rational approach to water allocation that facilitated orderly economic expansion.[11]

From these various sources of inspiration, the Colorado doctrine of water rights grew more or less organically from settlers' interactions with the environment. Settlers demanded a just distribution of the region's wealth. To achieve this ideal, Colorado's water rights system merged elements of rural agrarian populism, mining district water distribution rules, and *acequia* traditions of New Mexico and southern Colorado. For David Schorr, Colorado's territorial statutes, state constitution, and judicial decisions leading up to the groundbreaking *Coffin v. Left Hand Ditch Company* decision "were mainly concerned to prevent control of water by capitalists, and did so by breaking the common-law monopoly of riparian owners and opening access to the resource to all bona fide users."[12]

Today, Colorado's Prior Appropriation system has become a symbol for the preference of private property over common property, the privatization of public resources, and the rule of markets to distribute natural resources. Schorr recognizes the irony that we now have so little in common with the ideology of the people who framed the appropriation doctrine in the first place.[13]

I see additional ironic dimensions embedded in the Prior Appropriation doctrine. Settlers eventually set up farmers' unions (granges) to protect themselves from the corporate (mostly railroad) interests that were monopolizing access to markets. Settlers even organized cooperative mills as an alternative to corporate mills to process their grain. By today's standards, such homespun actions to protect their livelihoods might be denigrated as "socialist." The irony, of course, is that the descendants of those agrarian radicals—numerically most rural areas vote Republican—vigorously demonize anything that hints of socialism.

Even now, there are tensions between a populist desire for access to water and a capitalist desire to privatize that access. Echoes of that struggle reverberate today in conflicts over access to streams that pit wealthy landowners against fishermen and recreational boaters. It remains to be seen how this most recent conflict will be resolved. To better understand these modern tensions and how we got to where we are today, I think it makes sense to go back and examine how Colorado's appropriation doctrine crystallized into the form we now recognize. And there no better place to do that than by looking at the Left Hand Ditch Company.

THE LEFT HAND DITCH COMPANY

On Boulder and South Boulder Creeks, a large number of individual ditch companies serve water to their users and shareholders. This is in sharp contrast to Left Hand Creek, where a single ditch company controls, manages, and distributes almost all of the water that is used in the valley. This company is the Left Hand Ditch Company, and it owns the thirty-one originally adjudicated direct-flow decrees from Left Hand Creek along with two decrees that allow it to divert water from South St. Vrain Creek to Left Hand Creek. The Left Hand Ditch Company owns several reservoirs, including Allen Lake, Gold Lake, Lake Isabelle (in the Indian Peaks Wilderness), Left Hand Park Reservoir, and Left Hand Valley Reservoir, which it uses to store water for its shareholders. The Left Hand Ditch Company also uses Colorado River water from the Colorado–Big Thompson Project, both directly and through exchanges to increase water yields. As such, the Left Hand Ditch Company represents aggregate interests of all of the major ditches and water rights within the Left Hand Creek Watershed. A map showing the service area for Left Hand Ditch is shown in Figure 7.1.

The Left Hand Ditch Company itself has historic significance in Colorado water law and management. In 1882, the Colorado Supreme Court rendered its seminal decision in *Coffin v. Left Hand Ditch Company* that affirmed the Prior Appropriation doctrine as the fundamental governing principle in Colorado water law. In many ways, the story of the Left Hand Ditch is the story of water in the West.[14]

Little is known about what inspired the construction of a ditch deep in the mountains west of the small settlements and farms that were springing up on the High Plains along Left Hand Creek. Porter M. Hinman, the Left Hand Ditch Company secretary at the time it was incorporated, described the events in 1863 that led to founding the company. "The original construction

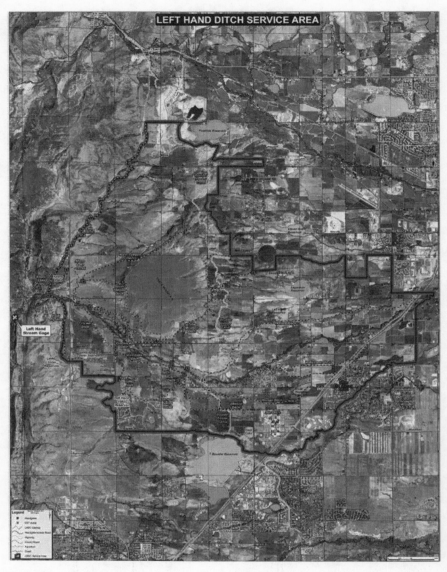

FIGURE 7.1. The Left Hand Ditch service area. Permission courtesy of the Left Hand Ditch Company.

of the ditch was conceived by Joseph H. Jamison," Hinman recalled. "We had about 100 acres in cultivation that year and Left Hand had no water; and Jamison was not interested in Left Hand but was living in another place—farming another place; he said he knew a place in the mountains where water could be got from the South St. Vrain into Left Hand."[15]

Hinman explained that a "committee of two" consisting of Joseph H. Jamison and Porter R. Pennock were the first to go up to the mountains to scope out the route for the ditch. Pennock, in particular, was a logical partner for Jamison as he had recently spent time hunting in the upper reaches of Left Hand Creek

FIGURE 7.2. Porter Pennock around 1864. Photo courtesy of the Longmont History Museum. Reprinted with permission.

and even crossed over to the St. Vrain in the winter of 1862 or 1863 with his future brother-in-law, Morse Coffin. Pennock learned the risks of Colorado winter travel when a blizzard dumped "snow fully up to our waists." His hard-earned familiarity with mountain geography came in handy once he and Jamison began scoping the ditch alignment. A photo of Porter Pennock from around 1864 is shown in Figure 7.2.[16]

More than a century later, Frank Gould, a longtime board member and superintendent for the Left Hand Ditch relayed some of what he had heard. "The story was told to me, probably second or third hand, but I think Rudolph Johnson told me he had heard the story," said Gould. "They said 'Wonder where we can get some water we can divert into Left Hand?' He said there was an Indian, called him Indian Jack who said, 'I can show you where you can get some water out of the St. Vrain with just a short ditch.' So that was one story, they went up there and dug a ditch."[17]

If Frank Gould's story is based in fact, then it was Joseph H. Jamison who heard about the possibility of building the ditch from Indian Jack. Hinman

FIGURE 7.3. A photo mosaic of the Left Hand Ditch Company's South St. Vrain Diversion. Photograph by author.

stated that he thought there were perhaps fourteen people who were originally responsible for constructing Left Hand Ditch. Hinman himself did not help dig the ditch, but sent a man up with the others to work because he was too busy on his farm to leave.[18]

Work on the Left Hand Ditch began on June 1, 1863, when Joseph H. Jamison, Lorenzo D. Dwight, Porter M. Hinman, Samuel Arbuthnot, William Arbuthnot, and about nine others organized, surveyed, and constructed the Left Hand Ditch from the South Fork of St. Vrain Creek over to James Creek. Left Hand Ditch is located west of the town of Ward and diverts water from the South St. Vrain to James Creek (a tributary of Left Hand Creek). The ditch itself is located in rugged terrain and cuts along the north face of a steep granitic hill for much of its course. When they built the original ditch, it was about one-half mile long, three feet wide at the bottom, and thirty-six inches deep. The original Left Hand Ditch had a decree for 40.77 cfs. Left Hand Ditch stands out because it was probably the first major irrigation ditch built in Colorado in such a remote mountainous location.

Figure 7.3 is a photo mosaic of the Left Hand Ditch Company South St. Vrain Diversion taken in about 2005. On the left is the diversion dam. In the middle is a metal trash rack to keep debris from flowing into the ditch. On the right is the headgate, which is an eight-foot manually-controlled radial gate. The state records the capacity of this structure at 400 cfs, and an average of about 15,000 acre-feet of water per year is diverted. In the distance is the dewatered South St. Vrain. In the 1860s and 1870s the diversion weir was a pile of boulders, and the headgate was made from timber.

Porter M. Hinman's father, Porter T. Hinman, came to Colorado seeking land and gold. The older Hinman was born in upstate New York and later moved to Ohio, where he taught school and started a family. Eventually the Hinmans ended up in Des Moines, where Porter T. spent a year as an assistant in the US Land Office. The elder Hinman's experience there probably made him aware of possibilities farther west. In 1860 the family migrated to Colorado, bringing 300 head of cattle with them. They settled on a 320-acre ranch on Left Hand Creek near Niwot. Porter T. lived on his farm with his wife, Mary, and six children. It was here that Porter M. became involved with the Left Hand Ditch.[19]

Right after building the Left Hand Ditch, Hinman and the others were able "to irrigate a few small patches of ground on Left Hand . . . that was a dry year and there was no water in Left Hand." In the first couple of years, the diversion dam washed out. In 1864 they enlarged the ditch, but it was a wet year and the ditch washed out again. It was dry again in 1866. In 1867, they repaired and enlarged the headgate and diversion. The ditch washed out once more in 1868, only to be rebuilt. Around 1869 they built a diversion dam of boulders that was three or four feet high and spanned the entire South St. Vrain River. This allowed them to divert the entire flow of the creek.[20]

As the Gold Rush began in 1859, twenty-three-year-old Samuel (Sam) Arbuthnot (Figure 7.4) and his twenty-four-year-old brother William (Figure 7.5) crossed the prairie from Iowa to seek their fortunes in mining. The two brothers first spent time at Gold Hill, Russell Gulch, and Central City. William soon returned to Iowa, but Sam stayed on and stuck with mining for several years. Eventually, Sam preempted some land along Left Hand Creek and started a farm. Hearing about the free land Sam had acquired, William returned for good in 1863. That year, William and the others began constructing the Left Hand Ditch. William also established a farm on 160 acres of land near Left Hand Creek that became known as the old Haystack Mountain farm. William's place was next to his German neighbors, John and Mary Bader. William must have become quite friendly with the family, because he married their daughter, Mary E. Bader, in the spring of 1869. A year later, Sam married Mary P. Johnson, the daughter of another neighbor. The Arbuthnots, Baders, and Johnsons eventually built and managed several ditches together on Left Hand Creek. William Arbuthnot lived on his farm until April 1882, when he was kicked in the chest while branding a colt and

FIGURE 7.4. Samuel Arbuthnot. Photograph courtesy of Donlyn Arbuthnot.
Reprinted with permission.

FIGURE 7.5. William Arbuthnot. Photograph courtesy of Donlyn Arbuthnot.
Reprinted with permission.

later died from his wounds. His brother Sam lived on until 1915. William
Arbuthnot lived just long enough to see his rights in the Left Hand Ditch
Company secured by the Colorado Supreme Court in 1881.[21]

While Hinman and company kept work going in the mountains, others
incorporated the ditch so they could raise money and levy assessments. On
February 27, 1866, Jamison, Dwight, and Edward P. Kinney incorporated the
Left Hand Ditch Company. Prior to that, all those involved were "joint owners and tenants in common." On incorporating, they issued 100 shares and
capitalized the company at $5,000. Among the first subscribers to the company
were settlers whose lateral ditches bear their names: Bader, Baum, Caywood,
Goyn, Hinman, Holland, Hornbacker, Johnson, Way, and Williamson. At the
time, $50 could buy you a share in the Left Hand Ditch Company. For people
who, on a good day, made three dollars this was a lot of money. Then on
March 24, 1866, they met at the Lower School House on Left Hand Creek to
adopt by-laws. The purpose of the company, they said, was to provide water
for mining, milling, and irrigating.[22]

Some settlers did not have the resources to pay for the shares outright, but
as long as they worked to pay off the shares and kept up their assessments,

their ownership was secure. Also among those first shareholders were the Arbuthnots, Jamison, and Dwight. Nicholas E. Bader and Porter Hinman served as the new corporation's first president and secretary, respectively. Later Samuel Arbuthnot served as president while Porter Hinman remained the secretary.

Water and ditch building was on the minds of more people than just a few settlers meeting in schoolhouses along Left Hand Creek. For during that same year of 1866, back in Washington, DC, Congress took up the matter of ditches and enacted legislation that authorized granting of rights-of-way across the public domain to construct ditches and canals for mining, agricultural, manufacturing, and other purposes. Whether the settlers on Left Hand Creek knew it or not, Congress had explicitly acknowledged their right to build the Left Hand Ditch on federal land in the mountains west of Boulder.[23]

When the company was incorporated, the owners of the various lateral ditches assigned their ownership over to the Left Hand Ditch Company. By doing this, they could pool their resources and proportionately share (based on the number of shares they owned) the water flowing down Left Hand Creek. This allowed them to avoid performing complex calculations under the individual lateral decrees and the St. Vrain diversion decree. Frank Gould put it this way: "they just decided the ditches would give up their individual rights on Left Hand to the Left Hand Ditch Company. There were several shorter ditches. The Bader was one, I think Proctor was another one and I believe there was an Altona Ditch which it is Haldi now . . . So they apparently all agreed that they would give up their individual Left Hand [creek] rights and would just group it all together. We will just have one class of shares and they will all be equal."[24]

Frank Gould's understanding encapsulates how the Left Hand Ditch Company has operated for as long as anyone that is associated with it can remember. In recent years, court decrees have confirmed this understanding, stating that the Left Hand Ditch Company "owns all of the direct flow decrees on Left Hand Creek and James Creek." As the owner, the Left Hand Ditch Company operates the decrees, but the individual lateral ditches (below their measuring flumes) remain the property of the individuals owning shares or interests in the laterals.[25]

By 1870, the value of the St. Vrain diversion to the farmers along Left Hand Creek was clear. On June 1, 1870, the company began enlarging the ditch.

Given that the work was in a remote site and the ditch cut through granitic bedrock, it is not surprising that the company reported the work was "very difficult." After the company completed the enlargement, the ditch was four-teen feet wide on the bottom, twenty-two feet wide on the top, and four feet deep. This allowed the company to claim an additional 685.23 cfs from the South St. Vrain. According to the water right decree, Left Hand Ditch could irrigate 23,000 acres.[26]

For the first few years, there seemed to be plenty of water to go around. But in 1879 the summer began to shape up as hot and dry. By the beginning of June, farmers along the St. Vrain were looking at the meager streamflows with some anxiety. Rubin Coffin, who lived about two and a half miles east of Longmont, was particularly concerned about flows in the St. Vrain River. Coffin knew there was a diversion owned by the farmers on Left Hand Creek that diverted water from the South St. Vrain into James Creek and then on to Left Hand Creek. Coffin also knew that the Left Hand farmers were getting sufficient water for their crops and he was not. It is noteworthy that Rubin Coffin lived downstream from the St. Vrain–Left Hand confluence. Since there were more and older ditches located upstream from him on Left Hand Creek, his goal was to stop diversions into Left Hand from the St. Vrain. If he succeeded, there would be fewer senior ditches that could divert water before it reached his farm.[27]

Rubin Coffin surely knew all about the Left Hand Ditch. After all, in 1864 his sister Ellen married Porter R. Pennock, one of the committee of two who surveyed the original route for the Left Hand Ditch. Pennock's close ties to the Coffins included joining Morse, George, and Ellen when they crossed the prairie to Colorado in 1862. In addition, one of Rubin Coffin's neighbors on the St. Vrain, James Andrews, helped build the ditch back in 1863. Even though Rubin Coffin's brother-in-law Porter was receiving St. Vrain water, Rubin did not like the idea that the Left Hand folks were getting water and he was not.[28]

Rubin Coffin approached his neighbors about the water situation on the South St. Vrain. James Andrews shared his concern. George A Starbind, John Kitley, Charles Webb, R. J. Franklyn, John Heartley, Garrett Clawson, and Louis H. Dixon, all neighbors and friends, were also anxious. Kitley had helped found Longmont's Highland Ditch, Starbind helped survey it, and his father was an early shareholder. As the season got drier and their situation became dire, the nine decided to take action.[29]

Rubin Coffin came to Colorado in 1866 to join his siblings. Before that, Coffin served under Colonel G. B. Turchin in Company G of the Nineteenth Illinois Infantry. From the time he enlisted in July of 1861 until he was mustered out in June of 1864, Coffin participated in Civil War battles at Stone River, Chickamauga, Mission Ridge, Resaca, and Altona Pass. Coffin's war experiences must have bordered on the horrific. Stone River alone had the highest percentage of casualties for both sides during the entire conflict. At Chickamauga the Union lost and suffered its second-highest number of casualties,

FIGURE 7.6. Rubin Coffin. Photo courtesy of the Longmont History Museum. Reprinted with permission.

a number that was surpassed only at Gettysburg. Coming to Colorado to escape the war-ravaged East must have been something of a rebirth for Coffin. On arriving in Colorado, Coffin acquired 160 acres near his brothers Morse and George and settled there in 1871. The photo in Figure 7.6 is of Rubin Coffin that was likely taken in the 1870s or 1880s. He wasted no time developing his farm. By the late 1870s, Coffin's farm, located along the St. Vrain just east of Longmont on the Boulder-Weld county line, made him one of the most prominent agriculturists of Weld County.[30]

Before Rubin Coffin arrived in Colorado, settlers enacted various laws governing how to use and claim water rights in the territory. Although the new state constitution embraced prior appropriation, many key elements remained undefined and the courts had not figured out how to enforce the doctrine on the ground. What the courts needed was a test case.[31]

On about June 21, 1879, Rubin Coffin, James Andrews, and seven others headed out from their farms on the St. Vrain. Most likely, they rode up Left Hand Canyon along the new toll road out of Altona. Somewhere along the way, they were joined by George W. Wilson, who was the superintendent for Left Hand Ditch. Wilson was probably agitated and tried to talk them out of their plans. Coffin and his neighbors had nothing to hide, and they thought they were justified about what they planned to do. Eventually they rode through the mining town of Ward and on to the Left Hand Ditch head-gate. There they found the three- to four-foot-high diversion that spanned the South St. Vrain Creek. As they suspected, all the water in the South St. Vrain was flowing into the ditch. Wilson undoubtedly protested, but he was far outnumbered. Coffin and the others got to work breaching the dam, and in short order the ditch was dry with all the water flowing down the South St. Vrain.[32]

In 1879, George W. Wilson was the station agent, postmaster, and senior member of his firm of G. W. Wilson & Son, grain merchants and propri-etors of a steam feed mill at Ni Wot (soon to be renamed "Niwot"), near Boulder, Colorado. Wilson was also the superintendent of the Left Hand Ditch Company. Wilson came to Colorado in 1872 for health reasons and at first lived near the mouth of Left Hand Canyon. He later moved to Niwot, where he was elected justice of the peace.

On June 24, 1879, Superintendent Wilson attended a hastily called meeting of the Left Hand Ditch board. Hinman, among others, had noticed that the water had stopped flowing during the night. Wilson reported to board pres-ident Samuel Arbuthnot that "a party of men from the St. Vrain and vicinity had taken out the dam and turned off the water from the ditch on Monday June 23." Breaching the dam galvanized the Left Hand board to action. The company adopted a motion authorizing Porter Hinman to muster a "suffi-cient force of men to repair the ditch and dam immediately and leave a suf-ficient force in opinion to keep the ditch full of water." Next they approved a motion for Hinman to "procure legal advice and see what could be done to establish the rights of the company also get the names of those who had damaged the property of the company."[33]

Porter Hinman mustered a number of men and went up to the mountains and rebuilt the dam, spending about $150 to $250 on the work. Each man was paid about $2.50 per day. This means that the repairs took somewhere between 60 to 100 man-days. To protect the rebuilt dam, the company hired guards at $2.50 per day to stand watch. At first, the company stationed four men at the diversion; this was later reduced to two, and after forty-five days these last two men were withdrawn.[34]

On July 3, the Left Hand board reconvened. Hinman reported that he had employed Major Richard H. Whiteley of Boulder to prosecute the parties who tore out the dam. From Wilson's report, the company knew that Rubin Coffin, Andrews, and others were responsible. Hinman reported that he had Whiteley sue the offenders. The suit, filed the previously day by Whiteley in Boulder County District Court, asked for damages to repair the dam and pay for lost crops; it also requested an injunction against Coffin and his companions from doing further damage. The Left Hand board authorized the immediate expenditure of $100 to pay Whiteley to "vindicate the title and rights of said company by the supreme power of the Law."[35]

Major Richard H. Whiteley was well known in Boulder. On arriving, he joined the town's small bar and helped raise funds to build the county's first courthouse. Formerly from Georgia, Whiteley (Figure 7.7) was in the cotton and wool manufacturing business at the outset of the Civil War. While working, Whiteley learned the legal profession. At the onset of the war, Whiteley entered the Confederate Army and served with its Western Army until its final surrender. At the war's end, Whiteley held the rank of major in the infantry under the command of General Joseph K. Johnston. During Reconstruction, Whiteley was a proponent of reintegrating the South into the Union. Whiteley maintained that the duty of the South was to unconditionally accept the results of the war. Moreover, Whiteley believed that it was important to enfranchise and protect the late slaves of the South. His advocacy for the former slaves earned him the epithets "scalawag" and "radical." In 1868, while still in Georgia, he was elected to the US Congress, but "defrauded by a false count." On two other occasions, it seems that he was denied a seat in Congress because of vote fraud. Whiteley was then elected to the US Senate by the Georgia General Assembly, but that election was later deemed illegal. By 1877, Whiteley was convinced that "there was no hope for a change in the feelings or the policy of the South," so he uprooted himself and moved to Colorado, settling in Boulder.[36]

Rubin Coffin, James Andrews, and the seven other defendants hired two well-known Longmont-area attorneys, John H. Wells and Colonel Byron Leander Carr, to defend them. Wells was born in 1842 and had had a varied career. Prior to the war, Wells was an apprentice printer and attended Knox College. With the war's start, Wells enlisted in the Illinois volunteer infantry and rose to the rank of lieutenant, junior grade, by its end. His biographer

FIGURE 7.7. Major Richard H. Whiteley. Image from http://
www.cemeteryworks.com/cccwss/cccwss_whiteley.html,
accessed September 2, 2012.

described him as a "silver-tongued orator," amateur actor, and musician—
all excellent skills for a lawyer. He went on to read law and on admission
to the bar partnered with Carr. Wells invested in railroads, becoming the
vice president of the Colorado Central Railroad. He was then elected to
the Territorial Legislature in 1871. At various times Wells served as the Boulder County attorney and Boulder County judge. Coincidentally, Wells was
a good friend of Ed Kinney, one of the Left Hand Ditch founders. Wells
was with Kinney and narrowly escaped death on February 22, 1870, when

a revengeful highwayman gunned down his friend—killing him—near Burlington, Colorado.[37]

Colonel Byron Leander Carr had gained prominence around Boulder County before he was retained by Coffin and the others. One biographer called him a "father of Colorado irrigation law," so his water credentials were strong. Carr (Figure 7.8), too, was a Civil War veteran who had participated in some of the toughest fighting of the war. In April 1861 Carr volunteered with a New Hampshire battalion in the Army of the Potomac and saw service at the second Battle of Bull Run, the Shenandoah campaign, the siege

FIGURE 7.8. Colonel Byron Leander Carr. Photo from Smiley, Semi-Centennial History, vol. 2: 213.

of Richmond, and finally Appomattox. In September 1864, Carr's left thumb was shot off. He was not deterred and remained in the fight. Tragedy struck Carr at Appomattox on April 9, 1865—the day before Lee's surrender—when he was hit by grapeshot and so seriously wounded in his right arm that field doctors amputated it at the shoulder. After the war, he joined the other veterans in migrating west. Carr first went to Greeley but then "walked across the sagebrush and cactus prairie" to join the Chicago-Colorado Colony at Longmont. Once there, Carr became its secretary. Carr was eventually admitted to the bar, became the district attorney for the Second Judicial District, and served as a delegate at Colorado's Constitutional Convention. In Wells and Carr, Coffin and the other defendants had an adept legal team representing them.[38]

It took almost two years, but eventually a jury trial was held in Boulder County District Court on May 17, 1881, to establish the facts and to settle all the claims. Hearing the case was the Honorable Thomas Mitchell. Although he was the judge of the First Judicial District of Colorado, Mitchell had been in Colorado for only two years when Coffin and the St. Vrain farmers tore out the dam. Like many men of his time, he served in the Union

Army. After the war, Mitchell studied law and was admitted to the bar in 1867. When he came to Colorado, Mitchell settled at Georgetown, establishing a law practice. In January 1880, the judgeship of the First Judicial District opened up, and Governor Pitkin appointed Mitchell to fill the vacancy. As a circuit judge, Mitchell oversaw Clear Creek, Gilpin, Jefferson, Boulder, Grand, Routt, and Summit Counties.

When the Boulder trial convened, it was well attended. The trial would have been of keen interest to Coffin and his eight partners. Their attorneys, John H. Wells and Byron Leander Carr, sat with them. Sitting across the aisle was the Left Hand Ditch crowd. Samuel Arbuthnot, Hinman, Wilson, and others from the company had a significant stake in the outcome and were present. Major Whiteley was sitting with the Left Hand folks. It is also known that Harper M. Orahood, the district attorney for the circuit, was present. Orahood was well known and understood the capabilities of the men on both sides of the isle. He had served with some of them back in 1864, when he was in the 100 Day service as captain of Company B in the Third Colorado Cavalry commanding the east division of Chivington's forces at Sand Creek. John J. Ellinghaus, the Boulder County sheriff and deputy US marshal, along with Edward J. Morath, court clerk, was also there. And, of course, there was the jury of seven men, led by their foreman, J. M. Jones.

At the trial, Porter Hinman testified about the founding of the Left Hand Ditch Company, the construction of the ditch, and the events of 1879. Samuel Arbuthnot provided additional perspectives on the matter. George Wilson testified about how Coffin and the others tore out the dam. Counsel for Coffin admitted that Wilson was telling the truth. Then James Andrews testified that he had helped construct the Left Hand Ditch back in 1863, even though by 1879 he was living along the South St. Vrain and was one of Coffin's partners in tearing out the dam. Andrews said that he had never sold his interest in the Left Hand Ditch. When cross-examined by Whiteley, Andrews admitted that he abandoned his interest in the ditch, stating, "I guess so. I never done anything to it since."[39]

Wells and Carr argued, "we shall contend that the common law doctrine of riparian proprietorship is fully applicable to this county and is in full force." They argued that Coffin and the others were entitled to the water from the South St. Vrain because their clients settled along the creek. They also attacked the legality of the incorporation and early chain of title for the

Left Hand Ditch Company. In addition, they maintained that Coffin and the others were within their rights to tear down the dam.[40]

Whiteley countered that in 1861 the Territorial Legislature provided that when "lands are too far removed from the stream, and the owner has no water facilities on those lands, he shall be entitled to a right of way through the farms and tracts of land which lie between him and the stream to convey water." Whiteley argued that the Left Hand Ditch Company was legally organized and incorporated to supply water to the farmers along Left Hand Creek.[41]

At the conclusion of the trial the jury rendered its decision: "We the jury empaneled and sworn to try the issues in said case do hereby find the said issues for the plaintiff, against each and every of the above named defendants, and assess the plaintiff damages at $90.00."[42]

Left Hand Ditch won on every legal point, but Hinman, Arbuthnot, and the other shareholders were not awarded anywhere near the amount of damages they hoped. Coffin and his neighbors went away empty-handed.

Even after the trial concluded, emotions remained raw. On the same page of the *Boulder News and Courier* announcing an upcoming appearance in Boulder of P. T. Barnum's Greatest Show on Earth, a letter from "Pratt Boy" exclaimed, "'Thou shalt not steal' is both a human and a divine command. Some of the residents of Longmont and vicinity are totally indifferent thereto, or they would not deliberately appoint thieves to proceed to the point in the mountain where the left hand ditch was taken out, and *steal* water belonging to our farmers."[43]

Unhappy with their defeat in Boulder County District Court, Coffin and his neighbors appealed the decision to the Colorado Supreme Court. Chief Justice Samuel Hitt Elbert took interest and presided over the appeal and heard the arguments of Coffin and Left Hand Ditch.[44]

Chief Justice Samuel Hitt Elbert (Figure 7.9) was a well-known figure in Colorado who served as the secretary of the Colorado Territory between 1862 and 1867 and later as territorial governor between 1873 and 1874. Elbert's name was enshrined by the naming of one of Colorado's highest peaks after him. Elbert was a member of Colorado's early elite and married the daughter of Territorial Governor John Evans. Elbert was acting governor while Evans was in Washington during the 100 Day callup that culminated in the Indian massacre at Sand Creek. Elbert's name could raise emotional responses among fellow Coloradans. The historian Hubert H. Bancroft

FIGURE 7.9. Chief Justice Samuel Hitt Elbert. Photo from https://www.colo rado.gov/pacific/archives/samuel -hitt-elbert. Reprinted with permission.

described Elbert and Evans as "cold blooded mercenary men, ready to praise themselves and each other profusely, but have in reality but little patriotism." Bancroft felt that Elbert and Evans embodied the "quintessence of meanness in more ways than one." Nevertheless, Elbert was thoroughly familiar with the territorial laws that he came to interpret while sitting on the bench. Throughout his career, Elbert advocated irrigation development in the West and even founded the influential Western Irrigation Conference at Denver during the summer of 1873. Elbert helped draft Colorado's constitution three years later.[45]

While governor, Elbert outlined his views toward Colorado's evolving system of water laws. He held that the state should own "the water of its streams" but assign the "control of its distribution among canal owners." This principle would assure that "no one would be allowed to divert the water from the natural bed of the stream to the injury of those having previously acquired and vested rights." Events on St. Vrain Creek gave Elbert the chance to elaborate his ideas about prior appropriation in Colorado.[46]

When the Supreme Court reached its decision, it took the opportunity to articulate principles of water administration that were evolving since the earliest territorial days. Chief Justice Elbert wrote that the doctrine of priority of right to water by prior appropriation "has existed from the date of the earliest appropriations of water within the boundaries of the state." Because of Colorado's arid climate, Elbert found that "artificial irrigation for agriculture is an absolute necessity." A bit farther along Elbert continued:

> It has always been the policy of the national, as well as the territorial and state governments, to encourage the diversion and use of water in this

country for agriculture; and vast expenditures of time and money have been made in reclaiming and fertilizing by irrigation portions of our unproductive territory. Houses have been built, and permanent improvements made; the soil has been cultivated, and thousands of acres have been rendered immensely valuable, with the understanding that appropriations of water would be protected. Deny the doctrine of priority of superiority of right by priority of appropriation, and a great part of the value of all this property is at once destroyed.[47]

Elbert's court underscored that the riparian doctrine had no place in Colorado, concluding that "the common law doctrine of giving the riparian owner a right to the flow of water in its natural channel upon and over his lands though he makes no beneficial use thereof, is inapplicable to Colorado."[48]

With this decision, Elbert affirmed the doctrine of prior appropriation as the fundamental governing principle in Colorado water law. Coffin, Andrews, and the others had their answer in unsparing language: according to the verdict of the jury, they were the "wrongdoers" when they trespassed to take out the dam. To this day, Left Hand Ditch diverts the flow of the South St. Vrain to irrigate Left Hand Valley. An image of the water rights decree for Left Hand Ditch is shown in Figure 7.10.

THE LEGACY OF COFFIN V. LEFT HAND

The *Coffin v. Left Hand* decision effectively prevented speculators and corporations from buying up riparian lands and later denying water to settlers who had already established farms. It stamped out the prospect of corporations monopolizing water for their private gain. As David Schorr has pointed out, "the decisions of Colorado's Supreme Court in its first decades, including the Coffin decision itself, advanced a like commitment to equal access and the prevention of concentration of wealth in the form of water."[49]

In hindsight, Elbert's decision can also be seen as part of the agrarian-populist movement that was gaining ascendance during that time. Even though Elbert was a member of Colorado's elite and was in the position to profit from concentrating the ownership of water, he believed that the widest access to water possible was the best way to ensure Colorado's development and prosperity. Agrarian populism favored Jeffersonian values over the capitalist elite that wished to accumulate natural resources for themselves.

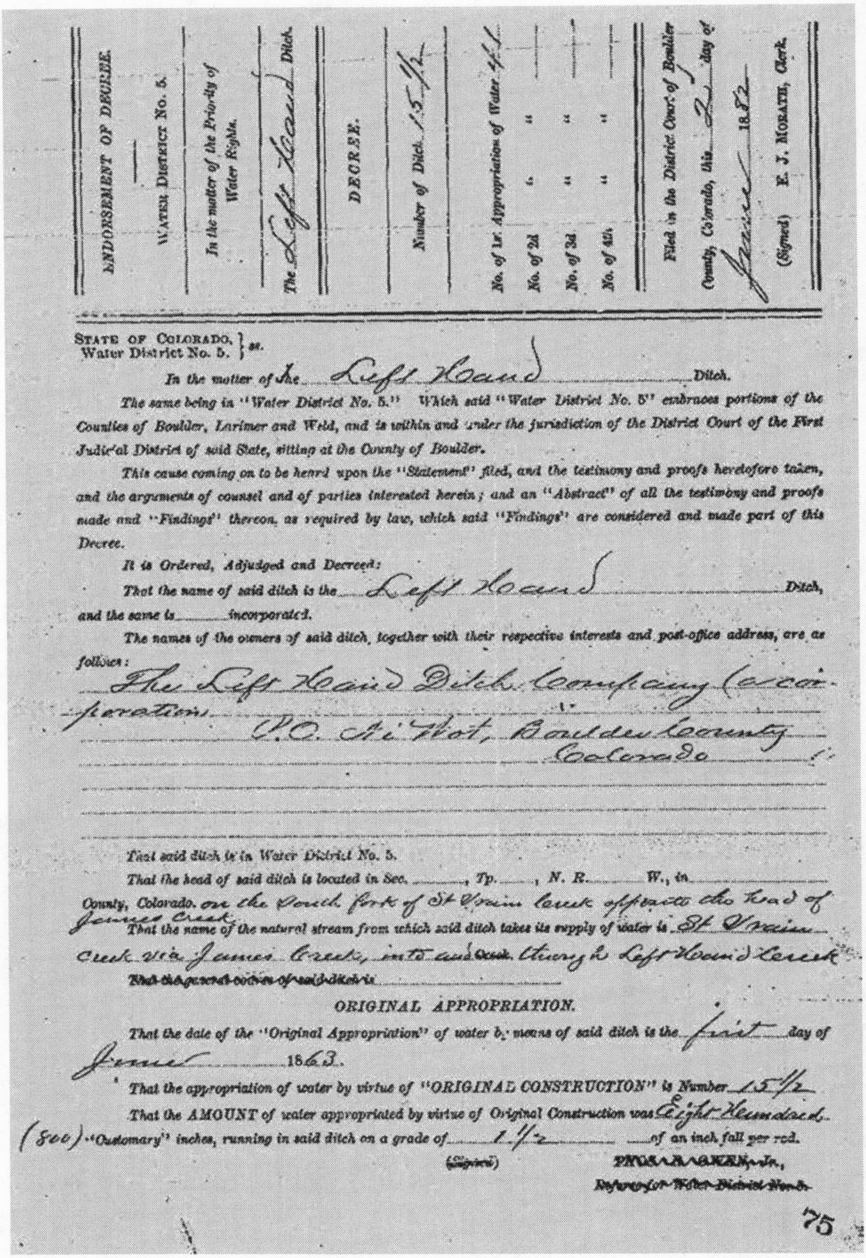

STATE OF COLORADO, }
Water District No. 5. } ss.

In the matter of the _Left Hand_ _____ Ditch.

The same being in "Water District No. 5." Which said "Water District No. 5" embraces portions of the Counties of Boulder, Larimer and Weld, and is within and under the jurisdiction of the District Court of the First Judicial District of said State, sitting at the County of Boulder.

This cause coming on to be heard upon the "Statement" filed, and the testimony and proofs heretofore taken, and the arguments of counsel and of parties interested herein; and an "Abstract" of all the testimony and proofs made and "Findings" thereon, as required by law, which said "Findings" are considered and made part of this Decree.

It is Ordered, Adjudged and Decreed:

That the name of said ditch is the _Left Hand_ _____ Ditch, and the same is _____ incorporated.

The names of the owners of said ditch, together with their respective interests and post-office address, are as follows:

The Left Hand Ditch Company (a cor-
poration)   P.O. Ni Wot, Boulder County
Colorado

That said ditch is in Water District No. 5.

That the head of said ditch is located in Sec. ____, Tp. ____, N. R. ____ W., in _____ County, Colorado, on _the South fork of St Vrain Creek opposite the head of James Creek_

That the name of the natural stream from which said ditch takes its supply of water is _St Vrain Creek via James Creek, into and across through the Left Hand Creek_

~~That the general course of said ditch is~~

ORIGINAL APPROPRIATION.

That the date of the "Original Appropriation" of water by means of said ditch is the _first_ day of _June_ 1863.

That the appropriation of water by virtue of "ORIGINAL CONSTRUCTION" is Number _15½_

That the AMOUNT of water appropriated by virtue of Original Construction was _Eight Hundred_ (800) "Customary" inches, running in said ditch on a grade of ____ _1½_ ____ of an inch fall per rod.

(Signed)   _THOMAS A. GREEN, Jr._
Referee for Water District No. 5

75

FIGURE 7.10. The water rights decree for Left Hand Ditch.

Coffin v Left Hand cemented democratic and egalitarian principles favoring a wide distribution of water rights to the maximum number of people.

With the *Coffin v. Left Hand* decision, the basic tenants of prior appropriation were settled. What followed was over 130 years of refinements to the basic laws of water rights management. For those who had the capital to buy water rights, such as cities and industries, they could work within the system to accumulate water rights to meet their needs. Eventually, the system became a symbol of entrenched interests and environmental degradation. Prior appropriation is now routinely attacked as denying widespread access to water even though it originated in a spirit of maximum utilization.

In 1991, Charles Wilkinson wrote an "obituary" of the Prior Appropriation doctrine. In it he traced the expansion of the system, from its roots in California and Colorado to Elwood Mead, the Wyoming Constitution, and its expansion across the arid states. Prior appropriation had become the law of the West. He saw the hand of prior appropriation guiding William Mulholland and his Owens Valley water grab. Prior appropriation would soon become the basis for building huge projects like Elephant Butte on the Rio Grande, which, in the name of progress, would smother the livelihoods of many small farmers the project was designed to help. Wilkinson recalled the "dam-building orgy of the 1930s through the 1960s" and the role prior appropriation played there. Glen Canyon would drown at the altar of prior appropriation. But prior appropriation meant progress in the American Century. To westerners, "water is our heritage. Take it—take it all, if you can. . . . Progress will result." At the pinnacle of its influence and through the sheer weight of its success, prior appropriation soon weakened as Indians, environmentalists, state water planners, and federal officials started to question its goals. And now prior appropriation has died, Charles Wilkinson maintained. It died of popular mistrust spread by the likes of the *Milagro Beanfield War* and President Jimmy Carter's 1977 "Hit List" of water projects. But most of all, Wilkinson asserts, it died close to where it was born on January 19, 1991, when the Environmental Protection Agency famously vetoed Denver's Two Forks Dam.[50]

But prior appropriation never died. It lives on in places like Boulder Valley each summer as ditch riders' call for water and the water commissioners dial back junior headgates to deliver the precious commodity. To many, prior appropriation is more important than ever. It lives on in the 22,000 ditches spread around Colorado and the many more that divert water across the West. What has changed is that prior appropriation must operate alongside the environmental laws and instream flows that muscled their way to the table. Diminished somewhat perhaps, but prior appropriation still dominates the phone calls between all the ditch riders and water commissioners in the American West. Even though ditch presidents fret over wetland permits and Corps of Engineer approvals for their projects, at the end of the day the water they receive arrives by virtue of a decision made a long time ago on Left Hand Creek.[51]

NOTES

1. Wilkinson, "Prior Appropriation," 5.

2. Colorado Const., art. XVI.

3. Act Concerning Irrigation, Dec. 7, 1859, Provisional Laws and Joint Resolutions Passed at the First and Called Sessions of the General Assembly of Jefferson Territory 214 (Omaha, Nebraska Territory: Robertson and Clark, 1860).

4. See Davis, *El Gringo*.

5. Matthew W. Irwin v. Robert Phillips and others, Supreme Court of California, 5 Cal. 140 (1855).

6. See Schorr, "Appropriation as Agrarianism." The overarching goal in mining camp rules, as Schorr points out, appears to be the widest possible distribution of water.

7. Ibid.

8. Bancroft, *History of Nevada*, 643; Hallett's decision would eventually come to be known as the Colorado Doctrine. It was one of the first expressions of the Prior Appropriation doctrine that would eventually be fully settled with the events on the Left Hand Ditch. For more on Yunker v. Nichols, accessed April 20, 2015, https://www.colorado.gov/pacific/sites/default/files/EarlyWaterLaw_0_0.pdf; see also Hobbs, "Colorado Water Law," 30, for an overview of Yunker v. Nichols; Colorado Const., art. XVI, § 7.

9. Schorr, "Appropriation as Agrarianism," 35.

10. Ibid., 27.

11. Ibid., 8.

12. Ibid., 3.

13. Ibid.

14. Coffin v. Left Hand Ditch Company, 6 Colo. 443 (1882).

15. Testimony of Porter M. Hinman, 1881, Boulder County District Court, Coffin v. Left Hand Ditch Company, Folio 141. Original documents of Coffin v. Left Hand Ditch, including the testimony and Supreme Court decision, are located in

the Colorado State Archives, filed under cases No. 885 and Boulder County District Court Cases No. 1103 and No. 1203.

16. Pennock helped build the ditch and years later helped found the Farmers Milling and Elevator Company, a farmer-owned and -operated company set up to protect shareholders from price fixing by leading grain mills. See Newby, *Longmont Album*, 61; Coffin, letter to *Longmont (CO) Ledger*, February 17, 1911.

17. See Ochs, *Water the Basis for Success*, 12.

18. Testimony of Hinman. Joseph Jamison came to Colorado from Kentucky in 1859 with his wife Ellen and six children. He was about forty years old in 1863 when work on the Left Hand Ditch began.

19. Bixby, *History of Clear Creek*, 644.

20. Testimony of Hinman, Folio 141.

21. Bixby, *History of Clear Creek*, 605; Donlyn Arbuthnot, personal communication, 2013.

22. Testimony of Hinman, Folio 144. Many years later, an additional 5 shares were issued, bringing the total number of shares in the company to 105. Between 1866 and 1868 they sold shares until all the shares were taken. Over the ensuing decades, shares and farms were sold and subdivided. The numerous transactions of stock resulted in a large number of fractional shares. This created significant accounting difficulties. To correct the problem, the Left Hand Ditch Company in 1969 executed a 160-to-1 stock split that resulted in the current 16,800 total shares that are outstanding.

23. The 1866 Mining Grant, H.R. 365, granted the rights-of-way for the construction of ditches and highways across the public domain to facilitate mining. The statute has given rise to considerable controversy and has been used by antienvironmental activists today as a justification for desires to plow roads into wilderness areas and national monuments.

24. Ochs, *Water the Basis for Success*, 81.

25. See, for example, Colorado Water Court Case No. W-7596-74.

26. Boulder County District Court Case No. CA1284.

27. Tree ring data suggest that 1879 was the second-driest year since active settlement began around Boulder in 1859. For hydrological reconstructions, see Smith et al., *Potential Consequences of Climate Change*.

28. *Portrait and Biographical Record*, 925; Newby, *Longmont Album*, 17.

29. John Kitley would later join Porter R. Pennock and others to form the Farmers Milling and Elevator Company; Articles of Incorporation of the Highland Ditch Company, Colorado Secretary of State, available at http://www.sos.state .co.us/biz/BusinessEntityHistory.do?quitButtonDestination=BusinessEntityDetail &pi1=1&nameTyp=ENT&entityId2=19871000986&srchTyp=ENTITY&master FileId=19871000986; Newby, *Longmont Album*, 61.

30. *Portrait and Biographical Record*, 925; see also Newby, *Longmont Album*, 20.

31. Schorr, "Appropriation as Agrarianism," 41; Colorado Const., art. XVI, § 5.

32. Testimony of James Andrews, Coffin et al. v. the Left Hand Ditch Company, 1881, Folio 183.

33. For Wilson, see Bixby, *History of Clear Creek*, 708; testimony of Hinman Coffin et al. v. the Left Hand Ditch Company, 1881; see also Left Hand Ditch Company Records of the Board of Trustees for 1879, 145, Left Hand Ditch Company files.

34. Testimony of Hinman, Coffin et al. v. the Left Hand Ditch Company, 1881, Folio 157.

35. Left Hand Ditch Company Records of the Board of Trustees for 1879, 146, Left Hand Ditch Company files.

36. Bixby, *History of Clear Creek*, 697.

37. St. Vrain Historical Society, *They Came to Stay*; Bancroft, *History of Nevada*; Allen, "Pioneer Life in Old Burlington."

38. St. Vrain Historical Society, *They Came to Stay*; Smiley, *Semi-Centennial History*, 2:213–17; Bixby, *History of Clear Creek*.

39. Testimony of Andrews, Coffin et al. v. the Left Hand Ditch Company, 1881, Folio 184.

40. Brief of argument of defendants, Coffin v. Left Hand Ditch Company, Supreme Court Case No. 885 (1881).

41. Brief of argument of appellants, Coffin v. Left Hand Ditch Company, Supreme Court Case No. 885 (1881), 9.

42. Verdict, Coffin v. Left Hand Ditch Company, Boulder County District Court Case No. 1103 (1881).

43. "NiWot Notes," *Boulder* (CO) *News and Courier*, July 23, 1880.

44. The appeal was heard on February 3, 1882, even though it was part of the December 1881 term.

45. Hubert H. Bancroft, Denver, 1884, transcribed by R. L. Hafen (Boulder: University of Colorado Archive, April 30, 1924).

46. Rocky Mountain News, January 2, 1878.

47. Ibid.

48. Ibid.

49. Schorr, "Appropriation as Agrarianism," 11, 63–64.

50. Wilkinson, "Prior Appropriation."

51. Hobbs, "Priority."

Corporate Opportunities

"Between 1880 and 1885 many parts of the state were
gridironed with canals built in advance of their need,
simply and solely because of the belief that by thus
securing possession of the water supply they controlled
the values of all the land tributary to their ditch."
—*Elwood Mead, 1888*[1]

By about 1870, the "pick and pan" era of the Gold Rush had mostly faded
away. Replacing it were industrial-scale mining operations. Equipment for
these endeavors required railroad transport and financial support from eastern and foreign sources. The railroads themselves were an expression of
Colorado's emerging industrialization. Suddenly Coloradans found themselves closely connected to commodity markets and manufacturing centers
such as Chicago and New York. This transformed Colorado's economy. It
was during this period that lignite and coal began to replace timber as a critical fuel, and with it, industrialized fuel mining emerged as an important local

DOI: 10.5876/9781607323822.c008

industry. With the new links to the outside, agriculture underwent a drastic transformation too, transitioning from farms that produced goods primarily for domestic consumption and local markets to commodity product agriculture (in particular, wheat and sugar beets), which was geared toward sending produce to distant markets. Likewise, the cattle industry evolved into a commodity industry as cattlemen discovered that they could transform the grass of the High Plains into beef and send it to eastern markets via railroads. It is within this economic context that ditches, once built by pioneers for their own needs, started to get constructed by land developers and entrepreneurs desirous of selling irrigated farms to Colorado migrants. These new water developers figured out that they could incorporate the ditches and sell land bundled with water in the form of ditch shares to prospective farmers. By corporatizing ditches, water rights became readily transferrable, and developers commodified and extracted profit from one of Colorado's critical natural resources. It is these innovations that ushered in what has sometimes been termed the "Corporate Ditch Era."

Corporations were revolutionizing the settlement process by the mid-1870s. Railroad companies led the way as they gained title to vast tracts of land on the High Plains in the aftermath of the Indian wars, and they wasted no time seeking ways to add value to their vast windfall. It was at this time that large infusions of capital from the eastern United States and Europe began pouring into Colorado. Once corporate capital became available, developers blazed roads and railroads into unoccupied areas to invite settlement and extract available resources.

The business model for corporate ditch building in Colorado was quite elegant in its simplicity. First, private investors, railroad companies, or other corporate developers would acquire a large block of undeveloped land. Railroads, for example, acquired huge tracts on either side of rail lines through government incentives to extend rail service. Some investors bought government or railroad land outright, while others acquired land for themselves and family members by preemption under the Homestead Act. Once the land passed to private hands, engineers developed plans and claimed the necessary water rights. They would then incorporate a ditch and sell enough shares to build the ditch while reserving sufficient stock to irrigate lands they owned. Elsewhere developers would sell the land and then rent the water to farmers. Using these tactics, irrigation companies profited by bringing new settlers to Colorado.

The economics of building ditches to add value to dry land was favorable. Investors in 1873 could purchase land from the US government for $2.50 per acre, and by digging a ditch they could turn around and sell land for $50 to $100 per acre. Advantageous economics like this led many people to build ditches. In 1874 alone, developers built more than fifty miles of ditches around the Boulder area. As historian Greg Silkensen put it, nineteenth-century irrigation developers were kindred spirits to the venture capitalists building the Internet in the 1990s.[2]

At first, the economics for the settlers buying land under the ditches was quite favorable too. This win-win arrangement between developer and farmer fueled market interest. A *New York Times* article from 1873 described the abundance that an irrigated Colorado farm might produce. For each acre planted to a crop, a farmer could expect to receive 28 bushels of wheat, 40 of oats, 150 of potatoes, 25 of corn, and 35 of barley, which were bountiful yields for that time. And because of the great demand coming from nearby mining camps, farmers were generally in the position to set and get the prices they wanted for their crops. If they could just obtain land and water, a farmer could build a profitable farm.[3]

Corporate ditch digging emerged in places like Boulder Valley as a consequence of the local geography. By 1862, the bottomlands in Boulder were spoken for, and settlers were left homesteading higher ground. Groups of private landowners began cooperating to raise the capital and labor to build more ambitious ditches. Farmers, North Boulder Farmers, Silver Lake, Davidson, Boulder and White Rock, and FRICO were all early Boulder-area corporate ditches that blazed the trail for the huge systems that would get built in the 1880s and 1890s elsewhere in Colorado and the West.[4]

As the corporate interest in ditch digging grew, so did corporate investment. Part of the trend was the Englishman Francis L. Carter-Cotton, who incorporated the North Poudre Land, Canal, and Reservoir Company in 1880 on Cache la Poudre Creek in Larimer County, Colorado. His plan was to irrigate 16,000 acres between the North Fork of the Poudre and Box Elder Creek. Carter-Cotton proposed building a fifty-two-mile-long ditch and estimated the cost at $175,000 to $200,000. A British company, the Colorado Mortgage and Investment Company of London, backed Carter-Cotton. Locally, Carter-Cotton's concern was nicknamed the "English Company." However, by 1880, the costs of ditch building had increased substantially, and to Carter-Cotton's disillusionment the first mile of ditch constructed cost a staggering $75,000, or nearly twenty times his initial per-mile estimate. These expenditures fore-shadowed problems to come. Carter-Cotton eventually lost control, other investors sank good money after bad, but the ditch was eventually built. Even so, the company fell into default. By 1901, a group of northern Colorado investors bought the company for $67,000—a fraction of its construction cost—and reincorporated it as the North Poudre Irrigation Company.[5]

Although corporate ditch building in places like Boulder never rose to the level seen elsewhere in the West as Elwood Mead's quote in the chapter epigraph suggests, the business model that others followed to great success had its inception along Foothills streams like Boulder and South Boulder Creeks. The reason for this is simply that these first corporate ditches were built near settlements, which meant that there was generally less land avail-able to develop. Early corporate ditches represented a progression in effort from the nearby pioneer ditches that had already proven the feasibility of irrigation. Corporations took the next logical step by designing schemes to develop the terraces between creeks. Farther east more land was available, but those areas would have to wait until someone demonstrated feasibility close to existing settlements. Once the feasibility of irrigating the terraces was proven, large systems like the North Poudre Land, Canal, and Reservoir Company or developments like the Greeley Colony became imaginable. A survey of some of Boulder's corporate ditches shows how these initial efforts paved the way for larger projects elsewhere.

EMERGENCE OF CORPORATE DITCHES

In the short span of just three years, the logic of geography and resource that facilitated Boulder Valley's earliest settlement had drastically changed. With the rush to acquire fertile bottomlands nearly complete, freshly arrived settlers were forced to devise new strategies to acquire water for their farms and ranches.

When twenty-two-year-old Lemuel McIntosh and his new wife, Angelina Stuart, started out for Colorado in 1860, he was thinking about mining, not farming. McIntosh was born in Indiana and later lived in Illinois and Iowa. He joined the state militia and was stationed at Spirit Lake in 1858 to help suppress the Indians. In April 1860, he married Angelina Stuart, and they decided to make the trip across the plains. The newlyweds traveled first to Omaha, where they acquired the ox teams for their long haul. Their migration brought them up the South Platte River and eventually to Gold Hill above Boulder. Once there, McIntosh tried his hand at mining and quit that for a homestead two and one-half miles south of Boulder that they acquired in 1862. The family built a log house, and McIntosh joined with neighbors to build the South Boulder and Bear Creek Ditch.[6]

With his farm situated above the creek, McIntosh had to consider other alternatives for irrigating his land. His solution was to start digging the ditch farther upstream along the creek and guide it along a shallow gradient to his land. This made the South Boulder and Bear Creek Ditch one of the first "high line" ditches in the state. Work began on May 25, 1862, and McIntosh and his neighbors had the ditch operating by July 1. With their ditch, the McIntoshes raised cattle, grew hay, and eventually planted an orchard of about 1,500 trees.

A few months later, on October 1, 1862, work on Farmers Ditch began. At the time, Farmers Ditch was the longest and most ambitious ditch undertaken in Boulder Valley. Its construction enabled the irrigation of about 3,000 acres of land north of Boulder Creek. With an investment of about $6,500, Jonathan A. Tourtellot and Jerome Thomas built the nearly six-mile-long ditch. Like McIntosh, Tourtellot and Thomas placed the headgate far upstream so that they could deliver water to the dry terraces where they owned land. Irrigation water brought immediate benefits, and by 1872 the debts to build Farmers Ditch were paid off. Most importantly, by building Farmers Ditch, Tourtellot and Thomas proved that irrigating otherwise dry terraces were both feasible and profitable.[7]

The principal motivator behind Farmers Ditch, Jonathan A. Tourtellot, was born in Rhode Island in 1812. He grew up on a farm, but by 1834 Tourtellot was working in the mercantile business. Then in 1836 he married Maria Wade, and they returned to his old farm for six years. In the early 1850s the Tourtellots moved to Illinois, where Jonathan got into the hotel business with his brother-in-law Frederick A. Squires, who was married to Maria's twin sister Miranda. Early on during the Gold Rush, the two families decided make a go of it in Colorado and traveled together, settling in Boulder. On arriving, they engaged in the hotel and merchandising businesses until 1865, and eventually lumber and mining.[8]

As soon as Farmers Ditch began delivering water, lands irrigated by it increased in value. Tourtellot, Squires, and business partner Jerome Thomas cashed in on the increased values by selling land (eventually much of it was annexed into Boulder) to new residents. Over the next decade they made dozens of land sales along the ditch. This put them at the forefront of investors to figure out that they could flip cheap land at a profit once they provided water.

When it was built, Farmers Ditch became the first source of water for most of Boulder. In 1869 the open ditch was still used for domestic purposes throughout the town. Laterals from Farmers Ditch distributed water parallel to city streets. So when the ditch froze, people who relied on it were greatly inconvenienced. One newspaper remarked, "there's no water in the farmer's ditch, which should supply the tidy housewives of Boulder who are grumbling considerably thereat." In addition to the threat of freezing, it was very difficult controlling water quality in open laterals during the age of horse transportation. In addition, leaking laterals and their repair and cleaning created ongoing concerns. Pipes eventually replaced the open ditch, and memories of these inconveniences faded.[9]

Unfortunately, Jonathan Tourtellot would not live long enough to see much of the dramatic growth that occurred along his ditch. Tourtellot died at age fifty-eight in 1870. His well-attended funeral celebrated Tourtellot's role in building Farmers Ditch. The image in Figure 8.1, believed to be of his funeral, shows mourners at the First Congregational Church wending their way toward the cemetery on Boulder's Sunset Hill. Water flowing through a lateral from Farmers Ditch dominates the image. Farmers Ditch itself is just barely visible in the distance at the top of the lateral.

Because of the company's seniority and its proximity to the city of Boulder, its shares have long been acquired by the city. Over the years, the city initiated seven water rights transfer cases involving nearly 40 percent of Farmers Ditch water rights. Its seniority gives Farmers Ditch a fairly long irrigation season. On average, Farmers Ditch is turned on in early May and is run until mid-September. Even in dry years the ditch has sufficient seniority that it might run water for about seventy-five days. Farmers Ditch was formerly used to power one of Boulder's first grain mills. The mill, once located near the mouth of Boulder Canyon, was built by Andrew Douty in 1866. It was later known as the Yount mill after Mrs. E. B. Yount, who began operating it in 1877.[10]

FIGURE 8.1. This photograph is believed to be of Jonathan Tourtellot's funeral. Mourners at the First Congregational Church wend their way toward the cemetery on Boulder's Sunset Hill. Water flowing through a lateral from Farmers Ditch dominates the image. Farmers Ditch itself is visible in the distance at the top of the lateral. Photograph courtesy of the Carnegie Branch Library for Local History, Boulder Historical Society Collection. Reprinted with permission.

Farmers Ditch jump-started development north of Boulder. As residential neighborhoods grew around the ditch, it became a neighborhood amenity. The ornamental bridge in the photo in Figure 8.2 hints at the affluence of the Mapleton Hill neighborhood. Notice the well-manicured ditch banks and the neat rock wall lining the channel. Farmers Ditch still flows through an open ditch in Mapleton Hill as it did in this photograph from over one hundred years ago.

Figure 8.3 is photo a taken about 1890 at the Orchard Grove Fruit Farm, owned by Joseph Wolff. Wolff's harvest suggests how productive the dry tablelands north of Boulder became once irrigation water was supplied. Wolff, a passionate abolitionist writer and acquaintance of John Brown of Civil War fame, moved from Ohio to Boulder and took up farming. Once here, Wolff created a prosperous fruit farm. He also grew hay and other

FIGURE 8.2. An ornamental bridge crossing Farmers Ditch (perhaps late 1880s to 1890s) in Boulder's Mapleton Hill neighborhood. Photo by J. B. Sturdevant, unknown date. Photograph courtesy of the Carnegie Branch Library for Local History, Boulder Historical Society Collection. Reprinted with permission.

crops. Before Wolff began irrigating, the area's aridity complemented the former name of the site, Rattlesnake Ranch. Wolff's farm was eventually annexed and subdivided. A Boulder neighborhood still carries the Orchard Grove name.[11]

As Boulder grew around it, Farmers Ditch has adapted to changing urban conditions. Ditch leakage became a nuisance in some areas. In response, the company installed a 2,300-foot-long, forty-three-inch-diameter siphon through North Boulder Park in 1953. Construction of the siphon freed up sixteen building sites in the Newlands subdivision of Boulder. One worker died of injuries sustained on the project.

As the city expanded, farms were annexed and subdivided, leaving fewer irrigated acres. Over the years, Boulder has continued to purchase Farmers Ditch shares. First, the city's water utility bought shares for municipal purposes. Later, as the city began buying open space, it acquired a number of farms irrigated by the ditch. With these purchases, the city now owns almost 75 percent of the outstanding shares in the company. Similarly, the City of

FIGURE 8.3. Joseph Wolff's Orchard Grove Fruit Farm about 1890. Photo by William Hassebroek, about 1890. Photograph courtesy of the Carnegie Branch Library for Local History, Boulder Historical Society Collection. Reprinted with permission.

Lafayette has purchased a majority of shares in the South Boulder and Bear Creek Ditch to feed its urban demand. Building these ditches opened up the possibility of irrigating otherwise dry lands far from creeks and created opportunities for entrepreneurs to build ditches as a gateway to real estate riches. While these ditches helped blaze the way for corporate opportunities, it was others who took the idea and ran with it.

REFINING THE CORPORATE MODEL: THE DAVIDSON DITCH AND RESERVOIR COMPANY

When Boulder was settled in 1859, the town was initially dominated by miners. Bucking the rush to the mountains was William H. Davidson and partner Samuel Breath, who knew that the real money to be made was in supplying the miners and not toiling in the mountains themselves. Davidson and Breath established Boulder's first grocery and mining supply store in a log cabin they built on the northeast corner of 11th and Pearl. Later their store became Boulder's first hotel, the Boulder House. Figure 8.4 is a photo of William H. Davidson later in life.[12]

Figure 8.4. William H. Davidson. Photograph courtesy of the Carnegie Branch Library for Local History, Boulder Historical Society Collection. Reprinted with permission.

Davidson, born in Philadelphia in 1817, spent about eight years in the California gold fields during the 1850s before coming to Colorado. While there he worked placer bars, built a sluice ditch, and engaged in farming and lumbering. Davidson's work brought him into many remote areas of California. On one of these occasions in 1857, Davidson was traveling in the mountains with partners John Wade and Morris Davis. One evening they settled into camp. As Davidson recalled it, they selected a secure camping site, one that looked defensible. This was necessary because they heard that potentially hostile Indians were in the area. Soon after darkness fell, the crack of a gun sounded, and Wade shouted, "I'm shot." Wade, bleeding from the chest, stumbled and fell into Davidson's arms. As Davidson rushed to help his friend, Morris was shot through his neck with an arrow. Davidson now had to contend with his mortally wounded friend Wade and the severely injured Morris while preparing for an inevitable rush of Indians intent on finishing them off. But the Indians did not charge immediately. As they waited, Wade died. Davidson hid near the edge of camp with his rifle and got ready. Eventually, when the first Indian rushed forward, Davidson took aim and shot him in the chest. At that, the remaining Indians backed off to regroup, so Davidson and Morris took their chance to escape, leaving everything behind, including Wade. They rushed to the nearest town to get medical help for Morris. Backed up by a large group of settlers, Davidson returned to the camp to retrieve the body. When they got there, they discovered that the Indians had burned Wade's corpse.

Although traumatic, Davidson's California experience did not deter him from pursuing his fortune in the gold fields. His western dreams were, however, interrupted when his brother died unexpectedly. With this personal tragedy, Davidson was forced to return to Iowa for several years to attend to family business.

But his yearning for gold did not diminish during his days in Iowa. Hearing of the Colorado gold strikes, Davidson lost no time to cross the plains to newly founded Boulder. Davidson spent the better part of 1859 in Boulder and in the fall moved on to Golden. At Golden, he built one of the first ditches in the territory to supply water to a placer called the Arapahoe Bar. This early ditch may have extended a structure begun by David Wall in the first days of the Gold Rush. Davidson's ditch to Arapahoe Bar was later incorporated into the Farmers Highline Canal and Reservoir Company. From his base in Golden, Davidson traveled around the territory looking for opportunities in mining and milling. Eventually, Davidson wound up operating a six-stamp mill near Ward.[13]

In 1864, Davidson traveled to New York where he organized the Ni Wot Company, a mining concern named after the Arapahoe Indian chief that the settlers would kill that winter. A year later Davidson, accompanied by partners Henry Dakin, C. S. Trowbridge, and others, went on a trip to help reconnoiter the best route for the Union Pacific Railroad and used this as an excuse to seek mining opportunities. In Idaho City, Idaho, his company purchased a gold mine. Meanwhile, Davidson ordered a fifty-stamp mill from Chicago and had it shipped to Iowa. Davidson then took a steamer from San Francisco to New York and from there traveled by train to Iowa to supervise the transfer of his stamp mill to Colorado. Getting the stamp mill to Colorado was a herculean effort requiring a wagon train pulled by 450 yoke of oxen. Davidson maintained through his life that this was the largest wagon train to have ever crossed the prairie. And that was near the height of Indian hostilities on the plains. By August of 1865, Davidson's company had the mill up and running. Then, after only three months of operations, the mill burned. Undeterred, Davidson got it back in operation where it ran for a couple of more years.

Eventually, Davidson helped pioneer the development of Colorado's coal and lignite industry. Davidson recognized the need for fuel for smelting ore and heating homes; he knew that it was only a matter of time before railroads would add to that demand. Then in 1870, Davidson started building a 600-acre farm east of Boulder. Davidson was joined by investors that included William

A. H. Loveland (railroad industrialist and town founder) and Henry Teller (Colorado's second senator) to form the Davidson Coal and Iron Company. This coal company acquired over 7,000 acres of land adjacent to Davidson's farm. The partners understood that water was critical for coal and iron mining and was essential to develop the area's agricultural potential.

Seeing the need for water, Davidson and his partners undertook building a ditch on South Boulder Creek east of Eldorado Springs to divert water to their properties. This placed them, like Tourtellot and Thomas on Farmers Ditch, among the first to recognize that by building a ditch they could make terraced lands arable and thereby turn a tidy profit selling land. We "want a fair price for the land, but give easy terms," Davidson said, adding, the "extra price is more than compensated by the advantage we offer. Without water the land was worthless for farming—we have made it all available, ready for the hand of the settler." Davidson's business model was frequently replicated. Their ditch ran along the northern slope of the Marshall bluffs and across what was later named Davidson Mesa, continuing north and east through Boulder Valley. Constructing Davidson Ditch (incorporated as the Davidson Ditch and Reservoir Company) cost a modest $13,000. Davidson claimed that in building the ditch a settler could grow thirty bushels of wheat per acre. With water Davidson's farm prospered. Upon his death, his obituary reported that there "are few people in Boulder County who do not know this bluff old pioneer, and all who know him cannot help but like and respect him."[14]

The emergence of corporate ditches was intertwined with the other two great corporate interests of nineteenth-century Colorado: mining and railroads. Perhaps nowhere is this more vividly illustrated than in the cancelled stock certificate from the Davidson Ditch (Figure 8.5). First, note that the stock was originally for the Davidson Coal & Iron Mining Company. Davidson had not yet printed dedicated stock certificates, so he used what was on hand. Davidson simply crossed out the words "Coal & Iron Mining" and wrote in the word "Ditch." As shown on the certificate, Davidson capitalized the company at $32,000, but as he later claimed, the ditch only cost $13,000 to build. By selling all of the outstanding stock, the initial investors more than doubled their money.

Shares on this certificate were issued to one of Davidson's partners, William A.H. Loveland. It was during 1864 that Loveland helped found the

FIGURE 8.5. A Davidson Ditch stock certificate that shows the interconnection of mining, agriculture, and transportation in nineteenth-century Colorado. Photograph by author.

Colorado, Clear Creek and Pacific Railway, which was later renamed the Colorado Central Railroad as a proposed (and never completed) connection to the transcontinental railroad in Cheyenne. The town bearing Loveland's name was eventually built along that line. Railroads became major landowners in Colorado and went on to develop ditches as a way to add value to their extensive landholdings and create customers for their freight service. Mines helped provide capital for both the railroad and ditch construction, and the ditches supported food production for all the workers. This triangle of industries converges in this single stock certificate.

William Davidson was a prolific ditch digger. In addition to the Davidson Ditch and the ditch he dug to deliver water to the Arapahoe Bar near Golden, also called the Davidson Ditch, he built a third ditch called the Dry Creek Davidson Ditch. This third ditch bearing the Davidson name takes water from South Boulder Creek to irrigate land Davidson formerly owned along Dry Creek.

Davidson Ditch construction began in April, 1872. Initially, Davidson reported that there were 7,152 acres being irrigated. With an 1872 appropriation date, the Davidson Ditch is considered a fairly junior water right for South Boulder Creek. Unless a shareholder has a supplemental water supply, the ditch right alone is insufficient to grow vegetable crops. Consequently, shareholders primarily use their water to grow hay, alfalfa, or to irrigate pasture grass. Even so, the ditch yields enough water that shares have been sold and transferred to municipal uses. This has resulted in four water rights transfers that have moved water out of the ditch to the cities of Lafayette and Louisville.[15]

William Davidson proposed filling "natural basins" along the ditch with "artificial lakes" to serve as reservoirs and fish preserves. However, these plans were never fulfilled. But this did not prevent other shareholders from using the ditch to deliver water to storage. Henry Teller took advantage of the ditch to carry water to his farm and stored it in lakes he had constructed. That put Teller on the forefront of settlers building reservoirs in Colorado. Teller's farm was located near the terminus of Davidson Ditch, where he eventually built five reservoirs for irrigation.[16]

The idea of building storage by the company lingered. In 1920, Davidson Ditch commissioned an engineering estimate for a reservoir on South Boulder Creek. The proposed 1,795-foot earthen dam, which was slated for construction on the Dunn Ranch, was to inundate thirty-five acres and hold 700 acre-feet. The company retained Fred Fair's engineering firm to prepare the estimate. Nothing ever came of the proposal, and the Davidson Ditch gave up pursuing storage.[17]

Bob Clyncke, a longtime Boulder Valley farmer, and his wife Bev live along the Davidson Ditch. Clyncke's farm has been in the family for 116 years. The Clynckes grow wheat and hay and raise cattle. For many years Bob served as the Davidson Ditch president and ditch rider and Bev as the corporate secretary. "I wound up taking care of the ditch," Bob said, "because I couldn't find anyone else to do it . . . Everyone said 'Hey you're doing all the work, you might as well get the money!', and so that's what I did." What Bob didn't say was how generous he has been over the years with his time and energy for the meager compensation he received. "Corn needs water in August, and Davidson is a junior ditch," Bob said, explaining, "We are out of priority around the fourth of July usually, and it was just too hard trying to get the yields." For that reason many shareholders grow alfalfa and hay rather than risk growing vegetable crops that need water to ripen in August. Like many ditch superintendents, Bob Clyncke gets frustrated by the way neighbors disregard his ditch: "People think the ditch is just a garbage disposal and they throw all kinds of trash in there. They don't think about the fact that someone has to pull OUT all the things they throw IN!"[18]

By "someone," Bob meant himself. Although Bob retired as president in 2010, he remains active on the ditch board. Bev served on the board for nearly as long as Bob was president. That makes the ditch something of a family affair. Both Bob and Bev's lives are deeply entwined with the ditch. One striking thing about working with them is how dedicated they are in keeping the ditch running. That's the kind of value you can't easily classify. Shareholders know that, with them around, the company is in good hands.

Operations on Davidson Ditch are fairly typical for companies its size. Since Davidson Ditch owns no storage, its operating season is limited. Davidson Ditch was built during the time when companies began realizing that direct-flow water rights alone were insufficient for many crops. Another ditch just downstream from the Davidson, the Goodhue, was built even later than the Davidson. Since it is junior to the Davidson, its season is even shorter. Once the Davidson and Goodhue were built, it was clear that any ditches built afterword would need storage or they simply wouldn't provide enough water for irrigating crops.

As early investors like William Davidson sold their interests, the farmers and ranchers that used the water took control. Eventually, the Davidson Ditch's location near Lafayette and Louisville led to those municipalities buying shares. By the 1970s, the City of Boulder began buying shares as it acquired land for its expanding Open Space program. Eventually municipal ownership overtook private ownership, and the company is now dominated by the cities. Municipal ownership notwithstanding, an active minority of farmers and ranchers participate in company affairs and take water to irrigate their properties.

William H. Davidson's entrepreneurial efforts at building ditches were soon emulated by others as the business model of corporate ditches spread. It is fitting then that one of the largest corporate ditch endeavors ever undertaken in Colorado, FRICO, has major components of its system paralleling William Davidson's ditch.

THINKING BIG: COMMUNITY DITCH AND FRICO

Where others sought their fortunes prospecting for gold hidden in the mountains, Joseph Marshall made his by mining something that was lying in plain sight: coal. Many settlers began digging for coal encased in the Cretaceous sediments on the eastern flank of the Front Range as early as 1864. But what set Marshall apart from others is that he and his partners quickly recognized that coal would be necessary for Colorado's industrialization. By 1866, Marshall had purchased a "lode" containing coal south of Boulder. Two years later he consolidated his holdings when he received a patent from the US government for additional lands in the area.[19]

When the Denver Pacific Railroad completed its connection between Denver and the Union Pacific Railroad in Wyoming in 1870, the demand for coal rapidly expanded. Marshall was in the right place at the right time to cash in on this new market. The Boulder Valley Railroad was soon built into Boulder, and David Moffat financed an extension to Marshall's coal fields. With the construction of the Colorado Central Railroad and other railroads that followed it, Marshall could readily sell his product to any number of customers. One customer was his neighbor William H. Davidson, who used Marshall's coal to smelt hematite into iron. This iron was then cast into a variety of products at the Colorado Territory's first foundry in Denver.

By the 1880s Colorado had moved away from its pioneer roots and was undergoing major transitions in the organization of its labor force. Previously, opportunities seemed to be plentiful for new migrants moving into the state to take up farms and make a go of life in Colorado. As the new state grew and industrialized, its emerging industries began employing large numbers of wage laborers. By this time there were far more opportunities for someone as an employee than as a self-employed pioneer. Although new migrants were fortunate to secure work, it often came at the steep price of dangerous work sites, low wages, and long days. Marshall's Consolidated Coal Company was at the center of this new industrial economy.

For Marshall, the owner, business was good and profitable. With his success, the value of the mines quickly increased, and by 1885 the Marshall Consolidated Coal Company issued some $2 million in capital stock. However, much of this wealth was achieved by exploiting the workers in his employ. While Marshall grew rich, many of his miners lived at or near poverty levels.[20]

Initially, while Marshall dug for coal, the agricultural potential of his land lay untapped. With the 1880s irrigation boom in full swing, anyone who could build a ditch and irrigate dry land along Colorado's Front Range was looking to make a profit in real estate. Marshall had undoubtedly seen what Davidson and others had done to develop their land.

It was in this setting that Joseph Marshall and two other well-known nineteenth-century coal magnates, Samuel F. Rouse and John Lathrop Jerome, built Community Ditch. At its outset, Community Ditch was essentially a coal company affair, but it allowed them to add an agricultural component to their land holdings. Like Marshall, his partners were successful industrialists. Samuel F. Rouse actively invested in coal properties and was a principal in William Jackson Palmer's Colorado Fuel Company, a precursor to Colorado's largest industrial corporation, the Colorado Fuel and Iron Company, or CF&I.

Marshall's other partner in Community Ditch was John Lathrop Jerome, also a coal magnate. Jerome came to Colorado in 1873 to become a public school superintendent but changed direction and studied law. After being admitted to the Colorado bar, his law practice grew and propelled him on to other endeavors. He eventually became a principal in the CF&I. Jerome also established the Overland Cotton Mill Company, investing in an industry that used coal to run the milling equipment. At CF&I Jerome became embroiled in the bitter power struggles over company ownership that John D. Rockefeller Jr. initiated. When the Rockefellers prevailed, Jerome left CF&I but exited a very wealthy man. Eventually, Jerome built a remote and opulent vacation retreat called La Hacienda, near Buffalo Creek, southwest of Denver. But happiness eluded him. Soon after he started vacationing there, Jerome was dead, apparently committing suicide by overdosing on opiates. He was forty-nine at the time.[21]

Work on Community Ditch (also known as Community Canal) began with its water appropriation on June 6, 1885. Community Ditch takes its water from South Boulder Creek near the mouth of Eldorado Canyon just north of the entrance to Eldorado Canyon State Park. When the water rights were appropriated, the company claimed that it would irrigate over 22,000 acres. Community Ditch delivers water to Marshall Lake and irrigates farms as far east as Broomfield, Colorado. Community Ditch was enlarged in 1905 to a capacity of around 575 cfs, but that capacity has diminished in recent years through nonuse to about 175 cfs.[22]

Eventually Marshall, Rouse, and Jerome sold their interests in Community Ditch to irrigators who were developing lands along the ditch. Chief among them was Charles Toll, whose descendants still actively farm and ranch in Boulder County. Toll had acquired extensive agricultural interests in Boulder and Jefferson Counties. But Toll would not own Community Ditch for very long. In 1902 FRICO purchased Toll's Community Ditch shares and took control of the company. It was at this point that Community Ditch became a division of FRICO, as it remains today.[23]

FRICO came into existence at the height of the corporate irrigation era. With FRICO, its principals embarked on an ambitious project to build an irrigation empire in northern Colorado. FRICO was incorporated in 1902 by Joseph Standley, Milton Smith, and Thomas B. Croke. To create their company, they bought several early ditches—including Community Ditch—and then set out to link them to new reservoirs and canals. This way, they could bring more land into production or sell water to existing farmers who needed additional supplies. They began in Jefferson, Adams, and Boulder Counties and soon extended their efforts to lands east of the South Platte River in Weld County. For its time, FRICO was a complex and expensive undertaking with an initial capitalization of $2 million.[24]

Standley, Smith, and Croke were prominent Colorado businessmen when they founded FRICO. Joseph Standley was among the earliest settlers in the state. Standley started out with several mining interests near Central City, and by 1859 he owned the California Mine. Standley later acquired interests in Denver National Bank and the First National Bank of Central City. Smith came to Colorado in 1889. An attorney, Smith specialized in mining, corporation, irrigation, and insurance law. Croke, a rancher, also owned a Denver furniture store and in 1911 was elected to the Colorado Senate.[25]

To develop FRICO, Standley incorporated a construction shell company to manage his projects and organized several quasi-municipal irrigation districts that sold nearly $4.3 million in bonds. Standley and his partners also raised cash through a series of complex stock deals involving construction contractors, the Franco-American Bank, and an insurance company. If this didn't make things complex and sufficiently opaque, they also formed at least four real estate companies to buy and sell lands that FRICO would irrigate. In all, they acquired or created about twenty-one different ditch, reservoir, land, and holding companies to build the system. To prove the feasibility of

FIGURE 8.6. Workers constructing a tunnel for Community Ditch east of Eldorado Springs. Photograph courtesy of the Carnegie Branch Library for Local History. Reprinted with permission.

their plans, they enlisted some of the leading hydraulic engineers of the time, including a Panama Canal commissioner and engineer Elwood Mead, who would later lead the Bureau of Reclamation.[26]

In 1909 FRICO began enlarging the Burlington Ditch, renaming it the O'Brian Canal (after its engineer, Peter O'Brian), and enlarged Barr Lake. FRICO performed major work on Community Ditch during this time. Figure 8.6 shows workers constructing a tunnel for Community Ditch east of Eldorado Springs.

Even though Marshall Lake was large, it was dwarfed by the far more ambitious Standley Lake project that FRICO was then building. Initially FRICO planned to construct a 100,000-acre-foot lake behind a 140-foot-high earthen dam. Had FRICO completed the initial plan, it would have been the largest earth-filled dam in the world. The Standley Lake project was so grandiose (see Figure 8.7), that some boosters even made comparisons to parts of the Panama Canal. Standley Lake construction started in 1907, but plans were scaled back, and a smaller reservoir was completed in 1912. As construction progressed, a dedication was attended by the Colorado and

FIGURE 8.7. Construction of Standley Lake in 1909. Reprinted with permission.

Wyoming governors and many other dignitaries. "Cultivation and irrigation will transform the face of Nature," the effusive US Secretary of Agriculture James Wilson claimed, adding that the Standley Lake project "seems certain of great success."[27]

But in their haste to construct the Standley Lake, FRICO took shortcuts—such as using inferior fill in the critical core of the dam—that soon had serious repercussions. In a properly constructed dam, this fill prevents water from seeping through the face of the earthen structure. Within a year of construction, cracks began to appear, and in 1914 a major slide occurred on the dam's downstream face. FRICO repaired this, but then a second major slide occurred in 1916, this time on the upstream face of the dam. The dam stood in a state of disrepair until 1922. Standley and his partners drastically underestimated the costs of building so many canals and reservoirs. By 1910, FRICO's rapid expansion led to significant financial difficulties. One of most troubling was that that FRICO owed a Kansas City contractor about $900,000. FRICO

FIGURE 8.8. Construction of the enlarged diversion dam for the Community Canal in February 1909. Photograph courtesy of the Carnegie Branch Library for Local History. Reprinted with permission.

soon fell behind on payments to Toll for its Community Ditch purchase just as other creditors began clamoring for payment. Bonds issued by the irrigation districts began to default. With the company unable to repay its debt, FRICO was forced into receivership and Standley and his partners lost control.

FRICO was reorganized, and since much of the construction had already been completed, the company remained a valuable irrigation concern when it emerged from receivership in the early 1920s. FRICO's financial troubles demonstrated for many that private capital was no longer sufficient to build large irrigation systems. In the future, large irrigation projects along Colorado's Front Range would need some form of federal or state subsidy to succeed.[28]

Figure 8.8 shows the construction of the enlarged diversion dam for the Community Canal in 1909. Enlarging the dam allowed FRICO to expand

Community Ditch diversions nearly 700 percent. Eldorado Springs resort is in the background of the photo.

Construction of Marshall Lake was one of FRICO's early successes. Work began in March 1902. Originally the dam was twenty-three feet high, but it was later enlarged twice so that the total depth of water now exceeds seventy-two feet. Today Marshall Lake has a total decreed capacity of 20,952 acre-feet of water. Because of the seniority of its decrees, when the company fills Marshall Lake, it often diverts the entire flow of South Boulder Creek during the winter at its Community Ditch diversion. This practice dries up South Boulder Creek for some distance below Eldorado Springs.[29]

Community Ditch and the Marshall Division are a small part of the FRICO system, accounting for only 6 percent of the company's 8,000 total shares. FRICO's system is organized around its reservoirs. Other FRICO units include the Standley Lake, Milton, and Barr Lake Divisions. FRICO serves municipal and agricultural users in Louisville, Broomfield, Superior, Northglenn, Thornton, South Adams County, Brighton, and East Cherry Creek Valley. FRICO operates four major reservoirs and about 400 miles of canals. Its service area extends across 3,500 square miles from Denver to Greeley. On the west side of the FRICO system, the Standley and Marshall Divisions are largely urbanized. East of the South Platte River, FRICO's Barr, Henrylyn, and Milton Divisions remain largely agricultural. FRICO's Henrylyn Division alone provides irrigation supply for more than 60,000 acres.

Today FRICO is the largest private ditch company operating in Colorado. FRICO's Marshall Division includes Community Ditch and Marshall Lake and is commonly referred to as FRICO Marshall. Because of its strategic location to Louisville, that city has purchased approximately one quarter of the company shares for its water supply.[30]

FRICO is known for aggressively pursuing opportunities for generating income to subsidize its operations. By the early 2000s the company had about $2.2 million in reserve and, unlike most ditch companies, did not need to charge its shareholders any assessment. With FRICO's pursuit of income, the company gained a reputation for being difficult to work with and litigious. In the mid-2000s the company's fortunes began to change when it lost a major proceeding in front of the Colorado Supreme Court. FRICO had attempted to market surplus yield and applied to water court to gain flexibility in managing its system. As part of its efforts, it planned to sell excess water to the East Cherry Creek Valley Water and Sanitation District. In water court, objectors challenged FRICO's estimates of historical consumptive use of water rights, the effect of historic decrees and new structures related to FRICO's use of its Burlington Canal, the FRICO's application of the so-called "one-fill rule" (which limits how many times a company may fill a reservoir under a storage right), and how these actions might affect other senior rights to use the waters along the South Platte River. After an expensive, multi-year court proceeding, the Colorado Supreme Court ruled in favor of the objectors who opposed FRICO. Shortly after the decision, FRICO's longtime attorney was replaced, and its general manager retired. Also, with a nearly depleted reserve, the company began setting assessments for stockholders.

BOULDER'S LAST CORPORATE DITCH

Silver Lake Ditch is sometimes termed Boulder's "last ditch." Although many small ditches and laterals were constructed in Boulder Valley after Silver Lake, it was the last corporate ditch built in the valley. Once built, there was simply not enough land available to justify another project of its size near Boulder. By the time George Oliver and James P. Maxwell decided to build the ditch, the script for corporate ditch building was well rehearsed. Their plan, like the other corporate concerns before them, was to build a ditch and reservoir system so that they might bring water to land they owned and cash in on its enhanced value.

Begun in 1888, Silver Lake Ditch was originally referred to as Maxwell and Oliver's Ditch and later, after Oliver sold out, just Maxwell's Ditch. When it was constructed, Maxwell and Oliver estimated that it could irrigate just over 1,000 acres of formerly dry land. Silver Lake Ditch flows just below Maxwell's old house, which still stands on a mesa in northwest Boulder.[31]

James Philip Maxwell, the man most closely associated with the ditch, was born on a farm in Walworth County, Wisconsin, in 1839 to James A. and Susan Maxwell. Maxwell studied at Lawrence University of Appleton, Wisconsin, and graduated in 1859. In 1860 Maxwell joined his father at Omaha, Nebraska, and took six weeks to travel by horse across the plains to Denver. Maxwell's first wife passed away in Wisconsin before he came to Colorado. Maxwell went first to Central City, then to Nevadaville and Lump Gulch, where he engaged in placer mining. Soon afterward, Maxwell was elected sheriff of

FIGURE 8.9. James Philip Maxwell.

the Gold Dirt District and stayed with it for about a year. Maxwell moved on and was soon involved with one of the many sawmills that were being erected in the mountains west of Boulder. Ever busy, he assisted building the Boulder and Blackhawk wagon road and then operated it as a toll road for several years. Once in Colorado, Maxwell married Francelia O. Smith, who was also a Wisconsin native.[32]

In 1863, Maxwell partnered with his brother-in-law, Clinton Monroe Tyler, to build a steam sawmill on South Boulder Creek. Tyler gained some notoriety a year later when Governor Evans commissioned him as a captain of US Volunteers during the Indian hostilities of 1864. At their mill, Maxwell and Tyler manufactured lumber that they marketed in Central City, Blackhawk, and Cheyenne. Later Maxwell sold his interest to help his father operate a sawmill at the mouth of Four Mile Creek in Boulder Canyon. In 1870 Maxwell moved into Boulder. For several years, Maxwell served as deputy US mineral and land surveyor. Then, in 1872, Maxwell was elected to the Territorial Legislature. When Colorado was admitted to the Union in 1876, Maxwell (Figure 8.9) became a member of the first state senate and served as president pro tem in 1879. Maxwell's political ambitions were not confined to state politics. In 1878 he was elected Boulder's mayor and served for two years. Maxwell's engineering expertise led to his hiring by a number of ditch companies to testify as an expert witness in Boulder County District Court in the first general stream adjudication for Boulder Creek in 1882. Then from 1882 until 1888 Maxwell worked as a surveyor in western Colorado. It was during this time that he gained his familiarity with the upper Boulder Creek Watershed, where he would later enlarge natural lakes for reservoirs. If all of this did not keep Maxwell busy, he also served as a director of the Anderson and Leggett ditches. Boulder's Maxwell Street is named after him.[33]

In 1888, the same year he started digging the Silver Lake Ditch, Maxwell was appointed state engineer and served until 1893. In that position, Maxwell

oversaw the development of irrigation and the construction of reservoirs, bridges, and roads throughout
Colorado. By this time, Maxwell
was regarded nationally as irrigation
expert. This earned him a spot on
the front cover of the first issue of
Irrigation Age, the influential magazine published by William Ellsworth
Smythe, whose nearly evangelical
promotion of irrigation helped lead
to the passage of the Reclamation
Act by Congress in 1902. Concurrently, Maxwell engaged in the cattle
business, purchased ranches, and
made various real estate investments.
Along the way, Maxwell became the
president of the Steamboat Springs
Company, which platted the town of
Steamboat Springs. Back in Boulder,
he platted the fifteen-acre Maxwell's
addition and became the owner of
the Maxwell block in Boulder. He

FIGURE 8.10. George Oliver. Photograph courtesy of the Carnegie Branch
Library for Local History, Boulder
Historical Society Collection,. Reprinted
with permission.

even served as vice-president of the Boulder Land and Improvement Company, which developed Boulder's Mapleton Hill neighborhood. In 1899 Maxwell
was appointed city engineer of Boulder, where he helped build the city's
water system. Other accomplishments included his surveying the Town
of Boulder Ditch and serving as the state water commissioner for Boulder
Creek. Around 1888, Maxwell tried but failed to convince the Boulder City
Council to expand the municipal water system to serve land he owned on
Mapleton Hill. Determined to get water to his land, Maxwell and his partner,
George Oliver, formed the for-profit Silver Lake Ditch and Reservoir Compa-
ny (Silver Lake Ditch) in 1887 to serve their developments.[34]

James Maxwell got to know George Oliver (Figure 8.10) while working
on various road and engineering projects. Oliver, a civil engineer, worked
to design and built the Silver Lake Ditch and several reservoirs that supplied

it water. Oliver and Maxwell started implementing their plans in 1887 when they built a low earthen dam to enlarge Silver Lake, a natural lake located near the Continental Divide northwest of Nederland. It made sense to start with the reservoir as most direct-flow rights from Boulder Creek were essentially appropriated, meaning they would need storage water to supply their ditch. A year later, in 1888, Maxwell and Oliver incorporated the Silver Lake Ditch with 250 shares of stock outstanding. Rather than sell shares outright, they organized Silver Lake Ditch as a for-profit company. This allowed them to retain ownership of the water rights by leasing water from the ditch.[35]

Ditch construction itself got under way in February 1888. With Maxwell's land located far from the creek, Maxwell and Oliver had to resort to building the ditch much farther up in the canyon than anyone before to get water to their more remote dry lands. This forced them into innovative engineering solutions to construct their ditch in a narrow, cliff-lined section of Boulder Canyon. Structures they built included five wooden flumes 1,300 feet long lashed to Boulder Canyon's walls and a 185-foot-long tunnel dug through a granite outcropping known as Elephant Buttress. According to Maxwell, the ditch cost about $15,000 to build. A photo taken around 1888 of one of the flumes under construction is shown in Figure 8.11. Notice that there is very little vegetation along the hillside below the ditch. This is because leakage from the ditch had not yet allowed riparian vegetation to take root on the steep slope. When completed, the ditch wound around the foothills above Boulder.[36]

Following in the footsteps of their work at Silver Lake, Maxwell and Oliver built a second earthen dam in 1890 on North Boulder Creek just upstream from Silver Lake at Island Lake. Both of these lakes collect melt from the Arapaho Glacier. Maxwell later stocked Silver Lake with fish to develop the area as a resort. Then, in December of 1893, they began work on Mesa Reservoir at the far downstream end of Silver Lake Ditch.

A number of productive truck farms prospered using Silver Lake Ditch water. One of these was the Long Farm in north Boulder. Here the family initially grew gladiolas and later switched to irises. Three generations of Longs have worked the property. Catherine Long Gates, who represents the third generation on the property, grows irises and leases land to several community-based farming organizations nearly one hundred years after her family first started using the ditch.

FIGURE 8.11. A flume for the Silver Lake Ditch under construction in Boulder Canyon. This photograph was probably taken in 1888. Photograph courtesy of the Carnegie Branch Library for Local History, Boulder Historical Society Collection. Reprinted with permission.

Maxwell and Oliver found themselves on the rising tide of the trend to build ditches to enhance the value of their land. However, by the dawn of the twentieth century, profits expected from many ditch development schemes were not materializing. Often the costs to build facilities were higher than expected. Many ditch companies, such as FRICO and Carter-Cotton's North Poudre Land, Canal, and Reservoir Company, went bankrupt. Whether or not Maxwell foresaw difficulties ahead in keeping his venture profitable is unknown. However, in 1906 Maxwell, then sixty-six years old, decided to liquidate his holdings and sold Silver and Island Lakes to the City of Boulder for $46,000. Boulder acquired the lakes for its municipal water system. The sale included "all water rights, storage rights, water decrees, reservoir decrees, and filings; and filings for further storage of water and all other rights of every kind and nature whatsoever . . . owned by [the Ditch Company]." Maxwell had finally convinced Boulder to purchase the project he pitched to it back in 1888.[37]

In the contract, Maxwell prudently retained the right to the top fourteen feet of water in Silver Lake and the top nine feet in Island Lake to supplement supplies to Silver Lake Ditch. Also, the Silver Lake Ditch Company agreed that if water is served to the lands "in any other manner," then the obligation to provide water from the lakes is reduced. Boulder has always claimed to understand this to mean that as the amount of land served by the ditch decreases, then the amount of water reserved in the lakes for the ditch is reduced accordingly. When someone annexes their land to the city and receives a city water tap or when a user simply stops irrigating, this provision applies. For this reason, Boulder has the incentive to track the number of acres served by the ditch very carefully. When Maxwell sold his shares in 1907, there were about 1,006 acres that could be irrigated. In 1963, about 662 acres remained. By 1998 there were 296 acres, and in 2007 only 248 acres remained. Boulder and the Silver Lake Ditch users have squabbled for decades about the exact meaning of the 1906 contract and subsequent revisions to it.[38]

It seems that relations between the Silver Lake Ditch and Boulder have been strained ever since James Maxwell sold his interest to the city. The contract terms gave later ditch users little incentive to cooperate with Boulder. The biggest source of tension is the provision that reduces the amount of water the ditch may receive as lands come to be served by Boulder. In the 1930s when the city attempted to conduct an inventory of irrigated lands, the company simply refused to cooperate. In the 1950s Boulder again demanded an inventory. City attorney Frank Moorhead questioned the amount of acreage the ditch users claimed to have under irrigation. This nearly led to litigation, and the original contract was amended in 1955. Two additional agreements followed most recently in 2010. It was only after the last agreement was signed that a comprehensive inventory of lands irrigated by the ditch, performed cooperatively by the ditch and city, was completed.

In 1907 Maxwell sold his remaining interest in the Silver Lake Ditch to William W. Degge for $25,000. Degge, like Maxwell before him, needed a ditch so he could supply water to land he was developing. For Degge, this was his Wellington Gardens property in north Boulder. Degge continued Maxwell's practice of managing the ditch as a for-profit company. Wellington Gardens included over 2,800 acres where Degge promised "prosperous homes for thrifty people," as in the advertisement shown in Figure 8.12. The water, Degge boasted, was "99.996 percent pure." Moreover, Degge claimed that Wellington Gardens had an "ideal supply of pure, cold water fresh from the melting snow and ice of the Glacier." If this didn't have you reaching for your

FIGURE 8.12. An advertisement for William W. Degge's Wellington Gardens development in north Boulder.

checkbook, perhaps Degge's advertisement of a "Wellington Stockholder," depicting a happy young girl, perhaps six or seven, sitting on a rock in the middle of a creek would, as it called fourth images of pure nature and youthful optimism. His shotgun marketing did not end there, as his maps prominently identified the location of nearby oil and gas wells, as if to suggest that investors would find additional wealth beneath their feet.[39]

Once Degge owned the ditch, he built Mesa Park Reservoir (now known as Wonderland Lake) to provide additional irrigation water. One flattering newspaper article told how "with plenty of Boulder county land and water enough to irrigate," Wellington Gardens "cannot fail of success." The article revealed that Degge's secret for success was that he "gives 'em dividends." Although Silver Lake Ditch never went bankrupt like other irrigation corporations, Degge never sold as many lots as he had hoped. Decades later, tracts of land he once owned is preserved as Boulder open space.[40]

Degge's endeavors sometimes drew controversy. In 1909 an investor from Washington, DC, sued him for fraud. Later the postmaster general of the United States issued a mail fraud indictment against him over irregularities in bond repayments. He eventually lost, but it seems that nothing much happened beyond that. William Degge lived on until 1918. After his death, his family retained its interest in the Silver Lake Ditch and Wellington Gardens and gradually sold off land. Dudley, William's son, and other family members continued marketing the property. They too found the enterprise was never very lucrative. Money to maintain the ditch was tight, and once the Great Depression hit, prosperity was delayed again. With many men out of work during the Great Depression, Dudley paid a miner $400 to blast a 100-foot-long tunnel to replace a failing section of the wooden flume at Red Rocks in west Boulder. After that came the war years and additional delay.[41]

Complicating management was the system of wooden flumes that conveyed water past cliffs and steep terrain in Boulder Canyon. By the 1940s these flumes had been in use for nearly a half century and were in poor repair. As former ditch president Everett C. Long later recalled, Dudley Degge used "scrap lumber and whatever was available, [but] he didn't have the money to maintain the ditch in the shape it should have been." This led to service outages during irrigation season that deprived users of critically needed water.[42]

By 1947, the ditch had deteriorated so badly under Degge family management that the water users, represented by J. F. Thompson, E. M. Antrim, J. K.

Edmonson, and Everett C. Long, approached the family to buy the ditch. Eventually, the Degges agreed to sell it to the users for $10,000 in installments of $400 per year for twenty-five years. No interest was charged. The buyers organized themselves as the Silver Lake Ditch Water Users Association. After completing the deal, Everett Long took charge of repairing the ditch, and between 1949 and 1952 the users replaced five wooden flumes with steel pipe. In 1955 they replaced the last 250 feet of wooden flume. Ditch users assessed themselves to fund the repairs and organized cleaning and maintenance parties ahead of the spring water run. The water users finally paid off their debt to the Degges in 1964 but did not receive the stock certificates until 1968 or 1969.[43]

After the water users bought the ditch, Everett Long became deeply involved in company affairs. He first served as company vice president and later president. Long's parents originally moved to Colorado in 1898 so that his father might recover from TB. Everett was born in Boulder in 1912 and on growing up, took over his father's farming operation. Everett was an avid mountaineer. Apparently while on honeymoon in the mountains with his wife Elizabeth, he saw Woodland Lake and recognized its potential as a reservoir site. They had always struggled to find supplemental the water for growing gladiolas on land they leased east of Boulder, and the Woodland Lake site met their needs. So in 1940 he filed on Upper Woodland Lake at an altitude of 11,215 feet to build Skyscraper Reservoir. Then Everett, Elizabeth, and others started moving supplies and machinery on pack horses to the site. They kept working until 1942, when they suspended operations until war's end. Once the war was over, Long acquired a Dodge power wagon with a winch. They then built a rudimentary road to the reservoir site to bring in supplies. The winch proved invaluable for, as Long put it, "the road was more like a mountain goat trail." Depending on conditions, they had to winch the Dodge over tough spots between four and seven times per trip. Prior to Long's completing the masonry dam, he was phasing out gladiolas in favor of more drought-tolerant irises. He could then run water from Skyscraper Reservoir into the Silver Lake Ditch and on down to his farm. Neighbors remember Long wearing a pith helmet as he drove an old Ford tractor to work his land nearly until his death at eighty-eight in 2000.[44]

Over the years rock slides, usually after thunderstorms, would take out sections of the metal pipe. At other times, debris choked sections of the open ditch in hard-to-reach sites. Once a rockslide destroyed the Parshall flume

FIGURE 8.13. Pipe replacement on Silver Lake Ditch in Boulder Canyon during 2007. Photograph by author.

FIGURE 8.14. Mesa Reservoir in 2007. Photograph by author.

near Boulder Creek. The water commissioner allowed the company to install a new flume at Sunshine Canyon to help avoid further damage. In 1956, Everett Long reported that a cloudburst in Boulder Canyon destroyed some of the pipes and stuffed the ditch "brim-full with sand and rocks and gravel." Starting about 1999, the users under the supervision of Superintendent Tim Ostwald began replacing sections of the rusting metal pipe installed by Long in the 1950s. Figure 8.13 is from work conducted in 2007. By 2010 nearly every section of the old pipe had been replaced.[45]

Silver Lake Ditch carries water to three reservoirs, Mesa Park (Wonderland Lake), Maxwell Lake, and Mesa Reservoir. In time, all three reservoirs were purchased by the City of Boulder. Mesa Reservoir, which is used for agricultural purposes, such as cattle watering, is also known for its migratory waterfowl habitat. Because of various difficulties, Boulder did not fill the reservoir for many years. However, in 1997, Boulder repaired the reservoir and, in 1998, restored annual water runs to Mesa Reservoir. Figure 8.14 is how Mesa Reservoir looked in 2007.

Over time, the Silver Lake Ditch seems to have evolved into a hobby rather than business for its many users. Often the company executes elaborate volunteer projects to mobilize manual labor to clean the ditch where other companies would assess shareholders to hire an excavation contractor. Granted, some locations are nearly inaccessible due to the mountainous terrain, which handicaps the company's ability to perform maintenance. To the company officers' credit, they seem quite selfless in their enthusiasm to keep the ditch operating. Cary F. Cook, who served as president from 1968 to 1982, typified this sentiment: in 1981 he spent 430 hours working on the ditch, for which he received only $360 in compensation. But even Mr. Cook had philanthropic limits, and he resigned as president the next year.[46]

Through the tenacity of the Silver Lake Ditch users, the company has managed to survive until now. However, its long-term prospects are uncertain. A steadily declining number of users means that there are fewer people to work on the ditch and pay for its upkeep. And as many of the remaining users age, its board is faced with the difficult task of recruiting new people able to work on this ditch.

Although the company has managed to replace the old flumes, deferred maintenance along the remaining ditch has meant that many trees and willows have cluttered the banks. Managing vegetation may be beyond the capacity of the company. As trees age, rotting roots along the steep banks of Silver Lake Ditch will likely mean increased seepage or bank breaches. Complicating matters is that all along the ditch neighbors have slowly encroached the ditch, making it increasingly difficult for the company to access and maintain its easement. For the company to survive, the company must preserve and reclaim its easement. If the company finds ways to overcome these obstacles, Boulder's last corporate ditch just may continue serving water for decades to come.

Backlash to Corporate Water: Radical Farmers, the Grange Movement, and Progressive Politics

Although profitable for many owners, corporate ditch building led to new challenges for Colorado farmers. While it opened up vast lands to farming, it undermined the individualism of the pioneer era. Even with the ascendance of agrarian populism brought about by Judge Elbert's *Coffin v. Left Hand* decision, it wound up representing only one step in the evolution of Colorado's water laws. Colorado was then in the midst of dramatic changes brought about by the construction of railroads that linked its farms to national markets. On one hand, farmers sought to benefit from the access to markets, on the other, they resented punitive transport fees that effectively siphoned off the fruits of their labor. Until a rail link was established, the great expense of freighting goods to and from Colorado across hundreds of miles of arid land to eastern markets effectively isolated the territory. Connecting Colorado to the rest of the country by railroad was seen by most as an essential step in its development. In 1865 the Union Pacific had begun building its line to California. By 1867 it was apparent that the Union Pacific would pass a hundred miles to the north of Denver through Laramie in the Wyoming Territory. This motivated John Evans, David H. Moffat, and others to secure the monies needed for a rail connection from Denver to the Union Pacific line. Work moved along rapidly, and in 1870 a company named the Denver Pacific Railway linked up with the Union Pacific tracks at Cheyenne. This railroad revolutionized communication and commerce in Denver and along the Front Range. It and other railroads that followed effectively tied the region to national markets.

In 1873 the Denver and Boulder Valley Railroad Company made the first rail link to Boulder. Among its founders were prominent territorial citizens, including former governor John Evans, Jerome B. Chaffe, Granville Berkley, Peter M. Housel, Walter S. Cheesman, David H. Moffat, and William J. Palmer. Denver Water's Cheesman Dam and Moffat Water Tunnel were later named after two of these people. The lesser-known Granville Berkley was involved with the early development of the North Boulder Farmers Ditch, and Peter Housel helped develop the Butte Mill and Marshallville ditches. For all of them, the success of Colorado's new communities—and their fortunes—rested on mining and farming linked by railroads.

The railroad founders represented Colorado's emergent elite. They were among the few who were positioned to profit from new links to faraway markets. Farmers migrating to Colorado were told they too could profit by selling agricultural commodities in eastern markets. But farmers soon learned that they had to first get their products to market by paying exorbitant freight rates set by the railroads. And so by the mid1870s the utopian ideals of Jefferson's independent yeoman farmers were clashing with the harsh realities of railroad capitalism.

The near monopolistic practices of the railroads worsened a mood of isolation, discontent, and social unrest among farmers. They initially responded by banding together within the emergent Grange Movement to protect their interests and assert their influence. Begun after the Civil War in 1867, the Grange Movement started as an agricultural advocacy group. Awareness of Granges rapidly expanded around the United States. In 1874, Colorado farmers started organizing granges to promote their interests. In short order there were at least eleven granges in Boulder County alone. Farmers along Left Hand Creek were among the first to sign on with this nascent movement. The Left Hand Grange was the ninth in Colorado, receiving its charter on January 24, 1874. From its inception in northeast Colorado, grange membership rapidly expanded. By 1888, the state held eighty-five granges and 2,390 members.[47]

The granges were soon advocating on behalf of farmers on issues such as the prohibition of margarine and liquor, but offered little to address more fundamental problems facing agriculture. One notable exception was an 1874 resolution of the State Grange urging the framers of Colorado's constitution to keep "the water of our rivers and streams . . . within control of the State for the benefit of the people." Their resolution urged the legislature to prohibit granting charters to corporations to control or use Colorado's water.[48]

Many farmers believed the concentration of granges in northeastern Colorado benefited that area to the detriment of other regions. Others complained that the granges were not vigorous enough in pursuing political action on their behalf. By the mid-1880s there appeared to be a pent-up demand for action beyond what the Grange Movement would offer.[49]

Concern among farmers was exacerbated as the scale of corporate ditch construction expanded in the 1880s. These new ditch and reservoir systems were far larger and even more capital-intensive than anything seen previously. More than ever before, farmers saw a grave threat from the growing corporate control of water.[50]

Under corporate ditch control, farmers were becoming "water tenants" as the companies retained ownership of the water rights and entered into lease agreements with water users. With water leases, prospects for a farmer's independence became more elusive. Between water leasing and high freight rates, farmers were squeezed by corporations on both the production and marketing sides of their livelihood.

Basic economic concerns were shared by farmers across Colorado. Simultaneously, wage-earning miners in the mineral districts were experiencing similar discontent as mine owners showed greater interest in profits than miner safety or living wages. It was from farm and mine worker restlessness that the nineteenth-century Populist Movement arose in Colorado. Although ideology played an important role in the movement, it was essentially a response to grievances arising out of economic dislocation and rapid social change.[51]

During the 1880s these kinds of grievances led farmers in Colorado to become increasingly anxious about the effects of corporate and foreign investment in water companies. Many farmers active in the Colorado State Grange began promoting progressive politics. In 1886 the Colorado State Grange, joining with the Farmers' Irrigation and Protective Association, successfully lobbied the Colorado Legislature to enact legislation to prevent corporations from charging excessive fees for carrying water in their canals. With their support, the Colorado Legislature also passed an antispeculation law directed at foreign companies. Farmers argued that deep-pocketed capitalists could purchase so much water that they would monopolize rivers much as the railroads had monopolized transportation. Colorado farmers termed these foreign and eastern capitalists as "water grabbers."[52]

As early as 1861, the Colorado Legislature began responding to worries over water price-fixing and within a few years gave county commissioners the authority to manage water markets by setting "reasonable" water rates. Soon another threat emerged involving large claims for water by corporations. The concern was that a big land and canal company would make a very large water right claim on a stream, so great that subsequent junior appropriators would never receive sufficient water. This would allow the company to leverage land prices even though water rates might be fixed. By speculatively claiming water rights, water companies could limit water supplies and force farmers to pay excessive land prices as a prerequisite to receiving water. Once a company made a water claim, it could wait for favorable conditions to sell land and maximize its profits. It was from abuses of this nature that Colorado's courts and legislature began to move against speculation. The legislature responded by setting time frames for water right holders to begin building their ditches or face forfeiture of their rights.[53]

Eventually canal owners hit upon a new way to increase profits at the expense of farmers. They began selling water to the farmers at county commissioner rates, but tacked on annual fees—which incorporated exorbitant profit margins—for using the ditch. Canal investors termed the charges as "royalties" or "bonuses" and argued that this was necessary to recoup their investments in the companies. Once again, farmers cried foul, complaining bitterly that the practice was "Un-American," and even invoked images of the British stamp act.[54]

Then Dr. Byron Wheeler, a member of the Grange Association and Farmers Protective Union, refused to pay the royalties to the High Line Canal near Denver, and the issue landed in court. Wheeler prevailed, with the court ruling that he did not have to pay the royalties. When Wheeler's case was appealed to Colorado's Supreme Court in 1888, it agreed, but added that because the state constitution reserved water as public property, canal companies were barred from charging excessive fees for furnishing water. Like the *Coffin v. Left Hand* decision before it, the courts adopted a populist position by placing the control of water with the people and rejecting back-door privatization efforts.[55]

It was out of the Wheeler case that most investor-held canal companies eventually passed into the hands of their water users. With royalties banned and speculation curtailed, canal companies began requiring that users buy shares in the company as a prerequisite for receiving water. As water users bought shares, the users themselves assumed greater roles in company operations. This drama bypassed most Boulder County ditches. However, investors in companies such as FRICO still managed to find ways to leverage land and water prices. FRICO was owned by a holding company that also owned several real estate companies. Through these corporate shell companies, FRICO's founders, Joseph Standley, Milton Smith, and Thomas B. Croke, simultaneously sold real estate and water to prospective farmers while managing to avoid embroiling themselves in speculation controversies. Even so, the era for large corporate ditches had passed. In the early twentieth century little land and even less unappropriated water remained. Large corporate ditches slowly shifted toward farmer ownership. Others, like FRICO, became overextended in this new era of constrained resources and went into receivership. Farmers who once resisted corporate power now found themselves controlling the very companies they had previously fought.

Radical farmers insisted on access to rivers and their water. Their activism insured that during the early years of Colorado's development they would have access to the rivers even if it meant condemning rights-of-way across others' land. They then ensured, through *Coffin v. Left Hand*, that all vestiges of riparian law were extinguished. Next they overturned corporate power in part through their advocacy of granges, farmers' unions, and progressive politics. Once the twentieth century rolled around, their rights secure, many of these struggles began receding into memory. Today all farmers know the value and importance of their water rights. Whether they realize why their rights came to be so valuable is an open question.

Colorado's founders recognized that accessing water was critical for the state's development. It remains to be seen how contemporary struggles over river access, such as landowner attempts to close off rivers to recreational users, will play out. Perhaps modern courts will continue the tradition of protecting public access to rivers as their predecessors once did.

NOTES

1. Mead quoted in Steinel, *History of Agriculture*, 211.

2. Silkensen, *Farmer's High Line Canal*; Perrigo, "Municipal History," 17.

3. "Colorado: Condition of Crops in the Territory," *New York Times*, August 4, 1873.

4. Coffin, letter to *Boulder* (CO) *County Miner*, January 8, 1914.

5. See Laflin, *Irrigation*, 24.

6. *Portrait and Biographical Record*, 690; Boulder County District Court Case CA1340.

7. Boulder County District Court Case CA1397; also Michael Holleran, *Farmers Ditch: A History and Guide* (Denver: University of Colorado, 2000).

8. Bixby, *History of Clear Creek*, 689.

9. Holleran, *Farmers Ditch*, 13.

10. Boulder County District Court CA1397. The ditch is smaller than that today, and the Colorado state engineer lists its capacity at about 55 cfs. The company was incorporated in January of 1880 with 100 shares outstanding. See also Boulder County District Court Cases 8407, 10518, 15012; and Colorado Water Court Division No. 1 Cases W7569, W8485, W9410, and 81CW466; Colorado state engineer, Enterprise Ditch Structure Summary Report, accessed November 18, 2010, http://cdss.state.co.us/DNN/ViewData/StructuresDiversions/tabid/75/Default.aspx.

11. Holleran, *Farmers Ditch*, 15; Wolff's Orchard Grove Fruit Farm was located on land bounded by Broadway and 19th and Alpine to Grape Streets in Boulder.

12. Sources for William H. Davidson include: Bixby, *History of Clear Creek*, 628–30; William H. Davidson, interview by Hubert H. Bancroft, May 24, 1886, University of Colorado Archive, Boulder; obituary of William H. Davidson, *Daily Camera*, May 19, 1892.

13. Silkensen, *Farmer's High Line Canal*.

14. Davidson quote from the *Boulder County News* 5, no. 7 (January 2, 1874); Davidson Ditch is owned by the Davidson Ditch and Reservoir Company; construction cost from the *Daily Camera*, May 19, 1892.

15. Boulder County District Court Case CA1344 and Colorado Water Court Cases W8348, 80CW469, 83CW319, and 85CW119.

16. *Boulder County News* 5, no. 7 (January 2, 1874).

17. Letter from Arthur J. Boase of the Fred Fair Engineering Association to William White, Davidson Ditch, Davidson Ditch corporate files, June 15, 1920.

18. Bob Clyncke, interview by Elizabeth Black for the Ditch Project, 2009.

19. Sampson, *Walking through History*.

20. Ibid.

21. National Association of Cotton Manufacturers, "In Memoriam, John L. Jerome," *Transactions of the New England Cotton Manufacturers Association*, no. 76 (Waltham, MA: E. L. Barry Press, 1904), 59.

22. Boulder County District Court Case 4842.

23. For the sake of brevity, I have simplified a complex series of transactions. Charles Toll controlled Community Ditch through his ownership of the Denver Land Company. It was his Denver Land Company holdings that he sold to Standley and his partners. At the time, Standley, Croke, and Smith were operating a holding company that controlled FRICO, the Denver Reservoir and Irrigation Company. It was this company that owned most of FRICO's stock that purchased Toll's Denver Land Company holdings. Much of the construction work for the FRICO system took place under the Denver Reservoir and Irrigation Company name. Because FRICO and the Denver Reservoir and Irrigation Company were essentially the same entity on all but paper and because it was FRICO that emerged from receivership, I use the FRICO name in the text to keep things from getting hopelessly confusing. Details on the financial dealings and the general history for this period come from Shaw, "Brief History of Denver Reservoir"; see also Lucas, "Denver Reservoir."

24. Although Croke remained active in the company, he lost much of his ownership interest shortly after the company was organized when he was unable to repay loans made to him by Standley. By about 1910, the costs to build the system had increased to over $10 million.

25. Sherow, Simmons, and Whitacre, "O'Brian Canal."

26. A quasi-municipal corporation is an entity that is vested with some governmental powers, such as taxation and bonding authority, but is often controlled by the founders or have a significantly limited scope of operations (limited to water supply, for example) relative to a city or county government. It appears that this multitude of companies was designed to circumvent Colorado's water antispeculation laws.

27. "The Standley System Opened," *Longmont* (CO) *Ledger*, September 15, 1911, 2.

28. Shaw, "Brief History of Denver Reservoir"; Michael Holleran, *Historic Context for Irrigation and Water Supply Ditches and Canals in Colorado* (Denver: Colorado Center for Preservation Research, University of Colorado at Denver and Health Sciences Center, 2005).

29. Storage decrees for Marshall Lake are included in several court cases, including Boulder County District Court Cases CA3944, CA6672, and CA12111 and Colorado Water Court Case 84CW0165.

30. There are 1,406 shares outstanding in FRICO Marshall.

31. Michael Holleran, *Boulder Valley Ditches: Silver Lake Ditch A History and Guide* (Denver: University of Colorado at Denver, 2000); Boulder County District Court Case CA5563.

32. Sources for James Philip Maxwell include *History of Colorado Illustrated*, vol. 4 (Chicago: J. S. Clarke Publishing Company, 1919); Bixby, *History of Clear Creek*, 660–61; *Portrait and Biographical Record*, 319–20; and Holleran, *Boulder Valley Ditches*.

33. Image from *Irrigation Age* 1, no.1 (1886), 1.

34. City of Boulder, *Source Water Master Plan*, 3–5.

35. Holleran, *Boulder Valley Ditches*; Boulder County District Court Case CA4842; Everett C. Long, "Random Remarks on the Silver Lake Ditch," 1948 (unpublished notes), Carnegie Branch Library for Local History/Boulder Public Library, Boulder; Silver Lake Ditch Articles of Incorporation, 1888, Colorado Secretary of State, http://www.sos.state.co.us/biz/ViewImage.do?fileId=19871009050&masterFileId=19871009050.

36. Holleran, *Boulder Valley Ditches*; Boulder County District Court Case CA4842; the Office of the State Engineer lists the physical capacity of the ditch at 6.5 cfs.; James P. Maxwell, "Irrigation and the Water Supply of Boulder County," *The Irrigation Era*, August, 1898, 9–13.

37. Deed Silver Lake Ditch & Reservoir Company to City of Boulder, Boulder County Clerk and Recorder Book 296 Page 104. The Silver Lake Ditch Company and the City of Boulder executed a contract on January 15, 1906, that allocated reservoir capacity in Silver Lake Reservoir between the City of Boulder and the ditch company. The agreement stipulated that the amount of water to be supplied by the City "shall be diminished by abandonment of their rights by contract holders, by forfeiture for non-payment of assessments, by other provisions for

water, or in any other manner" (contract is recorded in the Boulder County Clerk and Recorder Book 300, page 147; direct quote is on page 3 of the contract). Two weeks later a deed dated January 31, 1906, transferred ownership from the Silver Lake Ditch Company to the City of Boulder. Silver Lake Ditch is also used to fill Boulder-owned Wonderland (Mesa Park), Maxwell, and Mesa reservoirs. Typically, Silver Lake Ditch is turned on about May 21, and water is run until late September. Total deliveries have declined over the years as the number of users receiving water from the ditch has declined, see http://cdss.state.co.us/onlineTools/Pages /StructuresDiversions.aspx, accessed January 10, 2010.

38. Legal issues have arisen for over a century, including litigation (Boulder County Civil Action 17693) in 1964. Contract revisions to better define the relationship between the City and Silver Lake Ditch Company were executed on July 20, 1955, June 18, 1965, and in November 2009.

39. Wellington Gardens Prospectus, William W. Degge Papers, Call Number 998-3-3, Carnegie Branch Library for Local History, Boulder.

40. Undated newspaper clipping, William W. Degge Papers, Call Number 998-3-3, Carnegie Branch Library for Local History, Boulder.

41. Holleran, *Boulder Valley Ditches*.

42. Long, interview by Avery.

43. Long, "Random Remarks"; T. D. Waugh, "Value of Assets of Silver Lake Ditch Water Users Association and Silver Lake Ditch Company," Silver Lake Ditch Papers, 1888–1970, Call Number 998-12-17, Carnegie Branch Library for Local History, Boulder, undated.

44. Long, interview by Avery.

45. Ibid.

46. Cook, interview by Avery.

47. Colorado State Grange, *Colorado State Grange History* (Westminster, CO: North Suburban Printing and Publishing, 1975); "Left Hand Grange No. 9," accessed February 21, 2013, http://www.lefthandgrange.org/history.htm; Wright, *Politics of Populism*.

48. Colorado State Grange, *Colorado State Grange History*.

49. Wright, *Politics of Populism*, 42–43.

50. Schorr, *First Water-Privatization Debate*, 101–47.

51. Wright, *Politics of Populism*.

52. See Laflin, *Irrigation*.

53. Schorr, *First Water-Privatization Debate*.

54. Ibid.

55. Ibid.; Wheeler v. Northern Colorado Irrigation Company, 17 (Colorado 1888), 487, 491–92.

NINE

Colonizing Colorado

"The success of this colony was due to the
substitution of the combined effort of a community for the isolated efforts of individuals."
—*Edwin S. Nettleton, 1884*[1]

During the mid-nineteenth century, many people were seeking lifestyles away
from the industrialization and urbanization that was reshaping American life.
Some looked to utopian thinkers who preached alternatives to the capitalist economy that was expanding around them. One outlet to develop these
lifestyles was to turn to a variety of religious and social utopian groups who
were establishing communities of like-minded people across America. Some
were purely religious communes, while others were founded on a mix of
social, ideological, economic, and religious philosophies. At their core, each
of these utopian communities shared goals of developing better lives for its
members. Utopian communities often emerged as a backlash against social
injustices that members saw in the spread of ruthless capitalism prevalent
across mid-nineteenth-century America.

DOI: 10.5876/9781607323822.c009

Perhaps the best remembered today are the Shakers, who built village communities based on Christian communal principles. In Shaker villages the community was organized to promote their religious beliefs and put into practice self-reliant village economies. Their ascetic religious beliefs were translated into practice through building functional, well-built, but unembellished furniture and buildings. Shaker community leaders involved themselves in all aspects of religious, social, and economic life. Shaker communities often divided labor between genders, with men performing tilling and women overseeing domestic affairs. Many tasks such as food production and gathering firewood were performed cooperatively.

Although the Shakers are the most famous, many other social and religious communities emerged during the nineteenth century. Quite a few utopians established "colonies" to settle sparsely populated land in the West. Many communities centered around one or another Christian sect, and a few even promoted Jewish living. Utopian communities based on secular principles also gained in popularity. Places such as New Harmony, Indiana, and La Réunion in Texas were essentially socialist agricultural experiments. Other colonies catered to communities of newly arrived immigrants. Still others had philosophical underpinnings anchored by diverse ideas such as abolition or rigid temperance. With wide tracts of land thrown open to settlement in the aftermath of the Indian and Civil wars, Colorado was an obvious choice for idealists looking for a place to build communities.

Two idealists to emerge from the utopian movements of the 1850s were Nathan Meeker and Horace Greeley. Greeley and Meeker had previously traveled through Colorado and Utah and had seen firsthand the irrigation works built by early Colorado settlers and the Mormons in Utah. As a young man, Greeley embraced the communitarian ideals of the French socialist Charles Fourier and his chief American disciple, Albert Brisbane. Once Greeley achieved financial success as the editor of the *New York Tribune*, he invested thousands of dollars in communitarian settlements at Sylvania, Pennsylvania, and the North American Phalanx in New Jersey. Meeker, also a communitarian idealist, dreamed of organizing a colony in the West to put into practice his socialist ideology. Although Meeker was the elder, it was with Greeley's active support, encouragement, and money that Meeker organized the Union Colony, to be settled in the Colorado Territory.[2]

Nearly ten years before Greeley and Meeker began organizing settlement of agricultural colonies on socialist principles, they saw Colorado's potential. Greeley, in particular, actively wrote and lectured about Colorado's agricultural prospects. Greeley's introduction to the Colorado Territory began in 1859 when he toured the gold fields and Front Range. What he saw impressed him, and he almost immediately became the region's premier booster. No sooner than leaving the territory, Greeley began giving speeches extolling Colorado's virtues. On arriving in Laramie, Wyoming, fresh from Colorado, Greeley addressed a crowd about Colorado's great potential. Attending the talk were Hank, Lute, and Vane Wellman, who, taking a break on their westward migration, heard Greeley's spiel and abandoned their goal of California to redirect their sights south. Similarly, Morse Coffin had heard a "very gloomy picture of Colorado" and for a while thought he would head for Oregon instead. But on listening to the buzz surrounding Greeley's pronouncements Coffin, like the Wellmans, headed to Colorado. The Wellman brothers would settle along Boulder Creek and Coffin along the St. Vrain. In the years to come thousands more heeded Greeley's call to head west.[3]

Greeley freely acknowledged the difficulties in settling the lands of eastern Colorado. However, he was convinced that by pooling resources and acting collectively, settlers could succeed. As Greeley wrote in 1871, to "a stranger, these bleak uplands seem sterile; and, though such is not generally the fact, the presumption will repel experiments which involve a large initial outlay." And then in a subtle bit of self-serving advocacy, he suggested that "the railroad companies, which now own large tracts of these lands, will be obliged either to demonstrate their value, or to incite individuals and colonists to do it by liberal concessions."[4]

True to his socialist ideals, Meeker organized a colony whereby individual settlers would own their own farms and homes, but would be required to cooperate with their neighbors in building the community. Prospective settlers bought into the colony, and the labor and money they provided collectively built the settlement. As Meeker said after returning to New York from a trip to Colorado, advantages in building a communal settlement would include "easy access to schools and to public places, meetings, lectures, and the like . . . In planting, in fruit-growing, and in improving homes generally, the skill and experience of a few will be common to all, and much greater progress can be made than where each lives isolated." Meeker actively sought like-minded settlers who shared his moral and religious sentiments, for in his estimation, "without these qualities man is nothing." Contrary to contemporary myths of rugged western individualism, success required close cooperation and collaboration among settlers.[5]

The Union Colony and the town of Greeley that grew from it'were organized in New York in December 1869, and its colonists began arriving in Colorado during April and May 1870. Meeker's site for the colony was conveniently located near the mouth of the Cache la Poudre astride the new Denver Pacific Railway. They had to select this site far to the east of earlier settlements, as pioneers such as the Wellmans and Coffin had already taken the best bottomlands and corporatists like William Davidson had taken the best tablelands nearer to the mountains. The Union Colonists' first major undertaking, like anyone wishing to settle in the arid High Plains of Colorado, was to dig a ditch. The first ditch they completed (oddly named the Greeley No. 3 Ditch after a geographical plan) was made possible by colonists' labor and capital. It is from the Greeley experience that ditches built at these agricultural colonies have come to be called "colony ditches." Their effort remains notable because they believed that communal organization was superior to uncoordinated individual effort.[6]

Given all the work he put into the project, Meeker stayed at the Union Colony for only eight years before moving on. In 1878 Meeker was appointed the US Indian agent at the White River Ute Indian Reservation near the White River in western Colorado. Once there, he tried to replicate some of his successes at the Union Colony by promoting agriculture, ditch digging, and his Christian beliefs, but this time it was among the highly skeptical nomadic Ute Indians. The Utes resented Meeker's proselytizing, especially when he plowed under a track where they gambled on horse racing. Meeker, it seems, was trying to wean the Utes away from their horse culture and remake them in the image of white farmers. The horse-race-loving Utes were infuriated and responded by attacking and injuring Meeker. Relations between the Indians and whites deteriorated quickly, and the military was called in to protect Meeker and the agency. However, on September 29, 1879, before troops arrived, the Utes attacked again, and in the violence Nathan Meeker was killed.

While Meeker's sad ending played out, the Union Colony was well on its way to becoming the most successful experiment in agricultural settlement in Colorado. The Union Colony's early success inspired the founding of several other agricultural colonies in Colorado based on communal principles. Most were quite small, including the Wyandotte Colony of Illinois families, the German Colonization Company, which brought new German immigrants to the Wet Mountain Valley, and the St. Louis–Western Colony, which settled near Evans, just south of Greeley. In addition to these, there was the Chicago-Colorado Colony, which was ultimately second in size and success to only the Union Colony. The Chicago-Colorado Colony was essentially a Chicago response to the New York–founded Union Colony. Its settlement on the lower reaches of the St. Vrain resulted in the establishment of the town of Longmont and a number of ditches around it. But the Chicago-Colorado Colony had a very different origin than its neighbor at Greeley.[7]

Although the Chicago-Colorado Colony was eventually organized along ideological lines reminiscent of the Union Colony, its primary backers included successful capitalists such as John Evans and David Moffat, whose paramount concern was to offload their recently acquired real estate windfall. When the railroads were built across the West, the companies were rewarded with a government subsidy by the grant of alternate sections of land for twenty miles on both sides of the railroad right-of-way. Chief among the early Colorado railroads to receive land grants were Evans and Moffat's Denver Pacific Railroad. After securing the land grant, the Denver Pacific entered into a contract in 1869 with an outfit called the National Land Company of New York to market its land. In short order, advertisements began to appear offering the 4 million acres that the Kansas Pacific and the Denver Pacific companies had acquired.[8]

The general agent of the National Land Company was a fellow by the name of Colonel Cyrus N. Pratt of Chicago. Pratt worked closely with another Denver Pacific investor, William Byers, to sell the land. Pratt's marketing skills were vigorously supported by Byers's *Rocky Mountain News*, and together they set about to promote migration to Colorado. Their advertising campaign spun a yarn of Arcadian simplicity. With the ditches the colony would build, prospective farmers coming to Colorado were told that they might expect yields of wheat as high as eighty bushels per acre and grow sixty-pound cabbages, two-foot-long beets, and fourteen-pound sweet potatoes. Their marketing strategy reverberated for decades to come as real estate developers sold irrigation land to prospective farmers. It seems that the National Land Company's backers did not really care how the land was marketed or what the ideology of prospective buyers were, just whether they had the money to complete the sale.[9]

In November of 1870 Pratt initiated the process of organizing the new Chicago-Colorado Colony. Prospective colonists adopted a constitution and elected officers. Their slogan became "Industry, Temperance and Morality." Their first president was a Unitarian preacher and lecturer, Robert Collyer; Pratt was the secretary, and William Byers was conveniently chosen as chairman of the site-selection committee. Collyer articulated the communal values the settlers would need to survive on the frontier. In language mirroring Nathan Meeker, Collyer extolled the virtues of men pooling their labor, skills, and financial resources to achieve, in less time, what few men alone could do. The committee arrived in Colorado in January 1871, and eventually selected land marketed by the National Land Company on a hill above the St. Vrain River across from the old stage stop of Burlington. The town anchoring the colony was called Longmont for its excellent view of Long's Peak to the west. The first colonists began arriving in Colorado that March and started implementing Collyer's socialist vision.[10]

Originally, the plan was to buy 30,000 acres of checkerboard railroad land and preempt another 30,000 acres of interspersed government land. However, William Byers and the Denver Pacific reneged on their original sale price, with the result that the colony ended up with a total of 40,000 acres of railroad and federal lands. About 350 homesteads were made available to prospective colonists. With a payment of $155 to the colony, a settler would receive a forty-acre farm plot along with a perpetual right of irrigation water from the ditch that they were to build. Membership also enabled a settler to buy a lot in Longmont for another $50 payment. The small community of Burlington took advantage of the deal to be had at Longmont, and all of the homes and businesses were moved up the hill, jump-starting the new settlement.[11]

The Longmont town site was soon surveyed, and by July, Chicago-Colorado colonists were building a network of open ditches along every street and alley of their new community. Also during the summer of 1871, the colonists surveyed and began work on the colony-owned Excelsior Ditch, but the magnitude of the eighteen-foot-wide, three-foot-deep ditch outmatched their ambitions. The colonists soon decided to hire two contractors to dig the ditch, but it was November before the contracts were signed. Weather and delays then ended work for the season. One of the contractors, Holt and Company, built some shanties for workers to live in for the winter that quickly became known as Ditchville. By mid-February, work had resumed but was suspended when it was discovered that the colony treasurer fled to Canada with the colony funds.

With the money gone, the Chicago-Colorado Colony was on the verge of ruin, with no way to pay for building the ditch. Without water, there would be no food or community. Not only that, but most of the money that was still owed to the railroad was gone, so the fledgling community was at risk of losing its land too. It was under this financial cloud that the colony gave up all together on the Excelsior Ditch. Colonists decided to organize a separate ditch company to irrigate the land. These events led to the founding of the Highland Ditch Company. A number of settlers, including L.C. Mead and future ditch president John Kitely, began raising funds to build the new ditch. Mead took the lead and was able to sell $13,000 in stock subscriptions. The Chicago-Colorado Colony then exchanged its $7,000 in sunk assets in the Excelsior Ditch for shares in the Highland Ditch.[12]

Because the Highland Ditch was to serve the Longmont area and the surrounding Chicago-Colorado Colony farms, the ditch headgate needed to be situated far to the west (near present-day Lyons), within the mouth of the South St. Vrain Canyon, to provide sufficient grade for water to reach the dry terraces near the colony. Putting the headgate in the canyon created other problems. The biggest of these was that the company had to blast about 1,800 feet of rock near the canyon mouth. With the company short on money, the blasting had to wait until additional cash was raised from a Chicago investor.[13]

In November 1871 the cash-strapped company got the project going. However, the first digging did not start until nearly a year later. Even then, work progressed with numerous interruptions. Still feeling the cash crunch, the company accepted an offer by another stockholder, George Starbind, to pay fifty cents on the dollar, cash, to raise capital to pay the workers. This turned things around for a while and allowed the ditch construction to nearly reach Longmont. Besides financing the ditch, Starbind surveyed its alignment and much of the colony lands too.[14]

Finally, the first water was diverted out of the St. Vrain on March 30, 1873. When the company turned water in for the first time, a large party went into the canyon to watch, give speeches, and have a picnic. After all that it took to get the water flowing, the colonists felt it was indeed a time to celebrate. Upon opening, the Highland Ditch was very big: at over eight miles long, the ditch was twelve feet wide at the top and eight feet wide at the bottom, and able to divert about 205 cfs. Even with that impressive beginning, the company eventually made extensive enlargements to the ditch.[15]

Although the water was now running, the Highland Ditch Company was not out of the woods. Some sections of ditch leaked badly. Also, and more importantly, water had not reached nearly all of its subscribers. Over eighteen miles of ditch remained to be dug. First a railroad contractor was hired to dig, but after a time he lost interest and moved on. Eventually L. C. Mead stepped in again, as his farm remained dry. Mead offered ten or twelve men $10 in stock to help dig. Many of these men were just as desperate for water as Mead. Mead later said that he had "never seen so much dirt moved by the same number of teams in one day, before or since." Their work paid off, as Mead and the others got water to their farms in time to save their crops.[16]

The Highland Ditch was enlarged at least six times and remains crucial to Longmont and its surrounding farms. Claims for water on the South St. Vrain from the ditch eventually exceeded 2,832 cfs and ditch water goes to over twenty reservoirs strung out along its length. Its shares have been transferred to other ditches, and many more shares have been transferred into the City of Longmont water utility. As late as 2005, nearly 29,000 acres were still irrigated from this ditch. On average, the Highland Ditch diverts about 41,600 acre-feet of water per year.

Eventually, the Chicago-Colorado Colony had served its purpose, having seen the major ditches constructed and the town of Longmont established as the main community in the eastern part of Boulder County. The Chicago-Colorado Colony governed the community until a more traditional town government for Longmont was established in 1873. Once Longmont's town council was elected, it had the authority to raise taxes, so many of the functions the colony previously performed were transferred to the government. The colony organization continued on until at least 1890, during which time it disposed of the last remaining land that it held. Longmont became a major agricultural center, home to flour mills, sugar beet production, and related businesses. All the colony lands were parceled out and ditch shares subscribed. Although the Chicago-Colorado Colony long ago faded away, the ditch company it spawned continues to provide water to farmers and ranchers along St. Vrain Creek.

When considering Colorado's agricultural colonies, I think there are some interesting themes that emerge. Foremost is that the settlers used the word "colony" to describe their enterprise. As colonists they were "emigrants" to this land that only a few years before was Indian Territory. Once here, they became "migrants" or "immigrants." In promoting the colonies, their backers evoked images that previous migrants from Europe, the Pilgrims, the Huguenots, and so on would instantly recognize, namely, the goal of achieving economic independence and religious freedom. Real estate pitches resonated with nineteenth-century Americans by highlighting the economic opportunities that waited. Opportunities in land and water not available in the East were readily available in Colorado. Their forefathers and many colonists themselves had only recently arrived in America and were seeking a new and better life for themselves and their families.

The word "colony" also evokes images similar to the European enterprises of sending its excess people to faraway places to begin a new life. Like the Native Americans, the natives in those places were to be replaced, ignored, absorbed, or even exterminated as the new European civilization expanded into these lands. The removal of natives by Europeans and Americans was even more dramatic in Colorado than in many European colonies elsewhere in the world. So complete was the Indian removal from eastern Colorado that the memories and names of Native Americans were erased and replaced. It was now possible to create new place-names, memories, and narratives. The few Indian names that remain are mostly those given to places by nostalgic whites, such as the Indian Peaks or Niwot. Colorado's colonial period extended from the beginning of the Gold Rush through the establishment of the agricultural colonies. Although brief, Colorado's colonial history has cast a long shadow that extends to the present. During this time, Colorado was remade in both name and environment. For many, it is as if 1859 were year zero. Colorado's agricultural colonies, like the Territory of Colorado itself, were once at the periphery of an American empire expanding into the Great West. But projects like the Chicago-Colorado Colony ultimately brought the region into America's heartland.

By linking the words "agriculture" and "colony," these places were given a singular purpose that was different from other colonies, such as the all-encompassing thirteen original eastern colonies. They brought a highly focused purpose to develop thriving farming communities. Many migrants saw the communal aspects of the colonies as a necessary stepping-stone to independence. Others chafed under the requirements of temperance and were willing to do only enough communal work as necessary to be left to their own business.

Colony promoters leveraged the Jeffersonian ideal of the yeoman farmer and merged it with socialist rhetoric and Christian morality to promote the idea of families working collectively to carve out an independent lifestyle in an otherwise hostile environment. With this model, they could achieve, in less time and with less work, what was otherwise possible through individual effort.

The real estate promoters who backed the colonies and sold them the land, Evans, Moffat, and Byers, for example, were true capitalists. These men became Colorado's first oligarchs. By orchestrating force and politics they engineered the shift in title from Indian Land to Railroad Land. Once they controlled vast swaths of land, they seemed to have no qualms that the organizers of the colonies would employ socialist rhetoric to entice prospective migrants, provided they got their check at the end of the day.

Perhaps the greatest irony though is that communities built on socialistic principles have moved so far to the right in contemporary times. The *image* of the independent nineteenth-century farmer and rancher that we have today is far from the reality of communal cooperation that was in fact needed to build these successful farms and towns. Places like Greeley and Longmont incorporated socialistic principles into their charters and early identity. Somehow in the last century and a half, the narrative or origin myth for these and other rural communities has been transformed into something that their founders would scarcely recognize today.

Notes

1. Nettleton, *Report of the State Engineer*, 20.
2. Worster, *Rivers of Empire*, 83.
3. *Portrait and Biographical Record*, 951.
4. Greeley, *What I Know of Farming*, 275.
5. Willard, *Union Colony*, 2–3.

6. Nettleton, *Biennial Report*, 20.

7. Ibid.; Willard, *Union Colony*.

8. Principals in the Denver Pacific Railroad included Colorado territorial governor John Evans, David Moffat, and Walter Cheesman, who were instrumental in building Denver's water system, William Byers, founder and owner of the *Rocky Mountain News*, Joseph E. Bates, Bela Hugs, and Luther Kountze. Backers of the Chicago-Colorado Colony included the former lieutenant-governor of Illinois, William Bross, S. D. Kimbark, an iron company magnate, George S. Boden, a Chicago dry goods merchant, Henry Emery of the Prairie Farmer newspaper, Sidney Howard Gay of the *Chicago Tribune*, and William Byers. Willard and Goodykoontz, *Experiments in Colorado Colonization*. Evans's Denver Pacific Railroad also sold land to the Greeley colony but played no role beyond that.

9. Willard, *Union Colony*.

10. Willard, *Union Colony*; St. Vrain Historical Society, *They Came to Stay*; Newby, *Longmont Album*.

11. Newby, *Longmont Album*; Smith, "The Highland Ditch."

12. Smith, "The Highland Ditch."

13. Ibid.

14. Ibid.

15. Smith, "The Highland Ditch"; Boulder County District Court Case CA1645.

16. Smith, "The Highland Ditch," 6.

TEN

Making the South Platte

"We came to the shallow, yellow, muddy South Platte,
with its low banks and its scattering flat sand-bars and
pigmy islands—a melancholy stream straggling through
the center of the enormous flat plain, and only saved from
being impossible to find with the naked eye by its sentinel
rank of scattering trees standing on either bank. The Platte
was "up," they said- which made me wish I could see it
when it was down, if it could look any sicker and sorrier."
—*Mark Twain, Roughing It*[1]

Years ago, I remember Bart Woodward of the Riverside Irrigation District telling a curious story. I was at a meeting in Fort Morgan, Colorado, regarding federal efforts to protect rare species on the Platte River. Bart, who is now long deceased, represented the interests of farmers and irrigators along the South Platte in eastern Colorado. At lunchtime, we went to an unexceptional restaurant to get away for an hour. Here Bart described how settlers followed

DOI: 10.5876/9781607323822.c010

the South Platte across the prairie and first established farms along the tributaries at the base of the foothills. This, I knew, was where the oldest ditches in the South Platte drainage were located. Then Bart said that newer settlers began establishing farms out along the South Platte farther and farther east as they "followed the water." I did not quite understand, so he explained that once the tributaries at the base of the foothills were settled and the first ditches established, the hydrology of the upper basin was modified. Bart said to take a look at the appropriation dates for ditches: the oldest ones are on the west and the dates get younger as you head east. Along the mountain front in places like Boulder, Denver, and Golden, settlers' diverted water and irrigated fields, and the excess water found its way back to the stream either as groundwater or overland flows. This delayed water flowing down the upper tributaries and in turn altered the flow pattern in the South Platte. Suddenly water began to appear more regularly and later in the season on the South Platte. Soon there was enough water to support settlement farther down the river. Eventually it was possible to start farming in places like Fort Morgan and finally Julesburg. This explains why towns didn't spring up as settlers migrated west along streams, but first crossed over the arid plains to establish farms at the foot of the mountains and then built settlements by working back to the east.

It turns out that if you explore Bart Woodward's observation, you can trace the evolution of the entire watershed. Early travelers coming up the Platte and South Platte noticed how little water was present in these rivers, particularly during the summer months. First they had to cross over the area where much of the water seeped into the sandy bed of the South Platte. Only when they arrived at the mountain front did they encounter clear mountain streams. Stephen Long noted in his diary of June 20, 1820, that it was "unnecessary to dismount from our horses or unpack our mules" when crossing the South Platte, as there was too little water to give worry. Since most Rocky Mountain streams are in flood stage during June, one might expect a more difficult crossing. British traveler Thomas J. Farnham, who recounted his adventures to the Great Western Prairies in 1839, noted the scarcity of water in the South Platte: "This river is not navigable for steamboats at any season of the year," Farnham wrote. "In the spring floods, the batteaux of the American fur traders descend it from the forts on its forks. But even this is so hazardous that they are beginning to prefer taking down their furs in wagons."[2]

When John Fremont journeyed up the South Platte in July 1842, he noted that the stream was not navigable for any boat drawing more than six inches of water. Others had similar encounters with the river. The traveler Edwin Bryant recounted that he met a fur trader in 1849 who had started down the Platte with furs and was obliged to abandon his boats on account of the low water.[3]

With the Gold Rush, many more settlers began traveling up the South Platte. Well into the 1860s and 1870s people noted that the Platte and South Platte Rivers ran dry in many places for at least short periods. This happened at least eight times in these two decades, during the years 1863, 1864, 1865, 1866, 1871, 1873, 1874, and 1875. In these years, travelers often had to dig two or three feet into the sand to reach water.

Among the people noting the dry river was C. C. Hawley of Fort Collins, Colorado, who traveled along the South Platte River in the summers of 1863 and 1864. In those years, Hawley reported that from a short distance below the mouth of the Cache la Poudre all the way down below the Nebraska state line, the river was entirely dry. W. R. Bryant, of Cheyenne, Wyoming, had a similar experience in 1864, stating that to get water you had to dig "2 or 3 feet into the sand." John J. Brewer, of Irondale, Colorado, remembered hearing freighters say that in the years prior to 1870, the South Platte near the Colorado-Nebraska border "sank into the sand and they were obliged to dig holes to water their horses." This was corroborated by Eugene F. Ware of Topeka, Kansas, who observed buffalo pawing in the bed of the Platte to obtain water in 1865.[4]

Even the Platte River often dried up. John Evans of North Platte, Nebraska, saw the Platte River go dry in the years between 1895 and 1900. Others reported the Platte going dry in 1863, 1866, and 1871, and that it went dry for a number of years after 1885 or 1886.[5]

It is clear from these numerous accounts that the South Platte and the Platte Rivers either dried up or virtually ceased to flow during many years from the journey of Stephen Long in 1820 until the 1880s. By the 1870s and 1880s the South Platte seemed to have reliable flows near Greeley and Fort Morgan, but farther down it often went dry. After that, water regularly flowed farther downstream in places like Sterling and Julesburg. From 1900, water perennially flowed in the Nebraska reaches of the South Platte. This remarkable change is a consequence of water development and irrigation return flows.[6]

It turns out that Bart Woodward was not the first person to notice the curious irrigation flow patterns that developed in response to building ditches. People began reporting this phenomenon as little as ten years after the first ditches were established. Cyrus Thomas, the preacher and entomologist with the 1869 Hayden Expedition, attributed the increased flows to the now-debunked notion that "rain follows the plow." The premise was that once the sod was busted and the land brought under agriculture, more water became available via rainfall by some unexplained mechanism. Thomas wrote:

> When we reached the Cache a la Poudre, at Laporte, I heard it remarked that this stream now, and for a few years past, has been sending down a larger volume of water than it formerly did. I thought little of the matter at the time and let it pass, simply noting the statement. But when I reached the next stream in our journey south, the same thing was repeated in regard to other streams in that section. And to confirm the statement certain streams were pointed out, which, up to about 1862, had been in the habit of drying up annually at certain points, which since that time at these points have been constantly running. This caused me afterwards, during the whole length of our journey along the eastern flanks of the mountains, to make this a special subject of inquiry. And somewhat to my surprise, I have found the same thing repeated at almost every point as far south as Las Vegas, in New Mexico . . . Streams bearing down heavier volumes of water than formerly; others becoming constant runners which were formerly in the habit of drying up; springs bursting out at points where formerly there were none.[7]

Thomas later expressed a belief that as settlers migrated to Colorado, rain would somehow increase and provide more streamflow. When Thomas interviewed people along the way, he found that both the New Mexicans and Indians felt that "Americans bring rain with them." Thomas then summed up his thoughts about the matter: "All this, it seems to me, must lead to the conclusion that since the Territory has begun to be settled, towns and cities built up, farms cultivated, mines opened, and roads made and traveled, there has been a gradual increase of moisture . . . I therefore give it as my firm conviction that this increase is of a permanent nature, and not periodical, and that it has commenced within eight years past, and that it is in some way connected with the settlement of the country; and that, as the population increases, the amount of moisture will increase."[8]

And so it seems that the idea was born that rain follows the plow. Thomas was correct that many streams had been formerly dry, but failed to understand the cause. He also speculated that increased flows could be cyclical, but never outlined a plausible mechanism for that idea. He thought changes in the climate were not permanent, but were rather part of multiyear fluctuations. We know now that there are decades-long fluctuations in precipitation, but that is not the primary reason perennial flows developed on the South Platte. Thomas overlooked Bart Woodward's irrigation return flows, but the farmers and ditch builders saw what was happening. By the mid-1880s people were well aware that irrigation return flows contributed significant quantities of water to the South Platte.

Around 1870, B. S. La Grange, a Greeley colony pioneer and the first water commissioner on the Cache la Poudre, took note of water flowing back to the stream from irrigation. La Grange pressed the state engineer at the time, Edwin S. Nettleton, to investigate. Nettleton began studying the matter and concluded that river flow "is largely increased by seepage which is continually going on and increasing each year and also increasing as the area of irrigation is extended, thereby affording a more equal and continued supply of water both early and late in the season." On the Cache la Poudre alone, he determined that at least 30 percent of all water applied in irrigation returns to the river.[9]

In the early 1900s the economic and political significance of irrigation return flows became well known in Colorado. After all, within many people's lifetime, return flows had brought the lower South Platte to life, opening an entire new region to irrigation. The first ditches were relatively short and few reservoirs existed, so return flows were initially less. Later on, however, as longer ditches were built and reservoir construction increased, the magnitude of return flows expanded. Work by the Office of the Colorado State Engineer and the Colorado Agricultural Experiment Station (now part of Colorado State University) through the 1890s and early 1900s showed that there was a gradual yearly increase in what they termed "seepage" or "return" waters to the South Platte. In 1930 irrigation return flows to the South Platte River were estimated to have stabilized at an astonishing 1 million acre-feet per year.[10]

Eventually irrigation return flows became embroiled in interstate politics. During the early twentieth century as the role of the Colorado state engineer expanded from addressing issues within river basins to coordinating water use across state lines, Colorado became active in negotiating water compacts between neighboring states. As Colorado geared up to negotiate a compact over the use of the South Platte with Nebraska, many people in Colorado wanted to understand how much water was attributable to native flows versus irrigation return flows near the state line. After all, Coloradans argued that the compact should apportion flows naturally occurring near the state line, but increased flows attributable to water development upstream should remain in Colorado for use by its farmers.

Ralph Parshall, whose work advanced the science of flow measurement, was a natural choice to investigate irrigation return flows. Increased flows were due "without question to the application of irrigation water" in the South Platte and its tributaries, Parshall concluded. He also attributed increased flows to ditch and reservoir seepage and from water stored in the riverbank during times of high flow. The South Platte "has many depressions or arroyos leading to the stream, and before the extensive use of water for irrigation many of these water courses were dry except when carrying flood flow caused by heavy local showers or cloud-bursts," Parshall wrote. "Today," he added, "many of these formerly dry channels are carrying living or perpetual streams."[11]

It seems that the transformations to riparian ecology brought by irrigation were, by the 1890s, migrating downstream along with the farmers. As much as 20 percent of all water stored in reservoirs in the valley returned to the South Platte as seepage. Parshall concluded that return flows from Kersey (below Greeley) to Julesburg near the state line was approximately 750 cfs. These water rights supported agricultural output that amounted to about $2,250,000 in 1920.[12]

With the economic importance of seepage water firmly established, the matter of the growing river became a haggling point between Colorado and Nebraska during their compact negotiations. Colorado's chief negotiator, Delph E. Carpenter, was quick to stress the importance of return flows. Carpenter explained: "the disappearing river no longer exists. It is now a stream of constant flow, to and across the interstate line, although its waters have been repeatedly diverted, used, rediverted and reused for irrigation of 1,500,000 acres. The return waters of the South Platte and of the North Platte have stabilized the flow of the main river below North Platte and have made possible the adjustment between states, with assurance of increased future development in Nebraska."[13]

Without expressly stating the words "irrigation return flows," the South Platte Compact between Colorado and Nebraska implicitly recognizes the importance of this water source. Delph Carpenter and his Nebraska counterpart, Robert H. Willis, agreed that water originating in the upper reaches of the South Platte, west of Colorado's Washington County line, was not subject to stream calls by Nebraska. Moreover, in the lower river, if river flows remained at 120 cfs or above, Nebraska could not call out water rights with priority dates junior to June 14, 1897. And all water rights senior to that date in Colorado's lower reaches of the South Platte are not subject to calls from Nebraska. All of these provisions allow Colorado to use irrigation return flows and acknowledge that the stream formerly had little water in it.[14]

Starting with diversions on creeks like Boulder and Left Hand, the South Platte paradoxically grew into a permanent year-round river. It's doubtful that Mark Twain could ever have imagined that a sicker and sorrier river would, in a few decades, rise to support one of the nation's great agricultural districts.

NOTES

1. Twain, *Roughing It*, 60.

2. Long quote from James, *Account of an Expedition*, 2:153; Farnham, *Travels in the Great Western Prairies*, 106.

3. Teele, *Water Rights*, 44.

4. Ibid., 45, 46.

5. Ibid., 46.

6. At least some of the low flows are attributable to climate conditions. However, climate variation cannot account for the reliable flows that developed in the South Platte. For a discussion on climate impacts, see Lawson and Stockton, "Desert Myth."

7. Thomas quoted in Hayden, *Preliminary Field Report*, 140.

8. Ibid., 141.

9. Ralph L. Parshall, "The Importance of Return Flow to Colorado Irrigators," in Colorado Irrigation Centennial Committee, *A Hundred Years of Irrigation in Colorado: 100 Years of Organized and Continuous Irrigation, 1852–1952* (Denver: Colorado Water Conservation Board, 1952), 57–61; Nettleton, *Report of the State Engineer, Summary of Work Performed during the Years 1885–'86*, 22.

10. Parshall, "Importance of Return Flow," 59.

11. Parshall, *Return of Seepage Water*, 8.

12. Ibid.

13. Carpenter, *Colorado Proceedings*.

14. Colorado Revised Statutes, sec. 37-65-101, South Platte River Compact.

ELEVEN

Secondary Water Development in Boulder Valley

"Under present conditions the water used on the lands
near the headwaters returns in part to the streams to
be used again farther down along their courses."
—*Ralph Palmer Teele, 1905*[1]

Simultaneously with the growth of the South Platte, irrigation return flows
facilitated a further round of agricultural development along the river's
upper tributaries. Once the pioneer and corporate ditches were built, their
earthen channels naturally began leaking. Some water seeping from those
ditches would migrate downhill as groundwater and later emerge as springs
or as flow in otherwise dry channels. Also, irrigation water reaching the edge
of irrigated fields, known alternately as "wastewater" or "tail water," saturated the ground to increase groundwater levels or just collected and ran
along low spots where it became available for use.

DOI: 10.5876/9781607323822.c011

SEEPAGE DITCHES

Seeing new opportunities for appropriation, farmers, ranchers, and others began collecting and using seepage and tail water. Many people began filing claims for this water. They started by filing a "map and statement filing" with the county or state engineer and later submitting an application for a water right in court. In just a few years many ditches using tail water or seepage were dug in Boulder Valley. These ditches are generally quite short and irrigate a limited area. Because the water is derived from the earlier ditches, the appropriation dates for these seepage ditches tend to be many years after the direct-flow ditches were built. Early seepage ditch claims date from late 1870s and continue to the 1950s or later.

Because many of these seepage ditches represent a secondary phase of ditch development, their water rights adjudications took place long after the initial stream adjudications. For instance, about forty-seven small ditches, seeps, and pipelines that appropriated seepage or tail water were adjudicated in a single court case that began in 1953 and concluded in 1966. Many of these seepage ditches were assigned "non-stream priorities" in which the judge ruled that the "source of supply of said ditch are not tributary to any stream." With the award of a nonstream priority by the court, those ditches were made "independent of other priorities." Unless changed by later court proceedings, the language in those decrees remain binding on state water administration officials. In practice, this means that the local water commissioners generally do not administer these ditches, as they are not subject to calls by other water rights.[2]

A typical case is the unincorporated Arnold-Harrop Ditch, which derives its water from seepage of Farmers Ditch. It is located northeast of Boulder and now serves City of Boulder open space land. W. H. Arnold and Samuel Harrop made their appropriation in 1911 when they completed their map and statement filing. The water right was eventually adjudicated in 1953. The court ruled that the water supplying the ditch was "not tributary to any stream." As such, it is not administered by the water commissioner nor is it called out by other water rights. It is as if this ditch is independent of the priority system. The ditch is used to irrigate hay and pasture grass and supports wetland vegetation on what was formerly dry land.[3]

Another ditch in the Boulder area that diverts seepage water is the Economy Ditch. This one was appropriated in November of 1885 and takes water from Two Mile Canyon Creek, a tributary of Boulder Creek. J.O.V. Wise made the original claim to the ditch and had Fred Fair, the former City of Boulder engineer, prepare the map and statement filing. Wise spent about $200 building the ditch and stated that he began using the water "since its first appearance as seepage some time prior to 1897." Economy Ditch collected "surplus, waste, flood, seepage, drainage, and storm water" from Two Mile Canyon Creek. Economy Ditch was a short ditch with a decreed capacity of 5.25 cfs and, when built, was three feet across the top and one and one-half feet deep. Economy Ditch, which is now obliterated, existed in an area of rural north Boulder that is now completely covered in with housing developments. I have unsuccessfully looked for remnants of this ditch, but traces of it may still exist in various backyards in the area.[4]

Similarly, one short tail-water ditch that is still in use is the L. F. Spicer Ditch, which diverts "seepage, waste, surface, and flood waters derived and received from ditches from South Boulder Creek." L. F. Spicer appropriated water for the ditch on October 1, 1898. Like the Arnold-Harrop Ditch, many years went by before its water right was adjudicated. Now owned by the City of Boulder, it provides water to irrigate hay meadows and pasture grass and supports a very robust wetlands complex. The rare, federally protected Ute ladies'-tresses orchid occupies wetlands irrigated with water from this ditch, while adjacent nonirrigated land supports prickly pear cactus. Making this ditch particularly valuable is its 10 cfs decree that lists its source of supply as "not tributary to any stream," exempting it from stream administration.[5]

Today, within the Boulder Creek Watershed, there are 100 water rights that list their water source as "seepage." Of the South Platte tributaries, only the Cache la Poudre and St. Vrain have more seepage rights, with 133 and 117, respectively. Within the entire South Platte drainage, the Colorado Division of Water Resources lists a total of 600 seepage rights.[6]

Although numerous, the seepage ditches around Boulder are generally not well known beyond the water commissioner or their owners. Often only one or two individuals own these ditches. Rarely are they incorporated. Even though most are quite small and short, they often support wetlands and various rare species. But considering that hundreds of these structures exist, they cumulatively represent a significant hydrologic feature along the Front Range. These ditches came about only because earlier ditch-digging activities modified the hydrology sufficiently to enable their construction. Like the major water projects constructed along the South Platte River after the

1890s, digging ditches and building reservoirs altered the river basin's hydrology sufficiently to support later water development not previously imagined possible by the region's first settlers.

Redistribution of water through the construction of ditches and reservoirs enabled a secondary phase of water development both downstream along the South Platte and as infill between areas of already established ditches in the upper tributaries. This development in turn created secondary wetlands on formerly dry lands. For good or ill, as water rights are transferred away from agriculture and out of ditches, the hydrology supporting secondary water developments is slowly unraveling.

NOTES

1. Teele, *Water Rights*, 57.

2. Boulder County District Court Case CA12111. Within this single adjudication, the priorities for about 160 ditches, reservoirs, power pipelines, conditional water rights, and other structures were established.

3. Boulder County District Court Case CA12111.

4. Boulder County District Court Case CA6672.

5. Boulder County District Court Case 12111; map of the L. F. Spicer Ditch, Boulder County Colorado, filed with the Colorado state engineer, July 15, 1920.

6. The Colorado Division of Water Resources reports the water source for water rights. Some of this water ends up in either ditches or reservoirs.

TWELVE

Privatizing Nature

> "The necessity for a practical standard, or unit, of mea-
> surement of water is very urgent . . . At present we have
> no unit of measure in universal use throughout the State."
> —*Edwin S Nettleton, 1884*[1]

Boulder has at least a dozen great cafés and espresso bars, a handful of Starbucks, plus other places to get a good cup of coffee. But every Tuesday and Friday morning, Bob Carlson, the water commissioner for the Boulder Creek Watershed, sips coffee at the local Burger King on 28th Street. Twice a week various ditch riders, superintendents, and municipal water operations personnel join Bob to discuss the administration of water calls and water issues. It seems that they mostly talk about snowmobiling, hunting, fishing, or just about anything that is on people's minds that day. These are not the guys you see at an espresso bar with laptops nursing cappuccinos. These are the guys who look right drinking thin coffee from a Styrofoam cup. Nevertheless, Bob Carlson's orange Masonite booth at Burger King is

DOI: 10.5876/9781607323822.c012

the central operations clearinghouse for ditch management in Boulder Valley. It is also the place where a considerable number of cinnamon rolls are consumed each week.

Through the territorial days and on into the first years of statehood, settlers focused their energy on claiming water, digging ditches, and building their farms. They appropriated water rights, but most had only a vague understanding of how much water was actually flowing down each ditch. As the chapter epigraph suggests, water measurement was more subjective than scientific. There were no water commissioners like Bob Carlson to administer water rights, let alone measure how much water each ditch could receive. You could appropriate water and buy and sell your rights to it, but your tools for measuring how much water you or your neighbors used were rudimentary and relied mostly on guesswork.

The nineteenth century saw the emergence of vast commodity markets in grain, lumber, cattle, and other natural resources. To enable these markets, merchants devised clever ways to measure and price products they wished to buy but had not yet seen. This way, they might purchase grain from afar, comfortable in the knowledge that for the dollars they spent they would receive a product matching their expectations. The historian William Cronon showed how the American West grew as expanding metropolitan economies and the merchant class exploited distant rural environments. Critical to this expanding economy, Cronon asserts, was the commodification of nature. And the key to enabling commodity markets was the imperative to accurately measure your product.[2]

People squatting on public or Indian land, staking mining claims, and diverting water were all appropriating slices of nature. In the nineteenth-century West, one could occupy a piece of land and later gain a legal right to it. To get a land title, you needed an accurate survey of your claim. Security of your title rested on the accuracy of the survey. Accurate surveys made land a tradable commodity. Near Boulder, the federal Land Office took the first step toward privatization in 1859 by establishing a survey baseline along the fortieth parallel that would form the basis for future township surveys. By 1863, the Land Office had begun staking out townships and recording land titles.

Determining what water you owned was far more complex. Water is elusive; it flows away, seeps into the ground, and evaporates. The amount of water you need for farming varies from place to place. And you need lots of it to grow crops. Until simple, standardized, and accurate methods of measuring water were developed, there was no easy way to determine how much water a person was actually claiming, let alone how much he or she might sell the water for.

Nineteenth-century merchants developed ways to grade grain quality or price pork bellies, which paved the way for commodification of those products. Likewise, water users strove to develop methods to measure water flow and volume as a necessary step to privatize and commodify water. As more ditches were dug, users began seeking better water measurement and allocation practices. It was out of these necessities that the Colorado Legislature began assembling the modern institutions of water administration.

With the urging of water users in 1879, the Colorado Legislature took the first step by authorizing the creation of ten water districts aligned along watershed boundaries. The same legislation allowed the governor to appoint water commissioners in these newly established water districts and allowed the creation of additional water districts as needed. Figure 12.1 shows the map that the State Engineer produced for the Boulder Creek and St. Vrain Watersheds. Significantly, this groundbreaking act also initiated the court process to adjudicate the relative priorities of rights between ditches. This led to the first stream adjudications performed in the United States. When the adjudications got under way in 1880 and 1881, Boulder, Left Hand, and St. Vrain Creeks were among the first class of streams examined.

Because of discord on the streams, the 1879 act also authorized water commissioners to "divide the water" from streams among ditches and "shut and fasten" headgates when a ditch is not entitled to water by reason of priority. For this to be successful, the governor needed to appoint well-known, trustworthy locals as water commissioners.[3]

Early in 1880, William A. Davidson was appointed the first water commissioner for Boulder Creek. However, Davidson's tenure lasted less than one year. Perhaps he was too busy with all his ditches and mills to do the job justice. Davidson withdrew, and later that year Governor Pitkin appointed Hiram Prince as the District 6 water commissioner for Boulder Creek. Prince would stay in the position for many years. It was under Prince that the water commissioner position on Boulder Creek developed.[4]

Hiram Prince (Figure 12.2) was born in May 1824 and left home at ten to ship out on a whaling vessel. He stayed with whaling for twelve years and

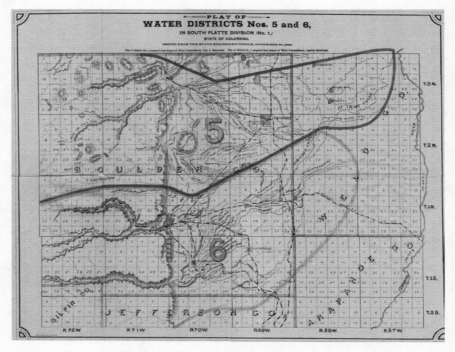

FIGURE 12.1. In 1879 the Colorado Legislature authorized the creation of water districts along watershed boundaries. This is the original state engineer's plat map of Water Districts Nos. 5 and 6, in the South Platte Division (No. 1), Denver, Colorado. Colorado state engineer, November 30, 1888. Image of map by author.

later became a second mate on a Mississippi steamboat. In 1851 Prince married Mary Lindsey, of Ohio, and they had six children together. The family moved to Denver in 1864, and Prince set himself up as a blacksmith. In 1870 they bought 250 acres of land in Boulder County and began farming. Prince's entire farm was under the South Boulder Canon Ditch. People often referred to it as the Prince Ditch due to his serving as company president for more than thirty years. When the South Boulder Canon Ditch was formed in 1870, Prince wrote the by-laws, articles of incorporation, and so on.[5]

Within two years of the appointment of the water commissioners, it became clear that someone was needed to coordinate their work. To do that, the legislature created the Office of the State Engineer. Eugene K. Stimson was appointed the first state engineer in June 1881 and served until April 1883.

Duties of the new state engineer included making stream measurements, determining carrying capacity of ditches, supervising the installation of measuring devices, and reporting to the governor. The same legislation created "water divisions" made up of all the water districts from within one large river basin. The first three water divisions were based on the South Platte, Arkansas, and Rio Grande Watersheds.

Curious parallels exist between Colorado's water districts and divisions organized along watershed boundaries that were created in 1879 and 1881 with John Wesley Powell's

FIGURE 12.2. Hiram Prince.

1878 recommendation in his *Report on the Lands of the Arid Regions of the United States* to organize political boundaries based on river basins. In Colorado the pressure to organize along watershed boundaries came from local ditch users who found themselves calling for state intervention to enforce the evolving Prior Appropriation system. Certainly many influential people working on water issues in Colorado had read or were aware of Powell's report, even if they did not consciously adopt his recommendations for water administration. Similarly, Powell, having traveled through Colorado, knew of its evolving legal institutions. Perhaps it does not matter if one was informed by the other; more importantly, it suggests that organizing water management by watersheds represented a rational progression in water administration practice in the later parts of the nineteenth century. It also shows that water governance institutions were evolving in scope from local to regional scales in order to balance the increasingly complex needs of water users. Powell certainly deserves credit for vocalizing this concept, but he was only the most prominent among a number of people who were thinking along the same lines at about the same time.[6]

Early efforts by the Office of the State Engineer primarily focused on measuring streamflow and ditch capacities. Elwood Mead, the future commissioner of the US Bureau of Reclamation, was one of the first to measure ditch flows on Boulder Creek. He summed up the problems he saw this way:

> When the men along the lower end of a stream see its waters shrink and their crops burning up for the lack of water they realize that it is due not to the absence of the snow in the mountains but to the fact that later ditches above them are robbing them of their just share. Before the farmers will permit the loss of their year's labor from this cause they will resort to almost any expedient to obtain what they believe belongs to them and so they organize raids to tear out the dams above or go into court to obtain legal redress. The remedy for this is to have water divided under public control.[7]

For Mead, the solution was careful water measurement and administration. In 1884 and 1885, when Mead was measuring ditch capacities in northern Colorado, he was struck by the discrepancy between the decreed appropriations and the actual carrying capacities he calculated. So great was the discrepancy that in some instances the ditch capacity and decree seemed to have no relationship to one another. He found ditches with decreed capacities "of two three and even five times the volume they were capable of carrying." Mead demonstrated what many water users already intuitively knew: many water rights decrees were "worse than useless" as a guide for a water commissioner trying to do his job. Even today many old decrees retain their originally decreed rates because they have never gone through modern water rights change cases.[8]

In Colorado water rights administration and adjudication are big businesses that employ numerous attorneys, engineers, and water planners. Water court cases often run into tens of thousands of dollars and take years to settle. Although most reach negotiated settlements, about 5 to 10 percent go to trial. Once the court renders a decree, its implementation shifts to the realm of the water commissioner and Bob Carlson's operations center at Burger King.

Soon after Colorado's first ditches were dug, it became apparent that there might not be enough water to go around. At first, miners and farmers alike used a very vague number called the "miner's inch" or "inch" to measure the flow of water. To everyone's consternation, miner's inches differed between mining camps and farming communities. Factors such as the slope of the channel, the size of the opening that the water flows through, or anything that affected water at the opening influenced flow measurements. Miners and farmers used crude wooden devices that were inaccurate and nonreproducible. It was hard enough to measure water at different sites along the same ditch, let alone compare inches of flow between a ditch near Greeley and a ditch near Longmont. Although a debate over how much water a miner's inch represents seems anachronistic today, it was critically important at the time because without knowing how much water a claim represented, one could not reliably buy or sell water rights. Questions over water measurement got the attention of Fredrick Watts, the US commissioner of agriculture, who asked the rhetorical question: "Why is there so much confusion? It is simply because everyone measures an inch of water to suit his own particular views."[9]

The Territorial Legislature tried to settle the issue around 1874 by adopting a formal definition by setting 1 cfs equal to 38.4 miner's inches. With this, the term "statutory inches" began appearing in water rights decrees. Soon after that, measurement of water rights and streamflow was standardized using cubic feet per second. People constructing reservoirs simply reported the storage in terms of cubic feet.

Colorado was not alone in its search for terms that conveyed water quantity. In the mid-1880s John Wesley Powell and his federal irrigation survey coined the term "acre-feet" to describe the amount of water that would cover an acre of land one foot deep. Acre-feet was a more convenient number for describing volume, because it allowed one to easily calculate how much water a farmer might need to irrigate his land.[10]

Figure 12.3 shows an early water measuring device invented by J. Max Clark of Greeley. The device is a rectangular orifice used for measuring miner's inches. It works by measuring the flow of water through a rectangular opening of known dimensions. Measuring water this way was difficult because the flow varied with the height or pressure of water weighing against the opening. Water first flows through a regulating gate on the left side and into the box where the level is kept steady. Water then flows out through the rectangular opening. It was important to carefully monitor the height of water in the box, as flow in the ditch would cause water level fluctuations. It was difficult to use but was better than no measurement at all.[11]

Another measuring device from the 1880s (Figure 12.4) is a rectangular weir and works by moving water through a notch or opening in an open channel.

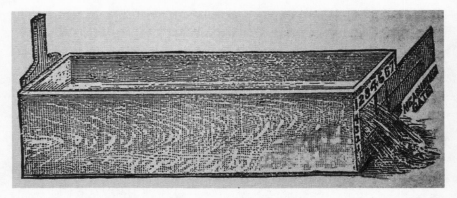

FIGURE 12.3. An early water measuring device invented by J. Max Clark of Greeley, Colorado.

The width of the opening is fixed, leaving the height of the water flowing over the square notch as the variable that the user measures.[12]

Water measurement became an early priority for the new Agricultural Experiment Station at the Colorado Agricultural College (CAC, now Colorado State University) in Fort Collins. One of its first engineers, Louis Carpenter, motivated by the wasteful irrigation practices he saw, studied water measurement technologies then in use. He found that devices such as Clark's rectangular orifice and the weir dam were loosely based on water measuring structures first developed in Italy, such as the Cippoetti weir. Carpenter's publications advanced water measurement technology in Colorado.[13]

Carpenter's advances notwithstanding, the problem of water measurement had become acute by the early 1900s. Many ditches did not even have headgates, let alone measuring devices. The few ditches that did have measuring flumes were rarely checked for accuracy. In 1907, for example, the 12th Street diversion for the largest ditch diverting water from Boulder Creek, the Boulder and White Rock, had a headgate but no rating flume or gage. This diversion also delivered water to other major ditches, including the North Boulder Farmers and the Boulder and Left Hand, along with several smaller ditches. Edward Autrey, then state water commissioner for District 6, simply "guessed in" the amount of water entering the Boulder and White Rock. For a ditch that could in theory divert about 180 cfs, Autrey's guess had major ramifications for everyone downstream. But one can't fault Autrey when he

FIGURE 12.4. A rectangular weir water measuring device from the 1880s.

guessed flow rates, as the funds to hire a deputy to make the measurements were "always vastly inadequate." Consequently, flow measurements were seldom performed.[14]

Into the twentieth century, the CAC remained a center for study-ing water flow and its measurement. Stepping to the forefront of water research at the college was engineering professor Ralph Parshall. Parshall started as an undergraduate at the CAC, pursued graduate studies at the University of Chicago, and returned to join the CAC faculty in 1904. His signature achievement was the perfection of a measuring flume that now bears his name. Figure 12.5 shows Parshall taking measurements at one of his Parshall flumes.

Parshall's hour-glass-shaped flume provided several needed improvements to previous designs. First, there were only two variables a user needed to

FIGURE 12.5. Ralph Parshall taking water measurements at one of his signature flumes. Courtesy of Colorado State University, Morgan Library Archives and Special Collections. Reprinted with permission.

measure to determine the flow rate. One was the flume width, which was set at the time of construction, and the other was the height of water flowing through the flume. As long as you knew the width of the flume and measured the water height, a user could look up the flow rate in an easily readable table. Second, the shape helped regulate water velocities and flushed sediment through the structure. Users could easily build different-sized flumes for small laterals or large canals without having to specially design flumes for every situation. More than any other device, the Parshall flume improved the science of water measurement to such a high degree of accuracy that it is still in common use today.

To accompany the flume, Parshall patented a recording device to measure flows continuously. His device coupled a drum and cylinder, clock, and float and counterbalance. A user would now have to visit the flume only every week or so to change a paper chart and rewind the clock to determine how much water passed the flume. With these innovations, Parshall revolutionized flow measurement. These two instruments effectively completed the process of commodifying water that began in the late 1850s with the first stream appropriations.[15]

Although the accuracy of water measurement has steadily increased in controlled environments, natural variations and irregularities along streams and in ditches make it exceedingly difficult to measure small variations in flow, let alone measure flow with very small error margins. Consequently, there is a gap between modern water rights decrees, which often mandate the accounting—on paper—of water diversions down to the tenth or hundredth of a cfs, and the practical ability by hydrologists or ditch riders to get accurate flow readings ten times that amount. In these instances, record keeping for water rights has become so detailed that users sometimes joke that more water exists on paper than in the stream.

Several years ago, I experienced this problem firsthand as a board member for a ditch east of Boulder. As part of a decree, the ditch company had to release about one one-hundredth of a cfs to the creek to make up for impacts to downstream users. When I asked the ditch rider to release the water, he pointed out that the amount we were talking about was less than the thickness of the painted lines on the staff gage. Since water sloshes up and down against the flume wall all day long, it's all but impossible to estimate the small flows that the decree mandates. So as Edward Autrey, the state water commissioner for District 6, did over one hundred years before, the ditch rider said that he would guess at how much additional water he was releasing when he adjusted the headgate. This made me think of the old saying that the more things change, the more things stay the same.

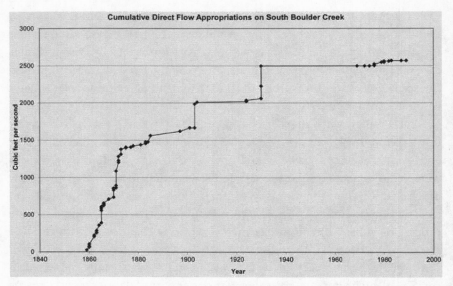

FIGURE 12.6. Cumulative direct flow appropriations on South Boulder Creek.

WATER RIGHTS AND APPROPRIATION IN THE BOULDER CREEK WATERSHED

Long before water users figured out how to accurately measure water flow, the amount of unappropriated water remaining in each creek steadily decreased. Consider the chart in Figure 12.6, which shows direct-flow appropriations on South Boulder Creek. From 1859 through the late 1860s direct-flow rights were rapidly claimed as settlers moved in. Starting around 1870 the rate at which new appropriations were made noticeably diminishes, and from about the 1930s through the present few new appropriations have been made. This is because these later appropriations are seldom in priority and are therefore of low reliability for many uses. Compounding this is the high cost to build structures for small quantities of water. For this reason most direct-flow appropriations from the mid-1880s onward, including the large spike in the early 1900s and the other spike in the mid-1930s, are associated with reservoir construction and not new ditches. Even the small direct-flow appropriations occurring from the 1970s onward are generally related to municipal storage projects.

As appropriations proceeded, the reliability of junior ditches to supply water decreased. Simply stated, junior ditches run for shorter periods of time

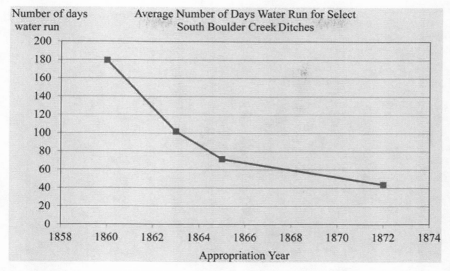

FIGURE 12.7. This chart shows the average number of days that a water right of a certain appropriation date will remain in priority for select South Boulder Creek ditches. Each point represents an average of fifty years of data.

relative to their seniors, as Figure 12.7 shows. After about 1872 all new ditches constructed on South Boulder Creek incorporated a storage component. Generally the number of days a ditch is run is related to the needs of water users, the call on the river, and the priority date of the ditch. Operational issues such as infrastructure repairs or farmers curtailing diversions so they might cut hay or other crops affect how long a ditch is run. The graph charts the average number of days water is run in ditches over a fifty-year period versus the water right appropriation date for those ditches.

As a completely predictable response to water scarcity and diminishing reliability of direct-flow rights, water users began to construct dams and reservoirs to collect water that flowed down the river during the winter, the spring snowmelt runoff, and other times of high flows. This process began when Charles Pancost built the first reservoir in Boulder Valley in 1863. Cumulative storage rights versus appropriation date for South Boulder Creek are shown in Figure 12.8. The big steps in the 1900s, 1920s, and 1950s correspond to the development of Marshall, Baseline, Valmont, and Gross reservoirs, respectively.

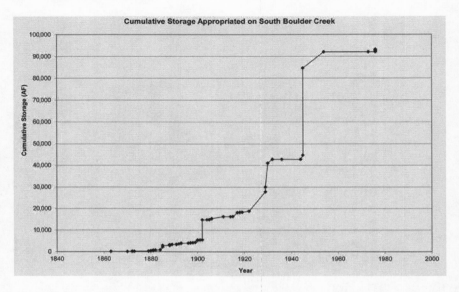

FIGURE 12.8. Cumulative storage appropriated on South Boulder Creek. The large jumps correspond to major reservoir construction projects.

These charts demonstrate what we already know: streams like Boulder and South Boulder were long ago fully appropriated. To provide one with a more nuanced sense of the spatial aspects to these appropriations, hydrologists produce "straight-line diagrams" to show the relationships between rights to the various streams, ditches, and reservoirs in a watershed. Straight-line diagrams, like the one for Boulder Creek (Figure 12.9), also hint at the magnitude of hydraulic alterations in any given watershed. It should be no surprise then, that the only options left for someone wanting water along Front Range streams was to develop more complicated projects such as transmountain diversions or pursue costly water rights transfers. But before turning to transmountain diversions and water transfers, it is interesting to consider how someone like Bob Carlson actually allocates water when he is standing near a headgate.

A CREEKSIDE LOOK AT STREAM ADMINISTRATION

"First in time, first in right" makes sense in abstract terms, but how is it implemented on the ground? With over 22,800 ditches scattered around Colorado,

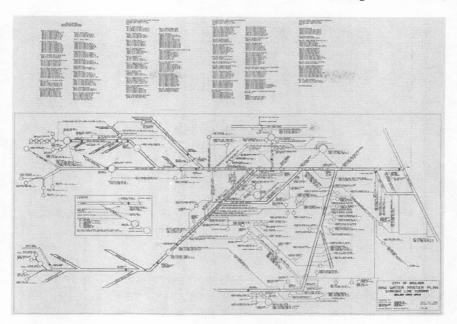

FIGURE 12.9. The straight-line diagram for the Boulder Creek Watershed. WBLA, Inc., Straight Line Diagram, Boulder Creek Basin, City of Boulder Raw Water Master Plan, 1988.

this is not an idle question. Allocation of water is based on a system of priority using the date that water was initially appropriated. A water user can divert streamflow when his or her water right is "in priority" or, in other words, when all water rights senior to the user are satisfied and streamflow is still available. Water users exercise their right by placing a "call" on the stream. When sufficient streamflow is available, a water user receives his or her entitlement. When insufficient water is available to satisfy senior calls, the water commissioner curtails diversions from junior water right users until there is just enough streamflow to satisfy the senior right.

An idealized example of water allocation in a stream using actual flow data and a simplified water rights list for South Boulder Creek can help one visualize how ditches come in and out of priority during any given season. I think the hydrograph data for 1963 is particularly well suited for this because it was a very low-flow water year that required careful administration of the

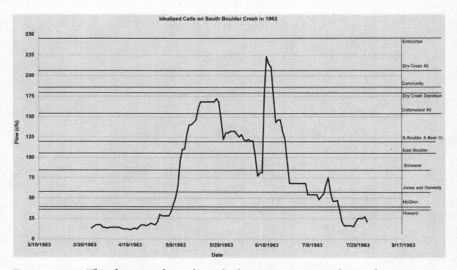

FIGURE 12.10. This diagram shows how ditches can come in and out of priority during an irrigation season. It charts the streamflow over time versus calendar date, and the horizontal lines are ditch appropriations stacked with the most senior ditch on the bottom.

stream. That year had some stream fluctuations that show how ditches may go in and out of priority. In Figure 12.10, the vertical axis depicts streamflow in cubic feet per second and the horizontal axis are dates between March 25 and August 12, which includes the spring snowmelt runoff and the highest water demands for irrigation. On the right side of the diagram are the names of the earliest water rights for South Boulder Creek. I omit several minor water rights to minimize clutter. Water rights appropriations are stacked in order of their seniority, with the oldest water right represented by a horizontal line at the bottom and successively younger water rights above it. Note that Figure 12.10 presents an *idealized* view of streamflows on South Boulder Creek during 1963. In reality, the Enterprise and Leyner Cottonwood ditches did receive some water in 1963.

On South Boulder Creek, Howard Ditch is the most senior water right, holding an appropriation date of April 1, 1860, for 36 cfs, so there is a horizontal line representing that decree. The McGinn Ditch is the second most senior water right and has an appropriation date of May 1, 1860, for 3.19 cfs, so there is a horizontal line corresponding to this appropriation at 39.19 cfs (36 cfs plus 3.19 cfs).

Additional horizontal lines correspond to each successive junior water right to represent how much water would need to be in South Boulder Creek for each of these water rights to come into priority. By constructing the diagram in this manner, it is possible to trace changes in streamflow to show which water rights come into and fall out of priority during the irrigation season.

From mid-March until about May 5, the flow in South Boulder Creek was only about 20 to 30 cfs. This means that only part of the Howard Ditch water right could be satisfied during this time and that no other water users were eligible to receive water so long as Howard Ditch was calling water. Howard Ditch shareholders calling for water during this time had no choice but to accept flows less than their full decree. By about May 5 the flow on South Boulder Creek started to increase as air temperature in the mountains warmed, inducing snowmelt. On this day, Howard Ditch received its full allocation of water, and then as streamflow increased the McGinn, Jones and Donnelly, Schearer, and East Boulder ditches came into priority, and the water commissioner allowed them to turn on in rapid succession. Several days later, sufficient water became available for the South Boulder and Bear Creek, Cottonwood No. 2, and the Dry Creek Davidson ditches, so they were turned on too. However, around May 20, the streamflow leveled off, and the water commissioner denied the calls of junior water right owners for the simple reason that there was insufficient water in the stream.

Around May 26, South Boulder Creek snowmelt peaked for the season, and the flow started to diminish. With less water available, senior ditches began calling out the juniors, first Dry Creek Davidson, then Cottonwood No. 2, South Boulder and Bear Creek, and so on. Around June 15 or 16, a welcome rain fell, and the flow in South Boulder Creek spiked, reaching its annual peak on June 18 at about 230 cfs. Several ditches came back into priority for a few days but were quickly shut off for the season as flows dropped again. Junior ditches, including the Enterprise and Leyner Cottonwood and others, never received water in 1963 because sufficient water never became available. After June 18, streamflow progressively decreased, and the water commissioner shut off ditches until finally about July 17 Howard Ditch was again the only ditch for which there was sufficient water in the stream.

When looking at the diagram, keep in mind that it represents an approximation of actual conditions and simplifies the progression of calls during a water year. Other factors make the actual situation on the creek more complex and often lead to junior ditches receiving water. Because the ditches are located downstream from the stream gage, more water was likely available than the chart suggests. Tributary inflows, irrigation return flows, and operations on the senior ditches (shutoffs for haying) add water downstream from the gage to provide water for ditches that might otherwise not come into priority.

When Bob Carlson meets water users each week at Burger King, they discuss whether the streamflow is rising or falling and which ditches will receive water. Each user knows his or her place in line, and watches how first-in-time, first-in-right plays out over streamflow and thin coffee.

Notes

1. Nettleton, *Report of the State Engineer*, 52.

2. Cronon, *Nature's Metropolis*.

3. Colorado Session Laws, *An Act to Regulate the Use of Water for Irrigation, and Providing for Settling the Priority of Rights Thereto* (Denver, 1879).

4. See Nettleton, *Report of the State Engineer*, 26–29.

5. Stone, *History of Colorado*, 367–68; *Daily Camera*, June 28, 1894.

6. Powell, *Report on the Lands*.

7. Mead, "Irrigation in the United States," 22.

8. Ibid.

9. Watts, *Report of the Commissioner*, 262.

10. Worster, *River Running West*, 477.

11. Pabor, *Colorado as an Agricultural State*, 51.

12. Ibid., 49.

13. Carpenter, *Measurement and Division of Water*.

14. Meeker, "Report on the Irrigated Area," 13–14.

15. Ralph Parshall was issued US Patent 1417941 on May 30, 1922, for his water stage recording instrument.

THIRTEEN

Great and Growing Cities

"No person shall put any carcass or any filthy animal or vegetable matter into the reservoir nor shall
any person bathe or swim therein or skate upon the
ice which may form thereon in cold weather."
—*Boulder's first water quality*
regulation, adopted January 23, 1877

Although Boulder's first settlers had mining on their minds, the winter
weather of 1858 to 1859 stymied prospecting until conditions in the mountains eased. To keep occupied, Alfred A. Brookfield "thought as the weather
would not permit us to mine we would lay out and commence to build what
may be an important town." In just a few months Boulder was "composed
of . . . some forty-odd log cabins or partial cabins, in various stages of completion, from foundations to a roof of shakes—split shingles some three
feet long and fastened with poles or small house logs laid on them and fastened in place," Morse Coffin later recalled. Municipal improvements were

DOI: 10.5876/9781607323822.c013

nonexistent. There were no paved streets, sewage disposal, garbage collection, or water system. During Boulder's early days, many people preferred to get water from a well located near the public square at 13th and Pearl. Their other options included procuring water from the creek or a ditch. Although going to the well was something of a social event, water delivery from a pipe to your home was a luxury to envy. A few ditches like Anderson and Farmers served water to neighborhoods, and then laterals brought water past the houses. Some people piped water from the ditch, and others just took water from the open laterals. While it was easy to supply a field with water from a ditch, it was far less desirable to supply a town with ditch water. So it was only a matter of time before agricultural and municipal interests in water delivery would diverge.[1]

For Boulder this process began with the formation of a private water supply company in May 1872 by Andrew J. Macky, Alfred A. Brookfield, and James P. Maxwell. Their enterprise, the Boulder Aqueduct Company, received a charter from the town trustees in November of 1872. The town gave them permission to lay wooden pipes in the city streets. Their plan was to lay pipes from Farmers Ditch to the homes and businesses desiring water.[2]

Piped water would increase the quality of life in Boulder and reinforce the town's position as the main commercial center in the county. Nevertheless, Boulder in the 1870s (Figure 13.1) had a long way to go before it would become a pleasant place to live. "Boulder" said Isabella Bird, the bourgeois British traveler who visited in 1873, "is a hideous collection of frame houses on the burning plain, but it aspires to be a 'city.'" Derisive comments aside, Boulder residents were actively thinking about ways to improve the quality of life in the community.[3]

Unfortunately for its founders, the Boulder Aqueduct Company's plans never got off the ground. Boulder would have to burn on the plains a little longer. In 1874, after a mass meeting of residents, a citizens committee was organized to determine if a private company should build the first waterworks. Sitting on the committee was Frederick A. Squires, Ephraim Pound, and Alfred A. Brookfield. Even though Brookfield was a part owner in the Boulder Aqueduct Company, the committee decided that the town should finance its own waterworks. Later that year, citizens filed a petition with the Town Board of Trustees requesting a vote on issuing bonds for the municipal water system. This led to the passage of an $18,000 bond issue in October

FIGURE 13.1. Boulder in the 1870s. Photograph courtesy of the Carnegie Branch Library for Local History, Boulder Historical Society Collection. Reprinted with permission.

1874. Eighty-eight votes were cast, with seventy-one voting for and seventeen against. It was official: Boulder would build its own municipal system. The trustees then appointed Ephraim Pound (Figure 13.2) as the town's first water commissioner; he served from 1875 to 1877. Perhaps it helped that Pound was previously the Board of Trustees president in 1873.[4]

Boulder's first municipal system run by Pound was a simple affair. Water was taken from Boulder Creek via the Town of Boulder Ditch, an open conveyance three feet wide and one foot deep. Responsibility for its construction fell to James P. Maxwell, who by then sat on Boulder's Board of Trustees. The ditch began with a wing wall in Boulder Creek and a set of headgates to regulate the water flow from the creek. It extended along the hillside, where it emptied into the small, now abandoned Town of Boulder Reservoir. By placing the intake upstream, the town avoided pollution emanating from the mills at the canyon mouth. John A. Ellet was paid $2,000 by the town to dig the ditch and reservoir. Ellet marshaled between fifteen and thirty men to complete the structures. The Town of Boulder Reservoir was located in a

FIGURE 13.2. Ephraim Pound. Photograph courtesy of the Carnegie Branch Library for Local History, Boulder Historical Society Collection. Reprinted with permission.

saddle between Settlers Park and Sunshine Canyon. This small reservoir was about 150 feet square and 12 feet deep and contained about one million cubic feet of water. Cast iron pipes delivered water from the reservoir to users along Pearl Street and downtown Boulder. When completed, the filler ditch cost $2,175; another $11,447 was spent on the reservoir, and additional money was spent on buying land.[5]

Although the earliest motivation for piping water into Boulder was ostensibly to facilitate firefighting, improved water quality soon took over as the primary benefit. During this time doctors around the country were beginning to suspect that poor water quality contributed to disease. Short notices in Boulder-area newspapers announced illnesses and deaths. Typhoid and other waterborne diseases were typical culprits. One article read, "Mr. Henry Neifkirk is quite sick with typhoid fever"; another announced, "Last Tuesday evening death, entered the home of Mr. P.A. Woodruff, and his boy of sixteen summers, was the victim. A relentless typhoid fever attacked a constitution that was never strong." Although typhoid epidemics made headlines, sporadic illnesses and deaths like that of Mr. Neifkirk were far more common. For the new town of Boulder, supplying clean water to its citizens was one of its first orders of business.[6]

In the late 1860s, with advances in France by scientists such as Louis Pasteur, the public became increasingly aware of the link between contaminated water and various diseases. The initial strategy for supplying pure water to a town was to simply move the water intake farther upstream to avoid pollution sources. Leaders in cities and towns began to make concerted efforts to abandon open ditches and replace them with a system of wood and clay pipes to deliver water to their citizens. Even with progress in piping, it was common in the late 1800s and up to about 1907 for water to flow in open ditches to rural water users. However, by then, domestic water service via pipes served nearly everyone in Boulder. Even though the water was piped, water treatment other than simple sand filtration was unknown, and the incidence of waterborne disease remained common. Deaths from typhoid and other diseases occurred throughout the 1920s.

Disease wasn't the only water quality issue. At least five mills and other industrial facilities contributed to turbidity, poor taste, and chemical pollution in Boulder Creek near the canyon mouth. Mills pulverized ore and extracted gold with mercury and other chemicals. Millers then dumped their tailings directly on the ground, often in drainages or within the creek bed itself. Similarly, mines discarded waste onto the hillsides below their workings and often directly into the creek, and once there minerals in the tailings, such as iron pyrite, degraded into iron hydroxides and sulfuric acid. Without careful vigilance these contaminants ended up in Boulder's water supply.

FIGURE 13.3. Water deliveries in Boulder's Mapleton Hill neighborhood from an open lateral of the Silver Lake Ditch. This photograph was probably taken in the late 1880s or 1890s. Photograph courtesy of the Carnegie Branch Library for Local History, Boulder Historical Society Collection. Reprinted with permission.

Despite the Town of Boulder Ditch diverting water above most mills, mines even farther upstream remained a problem. While touring Boulder Canyon around 1871, the writer John H. Tice noticed "the turbid waters of Four-Mile creek," remarking that it was "turbid because miners are washing the auriferous sands of the gulch in its limpid waves." This water flowed naturally down to the Town of Boulder Ditch headgate. Several more years passed before Boulder began addressing problems coming from higher up.[7]

Piping made it possible for the first time to bring water into homes. Figure 13.3 shows the Mapleton Hill neighborhood when it was still receiving Silver Lake Ditch water via an open lateral. Once the water was piped, people could shower and bathe without having to carry the water to the tub. They could also use the toilet in the convenience of their home rather than in an outhouse.

Domestic water soon became a necessity and not an amenity. The strategy for building the water system was twofold. First, extend pipes and ditches farther up into the mountains to access cleaner sources of water. Second, pipe water into town and deliver water directly to homes and businesses. Throughout the remainder of the 1870s Boulder continued to extend its water system. A second bond issue for $12,000, followed by another that raised $30,000, provided additional money for piping. Investments continued with a $50,000 bond issue in 1883. The work from these bonds included extensions of the pipe system, installation of fire hydrants, fixing leaking pipes that were already under the streets, and building a return flow to Boulder Creek. In 1883 pipe extended to the new railroad depot located on 21st Street.[8]

Initially, Boulder concentrated on getting the water system built. No rules or regulations existed for managing the system. Eventually on January 23, 1877, the town board got around to issuing its first operating rules. Among other things, these rules specified the duties for the water superintendent and required that users must pay for water. The operating rules also introduced Boulder's first water quality regulation, requiring that "no person shall put any carcass or any filthy animal or vegetable matter into the reservoir." If the old adage that new government rules treat known abuses, Boulder's water quality regulations reflected a sorry state of affairs. Another provision outlined how to install new taps and connections to the system. The town board also established its first rates for different water uses. A baker would pay $15 per year, barber shop chairs were $5, saloons $15, boarding houses $15, and each water closet seat and urinal was $3. Following on the heels of the first rates, the board added many more, such as a $50 per year fee for the State University, fees for ice cream saloons, boilers, street sprinkling, vinegar makers, and so forth. It would be years before the city would install water meters and set standardized rates for water use.[9]

The availability of piped water improved the quality of life in town in other ways. The Presbyterian Church installed a water-powered pipe organ, and the *Boulder County News* built a water-powered typesetting machine. Citizens placed fountains in their yards, and pipes were laid to schools and public buildings. People planted trees and other yard improvements. Soon the Town of Boulder Ditch and Reservoir struggled to meet all the demands.[10]

The 1880s brought more change and growth to Boulder. The town reincorporated as the City of Boulder in April of 1882. Town trustees were now aldermen. Population and with it water demand continued upward. New ways to meet demand were sought. One approach was through the purchase of ditch shares. The first purchase occurred in January of 1880 when the town bought three and one-half shares of Farmers Ditch. A month later, it bought an additional four and one-half shares of Farmers Ditch for $800. Then in 1886 the town bought eight shares in the Anderson Ditch for $400.[11]

During this time, James P. Maxwell had purchased land north of town in what would someday become the Mapleton Hill neighborhood. Maxwell and his partner, George Oliver, lobbied Boulder to supply water to their land. Boulder declined, so Maxwell and Oliver built the for-profit Silver Lake Ditch Company to meet their needs. Even without the additional burden on Boulder's water system that Maxwell's lands would have meant, the limits of the existing water system were becoming apparent. By 1886 some citizens were clamoring for a new reservoir. And by 1890, it was clear to everyone that the town had outgrown the Town of Boulder Reservoir and that ditch share purchases alone would not suffice. So in 1890 yet another bond issue passed—this one the biggest yet at $150,000. The vote approving the issue was overwhelmingly in favor at 459 to 39. With the money in hand, Boulder acquired land on the Gallop Ranch above town. George Oliver, as city engineer, surveyed the reservoir site. Oliver was the logical selection as he had engineered the Silver Lake Ditch a few years earlier. The site Oliver selected for the new Sunshine Reservoir was about 100 feet above the Town of Boulder Reservoir. In 1891 construction began. To improve water quality for the new reservoir, the water intake was moved far upstream on Boulder Creek to a site now known as Horseshoe Placer.[12]

The new Sunshine Reservoir was not without its problems. It was unlined, and when filled it leaked. In addition, users complained of turbid water. It did not help that some of the cloudy water came from mill tailings and other mine waste in Boulder Creek. But the leaks in particular grabbed the attention of the city council. A council committee visited the site, and the *Daily Camera* reported that they "found several feet of water which teems with fish and doubtless innumerable microbes." The city council went on to spend several sessions debating how to line the reservoir, and after it was lined, they spent more time debating how and why inferior cement was used. A photo of Sunshine Reservoir taken shortly after its completion is reproduced in Figure 13.4.[13]

FIGURE 13.4. Sunshine Reservoir taken shortly after its completion. Photo by J. B. Sturtevant about 1875 or 1876, courtesy of the Carnegie Branch Library for Local History, Boulder Historical Society Collection. Reprinted with permission.

Even with its problems, Sunshine Reservoir represented a significant improvement over the old Town of Boulder Reservoir, which by 1891 was described as "filthy with slime, mud and weeds." Boulder's health officer recommended against further use of the Town of Boulder Reservoir.[14]

As the nineteenth century closed, Boulder's population was approaching 6,600 people. Boulder's water system continued to expand. The city council decided to build a second reservoir at Chautauqua. Built in 1902, the reservoir got water from a new ditch dug from Gregory Canyon along with water pumped uphill from a steam plant near Boulder Creek.[15]

By the time Boulder completed Chautauqua Reservoir, a predictable cycle of events unfolded regarding the city's expanding system. First build a reservoir and intake ditch above town to address water shortage and water quality concerns. The new reservoir might be above town, but there were still mills and mines even higher that discharged some pretty nasty effluent. With growth, demand grew, and the new reservoir became overtaxed. Citizens began complaining about poor water quality and the need for additional water. They clamored for a larger reservoir with an intake ditch even farther upstream. The council continued authorizing service expansions, and the town would lay new pipe. Then the council completed the cycle by funding the construction of new ditches and reservoirs farther upstream. By the close of the nineteenth century, there was nowhere farther upstream to go than the Continental Divide.

BOULDER'S SILVER LAKE WATERSHED

By the early 1900s water management and technology had undergone major evolution. For many years, water development was dominated by private capital. Even so, populists and progressives in the West were vocal critics of corporations, particularly ones that dominated agriculture and water supply. Many people did not trust corporations to act in the public's interest. Their concern was justified, as many water companies had repeatedly set prices for land, water, and transportation at exploitive levels. Corporate interests, to be fair, were encountering the limits of their financial and technical abilities to construct large water projects. At the national level, former Grand Canyon explorer and US Geological Survey director John Wesley Powell saw the need for a strong government role both to fund water projects and counterbalance corporate influence in western development. Powell led the way toward advocating federally funded water development in the West. His efforts culminated several years after his death with the passage of the Reclamation Act in 1902 and the creation of the US Bureau of Reclamation. For the American West, the passage of the Reclamation Act marked the start of the modern era.

During the late nineteenth century, western cities were on the way toward building modern municipal water systems as they moved away from relying on open ditches. But the way forward was not clear. Water supplies in many cities were dominated by private corporations. Denver typified the private free-for-all in providing water to its citizens. At one point Denver had eleven private water companies vying for customers. Some even offered "free" water to anyone signing up for service. Charges of influence peddling were leveled at one Denver alderman who issued water franchises. Tough competition eventually bankrupted most water suppliers. Ultimately, a single powerful water monopoly emerged in Denver. Started in 1894 by Walter Scott Cheesman and David Moffat, the Denver Union Water Company aggressively consolidated water delivery while expanding water collection for Colorado's flagship city.[16]

Meanwhile, up the road in Boulder, citizens had long ago rejected the corporate route and began their own municipal system. Nevertheless, Boulder served as a revolving door between its private interests and local water officials. James P. Maxwell served as both a town trustee and mayor and eventually city engineer overseeing the water system while simultaneously building and promoting his private real estate and ditch projects. Others in the revolving door included George Oliver, an early Maxwell partner who surveyed both the Silver Lake and Town of Boulder Ditches. Another, John A. Ellet, served as president of the town trustees and contractor for water system improvements. Into the twentieth century the revolving door continued with the city employing the engineer Fred Fair, who continued to operate a separate engineering consulting business.[17]

Boulder's water managers gained experience through the 1880s and 1890s. And the town established a track record for getting the authorized projects completed. But major problems, once thought solved, kept resurfacing. Each time a new source of supply was added, new demand would quickly consume it. And water quality issues never seemed to go away. Eyes soon turned toward the glacial valleys in the high mountains west of Boulder, where a series of lakes formed during the ice age offered the prospect of clean, abundant water.

The twentieth century started off in Boulder by serving up a dry winter in 1901–1902. Streamflow on Boulder Creek was exceedingly low, and the city experienced its first serious water shortage. Demand had already overtaxed the Sunshine and Chautauqua Reservoirs, and when coupled with the low winter streamflow, the water system simply could not meet demand. The city turned to James P. Maxwell for help. By then Maxwell was not only the city engineer but also owner of the Silver Lake Reservoir in the high mountains west of Boulder. Coming to the rescue, Maxwell released water from his reservoir on an emergency basis to the town.[18]

In the aftermath of the 1901–1902 drought the possibility of storing pure water in a high mountain reservoir recaptured the attention of the city council. Although the city had previously refused to serve Maxwell's developments water, the tables were now turned. Suddenly the council took an interest in Maxwell's properties and visited Silver Lake to assess its potential. Maxwell saw an opportunity, and in 1903 he proposed a public-private partnership to build a pipeline from near Nederland to Boulder. Citizens met the proposal with skepticism because of perceived conflicts of interest. Although the partnership proposal went nowhere, negotiations continued, and eventually Maxwell and his family agreed to sell their water rights and facilities to the city.[19]

The first purchase occurred in January 1904 with Boulder's acquisition of storage rights in Triple Lake, Oval Lake, and Goose Lake from Clint J. Maxwell, James's son. Two years later, in January 1906, Boulder purchased various assets from the Silver Lake Ditch and Reservoir Company from James P. Maxwell. This included a portion of water rights in Silver Lake for $46,000 and Island Lake for $12,000. During the negotiations, former mayor M. S. Whiteley confidently remarked that this purchase would settle "the question of Boulder's water supply for all time to come." Although Maxwell and Boulder eventually finalized the sale, this, like the previous deals, was tainted by conflict of interest charges.[20]

About a year later, Maxwell sold his remaining interest in the Silver Lake Ditch to real estate developer William W. Degge. Maxwell, however, was not quite done with building Boulder's water system. In one last deal Maxwell bought the water rights in Lake Albion from Edgar S. Housel and quickly flipped it in a sale to the city.[21]

With Boulder's acquisitions from Maxwell complete, the city was well along the way toward assembling a system of reservoirs and land that became known as the Silver Lake Watershed. The next big step took place in 1907 when President Theodore Roosevelt signed a grant giving 1,524 acres of federal land to Boulder. The federal land allowed Boulder to access Lake Albion and Green Lakes. This gave Boulder a large contiguous tract isolated from the mining waste and pollutants that had made managing the Town of Boulder and Sunshine Reservoirs so difficult. The grant also angered boosters for the future Rocky Mountain National Park who wanted these lands included in the park. But it meant that Boulder achieved the twin goals of protecting the water supply and providing sufficient water for growth well into the future. Over the next century Boulder acquired nearly 6,645 acres of nearby federal and private lands. This included not only reservoir sites, but the surrounding watershed that supplied snowmelt to them. Boulder attained the enviable position of controlling both the source and quality of the water it received. With these acquisitions, the city could focus on integrating its water supply system and building up its storage and collection capacity.[22]

While assembling the watershed properties, Boulder also spent the early twentieth century taking action to extend pipe and services within town. It seemed that every few weeks the council considered and approved a new motion to extend water mains through the streets. At the same time citizens from around town petitioned for service extensions. The January 4, 1909, petition from I. T. Shockley was a typical request "for extension of water main . . . [from] 7th Avenue and Aurora Avenue; thence south on 7th Avenue a distance of 275 feet." Pipe extensions were piecemeal but ultimately comprehensive.[23]

While Boulder consolidated land and water holdings, it was also integrating the watershed with the rest of the municipal system. This included a pipeline to bring water to a settling basin on the Boulder County Ranch and another structure that later became known as the Lakewood Pipeline. Then in 1907 a water line was constructed across Como Creek to exclude polluted water from that area.[24]

Boulder wasted no time updating and enlarging the various reservoirs in the watershed. Many of its reservoirs were former glacial lakes that were dammed and enlarged to store water. In July 1906 the city employed a construction supervisor to oversee work at its Goose Lake Dam. Two years later a thirty-foot-high, rock filled, timber-crib structure was completed.[25]

In 1907, the torch of building Boulder's water system was passed to a young engineer by the name of Fred A. Fair, who began surveying for a possible rock dam at Lake Albion. Fair's plans evolved into a design for a sixty-foot-high concrete dam. Considerable preliminary work was needed to begin the project, including the construction of a road, bunk house, outlet channel, and other incidentals. With the passage of a $125,000 water bond in 1911, actual work on the Lake Albion Dam began. A crew of 175 men under the supervision of Clair V. Mann worked day and night. Even with a series of false starts and delays, Lake Albion Dam was finished by 1913.[26]

Fred Fair was intimately involved in developing Boulder's key watershed properties. Born in Iowa in 1880, Fair's family moved to Colorado in 1882. He started school at the age of twelve and later worked his way through the Colorado School of Mines selling sewing machines with his father. Fair (Figure 13.5) graduated with an engineering degree in 1902. In 1904 he is said to have discovered a glacier at the head of St. Vrain Creek that he named after his wife, Isabelle. After taking jobs around the state, Fair got his break

FIGURE 13.5. Fred A. Fair. Photograph courtesy of the Carnegie Branch Library for Local History, Boulder Historical Society Collection. Reprinted with permission.

when he designed Goose Lake Dam with James P. Maxwell. It is probably through this connection that Fair was named Boulder's city engineer, a position that he held from 1908 to 1910 and again from 1912 to 1916. Starting in 1932, Fair was employed as the Boulder County engineer. In the break between his stints with the city and county, Fair designed a number of other reservoirs, including Lake Isabelle on St. Vrain Creek, also named after his wife.

A flurry of work on other reservoirs took place as well. In 1911 the original rock-crib, timber-fill structure at Silver Lake constructed by James P. Maxwell was raised to thirty-five feet. The city also built additional storage at Green Lakes just upstream from Lake Albion. A private concern began the work on Green Lakes, but it was later taken over by Boulder. The survey work on Green Lakes Reservoirs was initiated by Fair in 1906, and construction began in 1908. Complicating matters was that Green Lakes were located above timberline, making them inaccessible for supply except by pack train. Financial difficulties of the original owner, F. L. Heseltine, and its builder, the Boston Power Company, further delayed construction.[27]

Primary development in the Silver Lake Watershed mostly wound down before the United States entered World War I. The main task that remained was to protect the water from possible pollution. In 1916 a health officer cited primitive sanitary conditions at Silver Lake from campers and tourists. Typhoid outbreaks continued in Boulder County, and the prospect of contaminated water remained a concern. With that, Boulder built its first chlorination plant at the Lakewood Pipeline intake. Even so, the city council seriously discussed the possibility of hiring guards to protect the watershed. Eventually, the council settled on the idea of a caretaker to watch the area and hired Alfred Wheeler for the job. Then in 1920 Boulder closed the watershed to public access, citing potential threats to public health. Boulder's Silver Lake Watershed remains closed to the public to this day.[28]

UNDER THE GREAT DIVIDE

In Colorado, moving water from one watershed to another began with the construction of the Left Hand Ditch in 1863. The close geographic proximity of James Creek, a tributary of Left Hand Creek, to the South St. Vrain River made building this early transbasin diversion feasible with the primitive tools then in use. Conflict and litigation over this diversion ended with the landmark court case, *Coffin v. Left Hand Ditch Company.* This decision shaped water development across Colorado and the West. Although ditch and reservoir construction continued at a brisk pace in Boulder County, no new transbasin diversions were built in the county for the remainder of the nineteenth century.

Nevertheless, in the late nineteenth century the idea of taking water across the Continental Divide began to grow in people's minds. Initial efforts focused on providing agricultural water, but cities soon became the main proponents for transmountain diversions. In 1889 Hiram Prince, Boulder Creek's water commissioner, urged the Colorado General Assembly to set aside $25,000 to survey a route to bring Colorado River water to the East Slope. Prince's idea was to develop a twenty-mile-long canal over South Boulder Pass to South Boulder Creek. As a major shareholder in the rather junior South Boulder Canon Ditch, Prince's idea seems self-serving today. Regardless of his motivations, this was likely Colorado's first formal proposal for a transmountain diversion. Although the legislature set aside some money for surveying, nothing came of the idea.[29]

Elsewhere along the Front Range, projects to divert Colorado River water moved forward. In 1890, the Water Supply and Storage Company of Fort Collins started work on a canal 1,000 feet above the Kawuneeche Valley in what is now Rocky Mountain National Park. The company appropriated 525 cfs of water from upper tributaries of the Grand River (now Colorado) and sent it by gravity over Poudre Pass to the Cache la Poudre River and on to farms east of Fort Collins. The remote location required much of the ditch to be dug by hand, and the company hired Japanese and Mexican laborers to do the work. Eight years elapsed from the first appropriation in 1892 to the first diversions across the divide.[30]

More years passed before other transbasin diversions were seriously considered for the mountains west of Boulder. In the early 1900s, a "Standley Canal Tunnel" and a Denver Northwestern and Pacific Railroad tunnel to be served by a "Moffat Tunnel Ditch" with water from the Fraser River on the West Slope were actively studied. Both tunnels would deliver water to the upper reaches of South Boulder Creek. Work for the Standley Canal Tunnel never progressed beyond the conceptual phase, but the railroad water tunnel went from concept to reality.

Transportation dreams led to the construction of the first major water tunnel under the Continental Divide. Denver businessmen had long sought rail links to simultaneously open Colorado to new markets and access the state's hinterland for further exploitation. In the forefront were David H. Moffat, Governor John Evans, and others who had financed Colorado's first rail link with their Denver Pacific Railroad to Cheyenne and the Union Pacific Railroad. Not satisfied with a single railroad, Moffat built other lines, but his long-term aspiration remained a rail link to the West Coast independent of companies he did not control. With this line, Moffat could liberate himself from eastern capitalists who owned competing railroads. A railroad across the Continental Divide would give Moffat a connection to Salt Lake and allow him to develop extensive coal holdings he acquired in northwestern Colorado.

Moffat eventually fulfilled his ambitions with the founding and construction of the Denver Northwestern & Pacific Railway, or "Moffat Road." Starting in 1902, construction progressed out of Denver and up South Boulder Creek. An exceptional engineering feat for its time, workmen dug well over thirty tunnels to reach the high country near Rollins Pass. The effort was enormous, and it consumed Moffat's health and vast fortune. Moffat died in 1911 with the railroad still under construction. Moffat's death notwithstanding, the road was completed, but winter operations over the Continental Divide at Rollins Pass proved daunting. Planning soon began to build a tunnel under the divide.[31]

Financing a Continental Divide tunnel was another hurdle, and promoters made appeals to the Colorado Legislature for assistance. Much of the work for raising the capital fell to William G. Evans, son of the territorial governor and a close Moffat associate. The first public effort to build a "Moffat Tunnel" came with an amendment to the Denver City Charter in May of 1913 to appoint a tunnel commission with the authority to issue bonds to help pay for the project. In the charter amendment, Denver reserved the perpetual right to use the tunnel as an aqueduct to bring water from the West Slope to Denver. After overcoming a number of setbacks, Evans's persistence was rewarded, and in 1923 the Colorado Legislature created a quasi-municipal agency called the Moffat Tunnel Improvement District. The tunnel eventually cost about $18 million to construct, or about three times the original estimate. Funds for the project were raised through bond sales.[32]

To determine the feasibility of the railroad tunnel, a somewhat smaller eight-by-eight-foot pilot, or pioneer bore, was cut parallel to the future railroad tunnel. Once the pilot bore proved the railroad's feasibility, it was completed for use as a water tunnel. Denver secured the lease for the bore and finished it as the Moffat Water Tunnel. The tunnel's name is appropriate, as David Moffat had helped found both the Denver Union Water Company, an entity ultimately taken over by the City of Denver and the Denver Northwestern Pacific Railway, for which the tunnel was eventually built.

The pilot tunnel was officially "holed" through on February 18, 1926. So important was the event for the region that boosters arranged for President Calvin Coolidge to press a key in Washington linked by telegraph to ignite the dynamite for the critical blast under the Continental Divide. It was a big news story at the time, meriting a live, nationwide broadcast transmitted from the heart of the mountain. Colorado governor W. H. Adams and the mayors of Denver and Salt Lake were on hand for the blast. The railroad tunnel itself was "holed" through on July 7, 1927, and then completed in February of 1928.

The railroad tunnel cut off 175 miles from the Denver route to the Pacific and, as promised, greatly eased winter operations. The pilot tunnel allowed Denver to divert water from the upper tributaries of the Colorado River. So critical was the water tunnel that Denver's Moffat Collection System now represents about 25 percent of Denver's total water supply. Construction did not occur without a steep human toll. On the evening of July 30, 1926, a rockfall estimated at 125 tons killed six workers instantly. Figure 13.6 suggests some of the working conditions in the Moffat Tunnel.[33]

The next major—and, for that matter, only other—transmountain diversion of water into Boulder County began with the creation of the Northern Colorado Water Conservancy District. Northern, as it's commonly known, was established in 1937 when the Colorado Legislature passed the Water

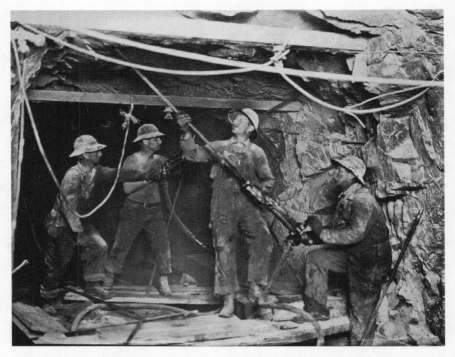

FIGURE 13.6. Construction work on the Moffat Tunnel. Reprinted with permission.

Conservancy Act. Northern's primary charge is to promote, develop, and distribute water from the US Bureau of Reclamation's Colorado–Big Thompson (C-BT) Project within the district boundaries. Construction of the C-BT Project began in 1936 with wide political support in northern Colorado. Much of northeastern Colorado is now supplied water by the vast system. Many saw it as needed stimulus to move Colorado out of the Great Depression. When the project was proposed in the depths of the Great Depression, proponents such as Ralph Parshall justified it using New Deal rhetoric of providing "social security" in the form of water for people in northeastern Colorado.[34]

Initial construction funds for the C-BT Project were provided in the Interior Department Appropriation Act of August 9, 1937. Secretary of Interior Harold L. Ickes determined the project was feasible in his efforts to stimulate the economy with New Deal public works moneys. Ickes's funding recommendation was then approved by President Roosevelt on December 21,

1937. C-BT diverts water from the Colorado River headwaters and delivers it to water users for agricultural, municipal, and industrial purposes. A central mission of the C-BT is to supplement existing water supplies. Initially, the C-BT primarily supplied agricultural water. Today many cities rely on the system to furnish municipal water.[35]

Water deliveries from the C-BT Project are restricted for use within the Northern district or its municipal subdistrict boundaries. Northern delivers C-BT water only to stakeholders or their lessees. Northern does not issue shares like one would expect from a corporation. Rather, Northern, as a quasi-public entity, issues contracts to deliver water to its stakeholders. These contract obligations are known as "units" and are bought and sold much as shares in ditch companies. There are 320,000 units outstanding. The City of Boulder eventually purchased a little over 21,000 units, making it one of the single largest stakeholders in the system. Other Boulder County municipal entities relying on C-BT units include Longmont, Louisville, Lafayette, Broomfield, and the Left Hand Water District.

The C-BT utilizes twelve reservoirs, ninety-five miles of canals, three pumping stations, and the thirteen-mile-long Alva B. Adams Tunnel to bring water from the headwaters of the Colorado River to the northern Front Range. Although development began with the creation of Northern in 1937, the complexity and magnitude of the project meant that supporters had to wait until 1957 to receive their first full year of deliveries. Northern continues to develop and expand to meet the water needs of its unit holders. Much of the recent development is focused on meeting growing municipal demand.

C-BT water begins its journey from the headwaters of the Colorado River and is first stored in Grand Lake (Colorado's largest natural lake), Shadow Mountain Reservoir, or Lake Granby (Colorado's second-largest reservoir). From there, the water travels beneath Rocky Mountain National Park and the Continental Divide via the Alva B. Adams Tunnel. After leaving the tunnel, water discharges into the Big Thompson River to flow through a series of canals and reservoirs. Water destined for Boulder flows through Lake Estes, Carter Lake, the St. Vrain Supply Canal, and then south via the Boulder Feeder Canal to Boulder Reservoir.

After more than a decade of work and countless hours spent in negotiations, planning, and construction, the first water came through the Alva B. Adams Tunnel on June 23, 1947. Among the onlookers was Greeley's W. D.

Farr, who eventually became the longest-serving member of the Northern board. In an interview with Daniel Tyler of Colorado State University, Farr described the day when the first Colorado River water came through the tunnel to the East Slope:

> "We had been there about an hour waiting," WD remembered. "Here is just the tunnel, and it is blank. Nothing! Very quiet! This group of men . . . we were up there to see what was going to happen. We had no idea. We stood around, fidgeted and talked. All of a sudden we heard a roaring noise, not like water or anything. It sounded like a train coming. We couldn't figure that out. Then the biggest cloud of dust I ever saw came out of that tunnel ahead of the water. You can imagine that. Thirteen miles long. It just covered us with dust. We were just filthy, our hats, our clothes. That dust hit us and we couldn't see anything. As that dust dropped down, then [came] the lighter dust behind it. Here was the water rushing out, and we knew it was going to work. We knew the water was there. I have never seen men as happy in my life. Never expect to [again]. Finally you had the water, and you knew it was going to change northern Colorado. You had no idea how, but that was the answer."[36]

The project succeeded beyond anyone's imagination, and Northern continues to grow today. When Northern was first proposed, Boulder citizens were skeptical about joining. Even in the late 1940s Boulder citizens remained ambivalent because they were not convinced about the long-term need for the water. Moreover, many were concerned that the Bureau of Reclamation had not firmly committed to build the Boulder Supply Canal, the essential feature necessary for Boulder to receive water. By 1950, Boulder, Northern, and the Bureau of Reclamation had reached an agreement to build the Boulder Supply Canal to Boulder Creek and the South Platte Supply Canal from Boulder Creek to the South Platte. Only after it was clear that these project components would get built did Boulder request admission to the district.[37]

Richard Behrmann, a longtime farmer on Left Hand Creek, recalled the bureau building the Boulder Supply Canal. According to Behrmann, personnel from Northern and the bureau were going around the valley offering to sell units to farmers for $50. Apparently they were eager to get as many farmers signed up as possible to show broad local support. With units selling in recent years for upward of $20,000, Behrmann said he wished he had bought many more of them.[38]

When the C-BT Project was originally built only 15 percent of the water went to cities and industries, with the remainder going to agriculture. However, with development, the amount of water consumed by cities and industries has steadily increased with conversions of agricultural land to subdivisions and other uses. By 2004, fully 60 percent of the C-BT Project was used for municipal and industrial purposes. Over the years, the ascent of municipal ownership has slowly shifted Northern's priorities toward serving its urban clients.[39]

As Boulder grew, it came to rely heavily on C-BT units. By 1967, Boulder gave top priority to construction of a new water filtration plant to treat its West Slope water. This plant, built near the terminus of Northern's Boulder Feeder Canal at Boulder Reservoir, came on line in 1971. Boulder's involvement with Northern continued to deepen in 1968 when the city council approved participation in the district's Windy Gap Project to pump additional Colorado River water to the East Slope.[40]

Concurrently with the shift from agricultural to municipal use, attitudes among Northern's users toward transmountain diversions have changed too. The public is increasingly aware of the steep environmental cost of transmountain diversions. On the West Slope, streams have been reduced to a trickle, wetlands destroyed, fish and wildlife damaged, recreational values diminished, future growth constrained, and farm economies shrunk. These effects have resulted in vigorous opposition to new diversions. As public attitudes have soured, West Slope politicians have called for compensation to offset the damage. However, attempts in the Colorado Legislature to compensate the so-called "basin of origin" have generally failed in the face of opposition from Front Range cities.

Environmental laws enacted starting in the 1970s have forced anyone wishing to divert water from the West Slope to go through an almost bewilderingly complex set of requirements to evaluate potential project impacts. West Slope rivers, once underutilized, are now fully appropriated, limiting the amount of water available to anyone on either side of the divide. As West Slope counties have grown, the demand for water along the upper tributaries of the Colorado River has increased. Consequently Summit and Grand Counties are setting high regulatory and political bars for anyone wishing to divert Upper Colorado River water. With these changes, new transmountain diversion projects face almost insurmountable odds for approval. The most that East Slope water developers can hope for is fuller utilization of existing West Slope infrastructure. And that is precisely where Denver Water and Northern have focused their attention.

With diminished opportunities to divert West Slope water, developers are left with few options for acquiring new sources of supply. Their chief option is to redirect water from existing uses through the purchase of agricultural water rights.[41]

GROWING CITIES, SHRINKING DITCHES

The author John Nichols got to the heart of tensions between water, land, and culture in his 1974 classic, *The Milagro Beanfield War*. In it the hero Jose Mondragon was an underdog fighting corporate interests who tried to pry water away from farmers to build a large resort development in northern New Mexico. Similarly, Jake, played by Jack Nicholson in Roman Polanski's *Chinatown*, was the underdog fighting seedy, big-money developers who were surreptitiously buying water rights in Owens Valley to feed the unstoppable growth of Los Angeles. In popular culture a mystique has developed around the perceived lack of ethics of transferring water from farms to towns. This isn't surprising, as water is fundamental to both the rural economy and our sense of place. Removing water can fray an area's economic and social fabric. Water transfers may support expanding regional economies and may make sense from a macroeconomic perspective, but they occur at the expense of the economic sustainability of rural communities.

Developers needing water are increasingly seeking supplies that are ripe for redevelopment or transfer. This has created markets for buying and selling water rights. However, once a water right is sold, the new owner, if he or she wishes to use it anywhere other than under the ditch from which it came, must submit applications to water court to authorize changing place, timing, or type of use.

Over time, people have appropriated thousands of water rights in the Boulder Creek Watershed. Water rights change cases modifying decrees now far exceeded the number of original water right appropriations in the watershed. On Boulder Creek and its tributaries there were 2,111 individually named water rights existing by the end of 1991. Of that number there were an

TABLE 13.1

Stream	Number of Individually Named Water Rights	Number of Water Rights Changes to Named Water Rights
Boulder Creek	206	533
South Boulder Creek	179	919
Middle Boulder Creek	25	48
North Boulder Creek	30	57
Coal Creek	85	149
Springs	183	202
Groundwater	944	1,016
Other Tributaries	459	547
Total Boulder Creek Basin	2,111	3,471

additional 3,471 changes to those named water rights, as summarized in Table 13.1. Mostly these changes modify the point or time of use, but include some augmentation plans and a few abandonments. Most changes involve only parts of individual water rights, such as when a municipality transfers ditch shares to its utility.[42]

Urban sprawl regularly makes newspaper headlines. One of the back stories to the urban sprawl issue is the conversion of farmland to urban uses. In Boulder Valley, when a new subdivision gets built, it usually means irrigated farmland is dried up and ditch diversions reduced. As urbanization advances, many ditch companies are now dominated by the municipalities that have slowly acquired shares. Often cities buy ditch shares outright or require developers to turn over their water rights as a prerequisite for annexation.[43]

When Boulder purchased its first share of Farmers Ditch in 1880, no one would have imagined that by 2012, the city would own nearly 74 percent of the company. Likewise, Boulder bought 8 of the 100 shares outstanding in the Anderson Ditch in 1886, and today the city owns about 63 percent of the company. On Howard Ditch, Boulder owns about 21 shares of the original 100 shares, and the cities of Louisville and Lafayette own another 65.

The fate of Farmers, Anderson, and Howard Ditches are typical. Few private shareholders remain in these companies. These companies long ago had to contend with municipal buyouts, the departure of private shareholders, and the urbanization of formerly irrigated lands. Other than the development happening earlier, the experience of many ditch companies, particularly those on the rapidly growing east side of Boulder County, is similar. Many ditches in urbanizing areas deal with a host of issues. These include interacting with real estate developers, paving and piping, construction of utilities over and under the ditches, easement modifications, grappling with storm water and runoff, and more odious things like water thieves, injury, and drowning.

Environmental impacts from water transfers are legion and stem directly from the hydrologic modification of streams and changed land management practices. As seen elsewhere, numerous environmental impacts occurred when the original ditches and reservoirs were constructed. With water transfers, a second round of environmental change materializes. Social scientist John Weiner has studied water transfers and has described their impacts as part of a cycle of change to an already dramatically altered environment. These impacts include drying up natural and man-made wetlands, reduced streamflows and lake levels (which affect fish and wildlife), changes in stream hydrology and morphology, dust storms, spread of noxious weeds, and changes in water quality and alteration of riparian flora. In addition, water transfers can change salt loads and affect the quantity of water available for dilution of pollution.[44]

Beyond environmental impacts, a "no-injury rule" evolved in Colorado water law to protect other water users from someone changing their water right. Starting in the mid-1880s the courts began setting limits on changes so that they do not harm other water rights. Generally, this no-injury rule limits the amount of water transferred to that historically *consumed* by the original user. However, determining consumption is a challenging engineering exercise. For agricultural uses, the consumed water is essentially the water that is evaporated by the plants. Detailed engineering studies estimating how much water has been applied each year versus the amount transpired have become standard analyses in change cases. Courts attempt to preserve historic return flow patterns, ditch seepage, transmission losses, and other factors to protect junior appropriators. Often the courts limit the rate of diversion, the total quantity of water to be diverted, and season of use.

Much of the pressure to convert agricultural ditch shares to municipal use originate with subdivision developers working with municipal governments to build tract homes in their jurisdictions. Typically there are two ways that water rights are transferred from agriculture to municipal use. First, developers acquire land and associated water rights for projects. Then during the development or annexation process the developer deeds the water rights to the city. The city in turn initiates the water court process to transfer the water to municipal use. Development fees are then levied to build the distribution system that the developer needs. Finally, the transferred water is served to the new development. The second way occurs when the developer pays tap fees to the municipality to obtain a water supply for the development. The municipality uses the tap fees to acquire water and build infrastructure that serves the development. Sometimes tap fees are used to purchase the very water rights that came off the developed land. All these fees are then imbedded in the price of the new homes, or in increased water rates paid by existing utility customers.

Many cities along the Front Range cooperate with developers to pursue projects that will expand the tax base. In 2001 the City of Broomfield reportedly paid a tax subsidy to the Flatiron Crossing mall developer in excess of $279 million dollars. The subsidy was intended to offset the cost of water, sewer, roads, and other infrastructure that smaller developments are normally required to pay. In addition, the Flatiron Crossing mall developer received a cap on water and sewer fees worth in excess of $50,000 per year.[45]

These transfers essentially pit municipalities against one another in water rights change cases. It sometimes leads to cities competing against one another by providing essentially free water and sewer service. While these transfers help fuel economic activity, they occur at the ultimate expense of the riparian and agricultural ecosystems.

DENVER WATER'S MOFFAT TUNNEL COLLECTION SYSTEM

During the time cities were purchasing agricultural rights, they were also actively developing projects to bring more water into their service areas. Throughout the twentieth century, many municipal water projects came on line within the Boulder Creek Watershed. First, Boulder assembled its Silver Lake Watershed facilities. Boulder then went on to build Boulder Reservoir to store Colorado River water and also began the process of acquiring Barker Dam, a hydropower reservoir on Middle Boulder Creek. Similarly, the towns of Lafayette and Louisville vigorously pursued storage with acquisitions in Base Line Reservoir and FRICO Marshall respectively. But in talking about water and the West, few systems surpass that built by the City of Denver to serve it and its suburbs. And within that system, some of Denver Water's most important facilities take water from Boulder Creek tributaries.

Denver collects water from a vast area spanning nearly 100 miles north to south, tapping water from the headwaters of both the South Platte and Colorado Rivers. Initially, Denver received water from Cherry Creek and the nearby South Platte. Once the Denver Union Water Company became the preeminent water supplier, it began developing more remote sites on the South Platte and completed Cheesman Dam, then Colorado's largest reservoir, in 1905.[46]

Eventually, Denver citizens voted to make the water utility a public entity and bought out the Denver Union Water Company for $14 million in 1918. The city created a new entity, the Denver Water Department (Denver Water), controlled by its powerful board of water commissioners. The new utility began aggressively developing plans to expand the system to serve an ever-growing city. In short order, Denver Water bought water rights in Antero Reservoir in South Park and the High Line Canal near Denver. Then it built its large Marston Water Treatment Plant and soon after that constructed Eleven Mile Dam on the South Platte. Eventually Denver Water's South Platte Collection System encompassed all of its South Platte facilities plus the Roberts Tunnel and Dillon Reservoir, which tapped the Blue River, an important Colorado tributary. Looking to diversify away from sole reliance on the South Platte, Denver Water set out to divert new supplies from the Upper Colorado via the Moffat Tunnel.

In the 1920s Denver Water began developing its Moffat Tunnel Collection System. This system captures water from the Williams Fork and Fraser Rivers on the West Slope, and South Boulder and Ralston Creeks on the east, and delivers it to the Moffat Water Treatment Plant in northwest Denver and various raw water customers. Several major facilities make up this system, including the Williams Fork River Collection System, Gumlick Tunnel, Vasquez Tunnel, the Fraser River Collection System, the Cabin-Meadow Creek Collection System, Moffat Tunnel, Gross Reservoir, South Boulder Diversion Dam and Canal, and Ralston Reservoir. Work on the South Boulder Diversion Dam and Canal began in September 1928. Figure 13.7 depicts the construction of the diversion dam for the South Boulder Diversion Canal. When this photo was taken in December 1935, the project was well advanced. Water is already

FIGURE 13.7. Work on the South Boulder Diversion Canal in December 1935. Photo courtesy of Denver Water. Reprinted with permission.

flowing through a small outlet gate. Before Denver Water could begin work on this structure, it had to construct a road in the narrow, near-vertical canyon along South Boulder Creek in what is now Eldorado Canyon State Park.

Water gathered in the Williams Fork Collection System is conveyed from high-elevation tributaries of the Williams Fork River to the Gumlick Tunnel. At 2.9 miles long, the Gumlick Tunnel carries water under the Continental Divide near Jones Pass to a second tunnel, the 3.4-mile-long Vasquez Tunnel, which passes back through the Continental Divide to deliver water into Vasquez Creek. Water in Vasquez Creek, along with water diverted from the Fraser River and its tributaries, plus Denver Water's Cabin-Meadow Creek Diversion System, are then collected and conveyed in a series of pipes, tunnels, siphons, and canals as part of the Fraser River Diversion System.

Located at the bottom of this massive water collection system is the 6.1-mile-long Moffat Tunnel, which conveys water under the Continental

FIGURE 13.8. To facilitate water flows from the Moffat Tunnel, Denver Water channelized South Boulder Creek from the tunnel's east portal to the Boulder County
hamlet of Pine Cliff. Photo courtesy of Denver Water. Reprinted with permission.

Divide into South Boulder Creek and on to Gross Reservoir. To better move
water, Denver Water channelized South Boulder Creek from the east portal
of the tunnel to the Boulder County hamlet of Pine Cliff. To accomplish this,
Denver Water acquired rights-of-way from the railroad and adjoining landowners. Figure 13.8 shows the channelization work. South Boulder Creek, a
formerly meandering stream in its upper broad glacial valley, was straightened and deepened to accommodate the additional 1,280 cfs of flow that the
Moffat Tunnel could deliver under the Continental Divide.

Water from Gross Reservoir is released into South Boulder Creek and then
diverted through the South Boulder Diversion Dam into a canal that leads
to yet another Denver Water facility, Ralston Reservoir. Completed in 1937,
Ralston Reservoir is an earth-fill dam 180 feet high with a storage capacity
of 10,749 acre-feet. After that, water reaches the Moffat Water Treatment
Plant and is delivered into Denver. Although largely hidden from view in
the canyons and mountains of western Boulder County, the Moffat Tunnel

and Gross Reservoir represent the single largest impact to water and riparian ecosystems in the region.[47]

Gross Reservoir's namesake, Dwight D. Gross, was the chief engineer for Denver Water from 1926 through 1951. Gross supervised much of the early survey work and managed the initial phases of reservoir construction. According to Gross, Denver Water "was looking for a site where a small dam would hold back a large quantity of water." Denver Water surveyed a number of sites between the Moffat Tunnel and Ralston Reservoir during the early 1940s. Denver Water eventually settled on a location that was recognized for its reservoir potential as early as 1914. With the start of World War II, defense programs caused water use in the city to increase by "leaps and bounds." With the war's end, demand remained high. Denver needed more water. Engineers soon drafted plans to build a 340-foot-high dam that would store 41,811 acre-feet of water. Denver Water's engineers found that the site could support an even larger dam with an ultimate height of 460 feet and maximum capacity of about 113,000 acre-feet.[48]

In 1949, when Denver Water's planning for the dam went into high gear, it unexpectedly found itself needing a permit from the federal government because of an obscure action by President William Taft in 1910. It turns out that during the early days of hydropower development, the federal government conducted surveys across federal land in the West to assess their potential as dam sites. Denver had approached the US Forest Service with a proposal to trade land in the reservoir area with land elsewhere. But some of the land that Denver Water wanted had been "withdrawn" from disposal or sale by President Taft and reserved for future hydropower development. In an attempt to complete the trade, Denver Water board president Karl C. Brauns appealed to President Harry S. Truman to use his executive authority to revoke President Taft's thirty-nine-year-old reservation. To Denver Water's consternation, President Truman demurred, stating that one request might lead to others and that they might "not be in the public interest." Instead, Truman suggested that Denver Water "could appropriately apply to the Federal Power Commission for a power project license."[49]

Denver Water quickly drafted plans to add hydroelectric generators and other facilities at Gross Reservoir and submitted an application to the Federal Power Commission (the predecessor of the Federal Energy Regulatory Commission) for approval. On the advice of Denver Water's chief council,

Glenn Saunders, the application specified that hydropower production would be incidental to water supply and that the facilities would be added *after* the dam was completed. Denver Water soon had a license from the Federal Power Commission to build its dam. But Denver Water took the word "after" literally and waited for more than fifty years until it needed to renew its license before grudgingly installing the generators.

In the late 1940s Denver Water claimed storage rights for the larger reservoir but elected to build the smaller dam. Denver Water also claimed water rights on South Boulder Creek that yield as much as 18,000 acre-feet during wet years. Once Denver Water claimed the storage rights, it could wait until Denver needed more water before enlarging the dam. Even at the smaller size, Gross Dam was both the highest and largest reservoir in the state when it was built. The reservoir itself is located in a rugged section of South Boulder Canyon above Eldorado Canyon State Park. Its gravity-arch concrete design was typical for large dams in the mid-twentieth century. At nearly 340 feet high, the dam remains an impressive structure. It is the single largest edifice within the Boulder Creek Watershed. Engineers estimated that nearly 650,000 cubic yards of concrete would be needed to complete the structure. To build it, Denver Water accepted bids for a little over $7 million from the Macco Corporation of Paramount, California, and the Puget Sound Bridge and Dredging Company of Seattle.

Dam construction did not occur without tragedy and controversy. On Friday, August 24, 1951, a lightning strike ignited dynamite, killing eight and injuring another ten workers. One of the injured later died from his wounds. Most of the casualties were from the Boulder area. One injured worker, Robert Greer of Boulder, recalled that the accident occurred just as it started to rain. Greer rushed toward a ledge when he saw lightning strike a nearby powder hole, detonating the charge. Rocks flew everywhere, knocking him unconscious. When he came to, his helmet was gone and he couldn't see out of his goggles due to blood streaming down his face. Men rushed everywhere to aid the injured.[50]

Among the rescuers, Captain E. G. Eyere of the Colorado State Patrol was prominent in directing stretcher crews in the hours after the accident. Figure 13.9 shows some of the casualties along with mangled compressors used to supply power to drilling equipment. An inquest initiated by Boulder coroner George W. Howe found two of Denver Water's contractors negligent. Even

FIGURE 13.9. Captain E. G. Eyere of the Colorado State Patrol directing stretcher crews at the Gross Reservoir work site after a lightning strike killed eight workers on August 24, 1951. Reprinted with permission.

though lightning was the immediate cause of the explosions, the inquest determined that there were too many men in the blast area and dynamite had been set long before they had intended to detonate the charges. The tragedy, bad as it was, was especially harsh for Betty Chaussart of Boulder, a mother of five, who lost both her husband and father to the blast.[51]

Accidents notwithstanding, work on Gross Dam forged ahead. When the image shown in Figure 13.10 was taken, about half of the concrete for the project was poured. Gross Reservoir was completed in 1954 at a cost of $16,837,184, or more than double the original contracts. Denver began storing water just as the region's most severe drought of the twentieth century reached critical proportions.

Once Gross Reservoir was operating, farmers in Boulder Valley, particularly those on junior ditches, began complaining of diminished water deliveries.

FIGURE 13.10. About one-half of the concrete for Gross Reservoir was poured by the time this photograph was taken on March 10, 1954. Image courtesy of Denver Water. Reprinted with permission.

Frank J. Montgomery, the former president of the Leyner Cottonwood Ditch, did not mince words when he discussed Denver Water. As Montgomery put it, his family used to "grow sugar beets, when there was enough water, until Denver stole all our water. We could grow beets, but after Denver put in Gross Reservoir, and their tactics for using the water, we didn't have enough water for sugar beets. We [now] just raise barley, oats, corn and alfalfa." It seems that the "tactics" angering Montgomery was Denver's practice of releasing constant flows out of the reservoir. Once the dam was built, the daily flow fluctuation, known as the diurnal, were averaged out with the effect that many junior ditches went out of priority earlier in the season than in prior years.[52]

In the late 1990s Denver Water relicensed Gross Reservoir with the Federal Energy Regulatory Commission. As a condition to relicense the dam, Denver

Water installed generators and made physical changes that would facilitate an eventual dam enlargement. As this book goes to press, Denver Water is seeking permits to enlarge Gross Dam from its current capacity of 41,811 acre-feet to about 119,000 acre-feet, which includes a 5,000-acre-foot environmental pool. Denver Water began a process of "scoping" potential projects in 2003 to enlarge its Moffat Collection System. By 2009, Denver Water had narrowed the list of potential projects to five. Denver Water's "preferred alternative," using the regulatory phrase, is to add about 131 feet to the top of the dam to increase storage by about 72,000 acre-feet. This would provide Denver with about 18,000 acre-feet of annual yield. The other options Denver Water considered all involve enlarging Gross Reservoir by fewer feet, but make up for that by adding other components, such as a possible second reservoir, pump back of wastewater, and so on. Until the federal permitting agencies, the US Corps of Engineers and the Federal Energy Regulatory Commission, issue a record of decision, a final configuration on the enlargement is unknown.

What is known is that Gross Reservoir, already the largest reservoir in the county, stands to nearly triple in size. Enlarging Gross Reservoir will impact Boulder citizens and the local environment regardless of the alternative the federal agencies select for permitting. Flows on South Boulder Creek, already reduced because of numerous ditch and reservoir diversions, will decrease further because Denver Water will enhance its ability to store water from that creek. From the Moffat Tunnel to the South Boulder Diversion Canal flows will actually increase as more West Slope water is brought across the Continental Divide. Taken as a whole, enlarging Gross Reservoir will affect the entire South Boulder Creek Watershed. To address adverse impacts to fish and invertebrates in South Boulder Creek, the City of Boulder, Denver Water, and the City of Lafayette developed an aquatic mitigation plan that offsets many impacts by providing water to the creek during the late summer, fall, and winter when ditch and reservoir diversions cause the greatest reductions in streamflow.

To improve streamflow, both the water and a place to store and release it is needed on South Boulder Creek. Boulder enlisted Denver Water, which has storage, and Lafayette, which has water rights, to work on the problem. In the mid-1990s Boulder and Denver Water accomplished a first step in establishing an instream flow program for South Boulder Creek. It did this by creating an "environmental pool" in Gross Reservoir that can be filled with water during the irrigation season for release later in the winter as instream flow. The environmental pool is similar to an empty bucket, because it must be paired with water rights to fill it. Unfortunately for the stream, storage was only accessible on an "as available" basis, and Boulder was unable to purchase the necessary water rights. Once Denver Water proposed enlarging Gross Reservoir, Boulder saw an opportunity to secure permanent storage rights to address the problem.

Consequently, Boulder initiated negotiations between Denver Water and Lafayette that resulted in an agreement to coordinate resources to solve the South Boulder Creek instream flow problem. This involves enlarging Gross Reservoir even further—an additional 5,000 AF—to create an environmental pool to store water rights owned by Boulder and Lafayette. The environmental pool, with an estimated cost of $8 million, has Denver Water contributing approximately $4 million while Boulder and Lafayette each contribute about $2 million. Water for the environmental pool will come from Lafayette, which owns numerous South Boulder Creek water rights, and Boulder, whose C-BT units can be stored in the reservoir and released for municipal or agricultural uses. It remains to be seen whether Gross Reservoir will be enlarged, but this mitigation plan holds promise that for once building a large dam may offset the long-term depletions experienced on an overtapped creek.

EXPANDING BOULDER'S WATER SUPPLY: BOULDER RESERVOIR AND THE BOULDER CANYON HYDROELECTRIC PROJECT

During the 1940s and 1950s it became increasingly clear that the Silver Lake Watershed could not provide all the water Boulder needed for its long-term growth. Compounding this problem, in the early 1950s Colorado experienced its most severe drought since hydrologists began keeping records. During the drought, water managers became alarmed that they might not meet existing demand, let alone the provide water for people and industries that had not yet arrived. Municipal systems across Colorado, Boulder included, raced to develop new supplies. Boulder was in a somewhat better position than most, as it had two options sitting nearly on its doorstep. The first was to further expand its holdings on Boulder Creek, and the second was to acquire water from the C-BT Project through Northern.

Situated above Boulder straddling Middle Boulder Creek is the Barker Meadow Dam. Located just east of the town of Nederland, Barker Reservoir was ideally positioned to supply water to Boulder. Boulder realized that Barker Reservoir, one of the first major hydroelectric projects in the state, could also supply water that the city badly needed.

During the early twentieth century, American cities underwent rapid electrification. In Colorado, two Colorado Springs engineers, Leonard Curtis and Henry Hine, developed plans to build a hydroelectric plant on the Grand (now Colorado) River in Glenwood Canyon. After Curtis and Hine completed a long series of tests proving their bold project's feasibility, investors incorporated the Central Colorado Power Company, raising a staggering sum of $22.5 million. Among its prominent backers were railroad magnate David H. Moffat and former Ohio governor Myron T. Herrick. Construction quickly started on what became known as the Shoshone Power Plant.[53]

With work progressing at Shoshone, some of its backers turned to a site on Middle Boulder Creek that also held significant potential for power generation. The site they chose was nearly ideal for a reservoir. A Pleistocene glacier had carved a broad U-shaped valley. At the terminus of the glacier, Middle Boulder Creek narrowed considerably where it entered a bedrock canyon that provided an excellent anchor for a dam.

A tangled series of owners came to develop and operate the reservoir project for Middle Boulder Creek. The first to produce concrete plans was a company known as the Denver-Eureka Power Company. This short-lived concern appropriated the first water rights for the project. However, it was some Central Colorado Power Company investors who formed a second company, the Eastern Colorado Power Company, in May of 1907 that began actual construction on the Boulder Canyon Hydroelectric Project (Boulder Hydro Project). But soon after they started, delays of nearly two years occurred as the company weathered an economic depression. Eventually work resumed full bore, and by 1910 the Boulder Hydro Project was operational. Then in April 1913 a new company, the Colorado Power Company, took over the assets of several firms, including those of the Eastern Colorado Power Company and its Boulder Hydro Project. Mergers continued, and in 1924 the Colorado Power Company became part of the Public Service Company of Colorado, which operated it until yet another merger resulted in its being taken over by Xcel Energy in 2000. In 2001, Xcel Energy sold the

FIGURE 13.11. Barker Meadow Dam under construction in April 1910. Image courtesy Colorado State Archives. Reprinted with permission.

Boulder Hydro Project to the City of Boulder, which continues to own and operate the system.[54]

The ambitious Boulder Hydro Project included building the Barker Meadow Dam, an aqueduct to bring water to a small holding reservoir (Kossler Lake), and a penstock to deliver water under pressure to a power plant in Boulder Canyon. A photo of the reservoir under construction from April 1910 is shown in Figure 13.11. As many as 350 men, including hammer men, horse skinners, and pick and shovel workers, to name a few, were employed at wages ranging from $2.50 to $3.00 per day. The aqueduct involved constructing an 11.7-mile, 36-inch reinforced concrete gravity pipeline through rugged terrain to connect the two reservoirs.[55]

Barker Dam was designed by the J. G. White Company of New York. The dam alone cost about $2.7 million. For the time, the 170-foot-high concrete masonry dam with a crest of over 660 feet was rare. Ironically the dam is named after Hanna Barker, the woman whose land the Central Colorado Power Company condemned for the project.[56]

FIGURE 13.12. The Boulder Hydro Project high-pressure penstock under construction. The method of "ball peen" welding was an innovation developed to stem
leaks from this penstock. This photograph was likely taken in 1910. Image courtesy
Colorado State Archives. Reprinted with permission.

To build the power plant, workers sent equipment and materials by train about halfway up Boulder Canyon to a place called Orodell, and from there loaded it onto specially constructed wagons for final shipment to the site. As this was in the days before the widespread use of gasoline-powered trucks, teams of up to sixteen horses were used to pull the wagons. During construction a temporary village catered to the workers, with living quarters, stables, a blacksmith shop, mess hall, and other buildings occupying the site.[57]

Once water arrives at Kossler Reservoir, it descends down the penstock 1,828 vertical feet to the power plant. The image in Figure 13.12 shows the high-pressure penstock under construction. Pipe rests on a tramway that workers built to carry materials up the steep mountain. When built, it had the highest head of any hydro plant in the United States. With the high head came high pressures. After penstock construction was completed, the company found that the riveted butt joints could not withstand the water pressure, leading to major leaks. To explore solutions, the company brought in a welder skilled in using acetylene gases from Kansas City, Missouri. Acetylene was just then coming into widespread use in welding. Between this welder and the workers at the plant, they discovered that by hammering the still-warm welds, the joints did not crack after cooling. This solved the leaking problem. Engineering reports credit the "ball peen" welding method as an innovation from this project.[58]

Major work on the dam and powerhouse was completed in August 1910. Producing power were two I. P. Morris waterwheels connected to two General Electric generators, each capable of producing 5,000 kilowatts. A number of families lived and worked at the plant. One operator, Everett H. Brines, raised six children there with his wife, Daisy Irene, until they moved out when Brines retired. To keep their home warm, Brines built electric resistance heaters out of wire. In Brines's words, the "coils had no insulation and they were dangerous. How we ever raised the kids without more accidents, I'll never know." But accidents did occur: first one daughter fell onto a heater, which burned and scarred her back. Next a son was scarred from burns, so they built screens to prevent further accidents. Then on November 1, 1933, Brines lost his right hand when he accidently touched one of the 13,000-kilovolt circuit breakers. The resulting electric arc burned his hand so badly that doctors had to amputate.[59]

With Barker Dam sitting above Boulder, it was only natural that the city would eventually take interest in acquiring the reservoir. Boulder's initial rights in Barker were established with a water storage agreement signed in 1955. By this time, the Public Service Company of Colorado (PSCo) owned Barker Dam and other properties, including the Shoshone Power Plant on the Colorado River and the Valmont Power Plant east of Boulder. The amount the city could store was later doubled in 1968 when PSCo and Boulder entered into a thirty-five-year, $1.4 million contract.

Then, in 1982, the Federal Energy Regulatory Commission (the federal agency that licensed Barker Dam) placed a storage restriction on the reservoir over concerns about the ability of the dam to withstand an overtopping event during a severe flood. In exchange for helping to pay for the necessary repairs to strengthen the dam, PSCo granted Boulder a perpetual interest allowing ongoing use of 8,000 acre-feet of storage and two-thirds of the capacity in the aquaduct.[60]

During the late 1980s and 1990s, Boulder sought to buy the entire Barker system, but PSCo refused to sell. However, through a series of corporate mergers PSCo ended up as a unit of Xcel Energy. When Xcel Energy expressed an interest in disposing of various assets, Boulder saw its chance and initiated negotiations to purchase the entire Boulder Hydro Project. The sale, which was completed in 2001, gave Boulder full control over Barker Reservoir. Boulder took over power generation and later claimed additional water rights to store municipal water in Barker Reservoir.[61]

Meanwhile, as Boulder made overtures to PSCo for Barker Reservoir, it worked on developing its supplies from the Northern. Once Northern completed the Boulder Supply Canal, Boulder needed storage so that it could use its C-BT units efficiently. This required the construction of new storage, later christened Boulder Reservoir. John M. Sayre, then Boulder city attorney, was instrumental in getting the reservoir built as a joint project between Boulder and Northern. Water rights from the Colorado River and several East Slope sources are stored there.

Sayre, who was born in Boulder, entered World War II as a naval officer just a few days after marrying his wife Jean. In October of 1944 he was seriously wounded on a mine-sweeper in the South Pacific. Sayre spent two years recuperating in a naval hospital in Oklahoma. Returning to Colorado, he earned a JD degree at the University of Colorado in 1948. He then served as the Boulder city attorney from 1952 to 1955. As city attorney he initiated the condemnation proceedings to acquire the land necessary for Boulder

Reservoir. Eventually Sayre served on the Northern board and helped organize its municipal subdistrict. At Northern, Sayre worked to finance and construct the Windy Gap Project, which provides West Slope water to participat-
ing municipalities. His experience in western water led to his appointment
as Assistant Secretary of Interior for Water and Science by President George
H.W. Bush. In that capacity, Sayre supervised the Bureau of Reclamation, the
US Geological Survey, and the Bureau of Mines. Sayre died in 2010 at the age
of eighty-eight.[62]

The Denver firm Colorado Contractors won the low bid to construct
the reservoir. Work began in May of 1954 and progressed rapidly, and the
1.2-mile-long earthen dam was completed in early 1955. When finished, it
could store 13,270 acre-feet. Even though Boulder Reservoir is a Northern
facility, Boulder took charge of building the reservoir, as it primarily benefits the city. In January 1957 the *Daily Camera* reported that the final cost of
Boulder Reservoir came in at $1,158,027. Of that, Boulder paid about $756,000,
and the remaining costs were borne by Northern. With Boulder Reservoir
completed, Boulder's main water supply projects were completed.[63]

THE QUEST FOR CLEAN WATER

Ever since the Town of Boulder Reservoir was built in 1875, one of the
main selling points for new water projects in the city has been to provide
safe drinking water. Boulder's citizens had firsthand experiences with poor
water quality and pushed for improvements to maintain public health.
Among Boulder citizens' earliest concerns were waterborne diseases and
industrial pollution.

Among the great scourges of nineteenth-century America was typhoid. A
vicious bacterial disease, typhoid is spread when a person ingests food or
water contaminated with the feces of an infected person. Tens of thousands
of soldiers were sickened or died from the disease during the Civil War. Many
people in the late nineteenth and early twentieth centuries who had firsthand
experiences with this and other devastating waterborne diseases supported
municipal efforts to stamp it out. Until sand filters and chlorination were
developed, Boulder's main water quality strategy available was to tap remote
and pure sources of supply. Eventually Boulder added filtration and chlorination to its water quality arsenal.

In what historian Martin Melosi terms the "Bacteriological Revolution," the period from 1880 to 1945 saw dramatic advances in knowledge about water quality and the importance of providing clean water to communities. Cities saw providing clean water as a key municipal enterprise that filled a necessary condition to support growth. As knowledge about water quality advanced, municipal engineers learned to translate those advances into projects that improved public health through safe water.[64]

During this time, municipalities began building complete water systems to collect and transmit water to their customers. Treatment began with filtration and later added chlorination to disinfect water before it entered the distribution system. And as water deliveries into cities expanded, engineers began to build storm and sewer systems to route excess water back to streams and away from towns where it posed a nuisance. Furthermore, they began building sewer treatment plants as neighboring communities complained about receiving degraded water from upstream sources. In all these ways, Boulder and the other towns of Boulder County were typical.

In 1875, Boulder's town trustees ordered that no privy or open sewer should be allowed to become "nauseous, foul, offensive, or injurious to the public health." Nevertheless, a number of serious epidemics struck Boulder between 1878 and 1934, including smallpox (1879, 1888–1889, 1901), diphtheria (1890, 1923), scarlet fever (1897, 1901, 1927), influenza (1918, 1920), typhoid (1917, 1922), and measles (1930, 1934). Although we now know that not all of these diseases are waterborne, the vectors for the spread of diseases were just becoming known when the epidemics occurred. With the public's health at risk, steps to protect the water supply were prudent. Boulder's initial action beyond moving its water intake west was to build its first chlorination plant at the inlet to its Lakewood Pipeline in response to the 1917 typhoid epidemic.[65]

Boulder's Silver Lake Watershed had such high-quality water that the city had little else to do to improve standards for decades to come. Finally, in 1963 Boulder built its Betasso Water Treatment Plant in the mountains west of town. The treatment plant is strategically situated on its Lakewood Pipeline from the Silver Lake Watershed. A new pipeline also connected the Boulder Hydro Project power plant to the Betasso Water Treatment Plant. Prior to this, Boulder could only get Barker Reservoir water via inefficient water rights exchanges. This new treatment plant helped the city meet ever-tightening drinking water standards after years of minimal treatment of water coming from the watershed.[66]

After the C-BT Project came on line, Boulder could supplement its supplies from this source. Initially, C-BT units were used in water rights exchanges to increase the amount of water available via the Silver Lake Watershed. By 1967, however, Boulder gave top priority to building a new water filtration plant to treat its West Slope water. This plant, built near the terminus of Northern's Boulder Feeder Canal at Boulder Reservoir, was completed in 1971. These two water treatment plants greatly expanded Boulder's options for delivering water into the city. From that point on, the city has undertaken many improvements to integrate the system and increase flexibility for the two plants.

As treated water use expanded, used water soon became a problem in and of itself. Initially citizens employed septic pits and other sewage disposal methods. But as Boulder grew, the septic pits and other methods were deemed wanting. Some citizens began agitating for sewers to convey waste away from town. In 1891 citizens petitioned the city to build sewers but were defeated at the polls in 1893. Two years later another petition followed, and this too was defeated. Apparently, most citizens did not see raw sewage as a problem meriting attention. Then in 1896, Boulder took action by raising bonds, and construction of the first sewer main to drain waste to Boulder Creek was soon under way. Once concentrated sewage began entering the creek, ranchers east of town began complaining of the nuisance, but it was not until 1934 that a sewage treatment plant was finally built.[67]

In the post–World War II era, Boulder continued to grow, and the city built a new wastewater treatment plant in 1957. By 1965 that plant could not treat waste fast enough, and the city was ordered to appear before the State Board of Health to explain why improperly treated sewage was discharging into Boulder Creek. For the remainder of the 1960s and into the 1970s Boulder grappled with its inadequate wastewater treatment plant. Boulder eventually constructed its present plant in 1968. Even with the new plant, treatment inefficiencies led local residents to complain about nuisance odors.

This latest plant was built at a time when Americans' awareness of water quality in streams and lakes was dramatically increasing. Between depleted flows and poor water quality, the fishery in Boulder Creek was in steep decline. At the federal level, the Safe Drinking Water Act was signed into law and led to tougher water discharge standards. Citizens began agitating for the city to address Boulder Creek's poor condition. Among them was Boulder resident Ruth Wright, who, from her seat on Colorado's Water Quality Control Commission, urged the city council to act so that Boulder Creek might again support fish.[68]

As water quality awareness expanded, the post–World War II era was one of construction and catch-up for Boulder's wastewater utility. Boulder explored various innovative ways to improve its sewer plant discharge. In one scheme, the city considered land application of sludge. In another, the city hired a local ecological consulting firm to plant willows and cottonwood trees downstream from the plant to shade the stream. The idea with the shading was to lower overall stream temperature to reduce the toxicity of nitrogen in the wastewater. Then in 1986 and 1987 Boulder implemented another innovative plan to collect methane produced by its waste to make electricity.

As chemists improved their analytical technologies, water managers became increasingly aware of changes in stream quality. In one startling discovery, researchers found sex organ changes in fish below Boulder's wastewater treatment plant. Investigators from the University of Colorado, led by John D. Woodling and David O. Norris, examined gender distributions in white suckers (*Catostomus commersoni*) near Boulder's wastewater treatment plant on Boulder Creek. They found that the effluent contained endocrine-active compounds and reproductive steroids of the kind used in birth control pills. Changes in gonads, including abnormalities and smaller ovaries, and other reproductive disruptions were found in white suckers downstream of the treatment plant but not at sites above it. Also, ratios of male to female suckers were skewed toward females below the treatment plant. Their research made national news and led to calls for stricter wastewater discharge standards.[69]

Other researchers identified water quality changes on Boulder Creek attributable to development. Many results were reasonably predictable, such as seeing more concentrated pollution at low flows than during the spring snowmelt. Likewise, the concentration of pollutants such as fecal matter gradually increases in Boulder Creek as it passes downstream through the city. And even though Boulder's wastewater treatment plant meets all state water quality standards, municipal discharge still dominates the water chemistry below the plant.[70]

Even with treatment, not every compound gets removed from the waste stream. For instance, a rare earth element, gadolinium, is present below but not above Boulder's wastewater treatment plant. It turns out that gadolinium is administered to patients at hospitals in advance of certain MRI examinations. Because it is an element, it does not decompose in the body or wastewater, and moves through the waste stream. Although there is no known impact from discharges of gadolinium, its presence is symptomatic of the many chemical alterations people make, however unintentionally, to our rivers.[71]

When we look at the growing cities along the Front Range, a general pattern to water development becomes apparent. First, cities chased the lowest-cost options to meet their growing demand. They initially appropriated water that was close at hand. In short order they were building structures farther and farther into the mountains, and eventually they tunneled right through the mountains to tap West Slope sources. Cities either dammed the best reservoir sites or bought existing reservoirs from farms and industry to meet their needs. All the while, cities bought ditch shares from farmers, drying up and developing former agricultural land in an ever-widening arc. By necessity cities began treating water, first by simple filtration, then by adding chlorine, and eventually by even more sophisticated methods. As water entered the cities, communities found that they needed to build separate systems to drain unwanted storm and sewage water. Eventually they began treating sewage and disposing waste from treatment plants. While this trajectory of development is quite rational, it is nevertheless remarkable that these dramatic innovations have taken place in the relatively short span of about 150 years.

LIMITS TO GROWTH?

In the 1980s environmentalists fought Denver Water's proposed construction of the Two Forks Dam on the South Platte tooth and nail because they believed that the project would accelerate urban development along the Front Range. At 1.1 million acre-feet, this reservoir would have been the largest water project ever constructed in the state. After mounting a massive public relations campaign, environmentalists celebrated Two Forks' veto in 1990 by the Environmental Protection Administration under George H. W. Bush.

Environmentalists at the time believed that in arid environments restricting water project construction could be used as a tool to curb urban growth. As it turned out, Two Fork's veto did little to reign in development in the Metro Denver area. Water providers turned to a number of smaller projects, demand management through conservation, and agricultural transfers to supply water to new developments. From 1990 to 2010, Metro Denver's population increased by about 1.3 million people. While there is a certain logic that one could curtail water supply to limit growth, the question remains why did this strategy fail so miserably in the ensuing years?[72]

As a semiarid state, it appears that Colorado has a water deficit, given all the demands on its rivers. For instance, in Boulder County there is simply not enough water to supply all the municipal, industrial, agricultural, and environmental needs. As we have seen elsewhere, water resources in the region were fully appropriated long ago, and we now import water into the county. Even so, a large hidden demand for water is met by indirect sources that do not place direct stress on local rivers. Because of much of our food is grown far from Colorado cities, we in effect use and import water resources from far away. This remote water is bound up in food and other commodities produced elsewhere and are what some water managers term "virtual water."

After all, if water were truly scarce, why isn't water extraordinarily expensive? Irrigation water prices are indeed high in Boulder but nowhere what they would be if we had no choice but to grow all our food locally. Agricultural water prices near Boulder are influenced by market forces far outside the region. As long as we have the ability to import food from other agricultural districts, local agricultural water (and land) prices must stay competitive if farms are to remain in business.[73]

This leads us to virtual water and its implications for regional development. Back in 2001 Tony Allan of the University of London's School of Oriental and African Studies published a book about Middle East water that I think is particularly relevant for helping us understand a largely overlooked aspect of water development in arid and semiarid regions such as Colorado. Allan asked the simple question as to why, with all the political intrigue in the Middle East, has there not been a major shooting war over water, perhaps that region's scarcest resource? To answer that question, Allan explained that water bound up or embedded in food commodities (his virtual water) that are transported from areas of abundant supplies to areas of water scarcity reduce competition for water in the water-short areas. Allen points out that even though water is scarce in the Middle East, food is grown in water-rich areas and imported into the region. This diminishes the pressure on local water sources. He illustrated the idea by pointing out that about 1,000 tons of water are needed to produce a ton of grain. So if the grain is grown in a water-rich area and then exported to the Middle East, the amount of local water supplies needed to produce food are dramatically reduced. Said differently, it makes more sense to transport one shipload of grain to the Middle East than 1,000 ships full of water to grow the grain there.[74]

If the Middle East can avoid a guns-and-bullets war over water, what does that say about water development in a place like Colorado? Because we can and do import inexpensive food from far away, it naturally affects the economics of local food production. It is for this simple reason that the prices of local produce must remain low to stay competitive. At the same time, the price for the land and water used to grow that food is high because real estate developers want it for subdivisions and homes. This explains why water transfers will continue to dry up agricultural land near Boulder, other Colorado cities, and the West in general for the foreseeable future. So long as we can grow food cheaply elsewhere, farm products produced near western cities must compete with lower-cost imports.

The economics of virtual water complicate policies intended to keep agriculture viable near our western cities. Through 2011, Colorado had about 5,117,000 people, and urban and industrial uses accounted for about 15 percent of all water consumed, with the remaining going to agriculture. If an imaginary policy dictator had the authority to issue a proclamation decreeing that Colorado agriculture was unimportant (not me!), that would free up 85 percent of the water supply for "higher-value" urban and industrial uses. If all that water were used domestically, we could theoretically stuff nearly 34 million people into the state. Before you shoot the messenger, let me be the first to say that this is not a future that I desire. I for one would move away long before Colorado became that overcrowded. The real point I wish to make is that *Colorado has plenty of water*. The question is not quantity per se, but allocation. We just do not have enough water to satisfy all of our desired uses without reallocation. It is the decisions about how to use the water that are difficult. Figuring out how to balance reallocation and meet new demands while preserving the things we value, like free-flowing rivers and local agriculture, is the real problem.

NOTES

1. Brookfield quoted in Hafen, *Colorado Gold Rush*, 248; Coffin, letter to the *Longmont* (CO) *Ledger*, July 19, 1907; Smith, "History of the Waterworks."

2 Smith, "History of the Waterworks."

3. Bird, *Lady's Life*, 230.

4. Ibid., 8.

5. The headgate for the Town of Boulder Ditch (also known as the City of Boulder Ditch) appears to have been just downstream from the location of Silver Lake Ditch. A year after beginning work on the Town of Boulder Ditch, John Ellet was elected the fourth president of the Town of Boulder Board of Trustees. The ditch carried about 6.19 cfs and was appropriated on June 17, 1875. Water from the Town of Boulder Ditch was eventually transferred to the Silver Lake Reservoir outlet in Boulder's Silver Lake Watershed in June of 1942. See Boulder County District Court Cases CA1400 and CA10518; Fair, "Report to E. O. Heinrich; see also Smith, "History of the Waterworks."

6. *Colorado Banner* (Boulder), November 23, 1876, and November 16, 1876.

7. *Over the Plains*, 97.

8. Smith, "History of the Waterworks," 11–14.

9. Fair, "Report to E. O. Heinrich," Exhibit B.

10. Smith, "History of the Waterworks," 12.

11. Ibid., 14–15.

12. Ibid., 15–17.

13. *Daily Camera*, October 20, 1891.

14. *Daily Camera*, September 8, 1891.

15. Fair, "Report to E. O. Heinrich."

16. Denver Water, *Denver Water Resources*; Limerick and Hanson, *A Ditch in Time*.

17. Maxwell's revolving door was not limited to the City of Boulder. On February 14, 1890, Maxwell and partner George Oliver filed their Map and Statement form for Round and Island Lakes with the Colorado state engineer in Denver. James P. Maxwell, State Engineer, signed the filing receipt.

18. City of Boulder, *Source Water Master Plan*, 2:3–6.

19. Ibid.

20. Smith, "History of the Waterworks," 22. Phyllis Smith points out that that the sale to the city in 1904 predates the deed from the US Land Office and asks if

Clint Maxwell sold the land "before he bought it?"; M. S. Whiteley quote in *Boulder* (CO) *County Miner* 1, no. 20 (October 12, 1905).

21. Smith, "History of the Waterworks," 24; Edgar S. Housel was the son of Judge Peter M Housel, founder of the Butte Mill Ditch.

22. In addition to the large land purchases, Boulder acquired smaller tracts such as a parcel from E. P. Hill for $400 and a 160-acre parcel for $1,500 from the Wood family at Silver Lake. This was the first of several grants of land to the city from the federal government. Boulder paid $1.25 per acre for land that was then in the Colorado National Forest. See Act to Grant Certain Lands to the City of Boulder, Colorado, approved March 2, 1907, 34 Stat. 1223. On March 4, 1927, Boulder acquired another 3,685 acres of federal land.

23. See Fair, "Report to E. O. Heinrich," Exhibit B.

24. Smith, "History of the Waterworks," 25.

25. Ibid., 29.

26. Fair, "Report to E. O. Heinrich"; Map and Statement Filing for Increase of Lake Albion Reservoir, Boulder County Colorado, May 4, 1908, Boulder County Clerk and Recorder.

27. Map and Statement Filing for Green Lake Reservoir, November 28, 1906, with supplemental statement, April 1919, Boulder County Clerk and Recorder.

28. Smith, "History of the Waterworks, 35; Perrigo, "Municipal History," 117.

29. Smith, "History of the Waterworks," 18.

30. http://grandcountyhistory.org/our-history/articles/. Then search Grand Ditch. Accessed April 22, 2015.

31. Bollinger, and Bauer, *Moffat Road*.

32. Morris, "Glimpse of Moffat Tunnel History," 63–66.

33. Image from Denver Water historic photo collection.

34. Laflin, *Irrigation*, 71.

35. A comprehensive overview of Northern and its history is far beyond the scope of this book. For anyone wanting to understand the history, development, politics, and layout of the Northern system, see Tyler's, *Last Water Hole*.

36. The W. D. Farr quote is reproduced from Tyler, "Daniel Tyler Completes Biographical Book," 27.

37. Tyler, *Last Water Hole*, 185.

38. Richard Behrmann, personal communication, 2010.

39. Laflin, *Irrigation*, 81.

40. Braddock, "Municipal Government History, 1965–1974"; Boulder has subsequently sold much of its interest in Windy Gap.

41. Colo. Rev. Stat. 37-82-106 (1); Colo. Rev. Stat. 37-82-106 (2).

42. An augmentation plan allows a person to release water from one source to satisfy senior water rights holders so they may divert water somewhere else. For example, someone may release water from a reservoir to a downstream senior ditch so they may pump a well that would otherwise be out of priority.

43. Boulder Revised Code, sec. 11-1-19, requires developers to turn over ditch shares as a requirement for receiving city services.

44. Wiener et al., "Riparian Ecosystem Consequences."

45. Mark Obmascik, "Mall Subsidy Tops $279 Million," *Denver Post*, April 16, 2001.

46. Denver Water, *Denver Water Resources*.

47. Before naming the dam after Dwight D. Gross, the structure was called Reservoir No. 22; most early water rights and federal permit filings are under this original name. *Denver Water News*, June 1951 and September 1952.

48. Dwight D. Gross, "Reservoir No. 22 Dam"; Colorado state engineer, Map and Statement Filing, Denver Municipal Water Works, Map of Reservoir No. 22, February 19, 1946.

49. Karl C. Brauns to Harry S. Truman, March 26, 1949; Harry S. Truman to Karl C. Brauns, July 13, 1949, Reservoir 22 files, Denver Water Central Records.

50. *Rocky Mountain News*, August 25, 1951.

51. Ibid.

52. Montgomery, interview by Hall. In questioning Denver Water staff about this practice, they are quick to point out that averaging the diurnal was with the consent of the District 6 water commissioner.

53. Stone, *History of Colorado*, vol. 1; Herrick is known for helping to start the National Carbon Company, which later became the Eveready Battery Company.

54. URS Consultants, "Modernization of the Boulder Canyon Hydroelectric Project."

55. URS Consultants, "Modernization of the Boulder Canyon Hydroelectric Project," 4.

56. URS Consultants, "Modernization of the Boulder Canyon Hydroelectric Project," 7.

57. Ibid., 9.

58. Ibid., 9.

59. Ibid., 10.

60. City of Boulder, *Source Water Master Plan*, 2:3–14.

61. Ibid., 2:3–15.

62. *Denver Post*, October 22, 2010, accessed March 3, 2013, http://www.legacy.com/obituaries/denverpost/obituary.aspx?page=lifestory&pid=146141187#fbLogged Out.

63. Boulder County District Court CA20716; *Daily Camera*, January 4, 1957.

64. Melosi, *Sanitary City*.

65. Perrigo, "Municipal History," 171–72.

66. City of Boulder, *Source Water Master Plan*, 2:3–17.

67. Perrigo, "Municipal History," 173–75.

68. Braddock, "Municipal Government History, 1965–1974"; Braddock, "Municipal Government History, 1975–1979."

69. Vajda et al., "Intersex and Other Forms of Reproductive Disruption."

70. Murphy, Verplanck, and Barber, *Comprehensive Water Quality*.

71. Ibid., chap. 4.

72. Environmental activists in Boulder pioneered the way in using service restrictions to limit unwanted development. In 1959, Plan Boulder proposed a city charter amendment that voters subsequently approved to establish a "Blue Line" along Boulder's mountain backdrop, at about 5,750 feet in elevation, above which city water or sewer services would not be permitted; see Smith, "History of the Waterworks." Developers wishing to build above the Blue Line were undaunted, and some of them formed the Pine Brook Hills Water District to serve lands no longer eligible for City of Boulder service. Others circumvented the Blue Line restriction by developing springs or gigging wells to serve their properties. Boulder ultimately found that the most effective way to control growth was to buy and set aside land as open space.

73. Agricultural water prices are low compared with water decreed for municipal use. In recent years, shares of the Left Hand Ditch, for example, that are decreed for agricultural use have sold for about $3,000 and yield about one acre-foot per share, while C-BT units that are authorized for municipal use may sell for over $12,000 and yield somewhat less than one acre-foot.

74. John A. Allan, *The Middle East Water Question: Hydropolitics and the Global Economy* (London: I. B. Tauris, 2001); John A. Allan, "Virtual Water—The Water, Food and Trade Nexus: Useful Concept or Misleading Metaphor?" *Water International* 27, no. 4 (2002): 4–10. Although the term "virtual water" itself has been criticized for being an inaccurate metaphor, I find that it succinctly describes the ephemeral nature of water bound up in commodities. For a critique, see Stephen Merrett, "Virtual Water and Occam's Razor," *Water International* 27, no. 4 (2002): 1–3.

FOURTEEN

People and Ditches

"There is a seldom-quoted maxim of the Colorado
law: An irrigation ditch is a structure which, upon
creation, will operate to convey controversy to landowners between the point of diversion and place of use."
—*Karl F. Kumli III*[1]

Today, as I see it, there is an uneasy marriage between the city and the ditch.
But that was not always the case. In western cities and towns, ditches are
a necessary but not necessarily wanted feature of the local landscape. We
need ditches for their water but don't want many of the management activities associated with them. It is common for people who own ditch shares
and manage ditches (if their shares haven't already been bought out by a
municipality) to feel under siege every time they get a phone call by someone
complaining about how their ditch is run, about the mosquitoes they bring,
or how field runoff is managed. Conversely, landowners along the ditch are
likely have their hackles raised whenever a ditch company crew walks down

DOI: 10.5876/9781607323822.c014

the ditch and throws leaves and branches on their lawn or cuts trees along the ditch and leaves them on the bank to rot.

In urban areas many people see ditches as anachronisms of an earlier time that are hanging on past their earlier utilitarian prime. For developers, ditches are to be piped or paved over to make way for subdivisions. Some people see the ditches as a link to an agrarian past. Others appreciate ditches for the ribbons of green that cross the community and see maintenance roads as a good place to walk the dog or take a morning run. Still others see ditches as an alternative for using tap water to irrigate the urban environment.

Fuzzy fault lines and uneasy dichotomies define the relationships people have with their ditches. Many of the thorniest and most emotional water conflicts in the modern West are found along the course of ditches. Many ditches are in the crosshairs of municipal water supply agencies, which see them as the source of cheap agricultural water ripe for transfer to urban uses. Many environmentalists would rather see a dried-up ditch than to see water out of a river. A whole host of tensions occur along ditches. People who live in rural areas but aspire to urban amenities are often put out when a ditch rider drives his backhoe across well-manicured lawns to clean the ditch. Ditch managers resent landowners who plant trees along the ditch or dispose of leaves in them. Private ditch shareholders view municipal shareholders sitting across the table at annual meetings with deep suspicion. Then there is always the worry, one that is not far off the mark, that a city will buy up enough shares to take over the ditch and push long-term shareholders off the board.

Among older shareholders there is often the sense of being the last of the Mohegans. In other words, even though their neighbors may have willingly sold their shares at great profit to a city, those who remain feel like they must make due with diminished supplies or authority as rural uses for the water fade away.

Ditches often cross prime land ready for subdivision and development. It is common to see developers try to bully ditch boards into accepting reduced easements, storm water discharge, bridges, and landscaping along the ditch with little compensation for the intrusion. Many ditch boards do not have the sophistication or financial resources to hire the engineers or attorneys to address changes along the ditch. Some ditch boards don't understand their legal rights well enough to craft deals that protect their interests. On one ditch east of Boulder a developer paid the ditch company to pipe the ditch through a new subdivision. The ditch company took ownership of the pipe and all responsibility for managing it. But pipe deteriorates over time, and some years from now how will that small company ever find the resources to pay to replace the pipe that goes under the lawns of million-dollar homes?

The shareholders of ditches have changed significantly over the years. Settlers worked ditches with their horse teams to maintain them to offset their assessments. Ditch company annual meetings were well attended, and announcements of meetings and director elections appeared in the newspaper. For many of these people, the ditch was a central feature in their livelihood. Sitting on a ditch board was prestigious. Community leaders, businessmen, and politicians highlighted their service on ditch boards. When the Leyner Cottonwood Ditch incorporated, for example, it recruited US senator Henry Teller to serve on its board. Today board duties generally fall on those who most need to keep their ditch operating. Farmers or ranchers may depend on their ditch but have their own wells or municipal taps. Many shareholders are now part-time users who have jobs elsewhere to supplement their income. Farmers in rural Boulder County often supplement their income driving school buses or operating a backhoe. Other shareholders are amenity ranchers or farmers who acquired their wealth independently from their land. For these people, living along a ditch is more of a lifestyle choice than an economic necessity.

Another fault line straddles the Continental Divide. The West Slope interests portray the East Slope as water-sucking leeches drying the headwaters of the Colorado River. And they are really not that far off the mark. Cities such as Denver once ran roughshod over West Slope interests in much the same way as William Mulholland dried up California's Owens Valley in his quest to provide water to Los Angeles. Boulder has largely escaped this bad press only because Northern, which serves Boulder its West Slope water, gets the bad press instead. The East Slope sees the West Slope as a playground to go fish, ski, and raft. Second homes of Front Range residents simultaneously support the West Slope's economy.

Many ditch companies often have to reconcile differences between private and municipal or institutional shareholders. Municipalities often assign professional water managers to sit on ditch boards while the private shareholders sitting across from them grew up helping a father or uncle irrigate with a shovel from the ditch. In these instances, perspectives and experience can create a great divide. Trust between private shareholders and their municipal counterparts are often difficult to establish. I have often heard private shareholders speak of "my" ditch the way someone may say "my spouse" or "my son." Sometimes it is never possible to get past differences in how one perceives ownership.

Private shareholders often wish to preserve the ditch and its operations. Municipalities often buy shares and then transfer water out of the ditch, leaving fewer private shareholders behind. For the remaining private shareholders, it gets mighty lonely as their neighbors sell out, leaving fewer people to manage the ditch.

Another contradiction that arises between the city and ditch comes from ditch leakage. Most ditches were simply excavated and never lined. Consequently they leak. Ditch leakage in turn supports urban forests that cool city streets with summer shade. Ditch leakage elevates groundwater levels and recharges aquifers, fills ponds, and supports wetlands. But this same leakage can flood basements. Mosquitoes breeding in ditches or nearby irrigated fields ruin backyard barbecues. This leads to angry phone calls from homeowners who, while appreciating the views across nearby farm fields, object to the inconveniences of living near the same field.

Also, as ditches cut across cities that have grown around them, all manner of accommodation has been made to reconcile demands for development with the superior easement rights that ditch companies usually possess. In Figure 14.1, for example, the Boulder and White Rock Ditch flows between a commercial development and one of Boulder's busiest streets. In this area, the company has entered into various agreements that allow encroachments on the historic easement. Even so, it is not uncommon for the company ditch rider to discover some new unauthorized encroachment that some neighbor has inadvertently (or sometimes deliberately) constructed within the ditch easement. When this occurs, the ditch company will work with the landowner to remove the encroachment or legalize it through an easement agreement or, barring that, turn the matter over to its attorney to force action.

Sometimes homeowners sue the ditch company that supplies water to the trees that shade their homes. A ditch I managed was once sued by a

FIGURE 14.1. The Boulder and White Rock Ditch flows parallel to Pearl Street in Boulder. Photograph by author.

landowner along it (he was also a shareholder!) because he was upset that the company cut down trees encroaching on the ditch bank. The ditch rider and I determined that the company needed to remove the trees to access the easement to maintain water flow. The suit was eventually dropped, but it sure consumed a lot of time and money. About a year after that, the same company was sued by a different person after a heavy rainstorm caused the ditch to overtop. Rainwater was everywhere, flooding both above and below the ditch. Rainwater concentrated in the ditch, and it overtopped. Never mind that the ditch was operating within its normal range and that the homeowner built her house in a low spot below the ditch. The homeowner asserted that the flooding was from the ditch and not the storm. She claimed the company not was performing sufficient maintenance along the ditch. The homeowner eventually dropped that suit, but not after the ditch and its insurance company spent a bundle of money showing that it had done nothing improper. For ditch companies sometimes it is damned if you do, damned if you don't.

Uneasy Neighbors

On the morning of February 2, 2012, Robert Davis was inspecting the Anderson Ditch. Davis works for the City of Lafayette, which runs water through the ditch in the winter to storage at Base Line Reservoir. When Davis stopped at 5th and Pleasant in Boulder to inspect a grate that sometimes catches debris, he came across "a white male wedged in the culvert" with nearly freezing Anderson Ditch water flowing around him. The man was initially unresponsive. Davis yelled at him and asked if he was okay several times before the man responded and began to struggle to get out of the ditch. It turns out that the nearly frozen man was twenty-two-year-old University of Colorado student Grant Munski, who had fallen into the ditch after an evening of hard drinking. Munski told Davis that he had been there since the previous night. Overnight temperatures had dipped as low as 19 degrees. Munski was stuck calf-deep in water and ice at the base of the ditch's six-foot embankment. Munski's foot and leg were positioned in such a way that he could not move. Davis called 911 and went back to Munski to stay with him until a rescue team arrived. Munski remained stuck but continued to struggle to get out of the water. Davis offered Munski the handle of a shovel to stabilize himself and began to converse with him until the police arrived. A Boulder police officer was first on the scene. Soon an ambulance and fire vehicles arrived. The fire department took over and extracted Munski from the Anderson Ditch. Munski was brought to the hospital for treatment of hypothermia and possible frostbite. Boulder Fire Department spokesman Kim Kobel later said that had Davis not come along, Munski "could have been there for days."[2]

My first thought on hearing about Grant Munski was relief that he was alive. My next thought was what kind of fool would get so drunk that he would fall into an irrigation ditch? As a board member for the Anderson Ditch, I also thought about the company's potential liability. The company is of course not liable for someone's drinking habits, but we live in a litigious society, and one claim can significantly increase insurance premiums. I'm relieved that Munski is alive after his ordeal. Others have not been so lucky. Although drownings and serious injury are uncommon, they do occur. Most recently, in June 2014, a young woman drowned trying to rescue a dog that fell into the Highland Ditch. Another tragedy occurred on May 31, 1984, when Butterfly Lee Xiong was playing along the Boulder and White Rock

Ditch near her home in the San Juan del Centro project where she lived. Butterfly fell into the ditch and nearly drowned. Horribly, by the time she was rescued, she was in a coma with irreversible brain damage. From the newspaper reports, it appears that a fence built along the ditch prevented her from climbing out. Sadly, this was at the very same location where a fence had been built after another child, Y Meng Than, had drowned in 1980. After Than's drowning, residents demanded the installation of a fence to prevent another tragedy. The housing project erected a fence that was eventually replaced by a newer fence. A blame game ensued, followed by litigation between Butterfly's family, the ditch company, the City of Boulder, the housing project, and others. As far as I am concerned, the lawsuit was a side spectacle. What matters is that a child's life was destroyed. Ditch companies, cities, landowners, and families must treat each ditch crossing, culvert, fence, and obstruction seriously.[3]

Ditch companies rarely want fences, culverts, bridges, and other potential hazards or constrictions placed in or across their ditch. Certainly no one wants a child injured, let along drowned. But ditch companies must contend with permitting potentially risky changes as the landscape around them urbanizes. The problem is that no one has yet designed a perfectly safe and effective fence or ditch crossing.

Beyond these serious safety concerns, ditch companies must contend with a host of small annoyances as a ditch winds through urban areas. Many people see the ditch paralleling their yard as a source for watering their garden. But if these people take water and are not a shareholder, they are stealing.

As a former member of the Davidson Ditch board, I had the occasion to walk long stretches of that ditch. A number of years ago Bob Clyncke, then Davidson Ditch president and superintendent, told me that he saw a pump on open space land with a hose extending to a private home nearby. The pump and hose did not belong to the ditch, and the homeowner was not a Davidson Ditch shareholder. Bob tried previously to get the landowner to stop pumping water without permission. Because of its proximity to Boulder's open space land, I told Bob that I would check it out. Sure enough, when I went out there, there was a pump right where Bob told me I would find it.

I unplugged the pump and disconnected the hose and put it into the back of my pickup truck. Later on, Bob got a call from the landowner, and Bob referred him to me. The landowner, whose name I no longer remember, was angry that I took his pump and asked for it back. I explained to him, as Bob had done in the past, that if you are not a shareholder and are pumping, you are stealing. I told him that I would happily return his pump. I said that we should set an appointment to give his pump back and that I would like to invite an officer from the Boulder County Sheriff's Department to attend so that when I give him the pump, I can make a report about water theft. He never set the appointment, and he never pumped from the Davidson Ditch again.

There is no one-size-fits-all management solution for ditches in urban areas. Themes like ditch safety and water theft are shared by all ditches. Even so, ditch boards, neighborhoods, and the ditches themselves vary widely from place to place. For the foreseeable future, ditches will both serve and burden western cities.

A Ditch Runs through It

For years I went through a tiresome ritual involving leaves and a ditch. The Dry Creek Davidson Ditch Company is a shoestring operation. Shareholders are quite conservative with the company finances, and everyone strives to keep the assessments low. One of the main ways the company does this is for the shareholders to walk the ditch each spring, pitching leaves out of the ditch, cutting willows, and performing assorted hand labor to get the ditch ready for the spring water run. Because Boulder owns just under half of the ditch shares, there was an informal understanding that I would assemble a crew and walk the upper half of the ditch, and the rest of the shareholders would walk the lower half.

For about fifteen years, we came to a property where the homeowner gathered all the leaves that fell from his trees onto his yard and dumped them in the ditch. It is backbreaking work to pitch all the leaves that naturally fall into the ditch, let alone dealing with leaves that someone intentionally dumped there. Even though I spoke to this fellow many times, he just did not seem to understand or care that you can't put leaves in the ditch and let the leaves wash down to become someone else's problem. So when the crew and I arrived, I'd have everybody pitch the leaves right back onto the lawn. On several occasions, the leaves were nearly three feet deep, so when we left, he had quite a soggy mess on his yard. But they were his leaves, so I felt no guilt giving them back.

Large ditch companies keep their easements denuded of vegetation. Small companies don't have the resources to remove every tree, and the landowners invariably grow fond of the vegetation. So putting up with some leaves and tree limbs seems a reasonable trade-off if it keeps a grand old cottonwood from being cut down.

On one ditch, I once heard the ditch superintendent joke about trees and ditches. He said something to this effect: "You see that tree over there next to the ditch bank? Well, that is the beloved property of the person that owns that beautiful house and neatly landscaped yard. You know, if I went over to cut back that tree because it is on the ditch bank, the landowner would raise hell. So it is amazing to me that, by some quirk of nature, when the leaves fall off that tree into the ditch, or when the tree itself dies and falls into the ditch, somehow the *title* to leaves and mess it creates seems to transfer from the landowner over to the ditch company and becomes our problem."

Controversies that arise along ditches, like tree cutting, often come down to what is or is not within the scope of the ditch easement across a property. But just as often it involves common sense. Several years ago, when I was on the Dry Creek No. 2 Ditch board, I received a call from an elderly shareholder. She was clearly very upset and on the verge of tears. It turns out that the company's ditch rider came through her place and left mounds of debris on her yard and truck ruts in her lawn. I took a look and was appalled. Not wanting to have the ditch rider go back to her property and make matters worse, I mustered a crew and cleaned up the mess. At the end of the season, the company thanked the ditch rider for his services and said that it wouldn't need him the next year.

You may ask, "How come there is such ambiguity around managing a ditch easement?" The answer is pretty easy if you think about it from the perspective of how ditches were developed. Simply put, if you needed water, you needed a ditch. Regardless of who built the ditch, it brought water to otherwise unproductive dry land, and few people objected to that. This was later affirmed when territorial courts and then the state constitution allowed one person to build a ditch across another's land.

Even though the Territorial Legislature and courts explicitly granted the right to condemn a right of way across another's land, it was rare for a condemnation proceeding to actually occur. Most of the earliest ditches were simply built, and no one worried much about obtaining written permission from the underlying landowners. Indeed, many ditches along the Front Range and northeastern Colorado were even built before the Indians began relinquishing title to those lands starting with the 1860 (revised 1861) Treaty of Fort Wise. What mattered for most people was to get water, so having a ditch nearby was seen as a benefit. Few people worried, let alone complained, about the construction of ditches across their land. Moreover, the same people who built the ditch often owned considerable land around it. These people did not draw up a document allowing themselves to build a ditch across their land. But, over time, lands are subdivided, water rights are sold, and the link between the original landowner and the ditch slowly becomes obscured.[4]

Ditch companies own a whole bundle of rights that go with ditch easements. Colorado's courts recognize that ditch companies have the right to inspect, operate, maintain, and repair the ditch. The courts have also held that the owner of a ditch easement "may do whatever is reasonably necessary to permit full use and enjoyment of the easement." For new landowners it sometimes comes as a surprise that the ditch owner has the right of "ingress and egress for maintenance, operation, and repair."[5]

Digging ditches often established what attorneys call "prescriptive easements." It's analogous to adverse possession, but the ditch company only has the right to move water and do what it takes to maintain the ditch.

Managing prescriptive easement is easily the most contentious aspect of water management I have ever experienced. From the perspective of the water user or the landowner, managing prescriptive easements represent different shades of gray in the management spectrum. Ditch presidents often speak with landowners who are angry to see a backhoe crossing what they thought was their private estate, piling buckets of debris along the ditch bank. Easement management priorities shift depending on your perspective. If you are the landowner, you think, how did the ditch company get the right to pile trash along the easement or blade a road next to the ditch? And if you are the ditch owner, you're thinking, this is how the company has managed its easement for a hundred years, why should we act differently now? Why, you ask, should the company spend money to remove debris when it never had to before? If the ditch manager and the landowner can't talk all this over in the field, both may find themselves in the middle of an expensive and frustrating legal battle.

These issues arise from the very nature of what a prescriptive easement is and how it was established. A prescriptive easement is acquired when a ditch is built across a piece of property, is used for a long time, and does not require the specific permission of the underlying landowner. The earliest ditch easements came into existence when teams of workers driving horses or oxen dug the ditch and placed the spoils alongside it. The teams would use a scoop or plow to drag dirt out of the ditch. Ditch companies maintained the ditch using teams of men and livestock working in and along the ditch bank. As time went on, the horse and ox teams were replaced by backhoes, but the width of the easement stayed more or less the same.

What exactly is width of a prescriptive easement? Unfortunately, there is no definitive width unless the ditch company and landowner previously negotiated a contract with a specified number. Essentially, it is the width that the company traditionally used on either side of the ditch to move equipment and keep it maintained. Ditch managers simply use their best judgment. This might be the width of a backhoe plus some additional space to turn it around or rotate its shovel. The width varies depending on whether the ditch is on a hill or flat land, or if some other feature is present to alter the access. Clear as mud, isn't it?

It is the very lack of specificity regarding the easement width and what management activities are needed that create the greatest tension between ditch companies and landowners. Disputes over what activities are appropriate often lead to lawsuits. Once in court, judges tend to defer to the expertise of the ditch company managers to determine what they need. However, if the landowner can show that the ditch company has not used its easement for many years or has acted arbitrarily, the court just may decide in the landowner's favor.

A prescriptive easement gives the ditch company the right to use the property for the purpose of delivering water and managing the ditch. Once established, a prescriptive easement exists as long as the ditch company continues to operate and maintain the ditch. And even if the company maintains the ditch intermittently, the prescriptive easement remains intact. What becomes particularly nettlesome for landowners is that once a prescriptive easement is established, it remains in place even if the underlying landowner sells out to a new person. Moreover, the prescriptive easement need not be mentioned in the conveyance contract or deed in order to remain in effect. So it often comes as a shock when someone from the East Coast moves into rural Colorado, buys a ranchette, and a year later sees a track hoe driving along the ditch through the property and placing muck on the easement.

A recent conflict over ditch easements on Colorado's West Slope has affected ditch-landowner relations all over the state, including Boulder Valley. The matter involved drastically different perspectives on ditch management that blew up into a drawn-out court battle pitting an old-school cattle-ranching family against a contemporary resort development. In many ways this case embodied the clash between the old and new West in Colorado. Tensions started in 1995 when a resort developer, the Roaring Fork Club, purchased land along the river of the same name and began implementing its plan to develop a high-end mountain getaway. The Roaring Fork Club, near the town of Basalt in Pitkin County, offers members "experiences to enrich, entertain and to educate." Club members enjoy "mountain biking to fly fishing, from world-class golf to culinary arts" and promises that members will live "life with the soothing qualities of the wilderness and the pursuit of sport."[6]

Just downstream on the Roaring Fork, Reno Cerise and his family own the 240-acre St. Jude Ranch. The Cerise family has ranched there for several generations. Their operation includes irrigating pasture for the cattle with three irrigation ditches that pass across Roaring Fork Club land. After buying the land, the Roaring Fork Club sought to alter the ditch course in order to accommodate its golf and fishing development. It attempted to negotiate a contract with the St. Jude Ranch to either to purchase portions of ranch's easement or to formalize a ditch maintenance arrangement. However, the ranch and club failed to complete an agreement. Undeterred, the Roaring Fork Club moved forward with its development. The club excavated within the ranch's rights-of-way, graded and destroyed ditch banks and portions of ditches, realigned ditch channels, modified ditch flows, piped portions of ditches, constructed cabins and golf course greens within the easements, and even temporarily piped wastewater into one of the ditches. Needless to say, the Cerises were very upset.[7]

The upshot of all this was that the St. Jude Ranch initiated a trespass action against the Roaring Fork Club in 1997 seeking a permanent injunction that would require the club to restore the ditches to their original location and course and to remove the improvements that prevented the ranch from maintaining the ditches. After a three-day trial, the court found that the Roaring

Fork Club had modified the ditches as alleged. The matter did not stop there, as the parties appealed all the way to the Colorado Supreme Court.

The Supreme Court ruled that the Roaring Fork Club trespassed on St. Jude's easements by unilaterally altering the ditches. The court conceded that rules guiding ditch easements are still murky and contested. But the Supreme Court concluded that ditch easements are a property right that the underlying landowner (or "burdened estate") may not unilaterally alter without the consent of the ditch owner.[8]

In the end, the Supreme Court had the common sense to say that the best course is for all "to agree to alterations that would accommodate both parties' use of their respective properties to the fullest extent possible." If they can't agree, a courtroom is the place to resolve the dispute.

With the St. Jude decision, the Colorado Supreme Court strengthened the position of ditch companies on the front end of conversations regarding possible changes to easements. If you are a landowner and want to change a ditch, you must first get permission from the ditch company. If you can't agree on a solution, you may sue the ditch. Then a judge who may never have seen the ditch will decide how to balance the interests and needs of everyone concerned.

Even with major decisions like St. Jude, controversies and tension continue to plague ditches and adjacent landowners. Take the case of Don Getman and the South Tollgate Ditch. Don, an old-time Boulder County rancher, has been working his land since the 1940s. Don is an affable guy who is now in his eighties. Like most ranchers I know, when he makes a decision, his mind is set. Someone else may call that stubborn, but when you need to get things done, I will go ahead and call it a virtue. In April 2009, Don decided to cut down a tree along the ditch that he thought would become a management problem if left unattended. He hiked up the hill behind his house with his chainsaw and prepared for the job. A neighbor came down the hill from his house and exchanged some words with Don. It seems that the neighbor liked the tree and would have nothing of Don's plan to cut it, saying it would hurt his view. Don said he planned to cut it, so the neighbor turned around, went to his house, and came back with a shotgun. Leveling it at Don's chest, he told Don not to cut the tree. Seeing no point in being killed over a tree, Don retreated and called 911. Don's neighbor was arrested for felony menacing. Don had a right to cut the tree, but as you can see, emotions can run high over even one tree along a ditch easement.[9]

Each and every ditch seems to have issues whenever there are easements involved. As long as a ditch runs through it, landowners and ditch companies will always find something to argue about. Clear as mud.

NOTES

1. Kumli, "A Ditch Runs Through It."

2. Robert Davis incident report to the Boulder Police Department, February 6, 2012.

3. Millard, "Fences and Ditches."

4. The Arapahoes and Cheyennes considered the Treaty of Fort Wise a swindle. Little Raven, the Arapahoe chief, later said that the Indians were simply told to sign a paper, adding, "we did not know what it was. That is one reason I want an interpreter, so that I can know what I sign." See Grinnell, *Fighting Cheyennes*, 126, 133.

5. Osborn & Caywood Ditch Co. v. Green, 673 P.2d 380, 383 (Colo.App.1983).

6. http://roaringforkclub.com/, accessed February 21, 2012.

7. Roaring Fork Club v. St. Jude Company, Colorado Supreme Court, No. 00SC372, November 19, 2001.

8. Ibid., V. B.

9. *Daily Camera*, April 11, 2009.

An Unnatural History?

"In a way, a skyscraper is really as natural as a birds' nest."

—*Alan Watts*[1]

When the Wellman brothers, Jonas Anderson, Charles Pancost, and other settlers began building farms, digging ditches, and constructing reservoirs, they took intentional steps to change Boulder Valley in ways that supported their livelihood. Later, as water managers began building pipelines, dams, and water treatment plants, they modified streams and waterways to benefit the people they served. At each step along the way these people felt that they were making Boulder Valley a better place to live.[2]

When we trace the history of water development and survey the various cultural and historic changes wrought by people on Boulder's streams and lakes, it becomes clear that we cannot understand Boulder's landscape apart from the cultural forces that created it. Human-induced changes to our streams and the outright construction of lakes make it increasingly difficult to distinguish between natural systems and those that are more or less derivative of human action.

DOI: 10.5876/9781607323822.c015

Looking across Boulder Valley, we see that lakes and streams are simultaneously natural and cultural in origin. Although natural, many of the region's freshwater ecosystems are affected by ongoing ecologic, hydrologic, chemical, and geomorphic modifications produced by human activity. Our long history of human occupation, exploitation, and development underscore how difficult it is to distinguish between human and natural processes. I like the term "hybrid freshwater ecosystems" to describe these human-derived freshwater ecosystems. People and nature were both active participants in creating these places. It may be impossible, and perhaps even detrimental, to try to delineate a bright line between the natural and the artificial in Boulder's lakes, streams, and meadows.

Since Boulder citizens began actively acquiring open space in the name of preserving nature, I think it is especially important to consider how the landscapes they are preserving came into existence in the first place. Perhaps even more important is that we need to examine the underlying values that we carry when engaging with these places. Also, let's not ignore that conservation-oriented sciences such as restoration ecology, which Boulder uses to manages its open lands, are value-laden practices that change landscapes.

ECOLOGICAL CHANGES

People have permanently and irreversibly altered the streams and riparian corridors along Colorado's Front Range, Boulder Creek included. As we have seen, people have systematically modified the area's streams through fur trapping, placer mining, road and railroad construction, timber harvesting and railroad tie drives, grazing, and recreation. Extensive development activities, including diversions, wastewater treatment, well drilling, and changes in urban hydrology, have contributed to the transformation of streams throughout the region.[3]

One way to visualize this transformation is from the perspective of historian Alfred W. Crosby's "ecological imperialism," whereby Old World peoples and the microbes, plants, and animals they brought acted in concert to conquer the peoples of the New World. Diseases such as smallpox, measles, and even the common cold cut down the populations of the New World in advance of European colonization. The colonists themselves chopped trees and introduced Old World plants and animals familiar to them. European livestock replaced native ungulates and opened the way for Eurasian weeds to become established within North American ecosystems. European bees and earthworms became established as settlers moved west. These changes led to the creation of "Neo-European" ecosystems in the wake of the foreign invaders. And even though a number of endemic species have sadly been lost, most have not, and grim prophecies of total elimination of endemic species have generally proven false. Native and foreign species now live side by side in Boulder Valley in newly emergent ecosystems that defy easy categorization.[4]

Today, in Boulder Creek's riparian forest, only one in four of the most common trees are native, the remainder being dominated by imported species. Moreover, the vast majority of the plants present in the forest understory are weedy exotics. These introduced species include escaped ornamentals and weeds that spread out from disturbed areas.[5]

The Boulder Creek fishery is just as altered. In Colorado deliberate fish introductions began in 1878 when 459 bass were placed in a variety of reservoirs. Three years later the first fish hatchery was built near Denver with an initial stock of 100,000 brook trout eggs. By 1916, there were twenty-three fish hatcheries in Colorado that turned out some 30,000,000 fry. Where those fish went is not known, but many were likely brought to the Boulder Creek Watershed. It is known that fisherman in Boulder County placed several thousand fingerlings in Boulder and Four Mile Creeks and "sixteen cans of fish eggs" in South Boulder Creek by 1910. That same year, 96,000 fish in milk cans were carried to the mountains to stock various alpine lakes. Eventually several fish hatcheries were built in Boulder County, and both wildlife managers and enthusiastic fisherman have been stocking area lakes and streams ever since.[6]

By the late 1990s the fishery in the Boulder Creek Watershed was dramatically different from presettlement conditions. Various studies show that ten of the twenty-six fish species currently present in the watershed are introduced. Two additional native fish species are known to be extinct within the South Platte basin while eleven others were found in the South Platte River and its tributaries, but not in the Boulder Creek Watershed. This suggests that as many as thirteen additional fish species may have once been present in Boulder Creek, but since comprehensive surveys were never undertaken before active settlement, the true number will never be known.[7]

This area was a center for nineteenth-century fur trapping. Mink and river otters lingered on, but were gone by 1911 and were not seen again for almost a century. Buffalo were gone by the 1860s. Other large mammals such as the gray wolf and grizzly bears were eliminated from the area by the 1890s. The consequences of these local extinctions may never be known. But biologists working in contemporary settings are identifying significant changes to ecosystem processes, such as stream morphology, scavenger subsidies, disease dynamics, and others when large predators are removed from an area. This suggests that Front Range and High Plains creeks may have endured similar impacts.[8]

OUT WITH THE OLD, IN WITH THE NEW

Some trees like the crack willow (*Salix fragilis*) are so common that many people are surprised to learn that this giant was introduced to Colorado long ago. These huge trees can easily exceed four or six feet in diameter. Crack willows arrived with good intentions along with some of the earliest settlers to Boulder Valley. Newly arrived settlers found an essentially a treeless plain, and they strove to transform it into a more familiar and comfortable place. Among them were David Nichols and his wife Elizabeth Atkinson, who arrived in 1860 and bought a ranch on the outskirts of Boulder. According to Nichols's biographer, there "was not a tree or shrub on the place, but as soon as Mr. Nichols had set out some [trees] they began growing at a wonderful rate, and in a few years the beholder could not have believed that his little paradise of greenery was the same desert-like, barren-looking property of yore." A friend of Nichols from Illinois had sent a small, six- or seven-inch branch of crack willow for him to grow. Nichols planted it, and from "the one tiny slip originally planted here, countless thousands of flourishing trees, in all parts of the state, have been grown." Today crack willows dominate many of the creek corridors around Colorado. Where David Nichols and Elizabeth Atkinson had their "little paradise of greenery," strip malls and big-box stores now occupy the farm site at the corner of 28th and Pearl Streets in Boulder.[9]

A further change to the streams is the introduction of fish disease and aquatic pests. Accidental introductions of whirling disease (*Myxobolus cerebralis*), Eurasian watermilfoil *(Myriophyllum spicatum* L.; discovered in Boulder Creek in 2001), and the New Zealand mud snail (*Potamopyrgus antipodarum*) have further altered the stream ecosystem. A photo (Figure 15.1) taken in 2001

Figure 15.1. Eurasian watermilfoil, an invasive aquatic plant, near the headgate of the Butte Mill Ditch in 2001. Photograph by author.

near the headgate of the Butte Mill Ditch is of one of the first times, if not the first, that Eurasian watermilfoil was identified in Colorado. Since then, it appears to have spread down Boulder Creek to the South Platte and was later found in other lakes and streams around the state.[10]

Once established in Boulder Creek, Eurasian watermilfoil quickly became a problem for farmers and ditch managers. Rosamond Sullivan, the ditch rider for the Green Ditch, has had to use a backhoe to control the spread of this weed in the canal. She and her brother, Floyd, have several times dried out the ditch and used a variety of herbicides licensed for use around water to control the weed's spread. Jules Reignier, a farmer on the Leggett Ditch, complains of continually fighting clumps of the weed, which clogs his irrigation sprinkler heads. These problems may seem minor, but for the folks who deal with them this weed amounts to a time-consuming headache. Plus as the weed spreads, the problems that Jules and Rosamond experienced are replicated on ditches up and down the creek.

Many other species have arrived in Boulder Valley in the last 150 years. Their proliferation elsewhere mimics what has occurred in Boulder. Mark Fiege, a historian at Colorado State University, has extensively documented a variety of invasive species as they spread across Idaho. Idaho farmers, for instance, deliberately introduced the common carp to ponds in the 1880s and 1890s for food. The carp soon escaped into rivers. Not surprisingly, people soon lost interest in the bony fish and now detest them because they compete with other more desirable species. Carp are common in Boulder's lakes and likely arrived in the same manner. Fiege also recounted how numerous weeds like Canadian thistle (*Carduus arvenis Bobs.*), sweet clover (*Melilotus* spp.), Russian thistle (*Salsolsa kali* L.), and cattail (*Typha* spp.), to name a few, have spread across Idaho. All these species and many more now reside in and along Boulder's ditches, streams, and lakes.[11]

Most invasive species are quite tenacious. I do not believe it is possible to eradicate many of these species once established. Nor do I especially believe that we should expend scarce resources on species unless they constitute a serious threat to human health, pose an economic risk, or are known to damage rare endemic species. I particularly don't think that a species should automatically get targeted for extermination simply because it is exotic. Some species, like the crack willow, bother many ecologists for the simple reason they are not native. But the nuisance or harmfulness of a species such as the crack willow is dubious at best. To eliminate species simply because they are "exotic" or "nonnative" is insufficient. We need to carefully choose our fights. If an exotic species is clearly damaging, we should act. But the reality is that some species have moved in and now share the ecosystem with the endemic species that were here first. We just need to recognize that in some areas, there is no getting around the fact that people have increased the species richness.

Many people organize their views of species as either "alien" or "native." The concept of native versus nonnative is fraught with problems: How long must a species be present for it to be called native? Should it be a year, month, millennia? How far must a species move from its place of origin to be called an invader? If a wetland species native to a stream corridor moves out along a ditch into formerly dry lands, does that make it an invader? How useful is it to define whether a species is native or alien based on some arbitrary spatial or temporal argument? Even the language used to describe exotic species is rife with xenophobic or militaristic terms where proponents of control urge "declaring war" to "eradicate" the "aliens" or "nonnatives." Taken to an extreme, the whole control-the-alien argument starts sounding uncomfortably close to the same xenophobic arguments that bigots apply to people who are different from them. At its furthest extreme, I have heard the agenda to eliminate exotics labeled as a form of "ecological fascism." This just shows that applying rigid ideology in the name of purifying nature puts one at the top of a slippery slope of some unsettling intellectual territory.[12]

Ecologists spend a lot of time measuring biodiversity, but how often are introduced species included in these calculations? All species present should be counted so that they do not live in the shadows of their endemic neighbors. After all, how do you characterize the biodiversity of modified ecosystems in places like lakes where none had previously existed? If we deliberately ignore introduced species when calculating biodiversity or species richness, do those figures have any meaning?

Water Development

Water development is often described as a top-down process that treats people as abstract concepts. This can be traced to the German philosopher Karl Wittfogel, who popularized the idea that water development is largely a top-down effort, that if not initiated by some elite, the water developers themselves eventually *become the elite* and may even go on to wield despotic power over those needing water. Wittfogel has always been something of an enigma since he was a lifelong Marxist who was simultaneously virulently anticommunist. Even though his work has largely been discredited due to numerous errors in his empirical data, his general perspectives have had remarkable staying power. Historian Donald Worster used Wittfogel's ideas as a foundation to develop his thesis that water development in the western United States is a top-down, state-dominated process. Likewise, Mark Reisner in *Cadillac Desert* focused on the role of the federal government as a driver of western water development. And, more recently, even though Patricia Limerick argued *against* the notion that "Power over water in the American West has been concentrated in the hands of a small, centralized, somewhat toxic elite," her narrow focus on the role that several influential men had in constructing Denver Water's vast system seems to betray her own argument. Perhaps the focus on elites misses the real point. This is because *hierarchies* within and between water management institutions do exist that were borne simultaneously out of environmental necessity and the historical evolution of these organizations. Water managers at various agencies do wield vast power specifically because they touch many lives, span vast geographic areas, and control large sums of money.[13]

In addition, others see development as a rich and somewhat chaotic process with complex interactions, hybridizations, and power relations between the various actors at all levels. Geographer Thomas Sheridan seems to exemplify this perspective in his study of water development in Arizona. I see something of a mixed bag. I believe that federal and state roles have been extraordinarily important in water resource development. And a number of individuals have had oversized roles in western water development. But I also think that that the role and impact of small ditch and reservoir companies and the many small to medium-size cities across the American West are long overdue to take their place alongside the states and federal government as agents of change for both society and the environment. As I see it, the large number of small ditches built by multiple individuals supports the view that water development and its environmental effects are the result of complex interaction between people with a wide diversity of motivations, political influence, and economic resources. If we keep in mind that there are over 22,000 ditches within the state of Colorado alone, the role of the little guy becomes inescapable.[14]

CONSERVING AND MANAGING HYBRID ECOSYSTEMS

To paraphrase the historian Richard White, we need to find better ways to live with our dilemmas. If we attempt to remove all human influence from a landscape in the name of conservation, some of the very qualities we wish to preserve may be eroded. But the flip side of this, namely that any human action is acceptable, is clearly not desirable either.

Several years ago, I had a very frustrating conversation with a young biologist about some ditch laterals that needed maintenance. He had found tadpoles for the rare Northern leopard frog (*Rana pipiens*) living in the laterals. He asserted that if I cleaned the laterals, I might destroy the tadpole habitat. He correctly pointed out that these frogs are a tier 1 "species of most concern" animal under the federal Endangered Species Act and that they were a candidate for federal protection. And I wholeheartedly shared his desire to protect the species. But the problem was that these frogs migrated into and now occupy habitat that was created by people. This young biologist was unconcerned that someone dug the laterals to irrigate otherwise dry land. Never mind that if someone (me) did not get these laterals cleaned, there would be no point for the rancher to turn water into the laterals so he might irrigate his hay meadow. The laterals would simply dry out and cease providing tadpole habitat or a source of water for the hay meadow. For the biologist, any action I proposed to clean the laterals was anathema for tadpole conservation. For him, the only acceptable state for the laterals was the current state, even though the current state was nonsustainable as the lateral was slowly filling in with sediment. It felt to me that he wanted the current condition frozen in time as if it were some kind of leopard frog Valhalla. Our conversation made me feel like a callous frog killer for even suggesting that it might be necessary to occasionally disturb the habitat by way of a backhoe so that we might perpetuate it.

Problems like this lie at the heart of conservation in managed ecosystems. Indeed, conserving freshwater ecosystems is essential for a variety of very good reasons. This creates ongoing, binary tensions between development and conservation, action and inaction, and nature and society that have complicated virtually every decision concerning freshwater ecosystem management. Finding ways to resolve these tensions is necessary to improve freshwater ecosystem management.[15]

On the rapidly urbanizing Colorado Front Range, water development and freshwater ecosystem conservation is contentious. Development of and our reliance on rivers and lakes to serve the growing population is accelerating. Many freshwater ecosystems are influenced by ongoing and historical modification by direct and indirect human activities, in some cases by their wholesale creation. Yet many of these same lakes and streams also contain valued assemblages of plants and animals that are the focus of vigorous conservation and restoration efforts. These lakes and streams look natural and are often very scenic. They contain individual elements that casual and professional observers may consider natural, such as riparian forests, wetland plants, and endemic fish populations. Nevertheless, human roles in the creating these systems are inescapable and often profound.[16]

Vigorous efforts to expand, protect, or manage freshwater ecosystems along the Colorado Front Range have wide public support. Open space programs in Boulder County and the cities of Boulder and Longmont have expended significant resources to protect riparian corridors. Also, at Barr Lake State Park, managers strive to preserve bald eagle (*Haliaeetus leucocephalus*) habitat in lakefront plains cottonwood (*Populus deltoides occidentalis*) groves. Barr Lake is an irrigation reservoir, and the cottonwood trees grew along the lakeshore where no trees had previously existed. At other sites, such as Barbour Ponds State Park, Walden Ponds Wildlife Habitat, and Sawhill Ponds Wildlife Preserve, migratory waterfowl, fish, wetlands, and vegetation are preservation priorities for the agencies that manage them. Significantly, these lakes and wetlands were created through aggregate mining.

In another twist, local streams, including Boulder, South Boulder, and Left Hand, have decreed water rights for instream flows based on the needs of exotic trout species. There is also the Rocky Mountain Arsenal National Wildlife Refuge's complex of constructed lakes and restored grasslands, located within a former Cold War chemical weapons and pesticide manufacturing plant. The refuge, once described as the most polluted site in North America, has been rebuilt on the ground, reimagined in the minds of people, and legislated into existence as a wildlife sanctuary of national significance. Each of these freshwater ecosystems is a unique product of its historic construction by human and nonhuman forces.

Back in 1991 the geographer Thomas Veblen, in talking about the forest lands fringing western cities, pointed out that the "public needs to know how past use and management policies have influenced the present land-scape." He added that an "informed historical perspective" is needed to make "informed choices about vegetation management options proposed by government agencies and special interest groups." His words hold equally well for our wetlands, lakes, and riparian lands. Understanding the historic construction of many of these sites through ditch and reservoir construction will help guide their future management.[17]

ROMANTIC LANDSCAPES AND THE PROBLEM OF RESTORATION

People have intentionally and unintentionally altered the climate, fauna and flora, soils, and physical landscape through the construction of roads and cit-ies, the cultivation of crops, farming and terracing, hunting, and the spread of weeds in the New World for at least 13,000 years. Consequently it is very difficult, if not impossible, to determine what original landscapes were or when they last existed. This activity has transformed the landscape to such an extent as to thoroughly obscure what would have actually been present if humans had never arrived. Calling some landscapes "natural," "cultural," or "artificial" ignores the fact that they are rarely one or the other. People who are accustomed to assuming that there is such a thing as a natural or original landscape that existed before the arrival of Europeans can feel disoriented in their search for this mythical place. When observing freshwater ecosystems, we need to recognize the difficulty in quantifying human influences and must be cautious about seeing unrealistic images of pristine rivers and lakes or pro-found human impact everywhere. We need to question the use of baselines for developing strategies to manage these lands. Searching for original land-scapes can complicate ecological restoration projects because they tend to rely heavily on environmental baselines for guidance. Baselines are inherently arbitrary and as such are a self-centered act that marginalizes and diminishes the reality of those people who were present or moved through the landscape before the baseline was set.[18]

Nevertheless, restoration ecology is a key technology that assists in the conservation of various ecosystem elements. Restoration itself serves to *hybridize* nature and society. Restoration influences the direction of landscape change. It is through restoration projects that ecologists imprint their notion of ideal landscapes on the ground. When undertaking restoration projects, we need to remain aware of the fundamental values and perceptions that gave rise to the technology in the first place. Ecologists working on land and water face the same dilemmas in identifying baselines as targets for their restoration activities. The geographer Cindi Katz framed the problem well, writing that restoration ecology "romanticizes certain historical geographies. It privileges certain landscapes over others, which begs the question of who determines what a 'good landscape' is." Katz adds, "Restoration ecologists appeal to 'nature' for the answers, and inevitably advocate, valorize, and fix a specific historical landscape as idealized and ahistorical, somewhat antithetical to the living, socialized ecology they set out to remake."[19]

From this perspective, any baseline we select produces a perceptual boundary that values human agency differently on either side of it. Baselines create arbitrary borders separating otherwise continuous human action on the landscape. Human activity occurring after the date of the baseline is often deemed "bad," while activity occurring before is often deemed "good" or is simply ignored altogether. When you hear about restoration plans on the Front Range, it often feels like you are listening to people who have watched too many reruns of Kevin Costner's *Dances with Wolves*. Many romanticize the days when Indians roamed the plains as if it were an ecological utopia and see settlement as a fall from Eden that happened with the discovery of gold and the rush of American settlement. Tracing Boulder's landscape history helps dispel this mythical nature and shows that the landscape we see is inseparable from the cultural forces acting on it.

It is no surprise that many ecologists select a preindustrial baseline as a target for their activities and fail to see that as an arbitrary imposition of their biases. After all, many people feel that industrial activities are intrinsically harmful and the preindustrial activities were good. Perhaps somewhere in our subconscious mind it stirs biblical notions of the garden and our fall from grace. Regardless, I believe that most ecologists are beginning to accept that almost all ecosystems are transient systems. Even so, many cling to the notion that predevelopment baselines should guide restoration. Perhaps it is time to recognize that rivers are irreversibly moving toward new states. We can no longer afford to ignore that newly functioning or self-regulating ecosystems are created by natural processes working within the constraints and limits of human actions. As author Michael Pollan wrote in *Second Nature*, "there appears to be no escape from history, even in nature."[20]

In constructed lakes or wetlands where none had existed before, the restoration or reclamation program is scarcely different from a gardener's decision as to which plants she or he wishes to plant given the local climatic and soil conditions. Many lake and river restoration decisions reflect the personal preference and values the ecologist wishes to promote: values and preferences that are derived from his or her life experience, discipline, and education.

Generations of ecologists and environmentalists have translated Aldo Leopold's *land ethic* (my emphasis) from a value system into a scientific imperative. I think there are many compelling reasons to protect ecosystems without hiding behind science as a front to project one's values. After all isn't it more honest to state that we value an ecosystem for what it is, rather than create weak scientific justifications that mask our actual intentions? As long we value wetlands, rare species, or habitats, we will seek ways to protect them. Consequently, carefully describing the underlying values that one wishes to promote should be the very first step in the conservation, preservation, and management of lakes and rivers.

In thinking about restoration, it is helpful to consider the underlying values embedded in the effort. Unfortunately, these activities are sometimes corrupted by "normative science," which fisheries biologist Robert T. Lackey describes as "information that is developed, presented, or interpreted based on an assumed, usually unstated, preference for a particular policy or class of policy choices." Clues that normative science is at hand arise when words like "degradation," "improvement," "ecosystem health," and "sick streams" are uttered to describe some new plan or policy initiative. These terms use science to direct desired policy outcomes. After all, who would not want to cure a "sick stream?" Policy-neutral words describing "change," "alteration," "increase," or "decrease" allow one to consider what is occurring without experiencing subconscious manipulation. Lazy (hopefully not dishonest) scientists will use normative terms to advance their agenda. In contrast, careful scientists will state the scientific results of their investigations and keep their policy recommendations separate.[21]

It is tempting to think of the world in terms of hard contrasts. We are bombarded with notions that things are either natural or artificial, wild or domestic, developed or undeveloped, and so on. In the jargon of social scientists, these either/or perspectives are termed "binary oppositions." Unfortunately, framing the world in terms of opposites tends to polarize rather than ease our conversations about nature and how we interact with it.

The geographer David Demeritt stresses the importance of thinking about how nature, science, and society are actually mutually constructed. One interesting aspect of Demeritt's work is that he explores how scientists embed (often in subtle and sometimes subconscious ways) political considerations into science when they first consider problems. He shows how the technical practices of science can create descriptions of specific environmental problems that are politically value-laden and anything but neutral. Once the technical questions are framed, he argues, scientists absolve themselves from seriously considering the underlying social causes of a problem. Scientists then do what they do best, which is find technical fixes rather than engage in messy social or political solutions.[22]

HYBRID FRESHWATER ECOSYSTEMS

Geographers and social scientists use the term "hybrid" to describe a landscape that is part natural and part social. Bruno Latour, in particular, traces complex networks between people and the environment to show how looking at environmental problems from a natural or social perspective alone severely restricts our options for addressing these problems. The geographer Sarah Whatmore explores how nature and culture are interrelated to create hybrid geographies that are inescapably partial, provisional, and incomplete. These landscapes are never really finished or stable. Whatmore asserts that culture and nature are not polar opposites but rather are intimately and variously linked. Here human agency affects nature and vice versa. Hybrid ecosystems are created through both cultural and ecological forces.[23]

Ecologists and resource managers use various terms that inadequately describe the broad character of these ecosystems. For instance, "modified" fails to describe those freshwater ecosystems that now exist where there were none before humans arrived (as in reservoirs and stock ponds). Similarly, the word "regulated" does not accurately convey a sense of human agency on freshwater ecosystems where there is no deliberate water management but very real human influences (consider riverbeds irreversibly modified by aggregate mining or lakes dominated by invasive aquatic weeds).

Others use the term "novel ecosystems" to describe how many ecosystems are transformed into "new, non-historical configurations owing to a variety of local and global changes." However, they do not seem to acknowledge the direct and ongoing human role in shaping these landscapes. And another term, "social-ecological systems" has been extensively used to analyze resource changes in human impacted ecosystems. Although the term explicitly acknowledges that all human used resources are embedded in complex, social ecological systems, it does not actively address geographies that are inescapably incomplete or inherently unstable. Moreover, the term is a mouthful that will find little use beyond academic journals.[24]

These hybrid ecosystems have also been described as "second nature." In these places we cannot take for granted that every action by people is necessarily bad. Quite to the contrary, many things people have done have been quite good for us. If everything we did was harmful, it is doubtful our species would still be around. As journalist and gardener Michael Pollan puts it: "[I]t should be acknowledged that man occasionally creates new ecosystems richer than the ones they replaced, and not merely on the scale of a garden: think of the tall-grass prairies of the Midwest, England's hedgerow landscape, the countryside of the Ile de France, the patchwork of fields of this part of New England. Most of us would be happy to call such places 'nature,' but that does not do them (or us) justice; they are really a kind of garden, a second nature."[25]

Clearly, a wide variety of people contemplate human-modified ecosystems. Depending on one's perspective, each of these terms has a greater or lesser value. I will stick with the term "hybrid ecosystems" because I think this comes closest to the mark for what is going on in places like Boulder Valley.

Hybrid ecosystems inevitably create intellectual challenges for people who work in these environments. For ecologists trained to think of themselves as scientists, accepting culture and history into their conceptions of ecosystem change can be a large pill to swallow. We must continually question what is presented as natural and strive to see it in the light of its landscape history. This reinforces the need to understand the social and historical construction of landscapes that we wish to preserve, conserve, or restore. Ignoring people neglects human agency as an ecosystem process. By recognizing a freshwater ecosystem as hybrid, conservationists can focus on consciously managing *the elements within the ecosystem* that we wish to privilege rather than disputing if one or another action is more or less consistent with a natural ecosystem. Perhaps it is more useful to think in terms of "less or more" rather than "either/or." I believe this will lead us to more honest political conversations when discussing how to manage these lands.[26]

MANMADE LAKES AND WETLANDS

By excavating ditches, water once confined to the stream corridor now flows across Boulder Valley. As we have seen previously, early settlers went to great lengths to get water to dry terraces often quite far from the stream. Ranchers and farmers who began applying upward of three to five feet of water per acre facilitated wetland development throughout the region. Riparian and wetland vegetation soon spread out along these ditches and began thriving in formerly xeric (dry land) settings.

All along the High Plains at the base of the Front Range, wetlands began developing with the start of irrigation. Less than thirty years after settlers dug the first ditches along the Cache la Poudre River, observers noted that some land was irrigated so heavily that even the higher terraces near the river had transformed into "cat-tail and rush-bearing swamps."[27]

Building lakes and the subsequent emergence of wetlands around them is another dramatic aspect of water development in Boulder Valley. Water that originally passed out of the watershed is now retained. Once dams were constructed and water impounded, the lake perimeters became perennially saturated and wetlands grew. Similarly, when aggregate miners dig gravel pits, their excavations often penetrate the groundwater table. If the pits are abandoned without backfilling or other remediation, as many older pits were, groundwater fills the excavations to create lakes. Saturated soils located around the perimeters of gravel pits soon support extensive wetlands.

The following series of air photographs illustrate the variety of wetlands that developed around ditches in Boulder Valley. In this first air photo from south Boulder (Figure 15.2), the difference between irrigated and nonirrigated lands is striking. The locations of the main ditches in the area are highlighted. Water is delivered by gravity and irrigates the lands below the ditch. The dark areas correspond to irrigated hay meadows. The light-colored areas are dry land prairie.

FIGURE 15.2. In this aerial photograph from 2008, the difference between irrigated land located topographically below the Davidson Ditch (top half of the image) and nonirrigated land above the ditch (bottom half of the image) is striking. Source of image and wetland mapping for this map is courtesy of the City of Boulder Open Space and Mountain Parks Department.

This next air photo (Figure 15.3) is the same area as the previous one, but with wetland mapping superimposed. Davidson Ditch runs diagonally across the middle of the image. Davidson Ditch typically runs water in May, June, and July, and depending on streamflow, occasionally in April and August. Between 1950 and 2008, annual water diversions into the Davidson Ditch

FIGURE 15.3. This aerial photograph is the same as Figure 15.2 and has the wet-land mapping for the area superimposed. Source of image and wetland mapping for this map is courtesy of the City of Boulder Open Space and Mountain Parks Department.

averaged 6,647 acre-feet per year. In 2005 about 503 acres were irrigated under Davidson Ditch. This probably represents a minimum value, as cities have bought many shares since 1950. Davidson Ditch has an earthen channel, so seepage is very high and perhaps only 50 percent of water diverted reaches the irrigated land. This means that each irrigated acre may receive about 6.6 feet of water during the three- to four-month irrigation season. It should be no surprise that the wetlands and irrigation under Davidson Ditch are closely linked. It is highly unlikely that any wetlands would persist under the Davidson Ditch if it were shut down for long periods of time. When considering all the seepage, one might suggest that the water is wasted. But is it wasted if the water supports a viable agricultural operation that contains rare plants and animals and manmade wetlands? Perhaps it is if you prefer subdivisions. Perhaps it isn't if you prefer rare orchids and local agriculture.

Figure 15.4 is an air photo taken south of Boulder in 2008 with wetland mapping superimposed. Community Ditch wiggles across the middle of the image. Davidson Ditch is downhill (on the upper left of the image) from Community Ditch. Both ditches have earthen channels. In the vicinity of this image, there is no intentional irrigation. All of the wetlands present below Community Ditch are related to ditch seepage. Wetlands are spread out along and below the ditch. Water flows generally toward the north in this image. Notice how wetlands are found within several gullies below the ditch where seepage water becomes more concentrated. Some wetlands are located above the ditch but are less extensive, largely confined to the bottom of drainages or in areas that receive road runoff.

Figure 15.5 is an air photo of Boulder Valley Ranch, a popular City of Boulder open space property. Farmers Ditch curves around the left side of the image. Nonirrigated lands are to the west of the ditch and irrigated lands to the east. The irrigated lands are darker than the surrounding nonirrigated lands. Wetland mapping for the area is superimposed. Tailwater running off the bottom end of irrigated fields supports the large complex of wetlands on the center-right of the image. These kinds of wetlands are common along the Front Range.

In this hydrologically replumbed region many ditches become surrogate riparian areas. This is not to say that the ditches function in precisely the same manner as nearby stream ecosystems. As people continue to manage ditches, the ecosystems supported by them will evolve. Elsewhere along the Front Range, wetlands derived from ditch seepage are at least as dramatic. In a recent study along the Cache la Poudre River in northern Colorado fully 92 percent of wetlands were visually connected to the irrigation infrastructure. Combining isotopic data analysis with groundwater investigations, the researchers concluded that the most of the wetlands in their study area were "recharged solely by canal leakage." This is neither a surprising nor

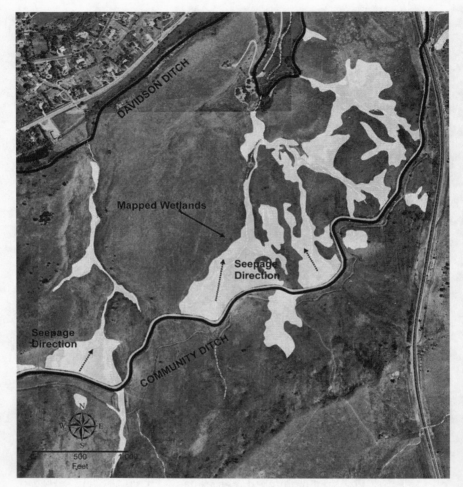

FIGURE 15.4. This is an aerial photograph from south of Boulder in 2008 with wetland mapping superimposed. The direction of seepage from the ditch and the resultant wetlands is indicated. Source of image and wetland mapping for this map is courtesy of the City of Boulder Open Space and Mountain Parks Department.

unexpected result. As people redistributed water across the landscape, the Great American Desert long ago became a High Plains oasis. With this redistribution of water, wetlands and riparian vegetation became firmly established in this formerly dry area. Anyone wishing to enforce hard distinctions

FIGURE 15.5. This is an aerial photograph of Boulder Valley Ranch showing Farmers Ditch curving around the left side of the image. Wetland mapping for the area is superimposed. Nonirrigated lands are to the west of the ditch and irrigated lands are on the east. Notice that the irrigated lands are darker than the surrounding non-irrigated lands. Tailwater running off the lower end of irrigated fields supports the large complex of wetlands on the center-right of the image. Source of image and wetland mapping for this map is courtesy of the City of Boulder Open Space and Mountain Parks Department.

between manmade and natural lake or wetland ecosystems fail to reconcile the broad range of cultural practices that affect these areas.[28]

In the Boulder Creek Watershed there are about 1,260 lakes and reservoirs. Of that number about 850 lie east of the mountain front. Back in 1999 and

2000, I had the opportunity to perform a water resources inventory for the City of Boulder Open Space and Mountain Parks Department (OSMP). I visited every pond and reservoir that we could identify on open space property. I counted 176 lakes on the system, representing about 21 percent of all the lakes east of the mountains within the Boulder Creek Watershed.

During the inventory, all open water bodies were characterized as either a permanent year-round feature or ephemeral. They were further characterized by their origin, such as a natural feature, gravel pit pond, stock pond, reservoir, and so forth. It turns out that over 99 percent of all lakes (by surface area) were built by people. This number is consistent with early survey maps of Boulder Valley that conspicuously lack natural lakes. Of these, reservoirs constitute 72 percent of the lakes by surface area, gravel pit ponds 24 percent, and stock ponds 3 percent. Evaporation from lakes east of the mountains consumes about 2.8 percent of the surface water flow in the basin. Since active settlement began, the number of surface water features in Boulder Valley has steadily grown (Figure 15.6). Most lakes built before 1950 are reservoirs and stock ponds. Starting in the 1950s a couple of large reservoirs were constructed just as aggregate miners began excavating gravel pits. Since about 1975, almost all new lakes are former gravel pits. Notably, all the ecosystems within these lakes are new to the region as well.

In 1932 historian Marjorie Large examined original public land survey maps and field notes from about 1863 for eight townships covering a 288-square-mile area roughly encompassing the St. Vrain and Left Hand Valleys from the mountain front east to the South Platte. These maps contained critical information needed for the prospective settlers, including location of streams and springs, character of the terrain, presence of timber (very little), potential for irrigation, location of roads, and so on. Notably, only two ponds were identified within the entire area. The maps do not reveal whether these two ponds, located north of the St. Vrain River, are man-made or not.[29]

Considering all this information collectively, I think we can safely state that east of the foothills from approximately Coal Creek on the south to St. Vrain on the north there were virtually no lakes present prior to active settlement. Extrapolating this to the Colorado Front Range, we can conclude that before the start of active settlement, outside of a few scattered oxbow or wind-scoured depressions, there were essentially no lakes present.

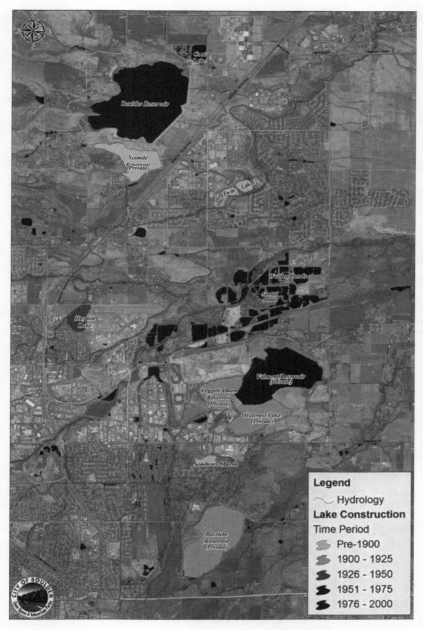

FIGURE 15.6. This map depicts the dates when lakes were created in Boulder Valley. Courtesy City of Boulder Open Space and Mountain Parks.

Making a Natural Area

On any given day, hikers, bikers, and runners enjoy the scenery along the South Boulder Creek Trail. It is one of Boulder's most popular destinations. People using the trail wind through the city's approximately 1,200-acre South Boulder Creek State Natural Area. It is an ideal place where we can explore how the cultural notions of "naturalness" create on-the-ground consequences for conservation. Designated as the South Boulder Creek State Natural Area in 1997, preservation rests on irrigation, grazing, and other active forms of management to support federally threatened orchids and mice, along with rare birds, fish, and globally rare riparian and wetland plant communities.

The city purchased the lands that make up the Natural Area from various owners between 1971 and 1992. Prior to city ownership, all of these lands were privately owned and were farmed or ranched. Starting in the early 1860s settlers such as the McGinn brothers, Norman Ross Howard, and others built ditches across the area to irrigate their homesteads. The settlers introduced cattle, farmed, tilled, and introduced a wide variety of species to support their livelihood. They were some of the first settlers to grow wheat and build fences along the Front Range. In time, the land was used primarily for ranching and hay production. By the late 1960s urban growth in the Boulder-Denver metropolitan region began exerting pressure on the farmers and ranchers to sell their land to developers. But in 1967, Boulder citizens approved a sales tax to buy land and prevent unwanted development. This enabled Boulder to purchase all the land now within the Natural Area and manage it as open space. As the land acquisitions progressed, some ranchers moved out, others became lessees, and the city's land managers took over. No people presently reside within the Natural Area, but remnants of several homesteads remain.[30]

As in the rest of Boulder Valley, water development has modified the stream hydrology, geomorphology, and the flora and fauna. South Boulder Creek, which runs through the site, bears little resemblance to its predevelopment conditions. Water diversions have virtually dewatered the creek. The reductions in flow are so dramatic that if the upstream gage on South Boulder Creek is used as a point of comparison, water diversions at the farthest downstream end experience the equivalent of repeated 500-year drought events year in and year out. Diversions make South Boulder Creek mimic the geomorphic pattern of a "loosing stream," one whose flow decreases as you move downstream. The result is that vegetation has encroached on the stream channel, and it becomes progressively narrower the farther downstream you go. At the downstream end, near its confluence with Boulder Creek, the stream width is only about one-fourth as wide as at the canyon mouth.[31]

And, since the 1950s, the South Boulder Creek channel has gradually eroded downward due to water developments like the construction of Gross Reservoir, channel straightening, and flood control activities, resulting in a new channel grade as much as three feet below the topographical elevation of the historic (Holocene) alluvial floodplain.

Land managers have modified the area in the name of improving nature. Boulder's OSMP has undertaken two projects over about a twenty-year period to "renaturalize" reaches of South Boulder Creek that were channelized over fifty years before. This involved building channel "improvements" such as meanders, placing riprap, inserting logs into the stream banks, and other channel modifications. These engineered structures translate the designer's ideas of what a natural stream channel should look like even though the stream has had more than fifty years to equilibrate to the changed hydrologic conditions.

Ditches irrigate over 60 percent of the Natural Area. About 18 to 20 percent of the riparian tree and shrub vegetation found within the Natural Area is located along the irrigation ditches and their laterals, and another 17 to 20 percent of the wetlands present are directly irrigated hay meadows or pastureland. Perhaps an additional 15 to 20 percent of wetlands are supported by irrigation return flows. All told, a significant percentage of wetlands, shrub, and riparian tree vegetation depend directly on human agency for their existence and persistence.[32]

The Natural Area contains Colorado's single largest known population of one species of plant, the Ute ladies'-tresses orchid (*Spiranthes diluvialis*). *Spiranthes* is federally designated as threatened and is endemic to wetlands. Inventories shows that fully 80 percent or more of the individually located orchid plants in the Natural Area are situated in irrigated hay meadows that would, in the absence of irrigation, be too dry for them to survive. Here a federally threatened species depends on irrigation and agricultural management for its survival.[33]

Shortly after *Spiranthes* was first listed as a federally threatened species in 1992, OSMP resource managers became alarmed that grazing would further imperil the orchid and ordered a halt to grazing to protect it. After removing the cattle, exotic species, including Canada thistle (*Cirsium arvense* [L.] Scop.), proliferated to such an extent that the orchid all but disappeared. With that, the resource managers reversed course and reintroduced cattle with the result that the thistle infestation was reduced and the orchid population rebounded. An ecologist studying *Spiranthes* remarked that orchids within the Natural Area "occurs in completely unnatural habitat which may not be viable without human intervention," adding that "any change in management regime from the traditional agricultural techniques tested would be detrimental to the population and increase the probability of extinction." Her perspective illustrates how some biologists see human intervention as inherently "unnatural" rather than as an ecosystem process itself. Nevertheless, the sensitivity of the orchid to changes in management demonstrates that ongoing irrigation and agricultural practices are central to its conservation.[34]

A notable animal species present in the Natural Area is the Preble's meadow jumping mouse (*Zapus hudsonius preblei*). Preble's was listed by the US government as a threatened species in May 1998. Considerable controversy surrounds this mouse, including whether it is even a legitimate species. Presence of a large population of Preble's helped support the state Natural Area designation. During four seasons of field trapping, biologists found higher mouse concentrations along ditches than along the South Boulder Creek stream corridor. They concluded that the irrigation ditches in the area function "analogously" to stream corridors in their ability to provide habitat for the mouse.[35]

During my time with OSMP, I was privileged to lead the staff effort to designate the Natural Area. OSMP was eager to see the designation, as staff believed that it would help thwart future plans to build recreational trails and expand a nearby highway (US 36) onto open space. While working on the Natural Area designation, I started to question many of my assumptions regarding the role of people in natural area management. While I remain committed to the protection of the Natural Area, my ideas evolved regarding what constitutes protection. I now believe that appropriate levels of grazing and irrigation are necessary for maintaining certain resources we wish to protect. In one meeting to promote the Natural Area designation, a member of the State Natural Areas Council (the state board that oversees Colorado's Natural Area

Program) asked why the state should designate this site as a "natural area" if it is so dependent on irrigation and other active forms of management. I encouraged the council to focus on all the individual elements that merit preservation. Some members of the council expressed political concerns that this site was not as "natural" as other sites that they had designated and worried that its proximity to the city and its urban pressures would undermine conservation. This prompted the council to engage in an animated conversation of what constitutes a natural area. In particular, the council questioned if an area should be considered natural in its entirety, or wondered if it is sufficient to consider only the individual species or plant communities it contains, as I had recommended. Some members noted that South Boulder Creek was the most modified site that it had yet considered for designation, that it was not as pristine as other natural areas in the state network, and worried aloud if there were political ramifications for designating such a place.

Their conversation got to the heart of the discourse on what is natural and the role of human activity as an ecosystem processes. It also exposed some of the political tensions involved in presenting a managed landscape as a "natural" area. Although the cultural practices of irrigation and grazing created favorable conditions for the threatened orchid, mouse, and wetlands to thrive, many people remain uncomfortable with the notion that cultural activities can support natural systems. Halting cattle grazing in Ute ladies'-tresses orchid habitat until the detrimental impact of cattle removal became apparent demonstrates how many land managers automatically leap to the conclusion that human practices are harmful.

Some individuals see South Boulder Creek as a site rich in biodiversity. Others see it for the historic ranchland and farmland it contains. Still others see the scenic benefits it provides Boulder Valley residents. Although all are viewing the same place, each distills his or her experience into a different understanding of the site. By carefully ordering and presenting the valued natural elements, it was possible to promote this site as a natural area.

In time the council recommended that the Colorado governor approve the natural area designation. Once the council made its recommendation, the remaining approvals became routine, and the site is now protected as a State Natural Area.

In talking about places like the Natural Area, I think it is helpful to visualize them as hybrid ecosystems. As a hybrid, the Natural Area is a product of human and nonhuman activity. First, it is a produced landscape formed through decades of direct human action such as irrigation and haying. Second, by representing it as natural and then taking the steps to formalize it as a "natural area," our perception of its naturalness crystallizes. This designation process now guides how the Natural Area is managed and will influence its future character. Politics help make the Natural Area a hybrid, even as some people try to purify various categories of nature by denying our role in creating it. Overall, the Natural Area's human and nonhuman characteristics are entangled, complex, mutually penetrating, and mutually dependent. Biophysical processes occur in the Natural Area but are dominated by water management and grazing activities along with indirect influences attributable to nearby urbanization. Because this place is scenic, the human forces that helped shape it are masked in ways that further strengthen our perception of naturalness.

Places like the South Boulder Creek State Natural Area defy contemporary views of a "natural area" as "untouched by humans." Here people and human practices, such as grazing and irrigation, interact with nonhuman processes to yield uniquely hybrid ecosystems. Historic practices like irrigation and grazing comingle in complex ways with nonhuman forces to create and maintain unique spaces.

BEYOND THE SOUTH PLATTE

At every scale we examine, it appears that the actions of people and nature have intertwined to create new ecosystems. Along ditches, lakes, and in whole natural areas, we see how people and the environment mingled to shape unique ecosystems. The South Platte River has evolved as irrigation gradually reshaped its hydrology. Taking a final step out to consider the Platte River, we find a vast ecosystem that was created from a complex engagement between people and nature. Streams such as Boulder and Left Hand remain part of this greater whole. So it is fitting to consider their place within the wider landscape.

Each South Platte tributary stream has experienced its own unique set of events and water developments over the past 150 years. Many events share common causes like emergence of prior appropriation, transmountain diversions, the spread of agriculture, urban development, expansion of commerce,

FIGURE 15.7. This photograph was taken along the Platte River near Cozad, Nebraska, around 1866. Image reproduced courtesy of the Union Pacific Railroad and the USGS.

and so forth. Like Boulder Creek, few bear much resemblance to the streams that Long or Fremont crossed so many decades ago.

In the Platte River of Nebraska, like Boulder Creek, hydrology, ecology, and human action are linked and not easily untangled. Here, too, we have altered the stream hydrology, changed the geomorphology, affected the patterns of vegetation, built lakes and made wetlands, flooded some areas while drying up others, and combined species in ways that will never allow us to go back to whatever past we wish to romanticize.

Invariably, alterations in one watershed translate into effects on the wider whole. With this in mind, changes on the Platte River resolve into a meaningful narrative. In the mid-nineteenth century, the Platte River of central Nebraska was wide and shallow and experienced bank-full flows during the spring and diminished to a nearly dry state by the late summer. In places, the Platte River was upward of one and one-quarter mile wide and occasionally

FIGURE 15.8. This air photo was taken in same general area as Figure 15.7, but in 1979. Image reproduced courtesy of the USGS.

up to seven feet deep. Timber was scarce, and if present it tended to be found on isolated islands that were protected from travelers.

By the late 1970s the width of the Platte River had shrunk dramatically, anywhere from half to one-twelfth of the width travelers noted during the 1860s. Water development reduced peak spring flows and altered the timing of water moving through the channel. Vegetation responded to this change and encroached on the formerly broad channel. The narrower channel now experiences more overbank events and seldom dries up.

A team from the US Geological Survey led by Thomas Eschner was among the first to describe these dramatic changes that took place on the Platte River. The two photos shown from their groundbreaking 1983 report speak for themselves.[36]

The first photo (Figure 15.7) was taken near Cozad, Nebraska, along the south bank of the Platte River around 1866. Notice the buffalo skull lying behind the lone man pensively contemplating the river. For me, the skull symbolizes the drastic changes that had already occurred. I have often wondered if this man is contemplating the future or just enjoying the view. Here the anonymous photographer has captured a nearly forgotten past within a long continuum of change.

By the time the second photo (Figure 15.8) was taken, much of the water development to affect the river was complete. This air photo was taken in same general area as the first image, but in 1979. A dense riparian forest swallows the vista where a man once gazed across a treeless expanse of shallow water. Formerly sandy river braids are now rooted by dense vegetation. Here people no longer cut down trees for fuel. Where bison once roamed cattle are confined to fields by fences. Gone are the multitudes of migrants driving hungry oxen along the river grazing everything in their path to dust. Today migrants travel a nearby interstate highway in cars propelled by fossil fuels, the memory of oxen relegated to history books. I think the conclusion we can reach is that the changes caused by water development are hidden in plain sight. You just need to recognize what you are seeing.

NOTES

1. Watts, Alan, *Taoism: Way Beyond Seeking*, 97.

2. Material in the chapter "An Unnatural History?" and the "Conclusion" rewrites, consolidates, and updates some material from two previous articles of mine. These are Crifasi, "Political Ecology of Water Use," and "Reflections in a Stock Pond."

3. Also see Wohl, *Virtual Rivers*.

4. Crosby, *Ecological Imperialism*.

5. Gershman, "City of Boulder Tributary Greenways Program."

6. Travis, *Fisherman's Paradise*.

7. Woodling, *Colorado's Little Fish*; Nestler et al., *Inventory and Status*; Bestgen and Kondratieff, *Fishes*; Randy VanBuren, "Fish Inventory Data."

8. Cary, *Biological Survey of Colorado*; Ripple et al., "Status and Ecological Effects."

9. *Portrait and Biographical Record*, 785.

10. Schisler, *Colorado Water Codes*.

11. Fiege, *Irrigated Eden*.

12. Warren, "Perspectives on the 'Alien' versus 'Native' Species Debate," 31, 427.

13. Wittfogel, *Oriental Despotism*; Worster, *Rivers of Empire*; Reisner, *Cadillac Desert*; Limerick and Hanson, *A Ditch in Time*.

14. Bebbington, "Reencountering Development"; P. M. Blaikie, "Development, Post-, Anti- and Populist: A Critical Review," *Environment and Planning* 32 (2000): 1033–1050; and T. Murray Li, "Marginality, Power, and Production: Analyzing Upland Transformations," in *Transforming the Indonesian Highlands: Marginality, Power, and Production* (Australia: Harwood Academic Publishers, 1999); T. Murray Li, "Images of Community: Discourse and Strategy in Property Relations," *Development and Change* 27 (1996): 501–27; Sheridan, "Arizona."

15. Cronon, "Trouble with Wilderness"; McCann, "Before 1492," part 2; Davies, Boon, and Petts, "River Conservation."

16 Wohl, *Virtual Rivers*; Wiener et al., "Riparian Ecosystem Consequences."

17. Veblen and Lorenz, *Colorado Front Range*, 1.

18. Denevan, "Pristine Myth"; McCann, "Before 1492," parts 1 and 2; Raffles, *In Amazonia*; Sheridan, "Arizona"; Crosby, *Ecological Imperialism*; Hunter, "Benchmarks for Managing Ecosystems"; Flores, "Great Plains"; Spirn, "Constructing Nature."

19. Katz, "Whose Nature, Whose Culture?" 57.

20. Hooper and Margerum, "Integrated Watershed Management"; Pollan, *Second Nature*, 187.

21. Lackey, "Normative Science," 38–39.

22. Demeritt, "Science"; David Demeritt, "The Construction of Global Warming and the Politics of Science," *Annals of the American Association of Geographers* 91, no. 2 (2001): 307–37; Demeritt, "What Is the 'Social Construction of Nature'?"

23. See Swyngedouw, "Modernity and Hybridity"; Robertson, "No Net Loss"; Gandy, *Concrete and Clay*; Raffles, *In Amazonia*; Latour, *We Have Never Been Modern*; S. Whatmore, *Hybrid Geographies: Natures Cultures Spaces* (London: Sage, 2002).

24. Quote from Hobbs, Higgs, and Harris, "Novel Ecosystems," 599; Ostrom, "General Framework for Analyzing Sustainability"; McCann, "Before 1492," part 2.

25. Pollan, *Second Nature*, 194.

26. Sivaramakrishnan, "Scientific Forestry"; Cronon, *Trouble with Wilderness*; Castree and Braun, "Construction of Nature"; Braun, *Intemperate Rainforest*; Raffles, *In Amazonia*; Keulartz, "Boundary Work."

27. Boyd, *Irrigation near Greeley*, 52.

28. Sueltenfuss et al., "Creation and Maintenance of Wetland Ecosystems."

29. Large, "Appropriation to Private Use."

30. Crifasi, "South Boulder Creek"; Crifasi, "Of Mice and Men"; City of Boulder, *South Boulder Creek Management Area*.

31. Richter et al., "Method for Assessing Hydrologic Alteration"; H. Hall, "South Boulder Creek Range of Variability Analysis," unpublished data analysis report, City of Boulder Open Space and Mountain Parks, Boulder, 2002.

32. Colorado Division of Wildlife, *Preble's Meadow Jumping Mouse*.

33. US Fish and Wildlife Service, *Ute ladies'-tresses.*

34. Arft, "Genetics, Demography, and Conservation Management," 150, 158.

35. Crifasi, "Subspecies No More?"; Krutzsch, "North American Jumping Mice"; T. R. Ryon, "Evaluation of Historical Capture Sites of the Preble's Meadow Jumping Mouse (*Zapus hudsonius preblei*) at the Rocky Flats Environmental Technology Site," M.S. thesis, University of Colorado, Denver, 1996; Carron A. Meaney, Anne K. Ruggles, Bruce C. Lubow, and Norman W. Clippinger, "Abundance, Survival, and Hibernation of Preble's Meadow Jumping Mice (*Zapus hudsonius preblei*) in Boulder County, Colorado," *Southwestern Naturalist* 48, no. 4 (2003): 610–23.

36. Eschner, Hadley, and Crowley, "Hydrologic and Morphologic Changes."

SIXTEEN

Conclusion

The New Nature

"The choice is not between two landscapes, one with and one without a human influence; it is between two human ways of living, two ways of belonging to an ecosystem."
—*William Cronon*[1]

When a rancher walks out to his field, shovel in hand to change his irrigation sets, is he thinking about the landscape he is creating? Walking down a ditch, pitching leaves for the spring water run brings you close to the earth. It makes you a companion with those around you and with the fields and trees that the ditch water maintains. Perhaps it brings you closer to the people who built the ditches. It is for you to decide whether transformations wrought by ditch diggers made this place better or worse. What is certain is that the appropriation of water and riparian resources set in motion a long arc of changes that continues to play out in a remarkable number of ways today.

When working on ditches and lakes and the various cultural ecosystems that they support, it is helpful to consider issues of nature, naturalness, perception,

DOI: 10.5876/9781607323822.c016

and value. It is especially important to look at an area's history to get a sense of how people have engaged with a landscape over time. Otherwise, we risk basing our choices and actions on dogma rather than insight.

I hope we can remain receptive to alternative approaches for organizing our thoughts on the natural world. Indeed, as we continue to extract resources from freshwater landscapes, the commodification process itself further alters perceptions and affect the actions of the very people creating and experiencing these landscapes.[2]

Biologists like to define biological communities as consisting of the species that occupy a shared locality along with the interactions between those species. Biologists also define an ecosystem as a biological community together with its associated physical environment. Neither of these definitions excludes humans and our social practices! All too often, the human factor in creating many freshwater ecosystems is overlooked or devalued. After all, one person's wetland ecosystem is often another's hay meadow. Ecology is crucial for understanding hybrid freshwater ecosystems, and ecologists must include people as an ecosystem actor when considering these landscapes.[3]

Managing these landscapes requires identifying all the forces responsible for their creation and understanding the human role that is involved. When we acknowledge human agency in making things like lakes and wet meadows, we create a space for politically balanced management to emerge. Similarly, representing certain freshwater ecosystems as hybrid allows us to explicitly recognize the human role in their creation and maintenance. It seems hypocritical for a land manager to prevent a rancher from cleaning a lateral to protect frogs and later bemoan the loss of the water that support the frogs as the lateral fills with silt and vegetation. It appears equally hypocritical for a rancher to dismiss the environmental amenities in these ecosystems as his livelihood ultimately depends on their integrity. If we helped make an ecosystem, ongoing management advances the conservation, preservation, and restoration of these sites.

As development on earth continues, people will continue to modify ecosystems to accommodate their needs and will increasingly devote time and energy in managing them. While we often value and preserve what we think are pristine examples of various freshwater ecosystems, we also value and preserve various modified ecosystems without necessarily acknowledging the human agency that created them or the need for active management to maintain them. In hybrid ecosystems, all decisions, including ones that reject actual on-the-ground management, are active in the sense that the pre-existing conditions have already been modified and the trajectory of future change has already been permanently altered.

Even small features on the landscape helps bring us to new understandings about nature. For in a lateral if the managers choose to walk away and do nothing, hay meadows, frog habitat, and wetlands will slowly revert to dry land. The very things we value and wish to preserve will disappear. Inaction can be every bit as destructive as a developer's backhoe. For conservation of these ecosystems to succeed, we have to get past any distaste for on-the-ground management if the features we wish to conserve are to be preserved. Removing the human or nonhuman agents in the landscape in the name of preserving nature creates an inherent contradiction: ecological change begins immediately with human action, and management intervention is often required to slow or control the change. Push that idea further, and accept that the human/nature divide is fiction and we see that withholding human action is the one profoundly unnatural action we can take. Land and water managers along with farmers and ranchers cannot forget that they are part of the ecosystems they manage and that these hybrid ecosystems are dynamic. By integrating considerations of human social practice with ecology, the understanding of these unique ecosystems can be developed far more than pretending that people are not part of them.[4]

Differences in perception about and priorities for conservation are profound and are manifested in the management of rivers. If we move beyond an absolute separation of nature and society, the politics become complex but liberating. Scientists and managers like to think that their decisions are derived from scientific facts based on what is natural. But once we recognize that these spaces are seldom purely natural, but rather intertwined with human influences, we must reevaluate decisions to confront the underlying human practices. Geographers Noel Castree and Bruce Braun urged working toward an environmental politics that neither loves nor hates technology. They caution about the extremes of either preserving Eden or rendering everything as resource. Castree and Braun understand the unease that many conservationists may feel toward these hybrid ecosystems. Recognizing the growing influence of humans on ecosystems does not, in their words, "argue against nature or for its 'destruction,' for social natures are no less ecological than so-called 'natural' systems from which humans have, in theory, been excluded." Instead, they urge us to focus on the social and ecological conse-quences that are everywhere intertwined. Social practices will always shape conservation priorities. Thinking about these places in terms of hybrids will make us reconsider using "natural" yardsticks to determine what is right or good and force us to confront the values we project.[5]

Overall, water development has depleted streams, altered the pattern, location, and timing of runoff, and affected water quality. It's irresponsible for water managers and ditch companies to walk away from these things, as they directly benefit from the water they use. Since water developers will continue to profit from the appropriation and removal of water from streams and agricultural transfers, they must shoulder greater responsibility for addressing the environmental problems stemming from these actions.

The streams in the Boulder Creek Watershed bear little resemblance to what once existed prior to active settlement. There is no indication that this process of development and environmental change will slow. Development has shifted the riparian ecosystem toward a new transient state. Land and water use has resulted in ongoing transformations of the aquatic and riparian ecosystem in the Boulder Creek Watershed, a situation replicated across the American West.

I do not wish to wax nostalgic for a paradise lost. Nor do I advocate dis-mantling our ditches and reservoirs or drying our fields to recreate some-thing that is long gone. There is, however, ample space to do things better. The people who built ditches sought a better life for themselves and worked hard to build a healthy community in which to live. Those values are time-less. As infrastructure is repaired or replaced, we need to improve it wherever possible. There is no excuse to divert water using structures that prevent migration of fish, block boaters, or diminish recreation along our streams. Using water to grow food locally is a laudable goal, if we keep in mind con-straints placed on us by geography and climate. There is no excuse to treat farmers as a foe that harms ecosystems, particularly when they are stewards to many of our finest wetlands and rarest species. Like the works of people, nature is never complete. Like nature, people must never remain passive if we are to preserve the things we value.

NOTES

1. Cronon, *Changes in the Land*, 12.
2. See, for example, Robertson, "No Net Loss."
3. Primack, *Essentials*, 34.
4. Neumann, *Imposing Wilderness*.
5. Davies, Boon, and Petts, "River Conservation"; Castree and Braun, *Construction of Nature*, 33.

SEVENTEEN

Epilogue

The Great Flood of 2013

"Emergency Alert 9/11/2013 Flash Flood
Warning this area till 10:45 PM MDT. Avoid
flood areas. Check local media."
—*National Weather Service*

WEDNESDAY, SEPTEMBER 11

I was just completing an evening class when my smart phone broadcast the warning in the epigraph above. It had been raining lightly for the past few days, but this evening it had really started to come down hard and steady. The National Weather Service issues a warning when "a hazardous weather or hydrologic event is occurring, is imminent, or has a very high probability of occurring." At the time, I knew that the warning was serious and that the agency released one only if its meteorologists believed the conditions posed a threat to life or property. Undoubtedly someone somewhere had already reported heavy flooding. Checking outside, I saw that there was water

DOI: 10.5876/9781607323822.c017

running everywhere, streaming down the roads and overtopping gutters, so I knew this was serious.[1]

Heading home, my wife and I drove across the 9th Street Bridge that crosses Boulder Creek. We paused and, although it was dark, could see from nearby streetlights that the creek was running uncommonly high for September. We passed North Boulder Park and saw water accumulating there and in the street. The rain quickened, and not long after arriving home we heard the alert sirens and muffled calls from emergency loudspeakers urging people to higher ground. Fortunately our home is located outside of all mapped floodplains, and given the lay of the neighborhood, I was not too worried about our house.

THURSDAY, SEPTEMBER 12

The rain never let up over the evening. More NWS warnings and public alert broadcasts arrived. On Thursday morning I turned on the news and learned that there was extensive flooding in the mountains west of Boulder and in the neighborhoods north of our home. Classes were cancelled, and the campus of the University of Colorado at Boulder was closed. Other schools were closed, and the City of Boulder shut down for all but essential personnel. And Governor John Hickenlooper declared a disaster and requested assistance from FEMA, the Federal Emergency Management Agency. After studying water resources for all of my adult life, I had to see Boulder Creek as it flooded. As soon as I left my house, it was apparent that I stepped into the middle of an extreme event. Rivers of water streamed down neighborhood streets. Broadway, one of Boulder's major thoroughfares, was inundated, and police had cordoned off sections of the road. Along 9th Street at North Boulder Park, the road was closed, and a lake had formed over it. I parked near Arapahoe Avenue and walked to Central Park in Boulder. I was surprised to see that a monument to Gilbert White, Boulder's renowned "father of floodplain planning," indicated that Boulder Creek was barely in flood stage. Yet what I saw all around me suggested that I was witnessing something else. From a bridge over the creek, I saw a kayak float by with a one-foot-diameter gash in it and no kayaker in sight. A few moments later I saw another pilotless kayak float downstream. This was big water and clearly beyond the capabilities of those boaters. I heard later that the kayakers got out of the water uninjured.

FIGURE 17.1. This is a still image from a video of flooding on Boulder Creek in September 2013. The full video is reproduced in the e-book edition and available online at http://www.upcolorado.com/university-press-of-colorado/item/2740-a-land-made-from-water.

Not long after, Tina, my wife, called me to say she received a warning that a "wall of water" was heading toward Boulder and that I should get to high ground (Figure 17.1 is a video clip that I recorded near here at about this time). What people reported was captured on a stream gage at Fourmile Creek, a tributary of Boulder Creek, that leapt from an already impressive eight feet to nearly thirteen feet in a matter of minutes, and from there it climbed to just under fifteen feet by evening. The most severe damage that happened in Fourmile Canyon likely occurred during this time. By then, the stream gage in Boulder had climbed off the scale. When the Fourmile Canyon surge reached Boulder, however, it was already absorbed into the mass of water churning in the creek, and the change in water elevation in this larger stream was all but lost to the eye.

It continued to rain all day. Disregarding all warnings, my friend Ian Huss and I headed back down to Boulder Creek on Thursday evening to see how it had grown. I sensed that we might see the flows near its peak. We immediately heard boulders knocking about under the waves. The water looked an almost angry red from the sediment it carried. Its color only served to

FIGURE 17.2. Boulder Creek at the Farmers Ditch diversion approximately 5:40 p.m. on September 12, 2013. Photograph by author.

reinforce the unharnessed power raging before us. As river runners, we figured that Boulder Creek was cranking at a Class VI level, which is considered unrunnable due to the severe, likely deadly consequence of a flip. But no one was braving the water, as the Boulder County sheriff had already banned boating earlier that day. Scarcely a week before, kids were floating this reach in inner tubes for relief from the late-summer heat. Figure 17.2 shows how Boulder Creek at the Farmers Ditch diversion near the mouth of the canyon looked at about 5:40 p.m. on Thursday.

During the day, Lyons was cut in half as the St. Vrain River overtopped and destroyed roads. As the waters rose, the central core of the town was submerged. Before long, both the water and wastewater treatment plants were under water and heavily damaged. Many homes and businesses were filled with water and mud; some were destroyed outright, while others were left unharmed but without gas, electricity, or running water. Farther south, Left Hand Creek overtopped the US 36 bridge, isolating residents of that area.

On Thursday evening at 11:15 p.m., the Boulder Office of Emergency Management broadcast a reverse 911 call to 8,000 phone numbers for residents along Boulder Creek, advising them to move to higher ground. Reports of road closures spread. President Obama signed an emergency order approving federal disaster aid for the county. At Boulder's 28th Street YMCA scores of residents began taking shelter. For still unexplained reasons, a number of homeless people were turned away from emergency shelters. Meanwhile, one fatality and one missing person were reported on Linden Street in Boulder. A debris flow crushed a home and killed a man in the mountain hamlet of Jamestown.

Past Boulder Floods

When the Justice Center at 6th Street and Canyon Boulevard in Boulder was built in 1975, a large number of stream boulders were taken out of the excavation. Many were too big to crush and remove. The mean diameter of the biggest boulders was 6.2 feet. As these boulders were Precambrian in origin, they had to come from within Boulder Canyon and moved a minimum of one-half mile to the Justice Center site. With an eye toward understanding large floods on Boulder Creek, geologists Bill Bradley and A. I. Mears set out to determine what kind of flows were needed to move those giants. Using various methods, they estimated that the flow velocities necessary to move 6.2-foot-diameter boulders would have to be in the range of 15 to 20 feet per second (10.2 to 13.6 miles per hour) with a water depth of 11 to 16 feet. Based on this, they estimated the flows were an amazing 22,000 cfs! By way of comparison, when I rafted the Grand Canyon of the Colorado, the flow was about 10,000 cfs, and our float averaged about 3 miles per hour. Bradley and Mears speculated that floods capable of moving the boulders occurred at least once, probably more than that, in the last 10,000 years.[2]

Within historic times, there have been big floods, but nothing like the one that moved the Justice Center boulders. On Boulder Creek and its tributaries a number of notable floods have occurred. In 1876 Coal Creek flooded and "Erie began to fill with water, and before an hour had elapsed, houses were flooded and the whole flat on which the town is located was swept by a muddy, roaring flood, over a quarter of a mile in width."[3]

On May 29, 1894, a warm spring rain that continued for nearly sixty hours melted the snow pack far too rapidly. This regional storm was similar to the September 2013 event, except that it happened during the spring snow-melt. Flooding on Boulder Creek began early in the morning of May 31. Mountain roads, bridges, rooming houses, and mines were destroyed. The track for the Greeley, Salt Lake City and Pacific Railroad, a narrow-gage line built in 1883 from Boulder Canyon to Sunset, was carried off. Both Boulder and Fourmile Canyon Creeks flooded, and the high water brought the St. Vrain out of its banks. Salina and Sugarloaf were damaged. According to historian Phyllis Smith, Left Hand Creek measured over 300 yards across and turned into a "howling river." Sections of Lyons were destroyed, and the Estes Park toll road was washed away. In Boulder the Sixth Street, Ninth Street, Twelfth Street (now Broadway), and Seventeenth Street bridges all collapsed and were swept away. Irrigation facilities were not spared, as the diversion for the Boulder and White Rock Ditch was destroyed. Water flowed uncontrolled down the ditch (the former Dry Creek) for several days before the water was stopped. Decades later, the US Army Corps of Engineers reported that the peak discharge for the 1894 flood on Boulder Creek was about 11,000 cfs.[4]

However, I remain highly skeptical that there is much, if any, validity in the 11,000 cfs estimate. First of all, no stream gages were then operating on Boulder Creek. So there is no stage information to reliably model flows. The flow estimate came from studies made "several years" after the flood but did not reference the source nor describe the data or methods used. Consequently, this number is essentially hearsay and should be disregarded. Moreover, consider that rainfall records for the time show that over a ninety-six-hour period the mountains west of Boulder received from 4.5 to 6 inches of precipitation, or about one-third the amount of rain that fell during the September 2013 storm. That too raises suspicions regarding the size of the 1894 flood. And as I explained previously, this flood came after decades of hydraulic mining and dumping of mill and mine waste directly into Boulder Creek. With the sediment-choked channel, the water had no alternative to go up and out of its banks in a destructive manner. That and subsequent floods likely flushed out the sediment, making it difficult to estimate channel conditions in 1894. Complicating matters was that this was at a time that virtually all the water-shed had been denuded after decades of logging and fires. With few trees, rainfall would have reached the creek rapidly. But that is also true for the 2013 flood, as the watersheds of Fourmile and Left Hand Creeks have experienced severe wildfires in recent years. It's highly likely that forest conditions present in the 1890s and today exacerbated the flooding.

One of the largest floods in the region occurred on South Boulder Creek on September 3, 1938. That day, thunderstorms dropped intense rain for seven hours. Over six inches of rain was reported in the mountains west of Eldorado Springs. Streamflow records show a rapid flow spike on South Boulder Creek. The flow increased from about 90 cfs at 7:00 p.m. at Eldorado Springs to 970 cfs by 8:00 p.m. and then peaked at 7,390 cfs about two hours later. After peaking, it rapidly receded, and nine hours later the flow was down to 1,020 cfs. Damage was severe along the creek. Catching the brunt of abuse was the Eldorado Springs Resort, which suffered extensive damage from eroded foundations.[5]

Around the region people have caused severe floods. Among the most famous was the Lawn Lake Dam failure in Rocky Mountain National Park on July 15, 1982, and the Castlewood Dam collapse on Cherry Creek on August 3, 1933. Perhaps the worst man-made flooding in Boulder County occurred from failures of the Left Hand Park Reservoir, located west of Ward. The reservoir was originally constructed under the supervision of Left Hand Ditch founder Samuel Arbuthnot. Construction on the twenty-eight-foot-high earthen dam began in 1896. Barely a year later, on July, 9, 1897, after a day-long rain, the dam breached. When it failed, a wall of water rushed down Left Hand Creek through California Gulch near Ward. The *Daily Camera* ridiculed the dam as a "loosely constructed affair." Six-foot-high waves carried everything before it, including the telephone lines between Ward and Gold Hill. Tragically, Mrs. James Matthews and her child, who lived along the creek, were swept away and killed. Her child was never recovered. Several bridges in Left Hand Canyon were destroyed too. The dam was repaired, and a second, smaller breach occurred on June 8, 1904. It was rebuilt again, and on July 15, 1918, the Left Hand Park Dam failed for a third time (see Figure 17.3). The *Daily Camera* reported that more than 50 million cubic feet of water rushed through its breach. This whole mass of water rushed down California Gulch to Left Hand Creek, just like it did twice before. Several railroad bridges belonging to the Denver, Boulder, and Western Rail Road washed away in the flood. Fortunately, there was no loss of life this time. Left Hand Park Reservoir stood empty until it was rebuilt to modern standards in 1966.[6]

FIGURE 17.3. The Left Hand Park Dam after it failed on July 15, 1918. Reprinted with permission. Image courtesy Carnegie Branch Library for Local History, Boulder.

FRIDAY, SEPTEMBER 13

Friday morning's *Daily Camera* led with the headline "100-YEAR FLOOD." Just below it was a photo of my friend, Sahand Tabatabi, untangling debris that washed into his north Boulder home. That image pained me, as it personalized the human toll. Although the force of the rain had abated somewhat, it continued to come down. Roads across the region were closed, including Interstate 25 and US 36 between Boulder and Denver. It seems that everyone we spoke to that morning had a flood story of their own—damaged basements, leaks, destroyed homes—or they knew someone affected by the unfolding events.

Overnight a large debris flow came down Flagstaff Mountain and took an office building off its foundation. On Linden Road in Boulder, another debris flow closed that road and caused extensive damage. Smaller landslides and debris flows were visible along the ridges north of Boulder. Ditches around Boulder, including Anderson, Silver Lake, and Farmers, were battered with debris and sediment.

Flooding extended across the Front Range from Fort Collins to Colorado Springs. Police remained in emergency mode throughout the day. It became apparent that multiple structures had collapsed or washed away in Jamestown, Salina, Lyons, and on Left Hand Creek. Longmont, cut in two on Thursday, remained isolated due to the swollen St. Vrain River. All the roads east of Estes Park were severed. Coal Creek swept away a new bike trail near Erie and eroded the road to Pinecliffe in the mountains west of Boulder.

The National Weather Service reported that Boulder was sandwiched between a "late season monsoonal low flow from the eastern Pacific and Gulf of California" and a "high pressure system" to the northeast that stalled the storm at Boulder. By this point, more than ten inches had fallen in three and one-half days in the mountains west of Boulder and even more at sites around the valley.[7]

Governor John Hickenlooper declared fourteen counties disaster areas and authorized $6 million in emergency aid. Hickenlooper, a trained geologist, undoubtedly understood the magnitude of the unfolding disaster. That day whenever the weather allowed, we could hear helicopter flights going back and forth between Boulder's airport and the mountains.

Meanwhile, we went back out to look at Boulder Creek during the day. Knowing that there were high flows on both Boulder and South Boulder Creeks, I wanted to see the area east of the two streams' confluence. The stream gage for South Boulder Creek (at Eldorado Springs) had gone offline for a while but indicated that the flows were about 640 cfs on Friday morning. The stream gage on Boulder Creek in town increased from about 200 cfs at around 6:00 p.m. on Wednesday and went off scale at about 1,000 cfs that midnight. It did not come back online until midday Friday, when it put out a reading of about 1,240 cfs. On Boulder Creek at 75th Street, where the combined flow of Boulder and South Boulder Creeks are measured, the flow increased from about 300 cfs in the evening of September 11 to about 6,200 cfs early on September 12. Around midday Friday when we were there the flow had decreased to a still impressive 4,000 cfs. The median flow over the previous twenty-six years of record was about 65 cfs. In other words, the flood peak was more than ninety-five times the median flow for that date in September.[8]

As Tina, Ian, and I drove along Pearl Parkway in east Boulder, we could see Boulder Creek overtopping its banks from our car. Goose Creek, then in the middle of a stream restoration project, was churning with mud as its banks eroded. Sixty-First Street was closed, so we walked north to investigate. Boulder Creek was out of its banks, and we encountered the first water from the creek about 880 feet south of the bridge over the creek. By this time water was only about shin deep along the road. When we arrived at the bridge, which was then out of the water, we could see that the water had overtopped it earlier. A deer was frantically swimming in the current on city open space north of the main channel. East of us, a car with Texas plates that had apparently washed off the road was sitting abandoned in the water. Unknown to us at the time, Boulder Creek was out of its bank to the west due to a bridge collapse on city open space, and the creek breached a sewer line to the east and destroyed a second stream crossing at that site. Although the rain intensity had abated, it continued to drizzle for the remainder of the day.

SATURDAY, SEPTEMBER 14

Clouds hung low and rain continued in Boulder on Saturday morning. But as soon as the rain relented and the clouds began to disperse, the whoop-whoop noise of Chinook and Back Hawk helicopters flying back and forth meant that rescue crews were out seeking stranded people in the mountains west of Boulder. Thousands of people were brought in during the day. Meanwhile farther north in the Big Thompson Canyon, two people were swept away and killed. Longmont staff estimated that flows over their Button Rock (aka Ralph Price) Reservoir on the North St. Vrain exceeded 10,000 cfs.

The flood peak and the damage it wrought moved downstream to the east. Near Fort Morgan, the South Platte jumped more than ten feet to a flow of approximately 50,000 cfs before the recording station failed. At Evans, the swollen South Platte flooded mostly Hispanic blue-collar neighborhoods. Mud and raw sewage poured into trailer homes around town. In nearby oil fields, oil tanks toppled and spilled their contents, further adding to the pollution. By this time seventeen counties in northern Colorado were under disaster declarations.

We were again out surveying the damage around Boulder. The debris flow at the top of Linden Avenue had swept through affluent Spring Valley Estates and deposited mounds of sediment along its path. Four Mile Canyon Creek (not the same as Fourmile Creek) had destroyed multiple homes both in the mountains and in north Boulder. Its sediments were deposited in braids typical of sediment-laden rivers except for the homes, trees, and cars complicating its path.

I received a call that morning from Terry Plummer of the Left Hand Ditch to assist the company to evaluate the damage and pick up the pieces. Within an hour I was touring the damage on Left Hand Creek. In Left Hand Canyon whole stretches of road had been swept away. The waters obliterated the Allen Lake diversion and cut a new channel, leaving the Left Hand Water District's Haldi diversion high and dry. Multiple bridges were out along Left Hand Creek. The stream once located south of a judge's home now flowed to the north of his house and between his barns. Elsewhere along the creek homes were surrounded by the floodwaters. Another home had the full force of Left Hand Creek directed against the side of the house that a few days before had not even been within a mapped flood zone. The diversion dams for the Table Mountain, Bader, Star, Williamson, Crocker, and other ditches were washed away, collapsed, or severely eroded from the floodwaters. Both spillways to Left Hand Valley Reservoir were overflowing for the first time ever. Offices for the Left Hand Water District were isolated by the floodwaters, and many water distribution lines were taken out. Figure 17.4 is a photo of the Left Hand Valley Reservoir Inlet Canal diversion taken that day.

I learned about the epic drive by Terry Plummer and one of the Left Hand Ditch directors, Joel Schapp, to the mountains west of Ward on Wednesday evening to shut down the Left Hand Ditch diversion. Unknown to the people of Jamestown, their drive prevented even more water from running through the besieged town. Returning down Left Hand Canyon late that night, they had to negotiate accumulating rockslides and debris along the road. Finally they had to turn around and wait out part of the night in the canyon until a rescue vehicle with a plow came across them at about 3:00 a.m. and helped them escape up Lee Hill Road. They were perhaps the last people to brave the canyon before the floodwaters destroyed the road.

Sunday, September 15

The rain continued, but not as vigorously, on Sunday, and swollen rivers eroded roadways and bridges throughout the region. An eighty-year-old Cedar Cove woman went missing in Larimer County. Teams of rescuers spread out to

FIGURE 17.4. The Left Hand Valley Reservoir Inlet Canal diversion on September 14, 2013. Photograph by author.

take residents out of mountain towns, some of whom declined assistance. In parts of south Boulder, high water pressure from shallow groundwater forced raw sewage back into homes, compounding the flooding problems. Meanwhile floodwaters continued migrating downstream to further damage Weld County towns. At least fifty bridges were seriously damaged or destroyed in that county. On a positive note, emergency officials significantly reduced the number of people unaccounted for as information on evacuees accumulated. For many victims, the shock and adrenaline of the emergency began to subside as the magnitude of their losses set in.

Damage that initially seemed somewhat random began to resolve into patterns around stream corridors, drainages, high groundwater, and blockages in roads and culverts. The worst damage was of course reserved for the corridors of the large creeks and their main tributaries, but the sheer amount of water meant that many otherwise seemingly secure areas experienced flooding.

THE RAIN STOPS: MONDAY, SEPTEMBER 16

Fog and drizzle welcomed the day, but by midmorning the weather broke and the sun finally emerged. Evacuations resumed as the emergency subsided and thoughts of recovery began. As the rain ended, about eighty-seven roads were closed in Boulder County due to bridge outages, landslides, and washouts. Many more were destroyed or damaged in surrounding counties. On the St. Vrain, every diversion dam between Lyons and Longmont was destroyed. The cities of Longmont and Loveland both lost critical water infrastructure, leaving each with a single pipeline to deliver raw water to their treatment plants.

Boulder County had at least 397 homes damaged and 340 destroyed by September 19. Another 7,685 households applied for and received about $4.3 million in FEMA assistance.[9]

On September 24, the state estimated that about 1,533 square miles were affected. The state's statistics hint at the human toll as some 5,958 people were under mandatory evacuations from their homes and 118 pets were placed in shelters. At least 1,882 homes were destroyed and another 16,101 were damaged. By then Colorado determined that fifty state bridges and 200 miles of state roads were damaged.[10]

Over the next several weeks Colorado refined its damage tally. Colorado's Office of Emergency Management listed twenty affected counties. Nearly 21,000 households were damaged or destroyed. As of September 30, 2013, eight people were known to be dead and another was missing and presumed dead. Damages to bridges and roads were estimated at about $475 million.[11]

HOW BIG WAS THIS FLOOD?

In the high-damage zones in Salina, Lyons, Jamestown, Boulder, Longmont, Evans, and elsewhere, the question of the flood magnitude really is a rather abstract and beside-the-point question. For the victims and all those who lost friends and family, that was a tragedy of the highest order. After all, knowing whether the flood was a 10-year or 500-year event doesn't change the fact that your home was destroyed or friends harmed.

But we like to classify and organize our understanding of events, and hopefully that will allow us to better plan and respond quickly to the next tragedy. Answering questions about the size of these floods really depends on understanding the variables involved in estimating the magnitude of the event. First of all, flood and storm frequencies require accurate data derived from the uncertain historic record. As I have explained elsewhere, I am very skeptical of flow data collected during the nineteenth and early twentieth centuries. To measure flow, we need to have accurate information on the stream channel conditions and the velocity of water moving through them. We really do not know what the channel conditions were, as there were likely significant amounts of sediment from hydraulic mining and mill tailings choking the stream bed. Also, the science of flow measurement was rudimentary in ways that make it particularly difficult to measure high flows. Not only that, but the forest cover was far smaller after decades of logging. That means that an identical rainfall event today would run off more slowly (more trees slows hillside runoff) than in the nineteenth century. An identical nineteenth-century storm would have reached the stream sooner, resulting in a higher peak even if the same amount of rain fell from the sky. If that were not enough to show that we are not comparing apples to apples, we need to keep in mind that storm intensity varies over the region. It is completely possible during a single storm for one area to experience a very rare downpour (perhaps a 1,000-year event) while somewhere nearby experiences much less rainfall. Furthermore, if the big downpour happens over an area recently affected by a forest fire, the resulting streamflow can be even greater.

Among scientists there is wide disagreement on just how rare large Front Range floods can be and what recurrence intervals they entail. Evidence from the geologic record gives different results than hydrologic analyses. Considerations of whether the flood was derived from snowmelt, rain events (as Boulder's September flood was), or a mixed snowmelt rain event affect the calculations. The amount of available sediment in the stream bed affects stage gage measurements and high-flow flood estimates. Uncertainty over high-water marks and the timing of erosion add additional variability to estimates. Also, if an identical storm happens a year after a large flood washed away the stream sediments, the second storm will manifest itself differently in the stream channel. In addition, scientists have developed many methodologies for estimating the size of large floods, and they all give different results. Compounding matters is that there is significant variability in the parameters used to perform the estimates with each method. Even for well-documented events such as the catastrophic Big Thompson flood of 1976, the calculated recurrence interval has ranged from a low of about 50 years to a high of about 17,500 years. One certainty is that the size and damage stemming from the September 2013 floods will generate a wide variety of opinions among experts versed in these methods for a long time to come.[12]

Colorado Water Conservation Board staff reported that the weather pattern for the storm was only moderate in short-term intensity. However, because it extended over so many days, the storm in many locations "exceeded a 1,000 year rainfall event." There is also anecdotal evidence that some rain gages filled and spilled, which artificially lowers the storm totals. When this water reached the rivers, a number of them experienced floods "equaling or exceeding a 100-year streamflow event." Although there is great uncertainty, this was undoubtedly the largest flood event in recent memory.[13]

Finally, public perceptions of flood intensity are influenced by the impacts to the built environment. A highly destructive flood in human and property terms will loom larger in the collective conscious than an even larger event remote from population centers.

THE SHADOW OF GILBERT WHITE

"For the most part, floods in the United States leave in their wake a dreary scene of impaired health, damaged property, and disrupted economic life." Gilbert White's prophetic words, published in 1942, encapsulated the situation in his adopted state seventy-one years later. Perhaps most importantly, he added, "Floods are 'acts of God,' but flood losses are largely acts of man."[14]

Gilbert White refined our understanding of floods. He articulated how engineers approach floods by inquiring if flood protection is warranted. His work helped emergency officials consider how to alleviate the distress floods cause. And he demonstrated the importance of forecasting to evacuate property and prepare for the worst. White was among the first to recommend relocating property and critical infrastructure out of the flood zone. Although this is easier said than done, this is the one sure strategy that can minimize damage.

Gilbert White's doctoral dissertation at the University of Chicago, "Human Adjustment to Floods," was often considered the "most influential ever written by an American geographer." White, a Quaker, was a conscientious objector to military service during World War II. He came to the University of Colorado in 1969 to teach geography. White believed that it was better for communities to adapt to or accommodate flood hazards through planning and zoning rather than resort to structural solutions such as dams and levees.[15]

The lessons of floodplain planning espoused by White are highly relevant here. As communities pick up the pieces, it is imperative to take steps to move homes and property out of high-hazard areas and harden other infrastructure to avoid or minimize the magnitude of future calamities. This may be a hard pill to swallow for the homeowners who are prevented from rebuilding on their land. But it is a necessary pill if we are to apply the lessons we have learned on how to better interact with the environment in which we live.

For communities like Lyons and Longmont, much of the damage was sadly predictable. Back in 1972 the US Corps of Engineers evaluated the flood damage potential along the St. Vrain corridor and largely anticipated the extent of flooding that occurred during the September 2013 event. In its study, the Corps estimated that a "standard project flood" on the St. Vrain in Lyons might carry 21,800 cfs of water. In some locations, the Corps predicted that a flood of that magnitude would expand the St. Vrain to an average of 550 feet and in a few sites up to 400 to 650 feet from the stream bank. The Corps observed that many homes in Lyons would be flooded in an event of that magnitude. Furthermore, the Corps predicted that trees and vegetation would be swept downstream to threaten or destroy bridges that lie in its path. Corps predictions for the lower St. Vrain through Longmont and for Left Hand Creek were similar. That over forty years passed without major efforts to relocate homes, businesses, and infrastructure out of the floodplain is something that those communities will have to face in the coming years. And while it is easy to be a Monday morning quarterback and point out planning failures, the flood risks were clearly known and in plain sight.[16]

Hopefully in the rush to rebuild, those communities affected by the floods will avoid mistakes of the past and take the difficult steps needed to minimize damage when the next event strikes. For the areas of high risk, there is a need to design with nature so that homes and valuable infrastructure are rebuilt out of harm's way. In some places there may be no alternative but to rebuild roads and other infrastructure within high-hazard areas. For these facilities, the engineers and planners will need to carefully consider what to harden or how to incorporate sacrificial structures that can be easily rebuilt with less expense. Ditch diversions should be rebuilt to modern standards and incorporate structures to resist floods and allow fish and boaters to safely navigate their structures.

Our experience with water and riparian development in the region is a long one. As we engage with nature along these rivers, we will continually find ourselves striking a balance in ways that will influence the course of future development and the ecosystems on which we depend. Here history and landscape are linked and our legacy of change endures.

NOTES

1. National Weather Service, "Glossary," http://w1.weather.gov/glossary/index.php?letter=w, accessed September 24, 2013.

2. W. C. Bradley, and A. I. Mears, "Calculations of Flows Needed to Transport Coarse Fraction of Boulder Creek Alluvium at Boulder, Colorado," *Geological Society of America Bulletin* 91, no. 3, part 2 (1980): 1057–90.

3. *Greeley Sun*, May 31, 1876 in Phyllis Smith, "History of Floods and Flood Control in Boulder, Colorado, " unpublished report for the City of Boulder Department of Public Works, Boulder, CO, 1987, 15.

4. Smith, "History of Floods," 16–30; US Army Corps of Engineers, Omaha District, *Flood Plain Information: Boulder Metropolitan Region, Colorado*, vol. 2, *Boulder Creek and South Boulder Creek* (Omaha, NE: US Army Engineer District, 1969).

5. Smith, "History of Floods," 41; US Army Corps of Engineers, Omaha District, *Flood Plain Information: Boulder Metropolitan Region*.

6. Map and Statement Filing for Left Hand Park Reservoir, November 1912, Boulder County Clerk and Recorder; *Daily Camera*, August 11, 1896; *Daily Camera*, in Ochs, *Water the Basis for Success*, 43–48.

7. Charlie Brennan, "Dueling Weather Systems Swamp Rain Fall Records, *Daily Camera*, September 13, 2013.

8. The flow numbers I refer to are the provisional real-time records for the stream gages.

9. Mitchell Byars, "Boulder County Ceases Air Rescue Operations as 2 Remain Unaccounted For," *Daily Camera*, September 19, 2013, http://www.dailycamera.com/news/boulder-flood/ci_24130691/boulder-county-ceases-air-rescue-operations-2-remain.

10. Colorado Division of Homeland Security and Emergency Management, "Statewide Flood Quick Facts: September 25 at 8 PM," http://www.coemergency .com/2013/09/statewide-flood-quick-facts-september_25.html.

11. Colorado Division of Homeland Security and Emergency Management, "Statewide Flood Quick Facts and Information: September 30," http://www .coemergency.com/2013/09/statewide-flood-quick-facts-and.html.

12. John E. Costa, "Colorado Big Thompson Flood: Geologic Evidence of a Rare Hydrologic Event," *Geology* 6, no. 10 (1978): 617–20; John E. Costa, "Paleohydraulic Reconstruction of Flash-Flood Peaks from Boulder Deposits in the Colorado Front Range," *Geological Society of America Bulletin* 94, no. 8 (1983): 986–1004; James D. Balog, "Flooding in Big Thompson River, Colorado, Tributaries: Controls on Channel Erosion and Estimates of Recurrence Interval," *Geology* 6, no. 4 (1978): 200–204.

13. Colorado Water Conservation Board, "Special Board Meeting Agenda Item 3—September 2013 Technical Flood Summary," October 21, 2013.

14. Gilbert F. White, *Selected Writings of Gilbert F. White*, vol. 1, ed. Robert W. Kates and Ian Burton (Chicago: University of Chicago Press, 1986), 11–12.

15. University of Colorado at Boulder, Natural Hazards Center, "Gilbert F. White—A Short Biography," http://www.colorado.edu/hazards/gfw/bio.html.

16. US Army Corps of Engineers, Omaha District, *Flood Plain Information, Boulder County, Colorado*, vols. 3 and 4.

Acknowledgments

The idea for this book began germinating in my mind shortly after I came to work for the City of Boulder Open Space (now Open Space and Mountain Parks) Department. My position afforded me with the opportunity to seek out information concerning Boulder's ditches. As I read old decrees, ditch records, and such, I became fascinated with the people and history those ditches embody. Working with them put a bug in the back of my mind that I might someday write about Boulder's water history. I warmly thank the City of Boulder and its dedicated staff for entrusting me with management responsibility for its extraordinary open space lands.

In 2009, I worked with Elizabeth Black, a Boulder artist, to organize the Ditch Project, a program to celebrate Boulder's ditches as part of the city's sesquicentennial celebrations. This afforded me the opportunity to assemble materials involving history and ecology that went into the project and an associated website chronicling Boulder's water legacy. I remain grateful for the partnership I shared with Elizabeth in bringing that project together. I especially wish to thank Justice Gregory Hobbs of the Colorado Supreme

Court for his early enthusiasm and generosity in support of the Ditch Project. Colorado is fortunate to have him on the bench.

Between my work with OSMP, the Ditch Project, and countless hours spent pouring through ditch records and other readings about western water history, I realized that I had collected sufficient material to begin this project.

I reserve special thanks for the various people who have worked alongside me on ditches. What I learned from them is at once unclassifiable and invaluable. Top among them is Duane Myers, to whom I owe a deep debt of gratitude. His on-the-ground ability to manage people and ditches is unparalleled. Other colleagues that I have spent long hours with in ditches include Craig Sommers, Kristen Weinberger, Pat Lemieux, Jake Cske, and Emily McMurtrery. Over the years I have benefited from their partnership, help, enthusiasm, and skill. I will always be indebted for their assistance and friendship. I thank Delani Wheeler, who passed away recently, for her mentoring and keen political acumen in moving through the minefields of shareholder politics.

I have served on many ditch boards and worked with many more board members over the years. All of them contributed to this book by educating me about their ditches. A titan among them is Richard Behrmann. Richard's knowledge and unassuming humor, along with his impeccable common sense derived from his life working the land, made my time on the Left Hand Ditch board a special privilege. Along with Richard, Terry Plummer, John Schlagel, Ron Sutherland, and Joel Schapp have all helped me better understand one of Colorado's most historic ditches. Others that I wish to thank include Jim Snow, Tim Ostwald, and Catherine Long Gates of the Silver Lake Ditch, Bob and Bev Clyncke of the Davidson Ditch, the Anderson family along with Gary Gisle of the Marshallville Ditch, Jeanette Hillery of the Howard Ditch, C. D. Bodam and Joe Kent of the Dry Creek No. 2 Ditch, John Brunner of the Boulder and Left Hand Ditch, and William Suitts (now deceased) of the McGinn Ditch. I appreciate the dedication of the Anderson Ditch board, in particular current and former board members Kim Hutton, Joe Taddeucci, and Carol Ellinghouse. On the North Tollgate Ditch I will always feel like a comrade in arms with my friend, rancher Larry Strear, and its other board members for the time we spent defending that ditch from blatant and illegal encroachments.

A diverse and welcoming group of people assisted me when I was researching this book. Wendy Hall and the rest of the staff at the Carnegie Library in Boulder deserve special thanks. Also, I truly appreciate the assistance provided to me from the staff at the University of Colorado Archives, University of Colorado Map Library, Longmont History Museum, Colorado History Museum, Colorado State Archives, Denver Public Library Western History Department, Colorado State University Water Archives, Boulder County Clerk and Recorder, Denver Water Central Records, the Water Court for Division 1 in Greeley, Colorado, and the National Archives and Records Administration in Broomfield, Colorado.

I was delighted when the names of two anonymous reviewers of my manuscript were revealed to me. Both I have held in the highest regard over my career. Their collective wisdom and knowledge of western water and water institutions and the importance of ditches are without match. Thank you, Dr. Charles Howe of the Institute of Behavioral Science at the University of Colorado at Boulder and Dr. Michael Holleran of the School of Architecture at the University of Texas at Austin, for reviewing this book.

My appreciation goes out to Theresa Cecot-Schearer for her careful review of chapter 1. I wish to thank both Jeff Campbell and Tom Meier for their generosity in taking the time to discuss Sand Creek and to share their deep insights and knowledge about the subject. Their scholarship has greatly improved our understanding of this tragic event.

Chapter 7, "Left Hand Ditch and the Emergence of the Prior Appropriation Doctrine," greatly benefited from my serving on the board of directors of the Left Hand Ditch Company and the company's kind permission for me to examine its records. I thank Donalyn Arbuthnot for information regarding her ancestors and Mike Adams, a fine poet and friend who is now deceased, for thoughtful commentary on the chapter. For chapter 10, "Making the South Platte," John Weiner provided a critical read and made helpful suggestions.

Material in chapters 15 and 16, "An Unnatural History?" and "Conclusion: The New Nature," consolidates and updates material from two previously published articles of mine that appeared in *Water International* and *Environmental Management*. I thank the four anonymous reviewers for reading the *Water International* article and providing useful suggestions that strengthened that work. I also thank the editors of *Environmental Management*, including Virginia H. Dale, and four reviewers, Becky Mansfield, Morgan Robertson, and two anonymous reviewers, for their careful and insightful suggestions that strengthened that work.

I want to extend a particularly warm thanks to Jessica d'Arbonne at the University Press of Colorado for all her efforts in bringing this book to print. I thank Alison Tartt for her hand in the careful copyediting that has greatly strengthened this book. To all the staff at the University Press of Colorado including Laura Furney, Kelly Lenkevich, Beth Svinarich, Daniel Pratt, and others unnamed, thank you! I find it is better late than never to thank all my teachers and family for helping instill in me a sense of curiosity and desire for learning. I especially appreciate Ed Larson and Bill Bilodeau for their encouragement and support in graduate school. And I reserve the greatest appreciation to the scholar, poet, and educator Rudolph Lindenfeld for inspiring me to trek down the road that I still follow. Thank you, Mr. Lindenfeld, wherever you are. To my parents, Paul and Loretta Crifasi, I owe a debt of gratitude and love that can never be repaid. Finally, but not least, I wish to thank my wife and best friend, Tina Tan, for patience in listening to oft-told stories of ditches and all the good years we have spent together.

Bibliography

Allen, Alonzo H. "Pioneer Life in Old Burlington." *Colorado Magazine* 14, no. 4 (1937): 154–57.

Arft, Anna M. "The Genetics, Demography, and Conservation Management of the Rare Orchid Spiranthes Diluvialis." PhD diss., University of Colorado, Boulder, 1995.

Armstrong, David. *Distribution of Mammals in Colorado.* Monograph of the University of Kansas Museum of Natural History, no. 3 Lawrence: University of Kansas, 1972.

Baker, F. P. "Report by States Respecting Their Forest Condition." In US Department of Agriculture, *Report on Forestry*, vol. 4, ed. N. H. Egleston, 183–85. Washington, DC: Government Printing Office, 1884.

Bancroft, Hubert H. *History of Nevada, Colorado, and Wyoming: 1540–1888.* Vol. 25 of The Works of Hubert Howe Bancroft. San Francisco: The History Company Publishers, 1890.

Baron, Jill S., Heather M. Rueth, Alexander M. Wolfe, Koren R. Nydick, Eric J. Allstott, J. Toby Minear, and Brenda Moraska. "Ecosystem Responses to Nitrogen Deposition in the Colorado Front Range." *Ecosystems* 3, no. 4 (2000): 352–68. http://dx.doi.org/10.1007/s100210000032.

Bartlett, Richard A. *Great Surveys of the American West*. Norman: University of Oklahoma Press, 1962.

Bebbington, Anthony. "Reencountering Development: Livelihood Transitions and Place Transformations in the Andes." *Annals of the Association of American Geographers* 90, no. 3 (2000): 495–520. http://dx.doi.org/10.1111/0004-5608.00206.

Benedict, Diane G. *Left Hand Canyon to the Plains: The Altona Community Boulder County, Colorado*. Lyons, CO: Applications Plus, 2005.

Beschta, Robert L. "Reduced Cottonwood Recruitment Following Extirpation of Wolves in Yellowstone's Northern Range." *Ecology* 86, no. 2 (2005): 391–403. http://dx.doi.org/10.1890/04-0964.

Bestgen, Kevin, and Boris Kondratieff. *Fishes, Macroinvertebrates, and Habitat of South Boulder Creek, Colorado, within City of Boulder Open Space Property*. Final report, January 31, 1996.

Bird, Isabella L. *A Lady's Life in the Rocky Mountains*. London: G. P. Putnam's Sons, 1886.

Bixby, Amos. *History of Clear Creek and Boulder Valleys, Colorado*. Chicago: O. L. Baskin & Co, 1880.

Blaikie, P. M. "Development, Post-, Anti- and Populist: A Critical Review." *Environment and Planning* 32 (2000): 1033–1050.

Block, Augusta H. "Lower Boulder and St. Vrain Valley Home Guards and Fort Junction." *Colorado Magazine* 16, no. 4 (1939): 186–91.

Bollinger, Edward T., and Frederick Bauer. *The Moffat Road*. Chicago: Sage Books, 1962.

Boyd, David. *Irrigation near Greeley, Colorado*. Water Supply and Irrigation Papers of the US Geological Survey, no. 9. Washington, DC: Government Printing Office, 1897.

Braddock, Virginia. "Municipal Government History Boulder, Colorado 1965–1974." Unpublished report to the Boulder Public Library Foundation, Inc., Boulder, CO, 1985.

Braddock, Virginia. "Municipal Government History Boulder, Colorado 1975–1979." Unpublished report to the Boulder Public Library Foundation, Inc., Boulder, CO, 1986.

Braun, Bruce. *The Intemperate Rainforest: Nature, Culture, and Power on Canada's West Coast*. Minneapolis: University of Minnesota Press, 2002.

Campbell, Jeff C. *Sand Creek Massacre Background Booklet No. 2 3rd Regiment Cavalry, Colorado Volunteers [US Army Volunteers] A One Hundred Days Regiment August to December 1865 Alphabetical Roll of Regiment and Alphabetical Roll of Regiment by Company*. Eads, CO: Jeff C. Campbell, 2006.

Carpenter, Delph E. *Colorado Proceedings of the South Platte River Compact*. Denver, January 7, 1925.

Carpenter, Louis G. *The Measurement and Division of Water*. Colorado Agricultural Experiment Station Bulletin, no. 13. Fort Collins, CO: State Agricultural College, 1887.

Carroll, John M. *The Sand Creek Massacre: A Documentary History*. New York: Sol Lewis Publisher, 1973.

Cary, Merrett. *A Biological Survey of Colorado*. US Department of Agriculture, Biological Survey. North American Fauna, no. 33 Washington, DC: Government Printing Office, 1911.

Castree, Noel, and Bruce Braun. "The Construction of Nature and the Nature of Construction: Analytical and Political Tools for Building Survivable Futures." In *Remaking Reality: Nature at the Millennium*, ed. B. Braun and N. Castree, 3–42. London: Routledge, 1998.

City of Boulder. *South Boulder Creek Management Area Inventory Report*. Boulder, CO: Open Space Department, October 28, 1998.

City of Boulder. *South Boulder Creek Area Management Plan*. Boulder, CO: Open Space Department, October 28, 1998. Accessed Mar. 11, 2004. https://boulder colorado.gov/openspace/planning/sbc/SBCArea.htm.

City of Boulder. *Source Water Master Plan*. 2 vols. Boulder, CO: Public Works Department, Apr. 7, 2009. Accessed Mar. 13, 2013. https://www-static.boulder colorado.gov/docs/volume-1-source-water-master-plan-1-201304021232.pdf.

"Clovis-era Tool Cache 13,000 Years Old Shows Evidence of Camel, Horse Butchering." *Science Daily*, February 26, 2009.

Coffin, Morse H. *The Battle of Sand Creek*. Ed. Alan W. Farley. Waco, TX: W. M. Morrison, 1965.

Coffin, Morse. Letter to *Boulder (CO) County Miner*, January 8, 1914. Accessed June 25, 2012. http://freepages.genealogy.rootsweb.ancestry.com/~mycoffinroots /ColoradoPioneers.html.

Coffin, Morse. Letter to *Longmont (CO) Ledger*, July 12 and August 2, 1907. Accessed June 25, 2012. http://freepages.genealogy.rootsweb.ancestry.com/~mycoffin roots/ColoradoPioneers.html.

Coffin, Morse. Letter to *Longmont (CO) Ledger*, February 17, 1911. Accessed June 25, 2012. http://freepages.genealogy.rootsweb.ancestry.com/~mycoffinroots /ColoradoPioneers.html.

Coffin, Morse. "Reminiscences." *Longmont (CO) Ledger*, July 19, 1907. Accessed July 11, 2012. http://freepages.genealogy.rootsweb.ancestry.com/~mycoffinroots /ColoradoPioneers.html.

Coffin, Morse. "Reminiscences." *Longmont (CO) Ledger*, July 26, 1907. Accessed July 11, 2012. http://freepages.genealogy.rootsweb.ancestry.com/~mycoffinroots /ColoradoPioneers.html.

Coffin, Morse. "Reminiscences." *Longmont (CO) Ledger*, August 9, 1907. Accessed July 11, 2012. http://freepages.genealogy.rootsweb.ancestry.com/~mycoffinroots /ColoradoPioneers.html.

Coffin, Morse. "Reminiscences No. Four." *Boulder (CO) County Miner*, January 15, 1914. Accessed July 11, 2012. http://freepages.genealogy.rootsweb.ancestry .com/~mycoffinroots/ColoradoPioneers.html.

Colorado Division of Wildlife. *Preble's Meadow Jumping Mouse Riparian Habitat Classification and Mapping Project*. Denver, CO, November 12, 1997.

Colorado State Grange. *Colorado State Grange History*. Westminster, CO: North Suburban Printing and Publishing, 1975.

Colorado Water Resources Research Institute South Platte Team. *South Platte River System in Colorado: Hydrology, Development and Management Issues Working Paper*. For Collins: Colorado Water Resources Research Institute, Colorado State University, 1990.

Colten, Craig. *An Unnatural Metropolis: Wresting New Orleans from Nature*. Baton Rouge: Louisiana State University Press, 2005.

Cook, Carey F. Interview by Sarah Binford Avery. Boulder, CO: Carnegie Library, 1985.

Crawford, Stanley G. *Mayordomo: Chronicle of an Acequia in Northern New Mexico*. Albuquerque: University of New Mexico Press, 1993.

Crifasi, Robert R. "Of Mice and Men: Boulder's Preble's Meadow Jumping Mouse Habitat Conservation Plan." In *Proceedings of the American Water Resources Association 2001 Annual Water Resources Conference*. Middleburg, VA: American Water Resources Association, 2001.

Crifasi, Robert R. "Political Ecology of Water Use and Development." *Water International* 27, no. 4 (2002): 492–503. http://dx.doi.org/10.1080/02508060208687037.

Crifasi, Robert R. "Reflections in a Stock Pond: Are Anthropogenically Derived Freshwater Ecosystems Natural, Artificial, or Something Else?" *Environmental Management* 36, no. 5 (2005): 625–39. http://dx.doi.org/10.1007/s00267-004-0147-1.

Crifasi, Robert. "South Boulder Creek near Boulder Colorado: A Description of Boulder's Instream Flow and Riparian Management Program." In *Watershed Management to Protect Declining Species*, ed. R. Sakrison and P. Sturtevant, 381–84. Middleburg, VA: American Water Resources Association, 1999.

Crifasi, Robert R. "A Subspecies No More? A Mouse, Its Unstable Taxonomy, and Western Riparian Resource Conflict." *Cultural Geographies* 14, no. 4 (2007): 511–35. http://dx.doi.org/10.1177/1474474007082292.

Cronon, William. *Changes in the Land: Indians, Colonists, and the Ecology of New England*. New York: Hill and Wang, 1983.

Cronon, William. *Nature's Metropolis: Chicago and the Great West*. New York: W. W. Norton, 1991.

Cronon, William. "The Trouble with Wilderness: Or Getting Back to the Wrong Nature." In *Uncommon Ground: Toward Reinventing Nature*, ed. W. Cronon, 69–90. New York: W. W. Norton, 1995.

Crosby, Alfred W. *Ecological Imperialism: The Ecological Expansion of Europe, 900–1900*. New York: Cambridge University Press, 1986.

Davies, Bryan R., P. J. Boon, and Geoffrey E. Petts. "River Conservation: A Global Imperative." In *Global Perspectives on River Conservation: Science, Policy and Practice*, ed. P. Boon, J. Bryan, R. Davies, and Geoffrey E. Petts, xi–xvi. Chichester: J. Wiley and Sons, 2001.

Davis, William W.H. *El Gringo; or New Mexico and Her People*. New York: Harper Brothers Publishers, 1857.

Dell'Amore, C. "Ancient Camels Butchered in Colorado, Stone Age Tools Show?" *National Geographic News*, February 27, 2009. http://www.dmns.org/science /the-snowmastodon-project, accessed June 27, 2011.

Demeritt, David. "Science, Social Constructivism and Nature." In *Remaking Reality: Nature at the Millennium*, ed. Bruce Braun and Noell Castree, 173–93. London: Routledge, 1998.

Demeritt, David. "What Is the 'Social Construction of Nature'? A Typology and Sympathetic Critique." *Progress in Human Geography* 26, no. 6 (2002): 767–90. http://dx.doi.org/10.1191/0309132502ph402oa.

Denevan, William. "The Pristine Myth: The Landscape of the Americas in 1492." *Annals of the Association of American Geographers* 82, no. 3 (1992): 369–85. http://dx.doi.org/10.1111/j.1467-8306.1992.tb01965.x.

Denver Water. *Denver Water Resources: Features of the Denver Water System*. Denver: Denver Water Department, n.d.

Dodge, Henry. *Journal of the March of a Detachment of Dragoons, under the Command of Colonel Dodge, during the Summer of 1835*. House of Representatives, 1st sess., Document No. 181. Washington, DC, 1836.

Dolin, Eric J. *Fur, Fortune, and Empire: The Epic History of the Fur Trade in America*. London: W. W. Norton, 2010.

Dyni, Ann. *Pioneer Voices of Boulder County: An Oral History*. Boulder, CO: Boulder County Parks and Open Space, 1989.

Eschner, Thomas R., Richard F. Hadley, and Kevin D. Crowley. *Hydrologic and Morphologic Changes in Channels of the Platte River Basin in Colorado, Wyoming, and Nebraska: A Historical Perspective*. US Geological Survey Professional Paper, 1277-A. Washington, DC: Government Printing Office, 1983.

Fair, Fred A. "Report to E. O. Heinrich, City Manager, on the Water Rights of the City of Boulder, Colo.: In Comparison with the Physical Facts that Affect Them." Unpublished engineering report, Boulder, CO, 1919.

Farnham, Thomas J. *Travels in the Great Western Prairies, The Anahuac and Rocky Mountains and in the Oregon Territory*. Vol. 1. London: R. Bentley, 1841.

Fiege, Mark. *Irrigated Eden: The Making of an Agricultural Landscape in the American West*. Seattle: University of Washington Press, 1999.

Flores, Dan. "Bison Ecology and Bison Diplomacy: The Southern Plains from 1800 to 1850." *Journal of American History* 78, no. 2 (1991): 465–85. http://dx.doi.org /10.2307/2079530.

Flores, Dan. "The Great Plains 'Wilderness' as a Human-Shaped Environment." *Great Plains Research* 9 (1999): 343–55.

Frazier, Kendrick. *The People of Chaco: A Canyon and Its Culture*. New York: W. W. Norton, 1999.

Fremont, John Charles. *Report of the Exploring Expedition to the Rocky Mountains in the Year 1842 and to Oregon and North California in the Years 1843–'44*. Washington: Blair and Rivers, 1845.

Gandy, Matthew. *Concrete and Clay: Reworking Nature in New York City*. Cambridge, MA: MIT Press, 2002.

Garrard, Louis H. *Wah-to-yah and the Taos Trail*. Introduction by A. B. Guthrie Jr. Norman: University of Oklahoma Press, 1955.

Gershman, Mark. "City of Boulder Tributary Greenways Program, Riparian Habitat Assessment, Vegetation Evaluation Final Report." October 1999.

Gleichman, Peter J., and L. Carol Gleichman. *Prehistoric Paleo-Indian Cultures of the Colorado Plains, Cs. 11,500–7500 BP*. Denver: Native Cultural Services, 1989.

Gleichman, Peter J., L. Carol Gleichman, and S. Karhu. 1995. "Excavations at the Rock Creek Site, 1990–1993." Denver: Native Cultural Services, 1989.

Greeley, Horace. *An Overland Journey from New York to San Francisco in the Summer of 1859*. New York: C. M. Saxton, Barker & Company, 1860.

Greeley, Horace. *What I Know of Farming: A Series of Brief and Plain Expositions on Practical Agriculture as an Art Based upon Science*. New York: W. W. Carleton and Co, 1871.

Gregg, Josian. *Scenes and Incidents in the Western Prairies: During Eight Expeditions, and Including a Residence of Nearly Nine Years in Northern Mexico*. Vol. 1. Philadelphia: J. W. Moore, 1857.

Grinnell, George Bird. *The Fighting Cheyennes*. Norman: University of Oklahoma Press, 1915.

Gross, Dwight D. "Reservoir No. 22 Dam." Paper presented at the Rocky Mountain Section Meeting of the American Water Works Association, September 25, 1951.

Hafen, LeRoy R. "The Early Fur Trade Posts on the South Platte." *Mississippi Valley Historical Review* 12, no. 3 (1925): 334–41. http://dx.doi.org/10.2307/1889565.

Hafen, LeRoy R., ed., *Colorado Gold Rush: Contemporary Letters and Reports 1858–1859*. Glendale, CA: Clark, 1941.

Halaas, David Fridtjof, and Andrew E. Masich. *Halfbreed: The Remarkable True Story of George Bent—Caught Between the Worlds of the Indian and the White Man*. Cambridge, MA: DaCapo Press, 2004.

Hart, Stephen H., Archer B. Hulbert, and M. L. Gardner. *The Southwestern Journals of Zebulon Pike, 1806–1807*. Albuquerque: University of New Mexico Press, 2007.

Hayden, Ferdinand V. *Preliminary Field Report of the United States Geological Survey of Colorado and New Mexico*. Washington, DC: Government Printing Office, 1869.

Hayter, Earl W. "Livestock-Fencing Conflicts in Rural America." *Agricultural History* 37, no. 1 (1963): 10–20.

Hewes, Leslie. "Early Fencing on the Western Margin of the Prairie." *Annals of the Association of American Geographers* 71, no. 2 (1981): 177–201. http://dx.doi.org/10.1111/j.1467-8306.1981.tb01347.x.

Hobbs, Gregory W. "Colorado Water Law: An Historical Overview." *Water Law Review* 1, no. 1 (1997): 1–161.

Hobbs, Gregory W. "Priority: The Most Misunderstood Stick in the Bundle." In *The Public's Water Resource*, ed. G. Hobbs, 303–21. Denver: Continuing Legal Education in Colorado, 2007.

Hobbs, Richard J., Eric Higgs, and James A. Harris. "Novel Ecosystems: Implications for Conservation and Restoration." *Trends in Ecology & Evolution* 24, no. 11 (2009): 599–605. http://dx.doi.org/10.1016/j.tree.2009.05.012.

Holleran, Michael. *Historic Context for Irrigation and Water Supply Ditches and Canals in Colorado*. Denver: Colorado Center for Preservation Research, University of Colorado at Denver and Health Sciences Center, 2005.

Holleran, Michael. *Farmers Ditch: A History and Guide*. Denver: University of Colorado, 2000.

Holleran, Michael. *Boulder Valley Ditches: Silver Lake Ditch A History and Guide*. Denver: University of Colorado at Denver, 2000.

Hooper, Bruce P., and Richard D. Margerum. "Integrated Watershed Management for River Conservation: Perspectives from Experiences in Australia and the United States." In *Global Perspectives on River Conservation: Science, Policy and Practice*, ed. P. J. Boon, R. Davies Bryan, and Geoffrey E. Petts, xi–xvi. Chichester: J. Wiley and Sons, 2001.

Hornaday, William T. *The Extermination of the American Bison*. Washington, DC: Smithsonian Institution, US National Museum, 1889. http://www.munseys.com/diskthree/exbi.pdf, Accessed January 25, 2010.

Hornaday, William T. *Our Vanishing Wild Life: Its Extermination and Preservation*. New York: New York Zoological Society, 1913.

Hunter, Malcolm. "Benchmarks for Managing Ecosystems: Are Human Activities Natural?" *Conservation Biology* 10, no. 3 (1996): 695–97. http://dx.doi.org/10.1046/j.1523-1739.1996.10030695.x.

Hyde, George E. *Life of George Bent*. Ed. Savoie Lottinville. Norman: University of Oklahoma Press, 1968.

Isenberg, Andrew C. *The Destruction of the Buffalo: An Environmental History, 1750–1920*. New York: Cambridge University Press, 1968.

James, Edwin. *Account of an Expedition from Pittsburgh to the Rocky Mountains Performed in the Years 1819, 1820*. 3 vols. London: Longman, Hurst, Rees, Orme, and Brown, 1823.

Katz, Cindy. "Whose Nature, Whose Culture? Private Productions of Space and the "Preservation" of Nature." In *Remaking Reality: Nature at the Millennium*, ed. Bruce Braun and Noel Castree, 46–63. London: Routledge, 1998.

Kelman, Ari. *A Misplaced Massacre: Struggling Over the Memory of Sand Creek*. Cambridge: Harvard University Press, 2013.

Keulartz, Josef. "Boundary Work in Ecological Restoration." *Environmental Philosophy* 6, no. 1 (2009): 35–55. http://dx.doi.org/10.5840/envirophil2009613.

Krutzsch, Philip H. "North American Jumping Mice (Genus *Zapus*)." *University of Kansas Publications, Museum of Natural History* 7, no. 4 (1954): 349–472.

Kumli, Karl F., III. "A Ditch Runs Through It: Title, Access and Maintenance Issues Regarding Irrigation Ditches for Real Property Owners." Unpublished white paper, Boulder County Bar Association, Boulder, 2005.

Lackey, Robert T. "Normative Science." *Fisheries (Bethesda, MD)* 29, no. 7 (2004): 38–39.

Laflin, Rose. *Irrigation, Settlement, and Change on the Cache la Poudre River*. Special Report, no. 15. Fort Collins: Colorado Water Resources Research Institute, 2005.

Large, Marjorie E. "The Appropriation to Private Use of Land and Water in the St. Vrain Valley before the Founding of the Chicago-Colorado Colony (1871)." Unpublished MA thesis, University of Colorado, Boulder, 1932.

Latour, Bruno. *We Have Never Been Modern*. Cambridge, MA: Harvard University Press, 1993.

Lavendar, David. *Bent's Fort*. Garden City, NY: Doubleday, 1954.

Lawson, Merlin P., and Charles W. Stockton. "Desert Myth and Climatic Reality." *Annals of the Association of American Geographers* 71, no. 4 (1981): 527–35. http://dx.doi.org/10.1111/j.1467-8306.1981.tb01372.x.

Lekson, Stephen H. *A History of the Ancient Southwest*. Santa Fe: School for Advanced Research Press, 2009.

Limerick, Patricia N., with Jason L. Hanson. *A Ditch in Time: The City, the West, and Water*. Golden, CO: Fulcrum Press, 2012.

Limerick, Patricia N., Jeffery Hickey, and Richard DiNucci. *What's in a Name? Nichols Hall*. Boulder: University Press of Colorado, 1987.

Long, Everett C. Interview by Sarah Binford Avery. Boulder, CO: Carnegie Library, 1985.

Lord, John. *Frontier Dust*. Ed. Natalie Shipman. Hartford, CT: Edward Valentine, Mitchell, 1926.

Lucas, Fred L. "Denver Reservoir and Irrigation Company Statement." Unpublished report, 1910.

McCann, Joseph M. "Before 1492: The Making of the Pre-Columbian Landscape. Part 1: The Environment." *Ecological Research* 17, nos. 1–2 (1999): 15–30.

McCann, Joseph M. "Before 1492: The Making of the Pre-Columbian Landscape. Part 2: The Environment." *Ecological Research* 17, no. 3 (1999): 107–19.

McHendrie, A. W. "The Hatcher Ditch (1846–1928): The Oldest Colorado Ditch Now in Use." *Colorado Magazine* 5, no. 3 (1928): 81–95.

Mead, Elwood. "Irrigation in the United States." Testimony before the United States Industrial Commission, Washington, DC, June 11–12, 1901.

Mead, Elwood. *Irrigation Institutions: A Discussion of the Economic and Legal Questions Created by the Growth of Irrigated Agriculture in the West*. New York: Macmillan, 1903.

Meeker, R. I. "Report on the Irrigated Area under Canals from Boulder Creek and the Relation of Volume of Water Required by this Area to the Water Supply of the Boulder Power Project." Unpublished engineering report to the Central Colorado Power Company, Colorado Springs, 1908.

Melosi, Martin V. *The Sanitary City: Urban Infrastructure in America from Colonial Times to the Present: Creating the North American Landscape.* Baltimore: Johns Hopkins University Press, 1999.

Mendoza, Patrick M. *Song of Sorrow: Massacre at Sand Creek.* Denver: Willow Wind Publishing, 1993.

Millard, S. "Fences and Ditches." *Sunday Camera Magazine,* October 7, 1984, 6.

Montgomery, Frank J. Interview by Steven Hall. Boulder, CO: Boulder County Folklore Survey, Carnegie Library, 1995.

Morris, Ernest. "A Glimpse of Moffat Tunnel History." *Colorado Magazine* 4, no. 2 (1927): 63–66.

Murphy, Sheila F., Philip L. Verplanck, and Larry B. Barber, eds. *Comprehensive Water Quality of the Boulder Creek Watershed, Colorado, during High-Flow and Low-Flow Conditions, 2000.* US Geological Survey Water-Resources Investigations Report 2003-4045. Denver: US Department of Interior, 2003.

Murray Li, T. "Images of Community: Discourse and Strategy in Property Relations." *Development and Change* 27 (1996): 501–27.

Murray Li, T. "Marginality, Power, and Production: Analyzing Upland Transformations." In *Transforming the Indonesian Highlands: Marginality, Power, and Production. Australia*: Harwood Academic Publishers, 1999.

Nestler, Thomas P., Randy VanBuren, J. A. Stafford, and M. Jones. *Inventory and Status of South Platte River Native Fishes in Colorado.* Fort Collins: Colorado Division of Wildlife, Aquatic Wildlife Section, 1997.

Nettleton, Edwin S. *Biennial Report of the State Engineer for the Fiscal Years 1881 and 1882.* Denver: Tribune Publishing, 1882.

Nettleton, Edwin S. *Report of the State Engineer to the Governor of Colorado for the Years 1883 and 1884.* Denver, 1884.

Netz, Reviel. *Barbed Wire: An Ecology of Modernity.* Middletown, CT: Wesleyan University Press, 2004.

Neumann, Roderick P. *Imposing Wilderness: Struggles over Livelihood and Nature Preservation in Africa.* Berkeley: University of California Press, 1998.

Newby, Betty A. *The Longmont Album: History and Folklore of the St. Vrain Valley.* Virginia Beach: Donning Company Publishers, 1995.

Obmascik, Mark. "Mall Subsidy Tops $279 Million." *Denver Post,* April 16, 2001.

Ochs, S. Alice. *Water the Basis for Success: Left Hand Ditch Company, the First 130 Years.* Longmont, CO: S. A. Ochs, 1996.

Ostrom, Elinor. *Crafting Institutions for Self-Governing Irrigation Systems.* San Francisco: Institute for Contemporary Studies, 1992.

Ostrom, Elinor. "A General Framework for Analyzing Sustainability of Social-Ecological Systems." *Science* 325, no. 5939 (2009): 419–22. http://dx.doi.org/10.1126/science.1172133.

Pabor, William E. *Colorado as an Agricultural State: Its Farms, Fields, and Garden Lands.* New York: Orange Judd Company, 1883. http://dx.doi.org/10.5962/bhl.title.40231.

Parshall, Ralph. *Return of Seepage Water to the Lower South Platte River in Colorado.* Bulletin 279. Fort Collins: Agricultural Experiment Station of the Colorado Agricultural College, 1922.

Perrigo, Lynn I. "A Municipal History of Boulder, Colorado, 1871–1947." Unpublished report to the Boulder County Historical Society and the City of Boulder, Boulder, CO, 1946.

Pollan, Michael. *Second Nature: A Gardener's Education.* New York: Grove Press, 1991.

Portrait and Biographical Record of Denver and Vicinity, Colorado. Chicago: Chapman Publishing Company, 1898.

Powell, J. W. *Report on the Lands of the Arid Regions of the United States.* Washington, DC: Government Printing Office, 1878.

Primack, Richard B. *Essentials of Conservation Biology.* Sunderland, MA: Sinauer Associates, 1993.

Raffles, Hugh. *In Amazonia: A Natural History.* Princeton, NJ: Princeton University Press, 2002.

Reisner, Marc. *Cadillac Desert.* New York: Viking-Penguin, 1986.

Richter, Brian D., Jeffrey V. Baumgartner, Jennifer Powell, and David P. Braun. "A Method for Assessing Hydrologic Alteration within Ecosystems." *Conservation Biology* 10, no. 4 (1996): 1163–74. http://dx.doi.org/10.1046/j.1523-1739.1996.10041163.x.

Ripple, William J., James A. Estes, Robert L. Beschta, Christopher C. Wilmers, Euan G. Ritchie, Mark Hebblewhite, Joel Berger, B. Elmhagen, M. Letnic, M. P. Nelson, et al. "Status and Ecological Effects of the World's Largest Carnivores." *Science* 343, no. 6167 (2014): 1241484. http://dx.doi.org/10.1126/science.1241484.

Robertson, Morgan M. "No Net Loss: Wetland Restoration and the Incomplete Capitalization of Nature." *Antipode* 32, no. 4 (2000): 463–93. http://dx.doi.org/10.1111/1467-8330.00146.

Romer, Mary C. "The Heritage and the Legacy of John Ramsey Rothrock: A Colorado Pioneer." Tucson: n.p., 1985.

St. Vrain Historical Society. *They Came to Stay: Longmont, Colorado, 1858–1920. Centennial Edition.* Longmont, CO: Longmont Printing Company, 1971.

Sampson, Joanna. *Walking through History on Marshall Mesa.* Boulder, CO: City of Boulder Open Space Department, 1995.

Schisler, G. *Colorado Water Codes Tested for Moxobolus Cerebralis, Causative Agent for Whirling Disease, by Pepsin-Trypsin Digestion Technique.* Denver: Colorado Division of Wildlife, 2000.

Schorr, David B. "Appropriation as Agrarianism: Distributive Justice in the Creation of Property Rights." *Ecology Law Journal* 32 (2005): 3–71.

Schorr, David B. *The First Water-Privatization Debate: Colorado Water Corporations in the Gilded Age.* Tel Aviv University Law Faculty Papers, no. 75. Tel Aviv: Buchmann Faculty of Law, 2008.

Shaw, A. J. "A Brief History of Denver Reservoir and Irrigation Company and Its Subsidiary Companies." Unpublished report, 1925.

Sheridan, Thomas E. "Arizona: Political Ecology of a Desert State." *Journal of Political Ecology* 2 (1995): 41–57.

Sherow, James E., R. Laurie Simmons, and Christine Whitacre. "O'Brian Canal, Adams County, Brighton Vicinity, Historic American Engineering Record." Unpublished report, National Park Service, Rocky Mountain Regional Office, Department of the Interior Colorado, Denver, 1988.

Silkensen, Gregory M. *The Farmer's High Line Canal and Reservoir Company: A Century of Change on Clear Creek.* Denver: North Suburban Printing, 2000.

Simmons, R. Laurie, and Christine Whitacre. *Highland Lawn.* Denver: Front Range Research Associates, 1988.

Sivaramakrishnan, Krishna. "Scientific Forestry and Genealogies of Development in Bengal." In *Nature in the Global South*, ed. Paul Greenough and Anna L. Tsing, 253–88. Durham, NC: Duke University Press, 2003.

Smiley, Jerome. *Semi-Centennial History of the State of Colorado.* 2 vols. Chicago: Lewis Publishing Company, 1913.

Smith, Joel B., Ken Strzepek, Lee Rozaklis, Carol Ellinghouse, and K. C. Hallett. *The Potential Consequences of Climate Change for Boulder Colorado's Water Supplies.* Boulder, CO: Stratus Consulting, 2009.

Smith, Phyllis. "A History of the Waterworks of Boulder, Colorado." Unpublished report to David Rhodes, Director, Public Works Department, City of Boulder, Boulder, CO, 1986.

Smith, Pauli Driver. "The Highland Ditch: Extracted from a Paper by the Same Name, Originally Written in 1889 by L. C. Mead." Unpublished report to the Highland Ditch Company, Longmont, CO, 2009. http://historichighlandlake.org/_assets/documents/Program_Highland-Ditch-annual.pdf, Accessed October 29, 2012.

Smits, David D. "The Frontier Army and the Destruction of the Buffalo: 1865–1883." *Western Historical Quarterly* 25, no. 3 (1994): 312–38. http://dx.doi.org/10.2307/971110.

Smythe, William E. *The Conquest of Arid America.* New York: Harper Brothers Publishers, 1900. http://dx.doi.org/10.5962/bhl.title.33648.

Spirn, Anne W. "Constructing Nature: The Legacy of Frederick Law Olmsted." In *Uncommon Ground: Toward Reinventing Nature*, ed. W. Cronon, 91–113. New York: W. W. Norton, 1995.

Steinel, Alvin T. *History of Agriculture in Colorado 1858 to 1926.* Fort Collins, CO: State Agricultural College, 1926.

Stone, Wilbur F., ed. *History of Colorado.* Vols. 1 and 4. Chicago: S. J. Clarke Publishing Company, 1918, 1919.

Sueltenfuss, Jeremy P., David J. Cooper, Richard L. Knight, and Reagan M. Waskom. "The Creation and Maintenance of Wetland Ecosystems from Irrigation

Canal and Reservoir Seepage in a Semi-Arid Landscape." *Wetlands* 33, no. 5 (2013): 1–12.

Swyngedouw, Erik. "Modernity and Hybridity: Nature, Regeneracionismo, and the Production of the Spanish Waterscape, 1890–1930." *Annals of the Association of American Geographers* 89, no. 3 (1999): 443–65. http://dx.doi.org/10.1111/0004 -5608.00157.

Taylor, Bayard. *Colorado: A Summer Trip.* New York: G. P. Putnam and Son, 1867.

Teele, Ray Palmer. *Water Rights on Interstate Streams: The Platte River and Tributaries.* Washington, DC: US Department of Agriculture / Government Printing Office, 1905.

Tice, John H. *Over the Plains and on the Mountains, or, Kansas and Colorado Agriculturally, Mineralogically and Aesthetically Described.* St. Louis: St. Louis Book and News Co, 1872.

Travis, Ella M. *A Fisherman's Paradise: The 100 Year History of the Boulder Game and Fish Club, Inc. 1908–2008.* Boulder, CO: Boulder Fish and Game Club, 2009.

Twain, Mark. *Roughing It, with an Introduction by Henry Nash Smith.* New York: Harper & Brothers, 1959.

Tyler, Daniel. "Daniel Tyler Completes Biographical Book, WD Farr: Cowboy in the Boardroom." *Newsletter of the Water Center of Colorado State University* 28, no. 3 (2011): 26–30.

Tyler, Daniel. *The Last Water Hole in the West: The Colorado–Big Thompson Project and the Northern Colorado Water Conservancy District.* Boulder: University Press of Colorado, 1992.

Udall, Stewart L. *The Forgotten Founders: Rethinking the History of the Old West.* Washington, DC: Island Press, 2002.

URS Consultants. "Modernization of the Boulder Canyon Hydroelectric Project, Documentation of Historically Significant Features and Equipment." Unpublished report to the City of Boulder, 2011.

US Army Corps of Engineers, Omaha District. *Flood Plain Information, Boulder County, Colorado.* Vol. 3, *Lower St. Vrain Creek.* Omaha, NE: US Army Engineer District, 1972.

US Army Corps of Engineers, Omaha District. *Flood Plain Information, Boulder County, Colorado.* Vol. 4, *Upper St. Vrain Creek.* Omaha, NE: US Army Engineer District, 1972.

US Fish and Wildlife Service. *Ute ladies'-tresses (*Spiranthes diluvialis*): Agency Review Draft, Recovery Plan.* Denver: US Fish and Wildlife Service, 1995.

Vajda, Alan M., Elena M. Lopez, Tammy A. Maldonado, John D. Woodling, and David O. Norris. *Intersex and Other Forms of Reproductive Disruption in Feral White Sucker (*Catostomus commersoni*) Downstream of Wastewater Treatment Plant Effluent in Boulder, Colorado.* Boulder: Department of Integrative Physiology, University of Colorado, 2004. http://bcn.boulder.co.us/basin/topical/haa/ Vajda_Intersex-suckers.pdf, Accessed March 19, 2013.

VanBuren, Randy. "Fish Inventory Data for Select Streams and Lakes on City of Boulder Open Space and Mountain Parks Lands." Unpublished report. Denver: Colorado Division of Wildlife, 1999.

VanBuren, Randy. "Fish Inventory Data for Select Streams and Lakes on City of Boulder Open Space and Mountain Parks Lands." Unpublished report. Denver: Colorado Division of Wildlife, 2000.

Veblen, Thomas T., and Diane C. Lorenz. *The Colorado Front Range: A Century of Ecological Change*. Salt Lake City: University of Utah Press, 1991.

Warren, Charles R. "Perspectives on the 'Alien' versus 'Native' Species Debate: A Critique of Concepts, Language and Practice." *Progress in Human Geography* 31, no. 4 (2007): 427–46. http://dx.doi.org/10.1177/0309132507079499.

Warren, Edward R. *The Mammals of Colorado*. New York: G. P. Putnam's Sons, 1910.

Watts, Alan. *Taoism: Way Beyond Seeking, Volume 5 of Alan Watts "Love of Wisdom."* Rutland, VT: Charles E. Tuttle, 1998.

Watts, Frederick. *Report of the Commissioner of Agriculture for the Year 1871*. Washington, DC: Government Printing Office, 1972.

Weber, David J. *The Spanish Frontier in North America*. New Haven, CT: Yale University Press, 2009.

West, Elliott. *The Contested Plains: Indians, Goldseekers, and the Rush to Colorado*. Lawrence: University Press of Kansas, 1998.

White, Richard. *The Organic Machine: The Remaking of the Columbia River*. New York: Hill and Wang, 1996.

Wiener, John D., Kathleen A. Dwire, Susan K. Skagen, Robert R. Crifasi, and David Yates. "Riparian Ecosystem Consequences of Water Redistribution along the Colorado Front Range." *Water Resources Impact* 10, no. 3 (2008): 18–21.

Wilkinson, Charles F. "Prior Appropriation 1848–1991." *Environmental Law (Northwestern School of Law)* 21 (1991): v–xviii.

Wilkinson, Charles F. *Crossing the Next Meridian: Land, Water, and the Future of the American West*. Washington, DC: Island Press, 1992.

Willard, James F. *The Union Colony at Greeley, Colorado 1869–1871*. Denver: W. F. Robinson Printing, 1918.

Willard, James F., and Colin B. Goodykoontz, eds. *Experiments in Colorado Colonization 1869–1872*. Vol. 3. University of Colorado Historical Collections. Boulder: University of Colorado, 1926.

Williams, Mark W., Jill S. Baron, Nel Caine, Richard Sommerfeld, and Robert Sanford. "Nitrogen Saturation in the Rocky Mountains." *Environmental Science & Technology* 30, no. 2 (1996): 640–46. http://dx.doi.org/10.1021/es950383e.

Winship, George Parker. *The Journey of Coronado Translated into English*. New York: A. S. Barnes and Company, 1904.

Wittfogel, Karl A. *Oriental Despotism*. New Haven, CT: Yale University Press, 1957.

Wohl, Ellen E. *Virtual Rivers: Lessons from the Mountain Rivers of the Colorado Front Range*. New Haven, CT: Yale University Press, 2001.

Woodling, John. *Colorado's Little Fish: A Guide to the Minnows and Other Lesser Known Fishes in the State of Colorado*. Denver: Colorado Division of Wildlife, 1985.

Worster, Donald. *A River Running West: The Life of John Wesley Powell*. Oxford: Oxford University Press, 2001.

Worster, Donald. *Rivers of Empire*. New York: Oxford University Press, 1985.

Wright, James E. *The Politics of Populism: Dissent in Colorado*. New Haven, CT: Yale University Press, 1974.

Wroten, William H., Jr. "The Railroad Tie Industry in the Central Rocky Mountain Region 1867–1900." PhD diss., University of Colorado, Boulder, 1956.

Yohe, Robert M., II, and Douglas B. Bamforth. "Late Pleistocene Protein Residues from the Mahaffy Cache, Colorado." *Journal of Archaeological Science* 40 (1956): 2237–343.

Index